Women and
Congressional Elections

TOWER CENTER POLITICAL STUDIES

James F. Hollifield, series editor

Women and Congressional Elections

A Century of Change

Barbara Palmer
Dennis Simon

LYNNE
RIENNER
PUBLISHERS

BOULDER
LONDON

Published in the United States of America in 2012 by
Lynne Rienner Publishers, Inc.
1800 30th Street, Boulder, Colorado 80301
www.rienner.com

and in the United Kingdom by
Lynne Rienner Publishers, Inc.
3 Henrietta Street, Covent Garden, London WC2E 8LU

Library of Congress Cataloging-in-Publication Data
Palmer, Barbara, 1967–
  Women and Congressional elections : a century of change / Barbara Palmer
and Dennis Simon.
        p.   cm. — (Tower Center political studies)
    Includes bibliographical references and index.
    ISBN 978-1-58826-815-0 (hardcover : alk. paper)
    ISBN 978-1-58826-840-2 (pbk. : alk. paper)
    1. Women—Political activity—United States—History. 2. Women legislators
—United States—History. 3. Women political candidates—United States—
History. 4. United States. Congress—Elections—History.
I. Simon, Dennis Michael. II. Title.
    HQ1236.5.U6P36 2012
    320.082—dc23
                                                                                                2012010117

British Cataloguing in Publication Data
A Cataloguing in Publication record for this book
is available from the British Library.

Printed and bound in the United States of America

The paper used in this publication meets the requirements
of the American National Standard for Permanence of
Paper for Printed Library Materials Z39.48-1992.

5 4 3 2 1

For their years of understanding, support, and encouragement

To Mary Ann and Otto Palmer
—Barbara Palmer

To Debbie, Jonathan, and Jennifer Simon
Valeria and Gary Simon and the memory of Michael Simon
Joan Roach and the memory of John Roach
—Dennis Simon

Contents

List of Illustrations   ix
Preface   xiii

1 Women of the Early Twentieth Century   1

2 A Long Slow Road:
The Integration of Women into Congress   29

3 Arrested Development:
A History of Careerism and Incumbency   63

4 Keeping It In the Family:
Widows, Daughters, and Mothers   91

5 Women as Targets:
Understanding the Competitive Environment   127

6 Red vs. Blue: A History of the Party Gap   161

7 Demographics Is Destiny: Where Women Are Elected   183

8 Women of the Twenty-First Century   217

Bibliography   241
Index   277
About the Book   285

Illustrations

Photographs

Representative Jeannette Rankin   4
The Women of the 75th Congress, 1938   6
Representative Clare Boothe Luce   14
Representative Helen Gahagan Douglas   15
Representative Margaret Chase Smith   40
Representative Shirley Chisholm   52
Representative Pearl Oldfield   98
Representatives Ruth Bryan Owen and Ruth Hanna McCormick   107
Representative Stephanie Herseth Sandlin   119
Representative Alice Robertson   136
Representative Linda Sanchez   221
Representative Jaime Herrera Beutler   223

Tables

1.1   The First Woman . . .   3
1.2   Profile of the Fifty-five Women Elected to the US House
         Between 1916 and 1956   8
2.1   Women Initially Elected to the US Senate   39
2.2   Sitting Female House Members Who Ran for the Senate   47
2.3   Women of Color Elected to the US House   54
3.1   Incumbents and Elections to the US House,
         by Redistricting Period, 1956–2010   68

x   *Illustrations*

3.2   Incumbents and Elections to the US Senate,
      by Six-Year Cycle, 1958–2010   68
3.3   Women Who Served Ten or More Terms in the US House   82
4.1   Women Who Succeeded Their Husbands in the US House   95
4.2   Women Who Were Appointed to the US Senate   101
4.3   Congressional Women Who Married Members of Congress   104
4.4   Congressional Women with Prominent Political Fathers   108
4.5   Congressional Women Whose Sons Served in Congress   110
4.6   Women Who Gave Birth While Serving in Congress   113
4.7   Women Under Forty Years Old Who Served in the US House   117
5.1   General Elections for the US Senate with
      Two Female Candidates   129
5.2   General Elections for the US House with
      Two Female Candidates, 1972–2010   131
5.3   Reelection Rates for Male and Female House Incumbents,
      by Redistricting Period, 1956–2010   133
5.4   Uncontested Primary and General Elections Among
      US House Incumbents, 1956–2010   146
5.5   Contested Primary Elections for the US House
      Within the Opposition Party, 1956–2010   147
5.6   Female Competition in Contested Primary Elections
      for the US House, 1956–2010   149
5.7   Women Winning the Nomination of the Opposition Party in
      US House Districts Where an Incumbent Seeks Reelection,
      1956–2010   150
5.8   Electoral Competition for Incumbents Seeking Reelection,
      1956–2010   151
5.9   Representative Connie Morella (R-MD) and Her Competition   153
7.1   The Shifting Demographics of House Districts Electing
      Democrats and Republicans, 1956–2010   188
7.2   House Districts Electing Men and Women, 1956–2010   200
7.3   The Shifting Demographics of House Districts Electing
      Men and Women, by Party, 1956–2010   202
7.4   House Districts Electing African American and Hispanic
      Male and Female Democrats, 1956–2010   208
8.1   Profile of the Sixty Women Elected to the US House
      Between 2002 and 2010   219
8.2   The Top Twenty Women-Friendly House Districts, 2010   233
8.3   The Bottom Twenty Women-Friendly House Districts, 2010   233

▓ Figures

1.1   Ideology of Female and Male Members of the US House,
        1916–1956   16
2.1   Women as Candidates for the US House, 1956–2010   30
2.2   Women as Candidates for the US Senate, 1958–2010   42
3.1   Women and the Pace of Change, 1940–2010   64
3.2   Open Seats in Elections to the US House and Senate,
        1956–2010   76
3.3   Careerism in the US House, 1800–1992   79
6.1   Women as a Proportion of Candidates Seeking Their Party's
        Nomination to the US House, 1956–2010   166
6.2   Women as a Proportion of Their Party's Nominees
        for the US House, 1956–2010   167
6.3   Women as a Proportion of Their Party's Delegation
        in the US House, 1956–2010   168
6.4   Women as a Proportion of Candidates Seeking Their Party's
        Nomination to the US Senate, 1958–2010   169
6.5   Women as a Proportion of Their Party's Nominees
        for the US Senate, 1958–2010   170
6.6   Women as a Proportion of Their Party's Delegation
        in the US Senate, 1958–2010   171
6.7   Proportion of Democrats and Republicans in the US House,
        1956–2010   173
6.8   Women as a Proportion of Their Party's Members
        in the Lower Chamber of State Legislatures, 1958–2010   174
6.9   Women as a Proportion of Their Party's Members
        in the Upper Chamber of State Legislatures, 1958–2010   175
8.1   Ideology of Female and Male Members of the US House,
        2002–2008   227
8.2   Probability of Electing a Woman to the US House,
        by Decade, 1972–2010   235

Preface

This project began casually, with the academic equivalent of a water cooler conversation. In the fall of 1998, we were colleagues in the Department of Political Science at Southern Methodist University. Dennis Simon was teaching a course on congressional elections. He divided the House and Senate elections among the members of his class and required them to gather data on the party, background, and gender of the candidates. In looking over their work, he noticed that there were fourteen races in which a woman ran against another woman. At the drinking fountain one day, he mentioned these races to Barbara Palmer, whose expertise included women and politics, and asked whether she found it surprising. Our discussion of this "tidbit" about the 1998 midterm elections raised numerous questions about women in the electoral arena and congressional elections. Thus began a project that has spanned more than a decade and has included conference papers, journal articles, and ultimately this book. We brought together two perspectives on politics in the United States and familiarity with two different bodies of literature. This project has been truly collaborative.

In the spring of 1999, the Research Council at Southern Methodist University awarded us a grant to begin the study. We used the funds primarily to hire research assistants to help in gathering and compiling what, in retrospect, turned out to be a staggering amount of data on US House and Senate elections. We wish to thank those assistants who were recruited from Barb's Women and Politics class at Southern Methodist University: Zhelia Bazleh, Diana Dorough, Cynthia Flores, Mandy Gough, Brooke Guest, Vanessa Hammond, Bernard Jones, Kristi Katsanis, Emily Katt, Albany Mitchell, Sheri Rogers, Heather Scott, Jessica Sheppard, Jennifer Sumrall, Andrea Swift, Natalie Thompson, Brenda Tutt, Amy Williams, and Kari Young. We owe a special expression of gratitude to those students who not only coded data but also "came back for more" to help us clean it and enter it into spreadsheets: Lindsay Abbate, Erin Echols, Elizabeth Myers, and Steve Schulte. We suspect that their experience in "doing real political science" was a deciding factor in their choice to attend law school. We also would like to thank those students who worked with Barb at American University, especially Amy Baumann, Meredith Hess, Cameo Kaisler, Alina Palimaru, and Laura Pautz. Christine Carberry at Southern Methodist University was both expert and meticulous in helping us proofread the manuscript and prepare the index. Barb would also like to thank Baldwin-Wallace College for granting her a 2011 Summer Research Grant, and Lauren Orrico, her undergraduate research assistant.

We wish to thank all the panelists and discussants who offered critiques of our work over the years, especially those at numerous Southern Political Science Association annual meetings. At Southern Methodist University, we regularly vetted our ideas with Brad Carter, Valerie Hunt, Dennis Ippolito, Cal Jillson, Joe Kobylka, Harold Stanley, Carole Wilson, and Matthew Wilson. Susannah Shakow and Coke Stewart of Washington, D.C., provided much-needed proofreading and a fresh perspective to our work, as did Mary Stegmaier at the University of Missouri and Melissa Deckman at Washington College. We are extremely thankful for the commentary and encouragement we received from the late David Broder of the *Washington Post.* Everyone's comments, questions, and encouragement were vital to this project, and we are grateful for their gift of collegiality.

Finally, we wish to thank Lynne Rienner for her invaluable ideas and feedback. We truly appreciate having the opportunity to work with her. Laura Logan, Karen Williams, and Sally Glover at Lynne Rienner Publishers were extraordinarily responsive and helpful throughout the process of creating the book.

Women and
Congressional Elections

ONE

Women of the Early Twentieth Century

"Today, we have broken the marble ceiling," announced Representative Nancy Pelosi, after she was sworn in as the new speaker of the US House of Representatives on January 5, 2007. "It is a moment for which we have waited over 200 years. To our daughters and granddaughters, the sky is the limit."[1] After receiving the gavel and becoming the first woman to lead the House, Speaker Pelosi brought all of the children who attended the ceremony up to the speaker's chair, presenting a visual image of power rarely seen in US political history: a woman surrounded by children. Without doubt, her swearing-in was a historic moment, but Speaker Pelosi led a House that was only 16 percent female.

On January 20, 2007, Senator Hillary Clinton (D-NY) ended years of speculation and formally announced her candidacy for president. In her webcast, seated on her living room couch, she stressed her Midwestern middle-class roots and that she was "in it to win."[2] Since the 1992 campaign, when presidential candidate Bill Clinton remarked, "Buy one, get one free," it has not been hard to imagine Hillary running in her own right.[3] She had a name recognition rate of 94 percent during the 2008 election.[4] During the first quarter of 2007, the first official fundraising period of the presidential campaign, Clinton raised a staggering $26 million, almost three times as much as any other candidate in history. In addition, she transferred another $10 million left over from her 2006 Senate race.[5] On the day of her announcement, polls showed her with a 24 percent lead over Senator Barack Obama (D-IL) among Democratic respondents. By December 2007 she was the presumptive Democratic nominee, and many predicted she would be the first woman president of the United States.[6]

On August 29, 2008, Republican presidential nominee John McCain announced that he had selected Alaska governor Sarah Palin to be his run-

1

ning mate.[7] Palin became, along with Geraldine Ferraro, chosen by Democrat Walter Mondale in 1984, one of two women nominated for vice president by a major party and the first woman on the Republican ticket. At the rally in Dayton, Ohio, where McCain introduced his choice to 15,000 supporters, Palin, a self-described "hockey mom," said, "We can shatter that glass ceiling once and for all."[8]

Without doubt, the story of women running for public office in the United States is one of transformation and change over the past century. However, Representative Pelosi lost her speakership when the Republicans gained control of the House in 2010. While the 2008 Democratic presidential contest was not decided until the very last states held their primaries, Senator Clinton was defeated by Senator Obama. Palin did not become vice president and, on October 5, 2011, announced she would not run for president in 2012.[9] As it turns out, the history of women in the US electoral arena is more accurately described as one of fits and starts. While there clearly has been progress, it has not been steady or particularly spectacular. The central question that motivates our book is: why has the integration of women into Congress taken so long?

◾ The Pioneers

Table 1.1 lists the "famous firsts" in the history of female candidates for Congress. The first woman ever to run for Congress was Elizabeth Cady Stanton, who is, of course, very well known for her dedication to women's suffrage and a wide variety of other women's rights issues.[10] Far less is known about her campaign for the House. Stanton, however, came from a political family. She was born in 1815, while her father, Daniel Cady, was serving in the House as a representative from their home state of New York. He served for one term as a member of the Federalist Party.[11] At the age of fifty-one and the mother of seven children, Stanton ran for the House in 1866 in New York as an Independent.[12] Her campaign was "neither extensive nor effective,"[13] but she ran to "impress the public with the fact that constitutionally women had the right to run for office," even if they did not have the right to vote.[14] She received twenty-four votes.[15] In *History of Woman Suffrage,* written in 1881 by Stanton, Susan B. Anthony, and Matilda Gage, the authors did note that Stanton, "in looking back on her successful defeat, regrets only that she did not . . . procure the photographs of her two dozen unknown friends."[16]

The first woman to serve in Congress, Representative Jeannette Rankin (R-MT), was elected to the House in 1916 at the age of thirty-six. Like Stanton, Rankin was very active in the suffrage movement, and it

Table 1.1   The First Woman . . .

	Name	When and Where
To run for the House	Elizabeth Cady Stanton	1866 in New York
To run for the Senate	Mary Elizabeth Lease	1893 in Kansas
To win a House election	Jeannette Rankin	1916 in Montana
To serve in the Senate (appointed)	Rebecca Latimer Felton	1922 in Georgia
To win a special Senate election	Gladys Pyle	1938 in South Dakota
To win a regularly scheduled Senate election	Margaret Chase Smith	1948 in Maine
Of color to win a House election	Patsy Mink	1964 in Hawaii
African American to win a House election	Shirley Chisholm	1968 in New York
Hispanic to win a House election	Ileana Ros-Lehtinen	1989 in Florida
Of color to win a Senate election	Carol Moseley-Braun	1992 in Illinois

Source: Women in Congress, 1917–2006, Office of the Clerk of the US House of Representatives (Washington, DC: US Government Printing Office, 2006).

was largely thanks to her efforts that her home state of Montana gave women the right to vote in 1914.[17] Rankin became a candidate for the House two years later after her brother encouraged her. She ran because "there are hundreds of men to care for the nation's tariff and foreign policy and irrigation projects. But there isn't a single woman to look after the nation's greatest asset: its children."[18] Four days after taking her oath of office, she cast a vote that would cost her reelection. With fifty-five other members, she voted against the United States entering World War I. Two years later, with her vote against the war seen as a liability and her at-large district dissolved, she did not seek reelection to the House and instead ran for the Senate. She lost the Republican primary, but ran in the general election as a National Party candidate, coming in a distant third. During her term in the House, Rankin cosponsored the constitutional amendment granting women's suffrage, but it failed to pass the Senate in that session. Because she was not reelected in 1918, she was not a member of Congress when the amendment finally passed in 1920. She became actively involved in the peace movement and secretary for the National Consumers League, lobbying for child labor laws along with minimum-wage and maximum-hour legislation. In 1940, at the age of sixty, Rankin ran again for the House and won. But on December 8, 1941, the day after the bombing of Pearl Harbor, she cast the only vote against the US declaration of war against Japan. Once again, she decided not to run for reelection and continued her work as a peace activist.[19] Rankin completed her House service as the only representative to oppose US entry into World War I and World War II.

Representative Jeannette Rankin, the first woman to serve in Congress, ran in 1916 at the age of thirty-six.

The first woman to serve in the Senate was Rebecca Latimer Felton (D-GA), who was appointed in 1922 at the age of eighty-seven. In addition to being the first woman, she also holds the distinction of having the shortest Senate career in history: two days. Felton was also a strong advocate of women's rights and was especially interested in the plight of rural women, although at one point she did support lynching blacks "as a warning against suspected rapists."[20] After Felton's brief appearance, it would be ten years before another woman would serve in the Senate. Senator Hattie Caraway (D-AR) was first appointed in 1931 after the death of her husband and then was reelected twice. In her bid for her third term, she was defeated in the primary by J. William Fulbright, who would hold the seat for the next three decades and chair the Senate Foreign Relations Committee. During her tenure, she earned the nickname "Silent Hattie" because of her rare speeches on the Senate floor. She explained, "I haven't the heart to take a minute away from the men. The poor dears love it so."[21] Caraway was given the same desk on the Senate floor that Felton had used and remarked, "I guess they wanted as few of them contaminated as possible."[22] Caraway served almost her entire thirteen-year career as the only woman in the Senate.

By 1929, the number of women in Congress reached nine and would hover around that number until the late 1940s. Even during World War II, the number of women in Congress remained stable, with ten serving in the 77th Congress (1941–1943) and nine serving in the 78th Congress (1943–1945). Exactly five decades after Representative Rankin broke the congressional gender barrier, the election of 1956 would be a high-water mark in the number of women running for the House: fifty-three women ran in Democratic and Republican primaries, with twenty-nine winning their primaries, fifteen winning election to the House, and one, Margaret Chase Smith (R-ME), winning election to the Senate. The nation elected President Dwight Eisenhower to a second term of office with 57 percent of the popular vote. Eisenhower's electoral appeal, however, was not sufficient to capture control of Congress. The Democrats enjoyed a 234–201 majority in the House of Representatives and a smaller majority, 49–47, in the Senate.[23] The national political agenda was crowded that year. President Eisenhower would address an international crisis triggered in late 1956 by the British-French-Israeli invasion of the Suez Canal. The successful launch of *Sputnik* by the Soviets added to the anxiety about the ongoing Cold War and sparked a debate about the quality of education in the nation. The debate would ultimately lead to the National Defense Education Act in 1958. In September 1957, the effort to desegregate Central High School would force President Eisenhower to send federal troops to Little Rock, Arkansas.

The 85th Congress (1957 session) is noteworthy for additional reasons. Congress enacted the Civil Rights Act of 1957, the first civil rights legislation passed by Congress since the Reconstruction era. Fourteen of the fifteen women in the House voted for the act, with Representative Iris Blitch (D-GA) casting the lone nay vote among them. Prior to serving in the House, Blitch had been one of the lone women in the Georgia house and senate and was known as the "Queen of the Legislature." One of her proudest accomplishments was passing legislation giving women the right to serve on Georgia juries. In 1956, however, she signed the Southern Man-

Photo courtesy of the Library of Congress

The women of the 75th Congress, 1938, left to right: Representative Caroline O'Day (D-NY), Representative Edith Nourse Rogers (R-MA), Representative Mary Norton (D- NJ), Representative Nan Honeyman (D-OR), Representative Virginia Jenckes (D-IN), and Senator Hattie Caraway (D-AR).

ifesto, decrying the US Supreme Court decision in *Brown v. Board of Education*.[24]

Many of the women of the 85th Congress would distinguish themselves as policy leaders in the House. Representative Martha Griffiths (D-MI) was a key force in the eventual passing of the Civil Rights Act of 1964 and later became known as the "mother of the Equal Rights Amendment."[25] Representative Leonor Sullivan (D-MO) was a cosponsor of the Equal Pay Act of 1963 and an early advocate of consumer protection.[26] Representative Edith Green (D-OR) "left her mark on nearly every schooling bill enacted during her twenty years on Capitol Hill" and was the author and principal advocate of Title IX of the Education Amendments of 1972.[27] Representative Gracie Pfost (D-ID), who became known as "Hell's Belle," was an opponent of private power companies and fought for federal intervention to manage the project planned for the Hell's Canyon branch of the Snake River.[28]

While the gains women in Congress made in the 1950s looked promising, their numbers would stall and actually decline in the 1960s. And as Table 1.1 shows, women in Congress were celebrating "famous firsts" well into the twentieth century. The first woman of color, Representative Patsy Mink (D-HI), was not elected until 1964. The first—and only—woman of color in the Senate, Carol Moseley-Braun (D-IL), was not elected until 1992.

▩ The Rules of the Game

That only fifteen women were elected to the House in 1956 provides a vivid example that women had "a very small share, though a very large stake, in political power."[29] For women, entry into the inner world of politics was largely blocked. Table 1.2 provides a profile of the fifty-five women who were elected to the House between 1916 and 1956. It suggests how women who were interested in politics during the first half of the twentieth century faced numerous barriers, including cultural norms and gender stereotypes that limited their choices, little access to the "pipeline" or hierarchy of political offices, and the politics of congressional redistricting.

Cultural Norms: Politics Is a "Man's Game"

In the 1950s, women were socialized to view politics as a man's game, a game that was inconsistent with the gender roles to which women were assigned. As Jeane Kirkpatrick explained:

Like men, women gain status for effective, responsible performance of culturally sanctioned roles. Any effort to perform roles assigned by the culture to the opposite sex is likely to result in a loss of status on the sex specific status ladder. The values on which women are expected to concentrate are those of affection, rectitude, well-being; the skills relevant to the pursuit of these values are those associated with nurturing, serving, and pleasing a family and community: homemaking, personal adornment, preparing and serving food, nursing the ill, comforting the downcast, aiding and pleasing a husband, caring for and educating the young. It is assumed furthermore that these activities will consume all a woman's time, that to perform them well is both a full time and a life time job.[30]

Women attending college in the 1940s, for example, reported being cautioned about appearing too smart and earning top grades, because displays of intelligence endangered their social status on campus. Women were also reminded, typically by their parents and brothers, that pursuing a career would reduce their prospects for marriage and motherhood.[31] In

Table 1.2   **Profile of the Fifty-five Women Elected to the US House Between 1916 and 1956**

	Number of Women	Percentage
Race		
Women of color	0	0.0
Background		
Lawyer	7	12.7
Prior elective office experience		
Elected to local office	6	10.9
Elected to state house of representatives	9	16.4
Elected to state senate	1	1.8
Elected to statewide office	1	1.8
Other political experience		
Served in appointed administrative office	10	18.2
Served in party organization	14	25.5
Lateral entry		
Widows	21	38.2
No prior elective office experience	6	10.9
Party		
Democrats	35	63.6
Republicans	20	36.4

Source: Data compiled by the authors.

1950, only 24 percent of bachelor's degrees were awarded to women.[32] The average age of marriage for women was twenty.[33] Traditional sex roles were widely accepted by men and women. In 1936, a Gallup Poll asked respondents whether a married woman should work if she had a husband capable of supporting her; 82 percent of the sample said no.[34] A similar question appeared in an October 1938 poll, with 78 percent (81 percent of male respondents and 75 percent of female respondents) disapproving of married women entering the work force.[35] Prior to World War II, the proportion of married women who worked outside the home was only 15 percent. Labor shortages during the war drew married women into the work force; by 1944, the proportion increased to 22 percent, and by 1956, to 29 percent.[36] Working outside the home and pursuing a professional career represented a rejection of tradition, socialization, and conformity.

Also accepted was the norm that politics was the domain of men. A 1945 Gallup Poll reported that a majority of men and women disagreed with the statement that not enough "capable women are holding important jobs" in government.[37] In the 1950s, voter turnout among men was 10 percentage points higher than among women.[38] One survey found that, compared to men, women were less likely to express a sense of involvement in politics; women had a lower sense of political efficacy and personal competence than men.[39] The political scientists conducting the survey reported that women who were married often refused to participate in the survey and referred interviewers "to their husbands as being the person in the family who pays attention to politics."[40] Moreover, these cultural norms about women and politics were slow to change. Indeed, as late as 1975, 48 percent of respondents in a survey conducted by the National Opinion Research Center agreed that "most men are better suited emotionally for politics than are most women."[41]

Against this cultural backdrop, it comes as no surprise that a "woman entering politics risks the social and psychological penalties so frequently associated with nonconformity. Disdain, internal conflicts, and failure are widely believed to be her likely rewards."[42] Entering the electoral arena was therefore an act of political and social courage. The example of Representative Coya Knutson (D-MN) poignantly illustrates that women with political ambitions were often punished. Knutson first ran for the House as a long shot in 1954, defeating a six-term incumbent Republican. During her campaign in the large rural district, she played the accordion and sang songs, in addition to criticizing the Eisenhower administration's agricultural policy. In 1958, Knutson was running for her third term. In response to Knutson's refusal to play along with the Democratic Party in its 1956 presidential endorsements, party leaders approached her husband, Andy, an alcoholic who physically abused her and her adopted son, to help sabotage her reelection campaign. At the prompting of party leaders, Andy wrote a letter to Coya pleading that she return to Minnesota and give up her career in politics, and complaining how their home life had deteriorated since she left for Washington, D.C. He also accused his wife of having an affair with one of her congressional staffers and threatened a $200,000 lawsuit. This infamous "Coya, Come Home" letter gained national media attention, and her opponent ran on the slogan "A Big Man for a Man-Sized Job." She was defeated by fewer than 1,400 votes by Republican Odin Langin.[43] She was the only Democratic incumbent to lose that year. Another woman would not be elected to Congress from Minnesota until Democrat Betty McCollum in 2000.

Serving in political office could also be extremely unpleasant. Women in Congress often had to fight for access and positions, such as committee assignments, that would have rightfully been given to them had they been men.[44] For example, in 1949, Representative Reva Bosone, a Democrat from Utah, requested a seat on the House Interior Committee. When she approached Representative Jere Cooper (D-TN), the chair of the Ways and Means Committee, who had the final say over assignments, he responded, "Oh, my. Oh, no. She'd be embarrassed because it would be embarrassing to be on the committee and discuss the sex of animals."[45] She shot back and said, "It would be refreshing to hear about animals' sex relationships compared to the perversions among human beings."[46] Cooper laughed and put her on the committee. In 1973, Representative Pat Schroeder (D-CO) did receive an assignment on the committee of her choice, Armed Services, but the chair, F. Edward Hebert, a seventy-two-year-old Democrat from Louisiana, made it clear he did not want a woman on his committee. Hebert was also outraged during that session because a newly elected African American, Representative Ron Dellums (D-CA), was assigned to his committee. Hebert announced that "women and blacks were worth only half of one 'regular' member," so Schroeder and Dellums were forced to share a chair during committee meetings.[47] Schroeder got the seat on the Armed Services Committee in the first place because of the pressure put on Hebert by Representative Wilbur Mills (D-AR), the head of the Committee on Committees. Normally, Hebert would have been able to veto Mills's decision to put Schroeder on the committee, but Mills pushed hard for Schroeder. Earlier that year, Mills was found "frolicking" in the Tidal Basin near the Jefferson Memorial with a stripper, Fannie Fox. Mills's support for Schroeder's appointment to the committee was an apparent attempt to appease his wife.[48] An apt summary of the congressional ethos facing female members was provided by Representative Florence Dwyer (R-NJ), who served her first term in the 85th Congress (1957 session): "A Congresswoman must look like a girl, act like a lady, think like a man, speak on any given subject with authority and most of all work like a dog."[49]

As Table 1.2 shows, none of the fifty-five women elected between 1916 and 1956 were women of color, who faced the "double disadvantage" of racism and sexism.[50] For example, as one historian explained, when the US Constitution was enacted in 1789, African American women, along with African American men, counted as three-fifths of a person in the infamous compromise over how to count slaves for the purposes of representation in the US House. The Fifteenth Amendment, passed in 1870, enfranchised only black men; now black women counted as zero under the Constitution. When the Nineteenth Amendment was passed in 1920, ensuring women the right to vote, Jim Crow laws and other restrictive means to disenfranchise blacks were in full force in the South. Thus, it was not until the Voting Rights Act of 1965 that African American women could actually exercise their right to vote.[51] However, after the passage of the Voting Rights Act, black women proved to be even more politically ambitious than their white counterparts, running for political office at the local, state, and national levels at higher rates than white women during the 1970s and 1980s.[52]

When Shirley Chisholm (D-NY) came to Washington, D.C., in 1968 as the first African American woman elected to Congress, she asked to be assigned to the Committee on Education and Labor. She was a former teacher with extensive experience in education policy while serving in the New York state assembly. Education was extremely important to her poor, black, Brooklyn district. The Democratic Party leadership in Congress, however, assigned her to the Agriculture Committee and the Subcommittee on Forestry and Rural Development. Outraged, she refused the assignment and took her case to Speaker of the House John McCormack (D-MA). He told her she should be a "good soldier," put her time in on the committee, and wait for a better assignment. Chisholm responded, "All my forty-three years I have been a good soldier. . . . The time is growing late, and I can't be a good soldier any longer."[53] She protested her committee assignment on the House floor, stating that "it would be hard to imagine an assignment that is less relevant to my background or to the needs of the predominantly black and Puerto Rican people who elected me."[54] She was reassigned to the Veterans' Affairs Committee. It was not her first choice, but Chisholm did note, "There are a lot more veterans in my district than trees."[55]

Entry Professions and the Pipeline

One of the most prevalent explanations for the slow integration of women into Congress is the "pipeline theory." In US politics there is a hierarchy of public office that functions as a career ladder for elected officials. A local office often serves as a springboard into the state legislature, which in turn provides the requisite experience to run for the US House of Representatives.[56] Both the state legislature and the US House serve as avenues to statewide office, the most prominent of which are governorships and the US Senate. Each successive office has a larger territorial jurisdiction, a larger constituency, and an increase in salary and prestige.[57] Before one can even enter this hierarchy, however, there are particular professions in the private sector that traditionally lead to political office, such as law and business. Although members of Congress come from a wide variety of career backgrounds, the most common by far is law. Those practicing in these professions typically form the "eligibility pool" of candidates for office. The pipeline theory maintains that once more women are in the eligibility pool, they will run for state and local office and then eventually "spill over" into Congress.

As Table 1.2 reveals, very few of the fifty-five women elected to the House between 1916 and 1956 advanced to Congress through this traditional pipeline. The primary reason for this is that for most of US history, women were barred from entering many of the professions in the eligibility pool; the pipeline was blocked.[58] In 1956, only 4 percent of law degrees were awarded to women. Prior to 1970, less than 5 percent of lawyers were women.[59] Of the fifty-five women elected to the House between 1918 and 1956, only seven were lawyers.

Very few of these women had prior experience in lower-level political office. Six women had won election to local office, and nine had served in their state house of representatives. Representative Iris Blitch (D-GA) was the only woman to serve in the state senate and the only woman elected to both the lower and upper chambers of a state legislature. Democratic representative Chase Going Woodhouse served as Connecticut's secretary of state and is the only woman of the fifty-five who had been elected to statewide office. Prior to pursuing a political career, she was an economics professor.[60]

Because the pipeline was largely off-limits, women relied on other routes to gain experience.[61] As Table 1.2 shows, ten of the fifty-five women, 18 percent, held administrative appointments, mostly at the local level, and fourteen, 25 percent, worked in some capacity for their political party. But even as volunteers in party organizations, women faced barriers. They were regularly confined to "expressive roles," while men assumed "instrumental roles";[62] women hosted social events and were assigned "menial tasks associated with secretarial work," while men worked at recruiting candidates and managing campaigns.[63] Moon Landrieu, former mayor of New Orleans and father of US senator Mary Landrieu (D-LA), described this division of labor as "women do the lickin' and the stickin' while men plan the strategy."[64] In the late 1960s, Representative Patsy Mink (D-HI) pushed the Democratic National Committee to put more women in party leadership and policymaking positions. She was confronted by another committee member, Edgar Berman, Vice President Hubert Humphrey's personal physician, who claimed that "if we had a menopausal woman President who had to make the decision of the Bay of Pigs," she would be "subject to the curious mental aberrations of that age group."[65] Mink demanded, and got, Berman's resignation from the committee. In response, he claimed he had been "crucified on the cross of women's liberation" and that her anger was "a typical example of an ordinarily controlled woman under the raging hormonal imbalance of the periodical lunar cycle."[66]

Because of such attitudes, the women who were elected to the House frequently gained their seats through "lateral entry" instead of climbing the public office career ladder. As Table 1.2 reports, twenty-one of the fifty-five women elected to the House between 1916 and 1956 were congressional widows; they ran for the House seats held by their deceased husbands. Six other women won their seats without the benefit of holding prior elective or party office. Occasionally, these women capitalized upon their "celebrity status" to launch a successful campaign for office. In other words, they relied on prior name recognition and acclaim they had earned outside the political arena.[67] For example, prior to running for the House, Clare Boothe Luce (R-CT) was a writer for *Vogue*. In 1932, at the age of twenty-nine, she was named managing editor of *Vanity Fair.* A collection of her articles satirizing the social life of New York City was published in *Stuffed Shirts.*[68] She left the magazine two years later to work as a playwright and had several of her plays produced on Broadway, including *The Women, Kiss the Boys Goodbye,* and *Margin for Error.* In 1935, she married Henry Luce, a founder and editor of *Time* magazine. Together, they developed *Life* magazine, which began publication in November 1936. In 1938, Luce's stepfather, Albert Austin (R-CT), won a seat in the House representing the Fourth District of Connecticut. Two years later, Austin was defeated by Democrat LeRoy Downs. In 1942, having never run for political office, Luce won the Republican nomination and then defeated Downs. During her second term, she battled the emotional trauma caused by the death of her daughter in an automobile accident. In 1946, Luce announced that she would not seek a third term.[69]

Representative Helen Gahagan Douglas (D-CA) was a contemporary of Luce. At age twenty-one, she made her Broadway debut in *Dreams for*

Photo courtesy of the Library of Congress

Representative Clare Boothe Luce was first elected to the House in 1942, having never run for office before.

Sale, a play that won its author, Owen Davis, a Pulitzer Prize. A Broadway critic called Douglas "ten of the twelve most beautiful women in the world."[70] She also pursued a career as an opera singer. In 1931, she married the well-known and popular actor Melvyn Douglas, and the couple left New York to pursue film careers in Hollywood. Helen appeared in one film, *She,* in 1935, in which she played Queen Hash-A-Mo-Tep of Kor, a beautiful 500-year-old queen of a lost arctic city who could die only if she fell in love.[71] The film lost $180,000 at the box office. According to critics, Douglas lacked "screen presence."[72] In Hollywood, Douglas became active in politics and testified before Congress on "the plight of migratory farm workers."[73] Her testimony attracted the attention of First Lady Eleanor Roosevelt. At Roosevelt's urging, Douglas became a candidate for Congress in 1944, when the retirement of Democrat Thomas Ford created an open seat in the Fourteenth District of California. She won the election with 52 percent of the vote and was reelected in 1946 and 1948 by more comfortable margins. As a member of the House, Douglas worked hard to emphasize her competence, in part by "consciously playing down her beauty under conservative garb and hair style."[74] During the 79th Congress (1945 and 1946 sessions), Douglas and Luce were colleagues in the House. Both had to contend with press coverage that tended to exaggerate personal rivalry between them.[75]

This attitude toward women who became involved in politics is reflected in the concluding chapter of *Political Life,* published in 1959 by Robert Lane, a political science professor at Yale. He explained:

> Broadly speaking, political affairs are considered by the culture to be somewhat peripheral to the female sphere of competence and proper concern. . . . It is too seldom remembered in . . . American society that working girls and career women, and women who insistently serve the

Photo courtesy of the Library of Congress

Representative Helen Gahagan Douglas first ran for the House in 1944, after being encouraged by First Lady Eleanor Roosevelt.

community in volunteer capacities, and women with extra-curricular interests of an absorbing kind are often borrowing their time and attention
and capacity for relaxed play and love from their children to whom it
rightfully belongs.[76]

John Lindsay, the mayor of New York City from 1966 to 1973, put it more
bluntly: "Whatever women do, they do best after dark."[77] Thus, it should
come as no surprise that many women who entered politics had very different career paths than their male counterparts.

Demographics and the Politics of Redistricting

Table 1.2 shows that of the fifty-five women elected to the House between
1916 and 1956, thirty-five, or 64 percent, were Democrats. This masks,
however, the relative equality between the parties for most of this time period. In fact, the number of Democratic and Republican women running
and winning in a given election cycle was remarkably equal. From 1916 to
1956, Democratic women outnumbered Republican women in only thirteen of the twenty-one election cycles. In the vast majority of elections, the
difference between the number of Democratic and Republican women running and winning was less than two. Thus, for fifty years, with a couple of
exceptions, there were approximately the same number of Democratic and
Republican women serving in Congress.

Regardless of their party, the women who served in Congress during
this time period were distinct from their male colleagues in one important
way: they voted differently.[78] Figure 1.1 provides a measure of ideology
for House members based on their House floor roll call votes. The measure provides scores from 0 to 100; scores closer to 0 indicate that representatives are more liberal, while scores closer to 100 indicate that
representatives are more conservative.[79] As the figure shows, women of
both parties were to the left of their male colleagues: on average, female

**Figure 1.1   Ideology of Female and Male Members of the US House,
1916–1956**

Most Liberal	Democrats		Republicans		Most Conservative
	Women	Men	Women	Men	
0.0	32.7	38.2	63.6	68.1	100.0

Source: Data compiled by Keith Poole and Howard Rosenthal, http://voteview.com/down
loads.asp.

Democratic House members were more liberal than male Democratic House members, and female Republican House members were more moderate than male Republican House members. For example, as noted earlier, fourteen of the fifteen women in the 85th Congress (1957 session) voted for the Civil Rights Act of 1957; the lone nay vote among these women came from a Southern Democrat.

One possible explanation for these differences may lie in the kinds of House districts that elected women.[80] Many of the successful female candidates who won election during this time period, regardless of party, came from large cities. For example, Representative Edith Green (D-OR) was from Portland, Frances Bolton (R-OH) was from Cleveland, Marguerite Church (R-IL) was from Chicago, Kathryn Granahan (D-PA) was from Philadelphia, Edna Kelly (D-NY) was from New York City, and Leonor Sullivan (D-MO) was from St. Louis. This suggests that women fared much better in urban districts. In 1956, the median urban population of districts electing men was 58 percent. In contrast, the median urban population in those fifteen districts that elected women was 87 percent. For the twelve women who won their party's nomination but were defeated in the general election, the median urban population in those twelve districts was only 54 percent. In addition, for the thirty-four women who were not congressional widows, only five, 15 percent, came from House districts in the South.

This "urban connection" becomes particularly important given the malapportionment across House districts that favored rural districts during this period. Prior to the early 1960s, most districts in the United States were malapportioned; in other words, districts did not have equal populations. After decades of dismissing malapportionment as a "political question," in 1962 the US Supreme Court finally ruled, in *Baker v. Carr,* that a challenge to the apportionment of seats in the Tennessee general assembly was a "justiciable issue." The standard established by this landmark case is often described as the "one person, one vote" rule and held that disparities in population across legislative districts were unconstitutional. Once implemented, the decision reduced the dominance of representatives of underpopulated rural districts in many state legislatures. In 1964 the Supreme Court announced its decision in *Wesberry v. Sanders,* a case that challenged the congressional district boundaries in Georgia. Here the Court applied the precedent from *Baker* and held that "construed in its historical context, the command of Article I, Section 2, that Representatives be chosen 'by the People of the several States' means that as nearly as is practicable one man's vote in a congressional election is to be worth as much as another's."[81]

According to the 1950 US Census, if districts had been apportioned with equal populations, they would have had approximately 349,000 residents.[82] The actual population of congressional districts, however, varied widely. In 1956, eighty-nine districts had fewer than 300,000 residents, and twenty-eight districts had fewer than 250,000 residents. There were also eighty-nine districts with populations exceeding 400,000, and twenty-eight with populations exceeding 450,000.[83]

This malapportionment created widespread disparities in representation that favored rural America. In essence, votes in less populated districts were worth more than the votes in highly populated districts. For example, the most populous constituency to elect a woman in 1956 was the Third District of Oregon, Democratic representative Edith Green's district. This district, with a population of 471,537, included the city of Portland. In contrast, the rural Fourth District of Texas, represented by Democratic speaker of the House Sam Rayburn, or "Mr. Sam," had 186,043 people. The value of an individual vote in Texas's Fourth District was over two and a half times the value of an individual vote in Oregon's Third. In addition to diluting the voting power of minority groups residing in urban areas, this rural bias limited the number of urban districts, which is where the women of the 1950s were most successful.

There were other apportionment issues that affected the electoral fate of women as well. Prior to the Supreme Court's decision in *Wesberry v. Sanders* in 1964, it was not unusual for a state gaining a seat in the reapportionment process to elect the new member at-large for one or two elections until the state legislature got around to redrawing the district lines and eliminated the at-large seat. Of the fifty-five women elected to the House between 1916 and 1956, eight were elected as at-large representatives. Only two, Representatives Isabella Greenway (D-AZ) and Caroline O'Day (D-NY), served more than one term in the House. Two women, Representatives Jeannette Rankin (R-MT) and Winnifred Stanley (R-NY), left the House after redistricting dissolved their at-large seats.

After the 1960 US Census and the Supreme Court's decisions in *Baker* and *Wesberry,* states began a wave of redistricting, and several other women who were first elected between 1916 and 1956 fell victim to reapportionment. Some states lost seats and existing districts had to be dissolved, as was the case for Representative Kathryn Granahan's (D-PA) district. As "compensation," Democratic leaders in Pennsylvania persuaded President John F. Kennedy to nominate Granahan for the post of US treasurer.[84] In some cases, redistricting forced two incumbents to compete for a single seat. In 1968, to comply with *Wesberry,* Ohio enacted a redistricting plan that pitted Republican representative Frances Bolton, who was seeking her sixteenth term in the House, against Democratic incumbent Charles Vanik, who defeated Bolton with 55 percent of the vote. Redistricting also forced incumbents of the same party to compete against each other. The 1968 redistricting plan in New York ended the career of Representative Edna Kelly when she had to run against fellow Democrat Emanuel Celler. In addition to the enforced sex roles that limited their choices and the denial of access to the political pipeline, this suggests that the success of some female candidates was often thwarted in the process of redistricting.

▨ Women and Congressional Elections: A Century of Change

Our overview of the barriers faced by women in the first half of the twentieth century begins to suggest why so few were elected to the House and Senate. The social and political culture was not amenable to female politicians. The preparatory professions and paths to public office were blocked. The geographic composition of House districts and the manipulation of those districts were additional challenges. Much has changed in US politics and culture since then. Our analysis is designed to further examine these clues to understanding the pace of women's integration into the electoral system.

Our Data

We developed three original datasets that span over a hundred years. The first dataset includes all primary and general elections to the US House of Representatives and US Senate from 1956 through 2010. Our major source for this "master file" is the *America Votes* series. For each district in each election year, we recorded the number of female candidates running for the Democratic and Republican nominations, the total number of candidates seeking each party's nomination, whether a woman won the Democratic or Republican nomination, and the outcome of the general election.[85] For each district, we also recorded the party and sex of the incumbent, whether the incumbent was seeking reelection, and the incumbent's share of the two-party vote in the prior election.

Identifying the sex of candidates was done by examining the names listed in each district in the primary and general elections provided by *America Votes* and, for more recent elections, by CNN's online Election Center. Occasionally, the sex of the candidate was not obvious from the first name. While the most common questionable names were Pat, Lee,

Terry, Leslie, and Robin (including Robin Hood), we also encountered the exotic Simone (no last name) and Echo in California. Other puzzlers included Kish, Avone, Twain, and Mattox. To investigate these unknowns, we consulted relevant editions of the *Almanac of American Politics* and the *Congressional Quarterly Weekly Report.* Quite often, the coverage in these sources provided information about the sex of the party nominees. For the more recent period (approximately 1974 onward), we conducted a Nexis or Google search of newspaper coverage. In almost every case, we were able to find media coverage that revealed the sex of the candidates. Finally, if these methods provided no information, the name was excluded from our count of candidates. The total number of exclusions was less than 2 percent of all candidate names. Applying these procedures to electoral data from 1956 through 2010, we coded 12,182 House elections involving over 38,200 candidate names, and 968 Senate elections involving over 4,660 candidate names.

Unfortunately, there is no reliable source of House candidates running in primaries across states prior to 1956, and thus we are limited to collecting data before this date only on those candidates who ran in general elections. For our data from 1916 to 1954, we relied on the *Candidate Name and Constituency Totals, 1788–1990* (5th edition) from the Inter-University Consortium for Political and Social Research. We then used the methods described previously to confirm the sex of the candidate if it was not clear from the name. This file includes 8,604 House elections involving 15,886 candidate names.

We also created a file with biographical information on all 239 women who served in the House from 1916 to 2010, including a wide variety of variables, such as the year they were elected, information about their district, their prior political experience, the number of terms served, and their age when they were first elected. These data are from the *Biographical Directory of the American Congress;* the *Biographical Dictionary of Congressional Women; Congressional Women: Their Recruitment, Integration, and Behavior* (2nd edition); *Women in Congress, 1917–2006;* and various editions of the *Almanac of American Politics.*

These three original databases were supplemented with additional information made available by Professors Scott Adler and David Lublin. For each congressional session between 1943 and 1997, Adler created a file that includes, for every congressional district, thirty-seven demographic variables from the US Census.[86] The *Congressional District Demographic and Political Data,* compiled by Lublin, includes electoral results and demographic measures drawn from the US Census for all House districts from 1962 to 1994.[87]

Our Analysis

Using the largest database in existence on women and congressional elections, we attempt in this book to unravel the underlying causes behind the pace of change in the integration of women into Congress.

Chapter 2 provides an overview of the number of women running in primaries, winning primaries, and winning general elections for the House and Senate from 1956 to 2010. The principal finding in this chapter is that the integration of women into Congress is best described as slow, irregular, and unremarkable. In fact, from 1956 to 1970, the number of women in Congress actually declined. Consistent increases in the number of female candidates did not begin until the early 1970s, when social attitudes about appropriate roles for women began to change; between 1972 and 1990, the number of women elected to the House would increase by one or two in a given election cycle. In the Senate, the integration was even slower. In 1992, the "Year of the Woman," a record number of women candidates ran and won, nearly doubling the number of women in the House, increasing the number of women of color, and tripling the number of women in the Senate. The conditions that produced this spike in the number of women running and winning have not, however, repeated themselves. In fact, in 2010, the "Year of the Republican Woman," the number of women elected to the House declined. Thus, trends in the number of women running and winning elections have shown anything but a steady, methodical climb.

Chapter 3 explores one possible explanation for this uninspiring and inconsistent pace. We place the integration of women into Congress in a larger context and investigate the historical development of careerism in Congress. For most of the nineteenth century, Congress actually did very little and was a notoriously unpleasant place; members who served more than one or two terms were rare. But around 1916, when women were first beginning to run for the US House, the average length of service began to steadily increase. By the 1950s, the power of incumbency was well established. For the past fifty years, incumbents, particularly in the House, have been virtually unbeatable. Even scandal only rarely dislodges them. Our analysis suggests a rather remarkable confluence of trends: just as women were starting to enter the political arena at the beginning of the twentieth century, careerism was just beginning to develop. And six decades later, when traditional gender stereotypes and social attitudes began to change and women began running in increasing numbers, the power of incumbency was firmly entrenched. Incumbency plays a major role in the "arrested development" of the success of women candidates.

In Chapter 4 we turn from the "big picture" and explore the individual decision to run for office. While incumbency is an almost insurmountable barrier, one factor has helped many aspiring candidates find their way around it: their family name. Many of the early women who successfully ran for the House were the widows of members of Congress, winning special elections to fill their deceased husbands' seats. Until the 1970s, given cultural expectations and traditional attitudes toward women's roles, the presumption was that after finishing her deceased husband's term, she would gracefully and willingly step aside, after a "real" replacement was found. This stereotype, however, did not match reality. Many congressional widows were experienced public servants and went on to long and successful House careers. As cultural expectations have changed, female candidates have transitioned from widows to mothers; as the widow route has become less frequent, the role of mother has gradually gained more acceptance. Because women are still the primary caregivers for children, they typically wait until their children are grown and thus are older than men when they run for office the first time. Voters still question whether women with young children will have enough time to devote to the demands of public office. However, there are now many examples of women who have successfully combined politics and parenthood.

We then turn, in Chapter 5, to the competitive environment faced by House incumbents seeking reelection and explore whether this environment is the same for men and women. Female House incumbents are actually reelected at rates slightly higher than male House incumbents. Female incumbents also win by larger margins than their male counterparts. These advantages are small, but reappear in election after election over the past five decades, suggesting that women have more than reached parity in the electoral arena. However, when we look beneath the surface, it turns out that female incumbents face a more competitive environment. They are much more likely to be challenged in their own party's primary, and candidates "come out of the woodwork" to run in the opposition-party primary. Male incumbents are more likely to run uncontested and get a "free pass," with no competition in their own primary and the opposition party simply conceding and not bothering to run any candidates. In other words, women have to work harder to keep their seats. In addition, the presence of a female incumbent draws more women into the race: female incumbents are more likely than male incumbents to face female challengers.

Chapter 6 investigates another unexplored inequality: the development of a substantial gap between the numbers of Democratic and Republican women in the House. As mentioned earlier, for most of the twentieth century there were relatively equal numbers of Democratic and Republican women in the House. However, in the 112th Congress (2011 session), Democratic women outnumbered Republican women in both the House (forty-eight versus twenty-four representatives) and the Senate (twelve versus five senators). In other words, Democratic women outnumbered Republican women two to one. In Chapter 6 we disaggregate the number of women running in primaries, winning primaries, and winning general elections for the House and Senate by party, to explore the development of this gap. The observed change in women seeking and winning office that is highlighted in Chapter 2 has not been uniform across both parties. Since the early 1990s, the growth of women as candidates and officeholders has occurred disproportionately within the Democratic Party. Further, this Democratic advantage in electing women is not restricted to the US House; it can also be seen in state legislatures. The development of this party gap is not particularly well explained by looking in the "pipeline." It is also not a function of the overall electoral success of either party. But if the road to Congress is through one party only, this further slows the integration of women.

Our results in Chapter 5 show that female candidates tend to cluster in particular districts, and Chapter 6 explores how party has played a role in the success of women candidates. Chapter 7 investigates how these two trends may be related. It boils down to the old adage that "all politics is local"; the key lies in the kinds of districts where female candidates are successful. Demographics are central to understanding the outcomes of US elections. Districts that elect Democrats share a particular demographic profile that is quite different from districts that elect Republicans. As it turns out, districts that elect women share a particular demographic profile that is quite different from the districts that elect men. Successful female House candidates come from districts that are smaller, more urban, more racially and ethnically diverse, wealthier, and more educated than districts that elect men. In other words, there are districts that are "women-friendly."

We began this book with a profile of the women who served in Congress during the first half of the twentieth century. Chapter 8 begins with a profile of the women who served in Congress during the first decade of the twenty-first century. Not only has there been a tremendous change in cultural attitudes toward women's "proper place," but there has also been a tremendous change in the career paths taken by the women who now serve in the House. The women of the twenty-first century are more racially and ethnically diverse, more likely to have law degrees, and more likely to have served in their state legislatures than their predecessors. The pipeline is now open to women. However, shifting demographics and redistricting also have the potential to dramatically shape opportunities for women. In fact, just as we can predict whether a Democrat or Republican will win a district by looking at factors like urbanization, racial and ethnic diversity, and income, we can also predict whether a man or woman will win a district. Using twelve demographic measures, we calculate, for each of the 435 House districts, the probability that a woman will win. While there are still far more districts that are highly unlikely to elect a female candidate than those that are "women-friendly," changes in the demography of the United States over the past fifty years—and those that are projected to continue into the twenty-first century—bode well for female candidates. As American society becomes more diverse, more urban, and more educated, opportunities for female candidates will expand. Demographics and political geography are critical to understanding the integration of women into Congress.

▓ Notes

1. Weisman and Murray, "Democrats Take Control on Hill."
2. Balz, "Hillary Clinton Opens Presidential Bid," p. A1.
3. Clift and Brazaitis, *Madam President,* 2nd ed., p. 149.
4. Newport, "Update: Hillary Rodham Clinton and the 2008 Election." See also Clift and Brazaitis, *Madam President,* 2nd ed., chap. 6.
5. Kornblut, "Clinton Shatters Record for Fundraising," p. A1.
6. Kornblut, *Notes from the Cracked Ceiling;* Traister, *Big Girls Don't Cry.*
7. Cooper and Bumiller, "Alaskan Is McCain's Choice."
8. Ibid.
9. Weiner, "Sarah Palin Not Running for President."
10. See, for example, Banner, *Elizabeth Cady Stanton;* Oakley, *Elizabeth Cady Stanton;* Stanton, Anthony, and Gage, *History of Woman Suffrage;* Stanton and Blatch, *Elizabeth Cady Stanton As Revealed in Her Letters.*
11. "Cady, Daniel."
12. Stanton, Anthony, and Gage, *History of Woman Suffrage,* p. 180.
13. Banner, *Elizabeth Cady Stanton,* p. 93.
14. Stanton and Blanch, *Elizabeth Cady Stanton As Revealed in Her Letters,* pp. 114–115.
15. Parsons, Beach, and Dubin, *United States Congressional Districts,* p. 126.
16. Stanton, Anthony, and Gage, *History of Woman Suffrage,* p. 181.
17. See Lopach and Luckowski, *Jeannette Rankin.*
18. Foerstel, *Biographical Dictionary of Congressional Women,* p. 225.
19. Ibid., pp. 226–227. See also Kaptur, *Women of Congress.*
20. Foerstel, *Biographical Dictionary of Congressional Women,* pp. 87–89.
21. Ibid., p. 51.
22. Ibid.
23. Alaska and Hawaii were not yet states, so the total number of senators was ninety-six.
24. Foerstel, *Biographical Dictionary of Congressional Women,* p. 27.
25. Ibid., pp. 109–111.

26. Ibid., pp. 263–265.

27. Ibid., p. 104.

28. Ibid., p. 218.

29. Kirkpatrick, *Political Woman,* p. 3.

30. Ibid., p. 15.

31. Komarovsky, "Cultural Contradictions and Sex Roles."

32. National Center for Education Statistics, "Table 279: Degrees Conferred."

33. "Families and Living Arrangements."

34. "Gallup Poll," p. 39.

35. Ibid., p. 131.

36. *Historical Statistics of the United States,* p. 133.

37. "Gallup Poll," pp. 548–549.

38. Campbell et al., *The American Voter,* p. 485.

39. Ibid., pp. 489–490.

40. Ibid., p. 485.

41. Mayer, *The Changing American Mind,* p. 394.

42. Kirkpatrick, *Political Woman,* p. 15.

43. Foerstel, *Biographical Dictionary of Congressional Women,* pp. 152–153; Haga, "'Come Home,' Coya Dies," p. 1A; Inskip, "A Revival of Sorts for Minnesota's Knutson," p. 11A.

44. Friedman, "House Committee Assignments of Women and Minority Newcomers."

45. Foerstel and Foerstel, *Climbing the Hill,* p. 95.

46. Ibid., p. 96.

47. Schroeder, *Twenty-four Years of House Work and the Place Is Still a Mess,* p. 41.

48. Ibid., p. 40.

49. Foerstel, *Biographical Dictionary of Congressional Women,* p. 79.

50. In 1956, three African American men and one Hispanic man won election to the House.

51. Locke, "From Three-fifths to Zero."

52. Clayton and Stallings, "Black Women in Congress"; Cohen, "A Portrait of Continuing Marginality"; Darcy and Hadley, "Black Women in Politics"; Darling, "African-American Women in State Elective Office in the South"; Handley and Grofman, "The Impact of the Voting Rights Act on Minority Representation"; Moncrief, Thompson, and Schuhmann, "Gender, Race, and the State Legislature"; Smooth, "African American Women and Electoral Politics"; Swain, *Black Faces, Black Interests;* Williams, "The Civil Rights–Black Power Legacy."

53. Chisholm, *Unbought and Unbossed,* pp. 82–83.

54. Ibid., p. 84.

55. Kaptur, *Women of Congress,* p. 149.

56. See, for example, Fulton et al., "The Sense of a Woman"; Sanbonmatsu, Carroll, and Walsh, *Poised to Run.*

57. See, for example, Canon, *Actors, Athletes, and Astronauts;* Francis and Kenny, *Up the Political Ladder;* Matthews, *US Senators and Their World;* Schlesinger, *Ambition and Politics.*

58. See, for example, Burrell, *A Woman's Place Is In the House;* Carroll, *Women as Candidates in American Politics;* Conway, *Political Participation in the United States;* Conway, Steuernagel, and Ahern, *Women and Political Participation;* Diamond, *Sex Roles in the State House.*

59. Epstein, *Women in Law,* p. 4.

60. Foerstel, *Biographical Dictionary of Congressional Women,* p. 281.

61. See, for example, Deber, "The Fault Dear Brutus"; Kirkpatrick, *Political Woman;* Welch, "Recruitment of Women to Public Office."

62. Constantini, "Political Women and Political Ambition"; Fowlkes, Perkins, and Rinehart, "Gender Roles and Party Roles."

63. Conway, Steuernagel, and Ahern, *Women and Political Participation,* p. 95.

64. Ibid.

65. Foerstel and Foerstel, *Climbing the Hill,* p. 27.

66. Ibid.

67. Canon, *Actors, Athletes, and Astronauts.*

68. Luce, *Stuffed Shirts.*

69. *Women in Congress,* p. 217.

70. Pitt, "Mrs. Deeds Goes to Washington," p. 477. See also Foerstel, *Biographical Dictionary of Congressional Women,* pp. 73–75; Scobie, *Center Stage.*

71. Internet Movie Data Base, http://imdb.com/title/tt0026983 (accessed June 13, 2005).

72. Ibid.

73. Pitt, "Mrs. Deeds Goes to Washington," p. 478.

74. Alpern, "Center Stage," pp. 967–968.

75. Ibid., p. 967.

76. Lane, *Political Life,* pp. 354–355.

77. Conway, Steuernagel, and Ahern, *Women and Political Participation,* p. 95.

78. For a review of the literature on this, see Swers, "Understanding the Policy Impact of Electing Women."

79. These scores are calculated from the data of Professors Keith Poole and Howard Rosenthal, available at http://voteview.com/downloads.asp. The original scores range from -1 to 1, but for ease of interpretation and comparison to other types of roll call indices, we transformed the scores to a scale ranging from 0 (most liberal) to 100 (most conservative).

80. See, for example, Gerrity, Osborn, and Mendez, "Women and Representation"; Simon and Palmer, "The Roll Call Behavior of the Men and Women in the US House of Representatives."

81. 376 US 1, p. 7.

82. Calculation of this target population excludes those at-large seats that have a statewide constituency and those states that are guaranteed one representative regardless of population (e.g., Vermont).

83. Simon, "Electoral and Ideological Change in the South."

84. Foerstel, *Biographical Dictionary of Congressional Women,* p. 100.

85. For primary elections, this count includes those candidates who received votes in the party primary. This differs slightly from those counts based upon those who filed to run but withdrew before the actual primary balloting. In gathering these data, we found several special cases. The states of Connecticut, Utah, and Virginia employ a mixed system of conventions and primaries to nominate their congressional candidates. The nominating conventions are held first, with primaries scheduled only if there is a significant challenge to the designated convention nominee. In instances where there is no primary, we coded the gender of the nominees only because the number of candidates seeking the nomination at the convention is unknown. Louisiana is yet another special case; the state employs an

open primary system in which candidates, regardless of party, run in a single primary. If a candidate wins an absolute majority of the primary vote, the candidate is elected to the House and there is no general election. For Louisiana, we coded the number of Democrats and Republicans (women and total) running in the initial primary. In instances where there was a general election, we followed the same conventions used with other states, noting, of course, instances in which the general election involved two candidates from the same party. Finally, there are states that have a primary runoff system. In these states, a candidate must win over 50 percent of the primary vote to obtain the party nomination. If no candidate wins over 50 percent, there is a runoff primary between the top two finishers. The winner of this runoff then becomes the party nominee. Our coding records the number of candidates (women and total) in the initial primary and the gender of the ultimate nominees.

86. These files are available at http://sobek.colorado.edu/~esadler/Data.html.

87. This file is available at www1.american.edu/dlublin.

TWO

A Long Slow Road: The Integration of Women into Congress

That politics has been a "man's game" for most of US history is best illustrated by the miniscule representation of women in Congress. Since 1789, less than 2 percent of the members have been women. Of the 10,739 people who have served in the House of Representatives, only 239 have been women, and only 39 of 1,930 senators have been women.[1] Only five states have been represented by two women senators serving simultaneously: California, Kansas, Maine, New Hampshire, and Washington. Nearly one-third of the women to serve in Congress are current members. In 2010, there were seventy-two women elected to the House and seventeen women serving in the Senate, making Congress 17 percent female. If current trends continue, the Senate will be half female by 2076. The House will be half female by 2156.

Our purpose in this chapter is to present both a statistical and descriptive history of women seeking and winning a seat in Congress. This history reveals that the growth in female candidates does not follow the pattern of a slow, steady climb. We show that, in fact, the years from 1956 to 1970 represent a period of modest decline. Consistent increases in the number of female candidates did not begin until the early 1970s. Between 1972 and 1990, the number of female candidates and nominees increased rather substantially, but the number of women elected to the House increased by only one or two in a given election cycle. In the Senate, the integration was even slower. In 1992, a record number of women candidates ran and won, nearly doubling the number of women in the House, including women of color, and tripling the number of women in the Senate. This much celebrated "Year of the Woman" has not, however, repeated itself. Modest gains best characterize the election cycles from 1994 through 2010, when the typical increase in the number of women in the House was three or four.

■ The Integration of Women into the House

Gaining a seat in Congress involves three distinct steps: seeking the nomination of a party, which in the vast majority of instances means running in a primary; winning the primary; and winning the general election. All candidates, whether they are incumbents, challengers, or running for an open seat, must go through these steps in every election cycle. Figure 2.1 provides an overview of the integration of women into the House from 1956 to 2010, showing the number of women running in primaries, winning primaries, and winning the general election.

As noted in Chapter 1, the first year included in our data, 1956, marked a high point in the number of women candidates; it would not be reached again until 1972. In 1956, fifty-three women ran in primaries, twenty-nine women won primaries, and fifteen were elected to the House. By 1968, this dropped to forty women running in primaries, nineteen women winning primaries, and ten winning election to the House. Commenting on their diminished and meager presence in the Congress, one female House member observed, "There are three times as many whooping cranes as congresswomen. . . . While many things are being done to protect the rare, long-legged bird, nobody seems concerned about our being an endangered species."[2]

Figure 2.1   Women as Candidates for the US House, 1956–2010

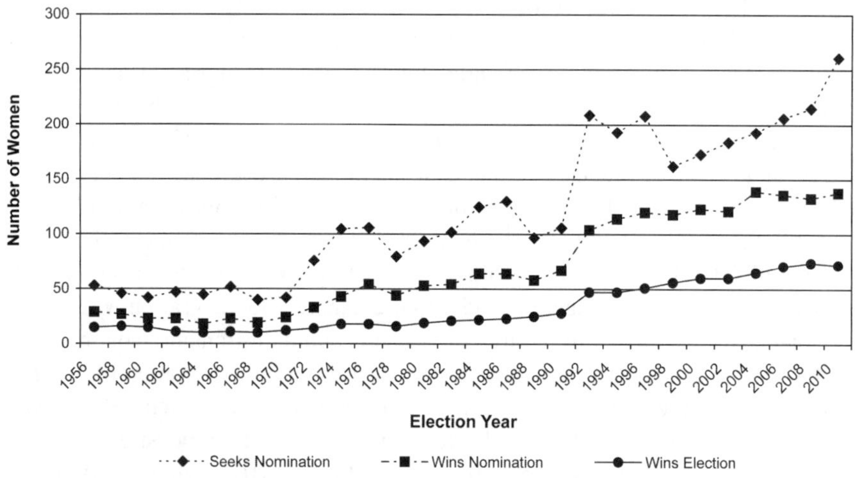

Source: Data compiled by the authors.

These declines seem especially surprising given many of the events of the 1960s. Women's rights were not a priority for President John F. Kennedy, but in 1961 he did create the Commission on the Status of Women and appointed former first lady Eleanor Roosevelt to be its chair.[3] In 1963, Betty Friedan's *The Feminine Mystique* brought "the problem that has no name" to the attention of millions of American women, and she toured the country talking about her book.[4] In 1964, Congress passed the landmark Civil Rights Act that banned discrimination in employment. The word "sex" as an illegal category of discrimination was added at the last minute by Representative Howard Smith (D-VA). The prevailing wisdom is that he did this in order to make the bill too radical and ensure its failure.[5] But the female members of Congress took the amendment very seriously, and this strategy to kill the legislation was ultimately unsuccessful. In 1966, the executive director of the Equal Employment Opportunity Commission, Herman Edelsberg, publicly stated that he had no intention of enforcing the provision. As far as he was concerned, "Men were entitled to female secretaries."[6] On September 7, 1968, a group of women led by Jo Freeman and Shulamith Firestone protested the Miss America pageant in Atlantic City, New Jersey, and received national news coverage; this would be "the first time the mass media gave headline coverage to the new feminist movement."[7] At the protest, demonstrators had set up a "freedom trashcan" and were encouraged to throw in things that represented traditional images of femininity, including high heels, curling irons, girdles, and bras. The coverage of the protest suggested that the women actually burned bras, leading to the term "bra-burners."[8] Despite the emergence of women's rights as a national issue, the integration of women into the House was slowing down.

These trends would change, however, in 1972. The early 1970s mark the beginning of a new era in the number of female candidates in House elections.[9] Between 1970 and 1974, the number of women running in primaries jumped from 42 to 105, the number of women winning primaries increased from 24 to 43, and the number of women winning the general election went from 12 to 18. The timing of this new era coincides with the dawn of the women's movement, marking the beginning of changing attitudes toward women as candidates and officeholders. "Like most social movements, the women's movement seemed to burst onto the political scene with little warning."[10] As Jo Freeman explained, "Within the short space of a few months the movement went from a struggling new idea to a national phenomenon."[11] In 1970, new women's rights organizations were forming at a rate faster than anyone could count.[12] Membership in the National Organization for Women exploded from 3,000 in 1970 to 50,000 in

1974.[13] *Ms. Magazine* was launched in 1972. Practical politics was emphasized as well. Organizations dedicated to recruiting and electing women to public office were created for the first time. In July 1971, Bella Abzug, Shirley Chisholm, Gloria Steinem, and Betty Friedan started the National Women's Political Caucus at a conference attended by over 300 women. In 1974, the Women's Campaign Fund was created to provide financial support directly to women candidates, to help women network with other powerful political action committees (PACs), and to make connections with political consultants.[14] Thus a new financial base for women candidates was established to increase their viability.

Other important events also took place during these years. The issue of abortion achieved national prominence after the Supreme Court handed down its decision in *Roe v. Wade* in March 1973. In 1971, the Court also reached its landmark decision in *Reed v. Reed* and for the first time ruled that discriminatory treatment based on sex was a violation of the equal protection clause.[15] That same year, the national Democratic Party approved the recommendations of the McGovern-Fraser Commission, a panel assigned the task of reforming the delegate selection rules. After adopting these reforms, the proportion of female delegates to the Democratic National Convention increased from 13 percent in 1968 to 40 percent in 1972.[16] Watergate and opposition to the Vietnam War mobilized women activists. In 1970, Bella Abzug, founder of Women Strike for Peace, organized Democrats in New York to oppose US foreign policy in Vietnam and also decided to run for Congress. On the day she was sworn in, she introduced a bill demanding that President Richard Nixon withdraw US forces from Vietnam.[17]

The 93rd Congress (1972 session) passed the largest number of bills on the "women's agenda" in congressional history, including Title IX of the Education Amendments.[18] One of the most galvanizing episodes of this period was the congressional debate over the proposed Equal Rights Amendment (ERA). Consideration of the amendment began on August 10, 1970. Representative Martha Griffiths (D-MI) organized an effort to use the discharge petition, a rarely used parliamentary maneuver, to wrest control of the resolution from the hostile chair of the House Judiciary Committee, Representative Emanuel Celler (D-NY), and bring it to the floor for debate. Celler had been a champion for the civil rights of African Americans, but was instrumental in keeping the ERA bottled up in committee for most of the 1960s.[19] His opposition to the ERA ultimately led to his primary defeat in 1972, when he ran for his twenty-sixth term; thirty-one-year-old Elizabeth Holtzman, who had never run for political office before, beat him by 600 votes, and then took his seat on the Judiciary Committee.[20] Celler's efforts to squash Griffiths's discharge petition were not successful, and the amendment passed in the House by a vote of 352 to 15. It was then "amended to death" in the Senate, including, among other things, a provision exempting women from military service and allowing school prayer. As a result, no final vote was taken on the ERA in the 1970 session of the Senate. However, the proponents of the ERA were successful in the 93rd Congress (1971 session), when a new version of the ERA was introduced. Attempts to amend the resolution failed, and bipartisan majorities voted to send the ERA to the states for ratification in March 1972.[21]

These events produced a substantial spike in the media coverage of women's issues in the early 1970s.[22] In effect, these developments constituted a declaration that politics was no longer an arena primarily reserved for men. The years from 1974 to 1990 were a period of modest but consistent gains; the number of female House nominees increased from forty-three to sixty-seven and the number who won a seat increased from eighteen to twenty-eight. Then came an astonishing turn of events in 1992. As Figure 2.1 illustrates, there was a dramatic spike in the number of women candidates. Often referred to as the "Year of the Woman," 1992 saw an unprecedented number of women running for office: 209 women ran in primaries, 104 women won primaries, and 47 women were elected to the House.[23] Only twenty-three of these women were incumbents. Along with their incumbent colleagues, twenty-four new women, including five blacks and two Latinas, were sworn in on January 5, 1993. Representative Henry Hyde (R-IL) remarked that with all the women now in Congress, the House floor was beginning to look "like a mall."[24]

Initially, there were few who thought that 1992 would become the tremendous victory for women that it did. The ousting of Saddam Hussein's army from Kuwait in the Gulf War of 1990 and early 1991 dominated news coverage. It was assumed that the success of President George H. W. Bush, foreign affairs, and military issues would be the top concerns on the political agenda during the election. This changed in the fall of 1991, when President Bush nominated Clarence Thomas, former chair of the Equal Employment Opportunity Commission, to fill a vacancy on the US Supreme Court created by the death of Justice Thurgood Marshall. During the confirmation hearings, it was revealed that Thomas was accused of sexually harassing Anita Hill, an attorney who had worked for the commission when Thomas served as chair. Many women were outraged as they watched the live broadcast of the hearings and saw the all–white male Senate Judiciary Committee badger Hill. She became "a symbol of women's status in American life and, in particular, their exclusion from the halls of power."[25] For the first time, the hearings brought national attention to the issue of sexual harassment. Moreover, as the economy slumped, the political agenda fundamentally changed; issues generally associated with women, such as education and healthcare, were now the major problems on the minds of voters.[26]

The Thomas-Hill hearings not only inspired women to run for office, but also inspired them to open their checkbooks. In 1990, PACs that supported women candidates contributed $2.7 million. In 1992, this increased to $11.5 million.[27] Female candidates also did particularly well among voters. Surveys taken in the spring and summer of 1992 showed that male and female voters believed that increasing the number of women in office would benefit the country.[28] Many women ran as "outsiders," which gave them a substantial advantage with the anti-incumbency mood of the electorate that particular year.[29] An exit poll indicated that voters actually preferred female candidates to male candidates.[30] As one journalist explained, "The farther away a woman was from power, the better her position to attain it."[31] Reactions to these events crystallized into the most spectacular success that female candidates have ever seen.

The following election cycle, however, was devastating for the Democratic Party. In 1994, the party lost fifty-two seats in the House. The 104th Congress would open with Republicans enjoying a 230–204 advantage. Thus ended the forty-year reign by Democrats as the majority party in the House. While 1994 was a historic loss for the Democrats, it was also dubbed the "Year of the Angry White Male." If 1992 had been a banner year for women candidates, 1994 was, by comparison, a setback; despite the tremendous shakeup in the overall composition of the House, the number of female members actually remained the same, at forty-seven.

This leveling-off, however, masked several crosscutting trends. The number of women running in primaries dropped to 193, but the number of women winning primaries increased to 114; in other words, women were more likely to win their primaries in 1994 than they were in 1992. Eleven new women were elected to the House, a higher number than usual, but eight female incumbents were defeated, six of whom had just been elected in 1992. As one journalist noted, "Marjorie Margolies-Mezvinsky was gone in less time than it takes to say 'Marjorie Margolies-Mezvinsky.'"[32] Margolies-Mezvinsky, a Democrat from Pennsylvania sometimes referred to as the "3-M Woman," won her first election to the House in 1992 by a margin of only 1,373 votes in a district that was solidly Republican.[33] Her defeat in 1994 is attributed to her vote for President Bill Clinton's budget plan. She had actually voted against Clinton's preliminary budget proposals three times and knew that voting for the budget would be "political suicide."[34] She promised Clinton, however, that she would not let the budget fail and would vote for it if hers would be the deciding vote. It was. Just after she cast her vote at the last minute, the Republicans on the House floor chanted, "Bye-bye Marjorie!"[35] She lost her reelection bid by 10,000 votes.[36]

The "Year of the Angry White Male" got its name in part because of the substantial increase in the gender gap among voters. Since the 1980s, approximately 52 percent of men had consistently identified with the Republican Party. But in 1994, 62 percent of men voted Republican.[37] In addition, the issues on the national agenda changed from education and healthcare to crime, which hurt many women candidates.[38] The same anti-incumbency mood that helped women win in 1992 made it difficult for them to retain their seats, as they were now perceived as "insiders."[39] Republican women, however, did relatively well. Of the eleven women first elected to the House in 1994, seven were Republicans, and all ten female Republican incumbents who sought reelection were successful. All eight of the female incumbents who lost were Democrats. In addition to Margolies-Mezvinsky, four other first-term female Democrats were defeated: Lynn Schenck (CA), Karen Shepherd (UT), Leslie Byrne (VA), and Maria Cantwell (WA). Many pundits felt that a more accurate label for the election would be the "Year of the Republican Woman."[40]

Although the number of women running in primary elections took a dive in 1998, the next several election cycles saw relatively steady growth in the number of women candidates. The election of 2006, like 1994, was another "wave election," but this time for the Democrats. Representative Rahm Emanuel, chair of the Democratic Congressional Campaign Committee, emphasized that George W. Bush was "going to be on the ballot like Clinton was in '94."[41] On the eve of the election, only 37 percent of the public approved of Bush's performance as president, a decline of 20 points since his second inauguration in January 2005. An even lower 34 percent approved of how the president was handling the war in Iraq.[42] It was also a year in which scandal played a major role. On September 28, 2005, the majority leader of the House, Representative Tom DeLay (R-TX), was indicted by a Texas grand jury for violations of the state's campaign finance laws.[43] DeLay subsequently resigned as majority leader and as a member of the House.[44] Representative Bob Ney (R-OH) withdrew from his reelection campaign in the face of charges that he had accepted illegal gifts from lobbyist Jack Abramoff.[45] Allegations that Representative Mark Foley (R-FL) had sent improper Internet messages to high school students in the House page program led to his resignation in September of 2006.[46] This chain of events allowed the Democrats to add charges of a "culture of corruption" to their campaign strategy.[47]

The 2006 midterms resulted in a thirty-seat loss for the Republicans. As a result, Republicans elected to the 110th Congress found themselves in the minority party, with the Democrats enjoying a 233–202 advantage. Representative Nancy Pelosi (D-CA) became the first female speaker of the House, with forty-nine Democratic female colleagues.[48] An additional twenty-one Republicans members were women. The number of women in the House increased from sixty-five to seventy-one, the largest net gain since 1992. Among the eleven new women in the House, eight were Democrats. All forty-two female Democratic incumbents who won their primaries held on to their seats.[49] All four of the female incumbents who lost were Republicans. Republican Katherine Harris of Florida did not seek reelection to her House seat because she decided to run for the Senate against Democratic incumbent Bill Nelson. Harris's management of her campaign suffered from a "seemingly endless exodus of staffers" and from troublesome gaffes.[50]

The election of Barack Obama as president in 2008 also widened the Democratic majority in the House, with the party gaining an additional twenty seats for a 257–178 advantage. The 2008 election is also noteworthy because the number of women elected to the House reached a historic high of seventy-four, including nine Democratic and two Republican women who were elected for the first time. Overall, the wave elections of 2006 and 2008 were advantageous to the electoral fortunes of female Democrats. Of the ninety-two Democratic women seeking reelection in these contests, ninety-one were reelected, the exception being Nancy Boyda (D-KS), who was defeated in 2008 by a female Republican, Lynn Jenkins. In addition, seventeen female Democrats were elected for the first time; seven of these women defeated Republican incumbents and four won their elections in open districts previously held by the Republicans.

The Democrats' euphoria and large majority in the House, however, were short-lived. The outcome of midterm House elections in 2010 is the most dramatic example of electoral change in several decades. The Democrats suffered a loss of sixty-four seats. As President Obama remarked, the Democrats got "shellacked."[51] The loss was larger than the party suffered during the Vietnam-era midterm in 1966 under President Lyndon Johnson (forty-seven seats) and larger than the Watergate-era loss for the Republicans in 1974 (forty-eight seats).[52] In fact, the election of 2010 produced the largest midterm setback for the party of the president since 1938, when the Democrats, under President Franklin Roosevelt, lost seventy-one seats. It was also the largest swing in seats for either party since 1948, when the Democrats, led by President Harry Truman, captured control of the House by winning seventy-five seats.

The 2010 campaign, however, featured a record number of female candidates: 264 women ran in primaries, a substantial increase from the 215 who ran in 2008, and 138 women won primaries, up from 133. These gains were largely the result in a surge in the number of Republican women running: the number of female Republican primary candidates more than doubled from 64 in 2008 to 130 in 2010. The election of 2010, it was claimed, would be like 1994, another "Year of the Republican Woman." In fact, a Google search for this phrase generated 221,000 hits.[53] Much of this media coverage focused on former Republican governor of Alaska and 2008 Republican candidate for vice president Sarah Palin. In many of her appearances and endorsements, Palin promised a "stampede of pink elephants" in 2010.[54] Palin was characterized as "building a pack of mama grizzlies" and advocating an "emerging conservative feminist identity."[55] And the number of Republican women in the House did grow, from seventeen to twenty-four, the largest increase in history. This number includes all fifteen of the incumbents seeking reelection along with nine members who won their first election. However, the number of Democratic women declined from fifty-seven to forty-eight, the largest decrease in history. Seven of the nine female Democrats first elected in 2008 were defeated. As a result, the number of women who won election to the House in 2010 declined from seventy-four to seventy-two, the first decline since 1968.

■ The Integration of Women into the Senate

The US Senate has been repeatedly called the "world's greatest legislative and deliberative body."[56] It is an institution dominated by history, tradition, and, until the 1970s, an "inner club" of "Senate types."[57] According to William S. White in *The Citadel,* a classic and reverential account of the institution published in 1956, a "Senate type" is, broadly speaking "a *man* for whom the Institution is a career in itself, a life in itself, and an end in itself."[58] That White would associate the "Senate type" with a man is not surprising given that the presence of a female member in the chamber was a rare event. Many of the women who served in the Senate obtained their seats first through appointment, rather than by election. While House seats that become vacant due to unscheduled retirements must be filled by a special election, Senate seats that become vacant can be initially filled by gubernatorial appointment. Then a special election is held in the next cycle to fill the remainder of the term. Fourteen of the thirty-nine women who have served in the Senate—over one-third—initially gained their seats through appointment.[59]

Table 2.1 lists those women whose initial entry into the Senate was the result of winning an election. The group includes fifteen Democrats and ten Republicans. Fourteen of these women won open seats in regularly scheduled elections; five won in special elections, including two who defeated an appointed incumbent; five defeated an incumbent in regularly scheduled elections; and one defeated an incumbent in a party primary. Eighteen of these senators were elected in 1992 or later.

The first woman to be elected to the Senate won a special election in 1938 in South Dakota and was never actually sworn in. Republican Gladys Pyle came from a political family. Her father, John, was the state's attorney general and her mother, Mamie, was head of the Universal Franchise League, an organization that successfully pushed for women's suffrage in South Dakota in 1918. After a career as a high school teacher, Gladys decided to enter politics. Her mother actually discouraged her, thinking her daughter would be accused of merely taking advantage of her family name, particularly her mother's high profile in the state. In 1922, at the age of thirty-two, Gladys became the first woman elected to the South Dakota house of representatives. In 1926, she became the first female secretary of state. After an unsuccessful run for governor, she ran for US Senate under rather unusual circumstances. After the death of Senator Peter Norbeck in 1936, Governor Tom Berry appointed Herbert Hitchcock. State law, however, required that Hitchcock step down before the next regularly scheduled election, in November 1938. A new senator would then be elected for the full term starting in January 1939. This meant, however, that the seat would be vacant for the two months between November and January. Typically, because the Senate would not be in session during those two months, the vacancy would not be filled. However, it was rumored that President Franklin Delano Roosevelt was going to call a special session. In response, the Republicans in South Dakota, who controlled the state's congressional delegation, pushed for a special election to fill the vacancy. With the support of the state party and the Republican National Committee, Pyle campaigned across the state and won with 58 percent of the vote. Unfortunately, Roosevelt never did call a special session, so Pyle was never sworn in. She did, however, still go to Washington, D.C., and during her two-month term she provided constituent services, secured several highway and Works Progress Administration (WPA) programs for her state, and convinced the crown prince and princess of Norway to stop in South Dakota during their North American tour.[60]

Because Pyle was never sworn in, Margaret Chase Smith (R-ME) is usually credited with being the very first woman elected to the Senate, in 1948. She ran after serving nine years in the House, having taken over that

Table 2.1   Women Initially Elected to the US Senate

	First Election	Dates of Senate Service
Gladys Pyle (R-SD)	Special election[a]	1938–1939
Margaret Chase Smith (R-ME)	Open seat	1949–1973
Hazel Abel (R-NE)	Special election	1954
Maurine Neuberger (D-OR)	Special election/open seat[b]	1960–1967
Nancy Landon Kassebaum (R-KS)	Open seat	1979–1997
Paula Hawkins (R-FL)	Open seat	1981–1987
Barbara Mikulski (D-MD)	Open seat	1987–present
Dianne Feinstein (D-CA)	Defeated Republican incumbent[c]	1993–present
Barbara Boxer (D-CA)	Open seat	1993–present
Carol Moseley Braun (D-IL)	Defeated incumbent in primary	1993–1999
Patty Murray (D-WA)	Open seat	1993–present
Kay Bailey Hutchison (R-TX)	Defeated Democrat incumbent[d]	1993–2013[e]
Olympia Snowe (R-ME)	Open seat	1995–present
Mary Landrieu (D-LA)	Open seat	1997–present
Susan Collins (R-ME)	Open seat	1997–present
Blanche Lincoln (D-AR)	Open seat	1999–2011
Debbie Stabenow (D-MI)	Defeated Republican incumbent	2001–present
Hillary Rodham Clinton (D-NY)	Open seat	2001–2009
Maria Cantwell (D-WA)	Defeated Republican incumbent	2001–present
Elizabeth Dole (R-NC)	Open seat	2003–2009
Amy Klobuchar (D-MN)	Open seat	2007–present
Claire McCaskill (D-MO)	Defeated Republican incumbent	2007–present
Kay Hagan (D-NC)	Defeated Republican incumbent	2009–present
Jeanne Shaheen (D-NH)	Defeated Republican incumbent	2009–present
Kelly Ayotte (R-NH)	Open seat	2011–present

Sources: Women in Congress, 1917–2006, Office of the Clerk of the US House of Representatives (Washington, DC: US Government Printing Office, 2006); "Women in the US Senate, 1922–2011" (New Brunswick, NJ: Rutgers University, Center for American Women and Politics, Eagleton Institute of Politics, 2011).

Notes: a. Pyle was elected on November 8, 1938, for a term that expired on January 3, 1939, but she was never sworn in.

b. Neuberger ran in both the special election to fill the seat of her deceased husband for the remainder of the 1960 term, as well as in the general election for the full term beginning in 1961.

c. In November 1992, Feinstein defeated Republican John Seymour, who was appointed when Pete Wilson resigned the Senate seat to become governor of California.

d. In November 1992, Hutchison defeated Democrat Robert Krueger, who was appointed when Lloyd Bentsen resigned his Senate seat to become secretary of the treasury.

e. In January 2011, Senator Hutchison announced she would not seek reelection in 2012.

seat after her husband died. In 1930, at the age of thirty-three, she married Clyde Smith, who was fifty-four years old. In 1936, Clyde was elected to the House as a Republican representing the Second District of Maine. Margaret worked on his staff; she answered constituent mail, wrote his speeches, and researched legislation. She was also part of the leadership hierarchy in the Republican Party of Maine. Just before his death in April 1940, Clyde asked the voters in his district to elect his "partner in public life."[61] She won with almost three times the vote her husband had received in his last election. When Senator Wallace White, the incumbent Republican, retired in 1948, she decided to run for the Senate. She faced three men in the primary and won with more votes than the combined total of all her competitors, and then won the general election. During the campaign, her opponents accused her of causing her husband's divorce from his first wife, despite the fact that she had met him three years after the fact.[62]

In the Senate, Smith gained national notoriety for her "Declaration of Conscience" speech on June 1, 1950, castigating Senator Joseph McCarthy

Photo courtesy of the Library of Congress

In 1937, Margaret Chase Smith was sworn in as a new member of the House of Representatives by Speaker William Bankhead, following the death of her husband. She successfully ran for the Senate in 1948.

for his reckless accusations and the way his committee conducted its investigations of communists. In the wake of this speech, stories in the media suggested her as a possible vice president for Dwight Eisenhower.[63] In 1964, during an event at the Women's National Press Club, she announced her candidacy for president. On the campaign trail, she handed out muffins, which generated so much publicity that one of her opponents, Nelson Rockefeller, tried to capitalize on her success by giving out his fudge recipe.[64] Smith became the first woman to have a major party place her name in nomination for president; she won twenty-seven delegates at the Republican National Convention.[65] Her congressional career ended in 1972 at the age of seventy-four, when she lost a close election for her fifth Senate term. She left the Senate fearful that "there is no indication another qualified woman is coming in."[66] While technically she was not the first woman elected to the Senate, Smith was the first woman elected to both the House and the Senate.

Figure 2.2 displays the number of women running in primaries, winning primaries, and winning general elections to the Senate.[67] The data are grouped into six-year periods. For each period, the membership of the Senate is divided into three groups, "Class 1," "Class 2," and "Class 3." In each two-year election cycle, one class—essentially one-third of the membership—stands for reelection. The six-year period thus represents the time span required for the entire membership of the Senate to stand for reelection. Two noteworthy observations can be drawn from Figure 2.2. First, it shows that prior to the 1970s, only a handful of women ran in Senate primaries, even fewer won their primaries, and hardly any won Senate seats in a general election. Second, the trends in the number of women running in primaries, winning primaries, and winning Senate seats match the trends in the House for the most part. The Senate numbers, however, are of course much smaller than those of the House. While the number of women running in Senate primaries did increase during the initial three periods in the series (1958–1962 to 1970–1974), the number of women winning their primaries remained flat. After Senator Smith's election in 1948, the only woman to join her for any length of time was Maurine Neuberger (D-OR), who served for one term.[68] After Senator Smith retired in 1973, there were no women in the Senate until Muriel Humphrey (D-MN) was appointed in 1978 to complete the term of her deceased husband, Senator Hubert H. Humphrey (D-MN).

Like trends in the House, the real increase in the number of female Senate candidates began in the late 1970s and early 1980s. EMILY's List, a PAC that raises money for pro-choice female Democrats, began to supply candidates with much-needed funds. The creation of EMILY's List was fostered by Harriett Woods's experience when she ran for the Senate in Missouri in 1982. Woods had twenty years of political experience on the city council and in the state senate. Even though no male candidates initially expressed interest, Democratic Party leaders told her, "We have to find a man for the job."[69] At the last minute, a lobbyist with no prior political experience filed, but Woods won the primary. Very late in the general election campaign, she received a "token contribution" from the national party.[70] To raise more money, Woods started calling other women, including philanthropist Ellen Malcolm, and raised $50,000, but it was not enough. She lost the general election to John Danforth by less than 1 percent of the vote. Woods and Malcolm realized that the $50,000 was "too little, too late," and founded EMILY's List. The name comes from the organization's mission: "Early Money Is Like Yeast. It makes the 'dough' rise." The PAC provides women with money early in their campaigns, when they need it most.[71] The first race it funded was Representative Barbara Mikulski's 1986 bid for the Senate in Maryland; it raised $250,000 for her primary.[72] Mikulski became the first Democratic woman elected to the Senate in her own right. In the 2008 election cycle, EMILY's List raised over $35 million.[73]

The "Year of the Woman" also had a notable impact on the number of women in the Senate, with the number of female senators increasing from

Figure 2.2   Women as Candidates for the US Senate, 1958–2010 (by six-year cycles)

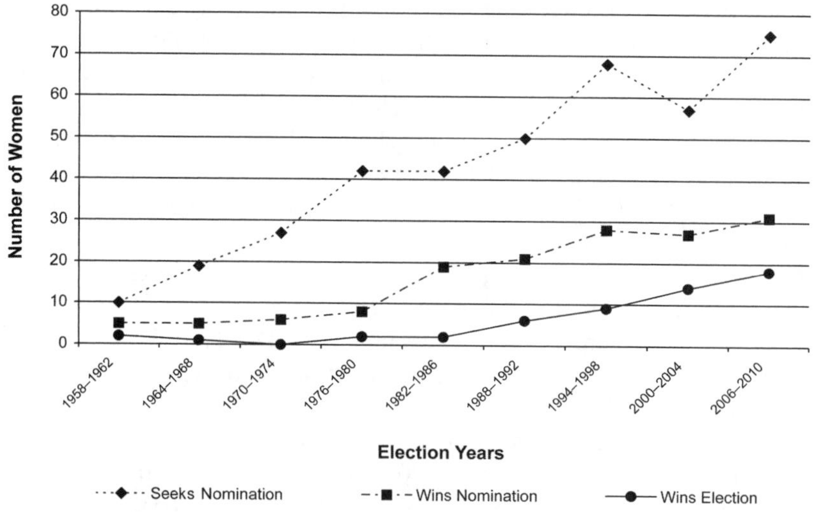

Source: Data compiled by the authors.

two in 1990 to six in 1992. The Thomas-Hill hearings, in particular, inspired women to run. For example, Patty Murray (D-WA) began her political career as a suburban mom in Seattle with two children and was very active in her children's preschool; in addition to leading sing-alongs, she taught parent education classes on nutrition and child development. In 1980, the Washington state legislature proposed cutting funds for parent-child preschool programs. Murray took her children with her as she lobbied legislators to fight the cuts. One male state senator told her, "You can't do anything. You're just a mom in tennis shoes."[74] A friend of Murray's said that this remark, instead of discouraging her, was like "wav[ing] a red flag in front of a bull."[75] She organized 12,000 families and successfully blocked the funding cuts. Eventually, she successfully ran for school board and state senate. In 1991, Murray was so angered by the way the fourteen white males on the Judiciary Committee treated Hill that she decided to run for the US Senate, using the "mom in tennis shoes" message as an integral part of her campaign.[76] Murray challenged first-term Democratic senator Brock Adams in the primary. The *Seattle Times* called her "the longest of long shots."[77] She received no support from the party or even EMILY's List. But then media reports revealed that Adams had sexually harassed and molested eight women. One of his former congressional aides publicly accused him of drugging her drink and taking advantage of her. Adams announced that he would not seek reelection.[78] After she won the Democratic primary, her Republican opponent, Rod Chandler, mocked her by carrying around a pair of sneakers.[79] By all appearances, Chandler should have cruised to victory: he outspent Murray two to one, had a great deal of campaign experience after five terms in the House, and was a former television anchorman. During their second televised debate, he hammered away at a shaky Murray. But instead of a closing statement, he sang a song made famous by Roger Miller: "Dang me, dang me. They ought to take a rope and hang me—hang me from the highest tree. Woman would you weep for me?" He continued singing the song, telling the tale of a philanderer who leaves his wife and child. The audience sat in stunned silence. Murray replied, "That's just the kind of attitude that got me into this race, Rod." She won with 54 percent of the vote.

In that same election cycle, Lynn Yeakel, who had never held public office, decided to take on incumbent Republican senator Arlen Specter of Pennsylvania. She explained that Specter's particularly aggressive questioning of Hill "pushed people like me over the line."[80] The ads she ran during the Democratic primary used footage of Specter from the hearings, with Yeakel asking, "Did this make you as angry as me?"[81] When she began her campaign, she was so unknown that she had less than 1 percent name recognition.[82] One Democratic Party official flippantly remarked to the press that all she had going for her was that she "had breasts." Claire Sargent, who was running for the US Senate in Arizona, quipped, "It's about time we voted for senators with breasts. After all, we've been voting for boobs long enough."[83] After defeating four men in the primary, Yeakel lost to Specter by less than 3 points.

In 1992, twenty-eight women ran in Senate primaries, a peak that would not be reached again until 2010. In fact, several election cycles after 1992 show substantially lower numbers. Sixteen women ran in primaries in 1998, fourteen in 2000, and only thirteen in 2008. In 1992, eleven women won primaries, a number that would not be exceeded until 2006, when twelve women won. That year, Claire McCaskill (D-MO) was the only female Senate candidate to successfully challenge a male incumbent, Senator Jim Talent (R-MO), in one of the closest general elections in the country. Stem-cell research became one of the key issues in the race, with a constitutional amendment on the ballot that would have protected all forms of such research allowed under federal law in the state of Missouri. Michael J. Fox appeared in an ad for McCaskill that ran during the World Series opening game featuring the St. Louis Cardinals. The ad featured Fox, shaking uncontrollably from his Parkinson's disease, endorsing McCaskill, a strong supporter of stem-cell research. Talk radio host Rush Limbaugh jumped into the debate, accusing Fox of "exaggerating the effects of the disease. He's moving all around and shaking and it's clearly an act."[84] The Republican National Committee ran an ad accusing McCaskill of "exploiting the medical tragedy of others just to get votes," and said her husband allowed "rape, poor care and even wrongful death" to occur in nursing homes that he owned.[85] Although Senator Talent outspent McCaskill, $16.5 million to $11.6 million,[86] she narrowly defeated him by less than 2 percent of the vote.

In 2010, a record thirty-eight women ran in Senate primaries and thirteen women won primaries. Sarah Palin, backed by the insurgent Tea Party, made several high-profile endorsements. In three Senate Republican primaries, Palin endorsed Carly Fiorina in California, Christine O'Donnell in Delaware, and Sharron Angle in Nevada, none of whom were ultimately successful. The endorsements of O'Donnell and Angle were especially newsworthy, since each won their primary over a well-known candidate endorsed by the state Republican leadership, and each emerged as a controversial candidate over the course of the general election campaign.

O'Donnell won her Republican primary by defeating Michael Castle, a former governor and nine-term member of the House. During the campaign, Castle had filed a complaint with the Federal Election Commission accusing O'Donnell of illegally coordinating her campaign with the Tea Party Express. In response, during a radio show, O'Donnell said, "These are the kind of cheap, underhanded, un-manly tactics that we've come to expect from Obama's favorite Republican . . . this is not a bake-off. Get your man-pants on."[87] She won the primary with 53 percent of the vote. Her general election campaign against Democrat Chris Coons was plagued by controversial statements from her past, particularly one she made in 1999, when she was a regular on *Politically Incorrect* with Bill Maher. In a segment that was actually cut from the original broadcast, she said, "I dabbled into witchcraft—I never joined a coven. But I did . . . I dabbled into witchcraft. . . . One of my first dates with a witch was on a satanic altar, and I didn't know it. I mean, there's little blood there and stuff like that. . . . We went to a movie and then had a midnight picnic on a satanic altar." The clip received over 800,000 hits on YouTube.[88] O'Donnell attempted to poke fun at all the attention these comments provoked in her first television ad, which aired in early October 2010. The ad opened with quiet piano music and O'Donnell looking into the camera stating, "I am not a witch. I'm nothing you've heard. I'm you."[89] The ad was parodied on *Saturday Night Live* and ultimately brought even more attention to her witchcraft comments. She lost to Coons with 41 percent of the vote.

■ The House as a Steppingstone to the Senate

The research on office-seeking and elections in the United States emphasizes that, when viewed systemically, there is a hierarchy of elective office. This hierarchy is often described as a "pipeline," a sequence of increasingly attractive offices for the politically ambitious. One component in this hierarchy is the upward step from the state legislature to the US House. For example, among the 191 women elected to the US House from 1956 to 2010, 94 (49 percent) served at least one term in the state legislature. A second step in the hierarchy is the movement from the US House to the US Senate. Given the increasing number of women in the pipeline over time, this latter step is one avenue for women to enter the Senate.

What makes a seat in the Senate attractive to a House member? As a smaller chamber whose members are accountable to a statewide electorate, a seat in the Senate is perceived as more prestigious. As an institution, the Senate is less hierarchical; given the tradition of the filibuster, individual senators have a great deal of power, and authority within the committee system is more dispersed. In the House, influence depends on long service and acquiring leadership positions within the party or committee system.

Senators, however, need not wait ten years to acquire these positions, and are, in general, considered "first among equals."[90]

However, campaigning and winning a seat are more difficult. Campaigns for the Senate have to reach a much broader constituency and require a shift from "retail politics," which involves cultivating a constituency through personal, one-on-one contact, to "wholesale politics," which requires attracting media attention, maintaining continuous fundraising, and running a media campaign.[91] In fact, many House members who ran for the Senate have lamented how they missed the intimacy and familiarity of their House district campaigns.[92] As Representative James Abourezk (D-SD), who served in both the House and the Senate, explained, "House members have a good sense of what their district is. Senators have a harder time getting a handle on a state."[93] Moreover, fundraising for a Senate race can be daunting. While the average House candidate in 2010 raised $574,000, the average Senate candidate raised $2.4 million.[94] The most expensive campaign in the 2010 election was Connecticut's open seat Senate race to fill the vacancy created after Senator Chris Dodd (D-CT) retired. Republican candidate Linda McMahon, the former CEO of World Wrestling Entertainment, spent over $50 million of her own money.[95] She lost to Democrat Richard Blumenthal, the former attorney general, who spent less than $9 million, which included $2.5 million of his own money.[96]

Table 2.2 summarizes the electoral fate of those sitting female House members who gave up their seats to run for the Senate.[97] Five of these women lost their primary, eleven lost in the general election, and five were elected to the Senate. The list also includes several campaigns that illustrate the intensity and, at times, nasty character of campaigns for the Senate.

Representative Helen Gahagan Douglas's (D-CA) 1950 contest for the open Senate seat in California ranks as one of the most unusual and bitter campaigns in modern history. The contest featured two members of California's delegation to the House: Douglas, first elected as a Democrat in 1944, and Republican Richard Nixon, first elected in 1946. Nixon had become a national figure through his service on the House Un-American Activities Committee and the celebrated conspiracy and perjury investigation of former State Department official Alger Hiss.[98] The campaign themes emerged during the primary season, when Manchester Boddy, the publisher of the *Los Angeles Daily News* and Douglas's opponent in the Democratic primary, charged her with being "part of a small subversive clique of red-hots" and giving "comfort to the Soviet tyranny."[99] Despite these attacks, Douglas defeated Boddy, but the divisive Democratic contest provided Nixon with a clear strategy. Using rhetoric that previously appeared in the

Table 2.2 Sitting Female House Members Who Ran for the Senate

	Year	Outcome
Jeannette Rankin (R-MT)	1918	Lost primary to Oscar Lanstrum (challenger)
Ruth Hanna McCormick (R-IL)	1930	Lost general to James Lewis (challenger)
Margaret Chase Smith (R-ME)	1948	Elected to the Senate (open seat)
Helen Gahagan Douglas (D-CA)	1950	Lost general to Richard Nixon (open seat)
Gracie Pfost (D-ID)	1962	Lost general to Len Jordan (incumbent)
Patsy Mink (D-HI)	1976	Lost primary to Spark Matsunaga (open seat)
Bella Abzug (D-NY)	1976	Lost primary to Patrick Moynihan (challenger)
Elizabeth Holtzman (D-NY)	1980	Lost general to Alfonse D'Amato (challenger)
Millicent Fenwick (D-NJ)	1982	Lost general to Frank Lautenberg (open seat)
Barbara Mikulski (D-MD)	1986	Elected to the Senate (open seat)
Bobbi Fiedler (R-CA)	1986	Lost primary to Ed Zschau (challenger)
Lynn Martin (R-IL)	1990	Lost general to Paul Simon (incumbent)
Claudine Schneider (R-RI)	1990	Lost general to Claiborne Pell (incumbent)
Patricia Saiki (R-HI)	1990	Lost general to Daniel Akaka (incumbent)
Barbara Boxer (D-CA)	1992	Elected to the Senate (open seat)
Olympia Snowe (R-ME)	1994	Elected to the Senate (open seat)
Linda Smith (R-WA)	1998	Lost general to Patty Murray (incumbent)
Debbie Stabenow (D-MI)	2000	Elected to the Senate (defeated incumbent)
Denise Majette (D-GA)	2004	Lost general to Johnny Isakson (open seat)
Katherine Harris (R-FL)	2006	Lost general to Bill Nelson (incumbent)
Heather Wilson (R-NM)	2008	Lost primary to Steve Pearce (open seat)
Mazie Hirono (D-HI)	2012	(running for open seat)
Shelley Berkley (D-NV)	2012	(running for open seat)
Tammy Baldwin (D-WI)	2012	(running for open seat)

Source: Data compiled by the authors.

California newspapers, Nixon commonly referred to Douglas as the "Pink Lady."[100] His campaign organization distributed "the pink sheet"—fliers critical of Douglas's voting record that were printed on pink paper.[101] In stump speeches, Nixon regularly criticized Douglas by asserting that she was "pink right down to her underwear."[102] For her part, Douglas popularized the term "Tricky Dick" and referred to Nixon as a "pipsqueak" and a "pee wee."[103] Ironically, Douglas's candidacy received the support of Ronald Reagan, who was then serving as president of the Screen Actors Guild, while John F. Kennedy, a member of the House, delivered a $1,000 donation to the Nixon campaign from his father, Joseph P. Kennedy. Capitalizing upon the unpopular Truman administration and the growing fear of communism, Nixon soundly defeated Douglas with 59 percent of the vote.

In 1982, an open Senate seat was created in New Jersey when Democratic senator Harrison Williams resigned in the wake of expulsion proceedings stemming from his indictment in the ABSCAM scandal. In 1980, the FBI conducted an elaborate sting operation and caught several House members on videotape taking thousands of dollars from a fake sheikh, Kambir Abdul Rahman (actually an ex-convict in disguise), in exchange for promises of influence on the Hill. One of the more infamous images was of Representative Richard Kelly (R-FL), who was videotaped stuffing $25,000 into his coat and pants as he asked, "Does it show?" Six members of Congress were ultimately sentenced to jail.[104]

Representative Millicent Fenwick (R-NJ), a Republican first elected to the House with the "Watergate Class" of 1974, entered the race to succeed Williams. Fenwick was the daughter of Ogden Haggerty Hammond, a New Jersey state legislator and ambassador to Spain. Her mother had been killed in 1915 as a passenger on the USS *Lusitania* when it was torpedoed by German U-boats. Fenwick worked as a model for *Harper's Bazaar* and became associate editor of *Vogue*. At the age of fifty-nine, she successfully ran for the New Jersey state legislature. With a reputation as a likeable, independent, and outspoken proponent of human rights, one of her aides described her as "the Katherine Hepburn of politics. With her dignity and elegance, she could get away with saying things others couldn't."[105] When she was asked for her reaction to the Republican Party's withdrawal of support for the Equal Rights Amendment from its platform in 1980, she said, "Absurd is the only word."[106] One of her well-known eccentricities was pipe-smoking; she took it up when her doctor advised her to stop chain-smoking cigarettes. Although there were always two pipes in her purse, she stopped being photographed with them because she believed "it would be a bad influence on the young."[107] Fenwick gained notoriety for her resemblance to Congresswoman Lacey Davenport, a popular character in the *Doonesbury* comic strip, by Garry Trudeau.[108] When she ran for the Senate in 1982, despite attacks on her House voting record as "too liberal," Fenwick defeated Republican Jeffrey Bell in the Republican primary. Frank Lautenberg, the multimillionaire CEO of Automatic Data Processing, surprisingly emerged from the field of ten candidates to win the Democratic nomination. In the fall campaign, Fenwick, a staunch supporter of campaign finance reform, refused to take money from political action committees; Lautenberg outspent her, $6.4 million to $2.6 million.[109] Despite polls showing him trailing Fenwick by eighteen points at the start of the campaign, Lautenberg won the general election with 52 percent of the vote. Fenwick was actually quite surprised about her defeat and admitted, "I never thought I would lose. . . . The fascination of that job is that I couldn't wait to get there." When asked what she would do after leaving Congress, Fenwick replied that she planned on "sleeping late, take up gardening and 'get fat on truffles and veal piccata.'"[110]

In 2006, Representative Katherine Harris (R-FL) took on Senator Bill Nelson (D-FL). Harris first gained notoriety as Florida's secretary of state during the controversy over the 2000 presidential election. In 2002, Harris won an open House seat previously held by Republican Dan Miller.[111] During the fall of 2003, Harris "entertained" the idea of running for the Senate seat that came open with the retirement of Democrat Bob Graham. Her decision not to run in 2004 was attributed to a visit from Karl Rove[112] and rumors that "the president did not want to share his re-election ballot with the Florida official so closely associated with his controversial 2000 win."[113] Harris then waited and announced in June of 2005 that she would challenge Democratic incumbent senator Bill Nelson, who had been elected in 2000 with only 53 percent of the vote. Her campaign, however, was at best characterized as a political nightmare. The reaction to her candidacy by both national and Florida Republican leaders was lukewarm. For nearly a year, there were efforts to recruit others to challenge Harris in the primary.[114] Harris's management of her campaign organization was chaotic and suffered from a "seemingly endless exodus of staffers."[115] Many of her public statements also got her into trouble. For example, in one interview she stated, "if you're not electing Christians, then in essence you are going to legislate sin."[116] As a result, Harris failed to mount a credible challenge and lost decisively to Nelson with only 39 percent of the vote.

The most recent example of sitting female House members running for the Senate is Representative Heather Wilson (R-NM). Elected to the House in 1998 from New Mexico's First District, Heather Wilson was the first female military veteran in Congress. She graduated from the Air Force Academy in 1982 and served in the Air Force until she worked on the staff of the National Security Council during the George H. W. Bush administration.[117] After five terms in the House, she decided to run for the Senate in 2008, when Senator Pete Domenici (R-NM) announced he was retiring. Wilson narrowly lost a two-way Republican primary by less than 2 points to Steve Pearce, another House member from New Mexico. Pearce was soundly defeated by Democrat Tom Udall, 61 percent to 39 percent. Wilson has announced that she will try again in 2012, this time for New Mexico's other Senate seat, to replace retiring senator Jeff Bingaman (D-NM).

These case studies illustrate the limitations of using a House seat to launch a Senate career. As Table 2.2 illustrates, very few women have forfeited their House seats to run for the Senate. In fact, these twenty-one women represent only 9 percent of all women who have served in the House. Their reluctance to vacate their seats may be well-founded: only five of the twenty-one women have been successful. Historically, of the 654 members who have served in both the House and Senate, only eight have been women, or 1 percent.[118] In addition to the five listed in Table 2.2, three more won election to the Senate after leaving the House for at least one term. Five of these eight women served in the 112th Congress (2011 session); four were elected and one was appointed. Of the seventeen women in the Senate in the 112th Congress, 29 percent had served in the House. Of the eighty-three men in the Senate, 53 percent had served in the House.[119] This suggests that the disparity between men and women in being elected to the House is matched by an accompanying disparity in their ability to move from the House to the Senate.

Despite this disparity, three female representatives in the 112th Congress have announced that they will run for the Senate in 2012. Representative Shelley Berkley (D-NV) was first elected to the House in 1998, when Republican House member John Ensign left the seat open and successfully ran for the Senate.[120] In an ironic twist of fate, Berkley is running for Ensign's Senate seat. Ensign left office in 2011, after he admitted he was having an affair with a woman who was married to one of his "best friends" and was the subject of investigations by the Justice Department, Federal Election Commission, and Senate Ethics Committee.[121] Representative Dean Heller (R-NV) was initially appointed to fill Ensign's vacant Senate seat. If successful in the Democratic primary, Berkley would then challenge Heller.

Representative Tammy Baldwin (D-WI) was initially elected to the House in an open seat race in 1998. Baldwin's victory was a double milestone, as she was the first woman from Wisconsin elected to the House and the first open lesbian elected to the House. Even before her career in national politics, Baldwin was a seasoned political veteran. She served for eight years on the Dane County board of supervisors and for six years in the Wisconsin house of representatives.[122] In her 2012 Senate bid, she will compete in the Democratic primary to succeed retiring four-term senator Herb Kohl (D-WI). If she wins the general election, she will be the first openly gay senator.

Representative Mazie Hirono (D-HI) was born in Fukushima, Japan, and immigrated to Hawaii with her mother when she was twelve years old. She served in the Hawaii house of representatives and as lieutenant governor before being elected to the US House in 2006.[123] Hirono decided to run for the Senate in 2012, after four-term senator Daniel Akaka (D-HI) announced his retirement. To fill Hirono's vacant US House seat, thirty-year-old Democrat Tulsi Gabbard has announced her candidacy. In 2002, Gabbard was elected to the Hawaiian house at the age of twenty-one, making her the youngest woman ever elected to state-level office. During her first term, Gabbard joined the National Guard and then gave up her seat to serve tours of duty in Iraq and Kuwait.[124]

▪ The Integration of Women of Color

The history of blacks serving in the US House of Representatives began during the Reconstruction era. From the 41st Congress (1869 session) through the 56th (1901 session), twenty black men were elected to the House. All represented states of the former Confederacy. Seven were from South Carolina, five from North Carolina, three from Alabama, and one each from Florida, Georgia, Louisiana, Mississippi, and Virginia. Ten of the representatives were former slaves.[125] Black membership reached its peak from 1873 to 1875, when seven members served simultaneously. After that, the number dwindled over time as the legislatures in the former Confederate states imposed a variety of restrictions that essentially disenfranchised black voters. In his departing speech from the floor of the House on March 3, 1901, George Henry White, the last of the era's black congressmen, proclaimed that "this, Mr. Chairman, is perhaps the negroes' temporary farewell to the American Congress, but let me say, Phoenix-like he will rise up someday and come again."[126]

It would take twenty-eight years for the phoenix to begin its rise. No African American would serve in the House until 1929, when Oscar Stanton De Priest, a Republican, won a seat in the First District of Illinois. In 1934, De Priest was defeated by a black Democrat, Arthur Mitchell, who served until 1943, when he was succeeded by another African American, Democrat William L. Dawson. That same year, Dawson was joined by Democrat Adam Clayton Powell, the first black elected from New York. The number of blacks in the House would not exceed the seven members of the Reconstruction era until ten members were elected in 1968. Representatives Barbara Jordan (D-TX) and Andrew Young (D-GA), both elected in 1972, were the first blacks from the former Confederate states to serve in the House since Reconstruction.

The ten black members in the "class of 1968" included the first African American woman to serve in Congress, Shirley Chisholm. She had been the second black woman to serve in the New York state assembly. After two terms in the state legislature, Chisholm decided to run for Congress when a constituent who was on welfare visited her home, offered her a campaign donation of $9.62 in change from a bingo game she won, and pledged to raise money for her every Friday night.[127] Chisholm noted, "When I decided to run for Congress, I knew I would encounter both anti-black and antifeminist sentiments. What surprised me was the much greater virulence of the sex discrimination. . . . I was constantly bombarded by both men and women exclaiming that I should return to teaching, a woman's vocation, and leave politics to men."[128] In 1972, she announced

Photo courtesy of the Library of Congress

Shirley Chisholm was the first African American woman elected to Congress, in 1968.

her candidacy for the Democratic nomination for president. Her name appeared on the primary ballot in twelve states. When the other Democratic candidates tried to exclude her from the televised debates because she was not "a real candidate," she went to the Federal Communications Commission and obtained a federal court order allowing her to participate.[129] On the first roll call at the Democratic National Convention, Chisholm won 151 votes.[130] She said, "I knew I wouldn't be president, but somebody had to break the ice, somebody with the nerve and bravado to do it."[131]

At the national level, as Table 2.3 shows, only forty-two women of color have served in the history of the US Congress, twenty-eight African Americans, eight Latinas, and six Asian Pacific Islanders.[132] Most of these women have been elected very recently; all but two have been elected since 1972. In the 112th Congress (2011 session), there were twenty-four women of color, all of them in the House. In fact, only one woman of color, Carol Moseley Braun, an African American woman from Illinois, has served in the Senate. All but three of these forty-two women—Representatives Jaime Herrera Beutler (R-WA), Ileana Ros-Lehtinen (R-FL), and Patricia Fukuda Saiki (R-HI)—are Democrats. The context of their initial election to the House is instructive. Nine women came to the House after winning a special election; eleven members were elected in newly created districts after the decennial reapportionment or in districts that were substantially redrawn; sixteen won election in open districts. Four women defeated an incumbent in the Democratic primary and, finally, two defeated Republican incumbents in the general election.

The first Cuban American to be elected to Congress, Representative Ileana Ros-Lehtinen (R-FL), is also one of three female Republican Latinas to be elected to Congress. Ros-Lehtinen won a highly contested special election for Democrat Claude Pepper's seat after he died in 1989. Born in Havana, Ros-Lehtinen immigrated to the United States when she was seven. She tends to vote with the conservative wing of the Republican Party in Congress the vast majority of the time and had strong ties with President George W. Bush; she was known for arriving early for the president's State of the Union address so she could greet him as he entered the House chamber.[133] In 2006, she won her tenth term, defeating six-foot-five-inch Democrat David Patlak, who ran with the slogan "Vote Big Dave." During the campaign, Oscar-nominated actress Sally Kellerman, who played "Hot Lips Houlihan" in the original movie version of *M*A*S*H,* came to Key West and hosted a fundraising concert for Patlak.[134] Ultimately, Lehtinen outspent Patlak, $1.4 million to $75,700.[135]

Following her reelection in 2008, Ros-Lehtinen gained national media attention when she hung up on President-Elect Barack Obama after he

Table 2.3   **Women of Color Elected to the US House**

	Context of First Election	Dates of Service
African Americans (28)		
Shirley Chisholm (D-NY)	Open seat after redistricting[a]	1969–1983
Yvonne Brathwaite Burke (D-CA)	New district	1973–1979
Cardiss Collins (D-IL)	Special election	1973–1997
Barbara Jordan (D-TX)	New district	1973–1979
Katie Hall (D-IL)	Special election	1982–1985
Maxine Waters (D-CA)	Open seat	1991–present
Barbara-Rose Collins (D-MI)	Open seat	1991–1997
Corrine Brown (D-FL)	New district	1993–present
Carrie Meek (D-FL)	Open seat after redistricting[a]	1993–2003
Cynthia McKinney (D-GA)	New district, open seat	1993–2003, 2005–2007
Eva Clayton (D-NC)	Open seat after redistricting[a]	1993–2003
Eddie Bernice Johnson (D-TX)	New district	1993–present
Juanita Millender-McDonald (D-CA)	Special election	1995–2007
Sheila Jackson Lee (D-TX)	Defeated incumbent in primary	1995–present
Julia Carson (D-IN)	Open seat	1997–2007
Carolyn Cheeks Kilpatrick (D-MI)	Defeated incumbent in primary	1997–2001
Barbara Lee (D-CA)	Special election	1998–present
Stephanie Tubbs Jones (D-OH)	Open seat	1999–2008
Diane Watson (D-CA)	Special election	2001–2011
Denise Majette (D-GA)	Defeated incumbent in primary	2003–2005
Gwen Moore (D-WI)	Open seat	2005–present
Laura Richardson (D-CA)	Special election	2007–present
Donna Edwards (D-MD)	Defeated incumbent in primary	2007–present
Yvette Clarke (D-NY)	Open seat	2007–present
Marcia Fudge (D-OH)	Open seat	2007–present
Terri Sewell (D-AL)	Open seat	2011–present
Karen Bass (D-CA)	Open seat	2011–present
Frederica Wilson (D-FL)	Open seat	2011–present
Latinas (8)		
Ileana Ros-Lehtinen (R-FL)	Special election	1989–present
Lucille Roybal-Allard (D-CA)	New district	1993–present
Nydia Velazquez (D-NY)	Open seat after redistricting[a]	1997–present
Loretta Sanchez (D-CA)	Defeated Republican incumbent	1997–present
Grace Napolitano (D-CA)	Open seat	1999–present
Hilda Solis (D-CA)	Open seat	2001–2009
Linda Sanchez (D-CA)	Open seat after redistricting[a]	2003–present
Jaime Herrera Beutler (R-WA)	Open seat	2011–present

continues

called to congratulate her on her reelection. She assumed it was a prank being pulled by a south Florida radio station. Moments after she hung up on Obama, Representative Rahm Emanuel, who had just been tapped to be Obama's chief of staff, called her, saying, "I cannot believe you hung up

Table 2.3   continued

	Context of First Election	Dates of Service
Asian Pacific Islanders (6)		
Patsy Mink (D-HI)	Open seat, special election	1965–1977, 1990–2002
Patricia Saiki (R-HI)	Open seat	1987–1991
Doris Matsui (D-CA)	Special election	2005–present
Mazie Hirono (D-HI)	Open seat	2007–present
Judy Chu (D-CA)	Special election	2009–present
Colleen Hanabusa (D-HI)	Defeated Republican incumbent	2011–present

Sources: Women in Congress, 1917–2006, Office of the Clerk of the US House of Representatives (Washington, DC: US Government Printing Office, 2006); "Women of Color in Elective Office, 2011" (New Brunswick, NJ: Rutgers University, Center for American Women and Politics, Eagleton Institute of Politics, 2011).

Note: a. "Open seat after redistricting" indicates that the boundaries of the existing district were substantially changed during the redistricting process.

on the President-Elect," and Ros-Lehtinen hung up on him too. Only after another call from Representative Howard Berman (D-CA), a colleague with whom she served on the Foreign Affairs Committee, was she convinced the call was real. When Obama called again, she joked, "You are either very gracious to reach out in such a bipartisan manner . . . or *Saturday Night Live* could use a good Obama impersonator like you."[136] In 2010, she was reelected with nearly 70 percent of the vote. As the most senior Republican woman in the 112th Congress (2011 session), she serves as the chair of the Foreign Affairs Committee.

Only one woman of color has served in the history of the Senate. Carol Moseley Braun defeated Democratic incumbent senator Alan Dixon in the primary the very first time she ran for the Senate in 1992. Motivated in part by the treatment of Anita Hill during the Clarence Thomas confirmation hearings, she ran because "it wasn't enough to have millionaire white males over the age of 50 representing all the people in the country."[137] After her swearing-in, she remarked, "I cannot escape the fact that I come to the Senate as a symbol of hope and change."[138] She felt the sting of racism early in her Senate career, after she single-handedly defeated an amendment proposed by Senator Jesse Helms (R-NC) extending a trademark to the Daughters of the Confederacy on their use of the Confederate flag in their logo. Shortly after the amendment was defeated on the Senate floor, Moseley Braun encountered Helms in the Senate elevator. As she recounted, "He saw me standing there, and he started to sing, 'I wish I was in the land of cotton . . .' And he looked at Senator [Orrin] Hatch and said, 'I'm going to sing Dixie until she cries.' And I looked at him and said, 'Senator Helms, your singing would make me cry if you sang Rock of

Ages.'"[139] Moseley Braun narrowly lost her reelection campaign in 1998, after being plagued by fundraising and sexual harassment scandals.[140] Following her defeat, she vowed "never to run for public office" again.[141] She was then appointed ambassador to New Zealand and Samoa by President Bill Clinton. In 2000 and 2004, she changed her mind about campaigning and ran for president.[142]

Patsy Mink, the first woman of color to serve in Congress, grew up on a sugar plantation in Maui. She served in the Hawaii territorial house of representatives in the 1950s and the Hawaii state senate in the 1960s. Much to the chagrin of state Democratic Party leaders, she ran for the Hawaii house in 1964, winning a four-way race for one of the state's at-large seats. Throughout her congressional career, the state party tried to push her out by supporting other Democratic candidates in the party's primary because of her "unwillingness to allow the party to influence her political agenda."[143] She finally ran unopposed in 1970. While in Congress, in addition to being an outspoken critic of the Vietnam War, she floor-managed the passage of Title IX, the legislation that banned discrimination in education. In 1972, she was asked by a group of antiwar progressives in Oregon to run for president. She often stopped there on her trips between Washington, D.C., and Hawaii. While her campaign was virtually unknown outside of Oregon, she received over 5,000 votes in the state's Democratic presidential primary.[144]

Passing up an all-but-certain reelection to the House, she decided to run for the Senate in 1976, but lost in the Democratic primary. For the next decade, she remained active in Hawaii politics, serving on the Honolulu city council and running for governor and for mayor of Honolulu. In 1990, she won both a special and a general election being held simultaneously for the House seat that became vacant after the appointment of Daniel Akaka to the Senate, and easily won reelection six more times. In September of 2002, Mink died after a month-long battle with pneumonia. It was, however, too late to remove her name from the ballot, and she was reelected posthumously with 73 percent of the vote.[145]

■ Conclusion

In light of the data and trends presented in this chapter, how do we best characterize the integration of women into Congress? Clearly, progress is evident. Seventy-two women were elected to the US House of Representatives in 2010, compared to fifteen in 1956. Those elected in 2010 included twenty-four women of color, compared to no women of color in

1956. In the 85th Congress (1957 session), Margaret Chase Smith was the lone woman in the Senate, while in the 112th Congress (2011 session), there were seventeen female senators.

This progress, however, must be qualified. In House elections between 1956 and 1970, women lost an average of half a seat in each election cycle.[146] This average did increase, however meagerly, to a gain just over one and a half seats in each of the election cycles from 1972 to 1990. The election of 1992 provides the sole example of a dramatic change, when forty-seven women were elected, a nineteen-seat increase over the number elected in 1990. It is the only double-digit increase in the history of Congress. From 1994 to 2010, the average increase in the number of women was three per election.

In addition, the progress of women has not been steady. In six election cycles from 1956 to 2010, the number of women elected to the House actually declined compared to the previous election. The most recent of these declines occurred in 2010, when seventy-two women were elected, compared to seventy-four in 2008. Thus the integration of women into Congress is best described as slow, irregular, and unremarkable.

▪ Notes

1. These numbers are as of July 27, 2011, and include Representative Kathy Hochul, who won a special election in New York in May, and Janice Hahn, who won a special House election in California in July. Five women served nonconsecutive terms; they have only been counted once. The overall number of people who have served in Congress is from Manning, *Membership of the 112th Congress,* p. 1.

2. Foerstel and Foerstel, *Climbing the Hill,* p. 25.

3. See Davis, *Moving the Mountain;* Harrison, *On Account of Sex;* Mansbridge, *Why We Lost the ERA.*

4. Davis, *Moving the Mountain.*

5. Ibid., pp. 38–45.

6. Freeman, *The Politics of Women's Liberation,* p. 54.

7. Ibid., *Rebirth of Feminism,* p. 123.

8. Ibid., pp. 123–124, 228–230.

9. When viewed historically, 1972 represents a "critical moment" analogous to the 1963–1964 period in the politics of race in the United States; Carmines and Stimson, *Issue Evolution.* See also Simon and Palmer, "Gender, Party, and Political Change."

10. Costain, *Inviting Women's Rebellion,* p. 1.

11. Freeman, *The Politics of Women's Liberation,* p. 150.

12. Ibid., pp. 147–148.

13. Davis, *Moving the Mountain,* p. 108.

14. Witt, Paget, and Matthews, *Running As a Woman,* pp. 136–137.

15. See Mezey, *Elusive Equality.*

16. Wayne, *The Road to the White House, 2000,* p. 120.

17. Foerstel and Foerstel, *Climbing the Hill,* p. 31.

18. Costain, *Inviting Women's Rebellion,* p. 10.

19. See Gillon, *That's Not What We Meant to Do.*

20. Foerstel, *Biographical Dictionary of Congressional Women,* p. 123. See also Holtzman, *Who Said It Would Be Easy?*

21. Mansbridge, *Why We Lost the ERA.* See also Boles, *The Politics of the Equal Rights Amendment;* McGlen et al., *Women, Politics, and American Society.*

22. Using the *New York Times,* Anne Costain's analysis shows a significant increase in both the number of issues covered and the number of reports for 1970, 1971, and 1972; see Costain, *Inviting Women's Rebellion,* esp. chap. 4.

23. The partisan split was thirty-five Democrats and twelve Republicans.

24. Foerstel and Foerstel, *Climbing the Hill,* p. 112.

25. Witt, Paget, and Matthews, *Running As a Woman,* p. 1.

26. Witt, Paget, and Matthews, *Running As a Woman.*

27. Bingham, *Women on the Hill,* p. 70.

28. Chaney and Sinclair, "Women and the 1992 House Elections," p. 127.

29. Dolan, "Voting for Women in the 'Year of the Woman.'"

30. Cook, "Voter Reactions to Women Candidates," p. 59.

31. Bingham, *Women on the Hill,* p. 28.

32. Foerstel and Foerstel, *Climbing the Hill,* p. 53.

33. Ibid.

34. Woodward, *The Agenda,* p. 300.

35. Ibid., pp. 300–302.

36. Foerstel, *Biographical Dictionary of Congressional Women,* p. 172. See also Margolies-Mezvinsky, *A Woman's Place.*

37. Witt, Paget, and Matthews, *Running As a Woman,* p. 298.

38. Foerstel and Foerstel, *Climbing the Hill,* pp. 50–51.

39. Ibid., p. 52.

40. Ibid., p. 48.

41. Traub, "Party Like It's 1994," p. 43.

42. PollingReport.com, www.pollingreport.com (accessed June 30, 2007).

43. Allison, "House Leader Hit with Indictment," p. 1A.

44. Weisman, "House Ethics Panel Begins Bribery Probe," p. 4.

45. Shenon, "Ohio Republican Tied to Abramoff Abandons Reelection Bid," p. 15.

46. Adair, Smith, and Kumar, "Lawmaker Quits Amid Scandal," p. 1A.

47. Traub, "Party Like It's 1994," p. 43.

48. See Peters and Rosenthal, *Speaker Nancy Pelosi and the New American Politics.*

49. One Democratic incumbent, Representative Cynthia McKinney of Georgia, lost her primary.

50. Lipman, "Ex-Harris Aides Reveal Why They Became 'Exes,'" p. 1A.

51. "Obama Blames Economy for Democratic 'Shellacking.'"

52. The information on seat change in previous elections was obtained from Stanley and Niemi, *Vital Statistics on American Politics, 2009–2010,* pp. 30–31.

53. The search was done on November 12, 2010, using the phrase "Year of the Republican Woman 2010."

54. Hennessey, "GOP Women Still Have Work to Do," p. A12.

55. Cillizza, "For GOP's Female Candidates, a Big-Name Den Mother," p. A2.

56. See, for example, Mervin, "United States Senate Norms and the Majority Whip Election of 1969," p. 321.

57. Polsby, "Goodbye to the Senate's Inner Club," p. 209.

58. White, *The Citadel*, p. 84, emphasis added.

59. For a complete list of all the women who served in the Senate, see "Women in the US Senate."

60. *Women in Congress*, pp. 177–179.

61. Foerstel, *Biographical Dictionary of Congressional Women*, p. 254.

62. Kaptur, *Women of Congress*, p. 89.

63. Foerstel, *Biographical Dictionary of Congressional Women*, pp. 253–256.

64. Kaptur, *Women of Congress*, p. 95.

65. Ibid.

66. Foerstel, *Biographical Dictionary of Congressional Women*, p. 256.

67. To preserve the three election groupings, the figure excludes the election of 1956. In that election, only two women ran in the primaries and neither was successful in winning the nomination.

68. Smith had personally encouraged Neuberger to run; Foerstel, *Biographical Dictionary of Congressional Women*, p. 201. Three other women did briefly serve with her: Eve Bowring (R-NE) for seven months and Hazel Abel (R-NE) for two months in 1954, and Elaine Edwards (D-LA) for three months in 1952.

69. Witt, Paget, and Matthews, *Running As a Woman*, p. 137.

70. Ibid., p. 138.

71. Ibid.

72. Ibid., p. 139.

73. "EMILY's List 2008 PAC Summary Data."

74. Bingham, *Women on the Hill*, p. 33.

75. Ibid.

76. Ibid., pp. 28–29.

77. Ibid., p. 35.

78. Ibid., p. 37.

79. Ibid., p. 43.

80. Witt, Paget, and Matthews, *Running As a Woman*, p. 4.

81. Ibid., p. 5.

82. Ibid., p. 213.

83. Ibid., p. 20.

84. Alberts, "Limbaugh Remains Defiant After Saying Fox Faked Illness," p. A4.

85. "What to Believe," p. B5.

86. Wagman, Franck, and Young, "McCaskill Prevailed Despite Cash Gap," p. A11.

87. Kane, "Mike Castle Won't Endorse Christine O'Donnell for the Senate"; Kleefeld, "O'Donnell Blasts Castle's 'Un-Manly' Tactics."

88. See www.youtube.com/watch?v=nECxQUi_pr0 (accessed July 7, 2011).

89. The ad in its entirety can be viewed at www.huffingtonpost.com/2010/10/04/christine-odonnell-witch-ad_n_750140.html (accessed July 7, 2011).

90. See Froman, *The Congressional Process;* Oleszek, *Congressional Procedures and the Policy Process.*

91. See, for example, Baker, *House and Senate*, pp. 49–50; Fenno, *Senators on the Campaign Trail.*

92. Baker, *House and Senate,* pp. 105–106.

93. Ibid., p. 115.

94. "2010 Overview: Stats at a Glance."

95. "Total Raised and Spent: 2010 Race, Connecticut Senate."

96. Ibid.

97. There have been a few additional female House members who ran for the Senate, but not as sitting House members. Blanche Lincoln (D-AR) ran for the Senate two years after leaving the House. Maria Cantwell (D-WA) ran for the Senate in 2000, six years after serving a single term in the House from 1993–1995. Heather Wilson (R-NM) unsuccessfully ran for the Senate in 2008 and will try again in 2012.

98. Ambrose, *Nixon,* pp. 166–196.

99. Ibid., p. 210.

100. Mitchell, *Tricky Dick and the Pink Lady.*

101. Ambrose, *Nixon,* p. 216.

102. Ibid., p. 218.

103. Mitchell, *Tricky Dick and the Pink Lady.*

104. Ehrenhart, *Politics in America,* pp. 745–746; Ross, *Fall from Grace,* pp. 257–261.

105. *Women in Congress,* p. 515.

106. Ibid., p. 516.

107. Sullivan, "US Senate Race Tops Jersey Elections," p. 40.

108. Barone and Ujifusa, *Almanac of American Politics, 1986,* p. 832. One Doonesbury website noted that "Lacy [*sic*] arrived in Congress two years before Mrs. Fenwick did, but the similarities seemed too distinctive to be coincidental. Indeed, so many people assumed Lacey was Millicent, it seemed ungallant to deny it"; www.doonesbury.com/strip/faqs/faq_ch.html (accessed June 20, 2005).

109. Norman, "Mrs. Fenwick and Lautenberg Meet in Final Debate," p. B13.

110. Norman, "Rep. Fenwick Tries to Figure Out Why She Lost," p. B15.

111. Barone and Cohen, *Almanac of American Politics, 2006,* p. 438.

112. Ibid.

113. Kumar and James, "Harris Announces Run for US Senate," p. 1A.

114. "Report: Pensacola Republicans Say Scarborough Courted for Senate"; Wallace, "At Final Hour, 3 Republicans Join Senate Race," p. B1; Wallace, "Harris Unfazed by Apparent Party Pressure," p. A1.

115. Lipman, "Ex-Harris Aides Reveal Why They Became 'Exes,'" p. 1A.

116. Ibid.; Ruth, "Memo to Harris Staff Members," p. 1.

117. *Women in Congress,* p. 926.

118. The total number of members is from Manning, *Membership of the 112th Congress,* p. 1.

119. Manning, *Membership of the 112th Congress,* p. 2.

120. Barone and Ujifusa, *Almanac of American Politics, 2000,* pp. 999–1000.

121. Demirjian, "Sen. John Ensign to Resign, Dean Heller Likely Replacement."

122. "Biography," Congresswoman Tammy Baldwin.

123. "Biography," Congresswoman Mazie K. Hirono.

124. "About Tulsi."

125. This information was gathered from *Biographical Directory of the United States Congress; Black Americans in Congress;* and Foner, *Freedom's Lawmakers.*

126. "George Henry White."

127. Foerstel, *Biographical Dictionary of Congressional Women,* p. 55.

128. Ibid., p. 54.

129. Clift and Brazaitis, *Madam President,* 2nd ed., p. xxii.

130. Foerstel, *Biographical Dictionary of Congressional Women,* p. 56. In 2004, a documentary of Chisholm's campaign was released titled *Chisholm '72: Unbought and Unbossed,* shortly before her death at the age of eighty on January 1, 2005.

131. Clift and Brazaitis, *Madam President,* 2nd ed., p. xxiii.

132. See, for example, Barrett, "The Policy Priorities of African American Women in State Legislatures"; Clayton, "African American Women and Their Quest for Congress"; Clayton and Stallings, "Black Women in Congress"; Gill, *African American Women in Congress;* Handley and Grofman, "The Impact of the Voting Rights Act on Minority Representation"; Lai et al., "Asian-Pacific American Campaigns, Elections, and Elected Officials"; Martinez-Ebers, Lopez, and Ramirez, "Representing Gender and Ethnicity"; Smooth, "African American Women and Electoral Politics"; Swain, *Black Faces, Black Interests.*

133. Yanez, "A Venerable Politician—and a Celebrity, Too."

134. Yanez, "Actress Plans Fundraising Concert for Patlak."

135. "Total Raised and Spent, 2006 Race: Florida District 18."

136. "Ros-Lehtinen Hangs Up on Obama."

137. *Women in Congress,* p. 725.

138. Ibid.

139. Foerstel, *Biographical Dictionary of Congressional Women,* p. 196.

140. Ibid., p. 197.

141. Ibid.

142. Fears, "On a Mission in a Political Second Act."

143. *Women in Congress,* p. 425.

144. Freeman, *The Women Who Ran for President.*

145. A documentary on her life, *Patsy Mink: Ahead of the Majority,* was released in 2009.

146. These averages are simply the difference in the number of women elected in a given election (e.g., 1958) compared to the number elected in the previous election (e.g., 1956). We then sum these changes over the period in question (e.g., 1956–1970) and divide by the number of election cycles in that period.

THREE

Arrested Development: A History of Careerism and Incumbency

Our discussion in the previous chapter demonstrates that the process of electoral change, as illustrated by the gain in congressional seats won by women, has been, with the exception of 1992, undramatic. These characteristics are especially perplexing given the broader shifts found in American society and culture over the past century. A few examples of these shifts are presented in Figure 3.1, where the progression of women as a proportion of all members of the House is compared to three indicators of social and cultural change. First is the proportion of married women in the civilian work force, second is the proportion of law degrees awarded to women, and third is a measure of attitudes toward women in business and government.[1]

These indicators demonstrate that, with respect to women, society in the United States today is substantially different from the way it was in the 1940s and 1950s. In 1940, only 15 percent of married women worked outside the home. This proportion first crossed the 50 percent threshold in 1986 and reached its peak of 59 percent in 2008. Although there are year-to-year fluctuations, our indicator of public attitudes displays a similar trend. In 1972, when the question was first asked, 47 percent of Americans agreed that women should have an "equal role with men." By 2008, this proportion had increased to 84 percent.

The patterns displayed by these two indicators exhibit slow but sustained change over an extended period of time.[2] In contrast, the proportion of law degrees awarded to women presents an example of a dramatic shift.[3] As late as 1968, women received fewer than 5 percent of all law degrees. Harvard Law School, for example, did not even admit women until 1950. But even law schools that eliminated their male-only admission policies during the 1950s and 1960s still opened their doors to women by only a crack. Beginning in the early 1970s, after the passage of Title IX, banning discrimination based on sex in education, the proportion began to increase rapidly, reaching 30 percent in 1980, 40 percent in 1988, and peaking at 50 percent in 2004.[4] This remarkable change provides one glimpse of the movement of women into a previously male-dominated profession typically regarded as "preparatory" for a career in politics.

When compared to all of these indicators, the election of women to the House appears as a case of "arrested development." As Figure 3.1 shows, in recent years over 80 percent of the American public has supported an equal role for women in business and government, nearly 60 percent of married women have been members of the work force, and nearly 50 percent of law degrees have been awarded to women. There have also been tremendous gains in other areas of higher education. In 1957, women earned 33 percent of master's degrees and 11 percent of PhDs. By 2008, women had surpassed men, earning 60 percent of mas-

Figure 3.1   Women and the Pace of Change, 1940–2010

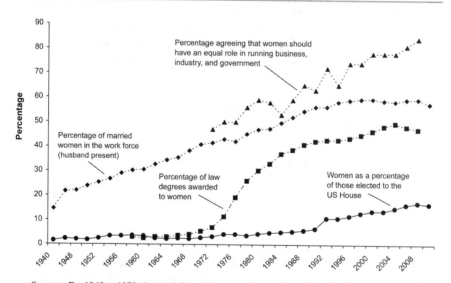

Sources: For 1940 to 1970, the work force data were obtained from *Historical Statistics of the United States,* p. 133. Data for subsequent years were gathered from relevant editions of *Statistical Abstract of the United States.* The proportion of the law degrees awarded to women is reported by the National Center for Education Statistics, "Table 279: Degrees Conferred." For our measure of public opinion, see endnote 1, p. 85.

ter's degrees and 52 percent of PhDs.[5] Yet the proportion of women in the US House hovers around 17 percent. Why?

In this chapter, we argue that a major culprit in creating this arrested development is incumbency. House and Senate incumbents are virtually unbeatable. They face little competition, and those who do face competition are likely to win in a "blow out." We show, however, that the phenomenon of long-term career incumbents is relatively recent. For the first hundred years of congressional history, most members of Congress did not serve more than one or two terms. This changed in the early part of the twentieth century, just as the first women began running for office. In essence, the growth of careerism occurred just as women were entering the national political arena. And by the time social attitudes about the role of women began to change in the 1970s, the power of incumbency was well established.

The Power of Incumbency

Today, one of the central features of US elections is incumbency.[6] Once candidates win an election and become members of Congress, they have substantial advantages when they run for reelection. Simply by virtue of being a member of Congress, incumbents have more name recognition than challengers. At least half of the people who voted in the last election can recognize the incumbent, while challengers are typically unknown.[7] Unless a major scandal develops, the local press is unlikely to provide any coverage of challengers at all, and if they are covered, the stories are usually about how they have no chance of winning. Many newspapers have a policy that if a challenger is running uncontested in their primary, they will not provide any coverage of the candidate until after the primary. If a state's primary is not until September, this means that the challenger only has six weeks to get press coverage.[8] Meanwhile, the incumbent is getting coverage of their legislative accomplishments in Washington, D.C.[9] As one political consultant explained, press coverage of incumbents and challengers is so unequal that "the local press is the unindicted co-conspirator" in perpetuating the invincibility of incumbents.[10]

One of the major ways incumbents keep their names in the minds of constituents is through the franking privilege. Since the First Continental Congress in 1775, members of Congress have had the right to send mail to every one of their constituents for free; in place of a stamp, they use their signature. The idea was that this would facilitate communication between representatives and their constituents. Members also discovered, however, that this could help their reelection campaigns. While reforms in the 1990s have substantially reduced abuse, the use of the frank typically doubles during election years. Representative Bill Frenzel (R-MN) commented that newcomers to Congress are taught three rules for getting reelected: "Use the frank. Use the frank. Use the frank."[11] More recently, members have been taking advantage of new media and other technology, such as phone franking, e-newsletters, and blogs, which have the advantage of being cheaper than traditional mailings, allowing members to spread their budgets even further and reach their constituents—potential voters—even more frequently.[12]

Incumbents also have the added advantage of having a well-established "money machine" at their disposal. Many candidates, regardless of whether they are incumbents, find fundraising not only time consuming but also humiliating. Rather than face his fourth reelection campaign, Senator John Glenn (D-OH) retired in 1998, commenting that "I'd rather wrestle a gorilla than ask anybody for another fifty cents."[13] Running for office requires the creation of a fundraising network, a network that can be used over and over again when candidates run for reelection. The experience that incumbents have in asking people for money makes it easier for them to raise more money. In addition, political action committees (PACs), a major source of campaign dollars, are much more likely to give to incumbents; in fact, incumbents receive seven times the PAC contributions that challengers do.[14] It is also not uncommon for incumbents to have money left from their previous campaigns; this provides the base for building substantial "war chests" to scare off future challengers. As a result, incumbents are able to outspend their challengers by substantial margins. For example, in the 2010 election cycle, House incumbents raised an average of $1.5 million, while their challengers typically raised less than $300,000. Senate incumbents raised an average of $11 million, while their challengers raised less than $1 million; incumbents outspent their opponents by a ratio of six to one.[15]

As a result, incumbents are virtually ensured reelection. As Table 3.1 shows, since 1956, 95 percent of incumbent House members running in the general election have been victorious. In eight of the election cycles during this period, the success rate for incumbents was 98 percent or higher. Only twice did the reelection rate for incumbents drop below 90 percent. In the Democratic landslide of 1964, the reelection rate was 89 percent, and in the 2010 midterm election, the rate was 86 percent. Both of these cycles were "wave" elections, in which national forces were quite strong and distinctly advantaged one party over another. In such elections, the re-election rate of incumbents in the advantaged party is higher than average, while the rate for incumbents of the disadvantaged party is lower. When Lyndon Johnson won the highest popular vote in the history of presidential elections in 1964, 98 percent of Democrat incumbents won, while the comparable success rate for Republicans was only 76 percent. Similarly, in the wave election of 2010, all but 2 of the 157 Republican incumbents won, for a success rate of 99 percent, while 53 of the 237 Democrat incumbents were defeated, giving them a success rate of only 78 percent.

Table 3.1 illustrates that not only do House incumbents enjoy spectacularly high rates of reelection, but over time they have also increasingly won by larger margins. During the 1950s, 79 percent of incumbents were reelected in "safe seats," which we define as winning with more than 55 percent of the two-party vote. From 2002 to 2010, the most recent redistricting period, 89 percent of incumbents were reelected with more than 55 percent of the two-party vote. In other words, incumbents have grown more secure electorally; almost all of them enjoy the comfort of safe seats.

Table 3.1 also reveals that for House incumbents, primary elections are strikingly uncompetitive. In an average election year, over 70 percent of incumbents have no opponent in the party primary. Moreover, since 1956, only 1 percent of incumbents have lost a primary challenge. Thus, as Table 3.1 shows, incumbents are virtually ensured renomination.

On the rare occasion when incumbents lose a primary, it is usually because they are running against another incumbent in the wake of redistricting. In 2002, for example, Michigan lost a House seat. The state legislature redrew the lines, pitting two Democratic incumbents against each other, Representatives Lynn Rivers and John Dingell. In a primary that split the party, Rivers received the support of women's groups, environmentalists, and gun-control advocates, while Dingell relied on a coalition made up of unions, the auto industry, business lobbyists, and the National Rifle Association. Dingell won with 59 percent of the vote.[16] In 2003, the state legislature in Texas conducted an unprecedented second round of redistricting after partisan control of the state house of representatives changed. Although the Texas case is unusual, it highlights the importance of redistricting for incumbents. Eleven of seventeen Democratic incumbents lost over half of the constituents who elected them in 2002. One incumbent, Ralph Hall, changed parties and became a Republican; another, Jim Turner, retired; and another, Chris Bell, lost his primary.[17] Four more were defeated in the general election, Max Sandlin, Nick Lampson, Charles Stenholm, and Martin Frost.[18]

Table 3.1 Incumbents and Elections to the US House, by Redistricting Period, 1956–2010 (percentages)

	Incumbents Running Who Are Reelected	Incumbents Reelected with a Safe Margin[a]	Incumbents Winning Renomination	Incumbents with No Primary Opponent	Incumbents with No Major Party Opponent	Incumbents with a Free Pass[b]
1956–1960	93.6	79.5	98.8	74.1	20.4	14.2
1962–1970	94.2	84.2	98.6	68.9	13.6	8.9
1972–1980	94.3	85.4	98.5	66.6	14.6	9.1
1982–1990	96.6	89.8	99.4	70.5	18.1	13.5
1992–2000	95.7	87.1	98.8	72.1	13.7	9.3
2002–2010	94.6	88.6	99.5	74.3	14.2	10.9
Overall	94.9	86.2	98.9	70.9	15.4	11.0

Source: Data compiled by the authors.

Notes: a. "Safe margin" is defined as winning with more than 55 percent of the two-party vote.
b. "Free pass" is defined as having no competition in the primary election and no competition in the general election.

Table 3.2 Incumbents and Elections to the US Senate, by Six-Year Cycle, 1958–2010 (percentages)

	Incumbents Running Who Are Reelected	Incumbents Reelected with a Safe Margin[a]	Incumbents Winning Renomination	Incumbents with No Primary Opponent	Incumbents with No Major Party Opponent	Incumbents with a Free Pass[b]
1958–1962	84.5	61.9	98.8	38.7	8.3	4.6
1964–1968	89.0	63.4	91.1	38.4	7.3	0.0
1970–1974	84.8	60.8	94.0	45.3	5.1	2.4
1976–1980	64.8	47.9	91.0	41.2	5.6	1.3
1982–1986	86.2	72.4	100.0	54.2	1.1	1.1
1988–1992	89.3	70.2	98.8	52.5	7.1	3.5
1994–1998	90.4	65.8	98.6	54.3	0.0	0.0
2000–2004	87.8	76.8	98.8	63.4	8.5	7.2
2006–2010	83.3	74.0	96.3	46.7	2.6	2.5
Overall	84.7	66.3	96.4	46.4	5.1	2.6

Source: Data compiled by the authors.

Notes: a. "Safe margin" is defined as winning with more than 55 percent of the two-party vote.
b. "Free pass" is defined as having no competition in the primary election and no competition in the general election.

In addition to facing little or no competition in their own primaries, it is not uncommon for incumbents to run uncontested in the general election. Historically, over 15 percent of House incumbents faced no opponent in the general election. While this phenomenon decreased following its peak in 1956–1960, it increased to 18 percent from 1982 to 1990. Despite the three wave elections in the period from 2002 to 2010, 14 percent of incumbents faced no major party opponent. Table 3.1 illustrates that, in every redistricting period, there is a substantial minority of incumbents who have no competition in the general election.

For obvious reasons, the most desirable state of affairs for any incumbent is the "free pass"—facing no competition in both the primary and the general election. As the last column of Table 3.1 shows, between 1956 and 2010, the proportion of free passes averaged 11 percent of those incumbents seeking reelection. In four election cycles, the proportion of free passes exceeded 15 percent (1958, 1988, 1990, and 1998). The election of 2010 is the only case where this proportion dropped below 5 percent. There is evidence, however, that the free pass is a disproportionately Southern phenomenon. For example, between 1956 and 1960, 46 percent of House elections in the South involved a free pass; in non-Southern congressional districts the proportion was only 3 percent. In the most recent redistricting period, the proportion in the South was 16 percent, while in the rest of the country it was 7 percent. In addition, the beneficiaries of the free pass have changed. Between 1956 and 1960, 99 percent of the free passes in the South went to Democrats. In the three most recent elections, 58 percent went to Southern Republicans. Overall, Table 3.1 demonstrates that defeating an incumbent, in either a primary or a general election, is a formidable task.

Reelection for Senate seats is a bit more competitive than for House seats, though reelection rates are still high. As we did in Chapter 2, we organize the data here in six-year election cycles. As Table 3.2 shows, Senate incumbents are, on average, reelected nearly 85 percent of the time. A substantial proportion of Senate incumbents also comes from safe seats, although there is much more variability across election cycles compared to the House. The most competitive period was the 1976–1980 sequence of elections. The success rate of incumbent senators reached a low point of 65 percent, as did the proportion who were reelected with a safe margin, 48 percent. Thereafter, the proportion who won with a safe margin increased substantially and topped 70 percent in four of the five subsequent six-year cycles. This includes the three most recent elections, during which, despite strong national forces, 74 percent of Senate incumbents won by 55 percent or more of the vote.

Table 3.2 also shows that there has been a substantial change in the proportion of Senate incumbents facing primary challenges. During the six-year cycle from 1958 to 1962, 39 percent of incumbents had no primary opposition, suggesting that there was substantially more competition in the Senate compared to the House. Thereafter, the proportion of incumbents facing no primary opponent increased, reaching its peak of 63 percent in the 2000–2004 sequence. In the three most recent elections, of 2006–2010, there was a significant change, as this proportion dropped to 47 percent. However, regardless of the level of primary competition, senators, like House members, are virtually ensured renomination, winning over 96 percent of their primaries. The proportion of Senate incumbents who run unopposed in the general election is much lower than for House incumbents. However, there are periods, such as 1958–1962 and 2000–2004, when a significant number of senators ran unopposed in the general election. Free passes, on the other hand, are relatively uncommon and typically much lower in Senate elections than in House elections.

Tables 3.1 and 3.2 suggest, then, that voters are extremely reluctant to oust a House or Senate incumbent. Occasionally, however, scandal will make incumbents vulnerable.[19] For example, in April 2001, Chandra Levy, an intern working in Washington, D.C., disappeared. Eventually, a connection was made between Levy and seven-term representative Gary Condit (D-CA). Condit initially refused to cooperate with police, and the story became a media frenzy. He appeared on *Prime Time Live* and on the cover of *People* magazine with his wife, denying that he was anything but friends with Levy. After four months, Condit admitted to police that he and Levy had had a sexual relationship.[20] Although the police never considered him a suspect in her disappearance, the damage was done. Condit lost his 2002 primary to Dennis Cardoza, 53 to 39 percent. Cardoza had actually worked on Condit's first House campaign and on his congressional staff.[21] Levy's remains were found over a year after she disappeared, in Rock Creek Park.[22] In November 2010, ten years after she disappeared, a jury convicted Ingmar Guandique of first-degree murder, although the prosecution could produce no witnesses or DNA evidence linking him to the crime.[23]

The campaign of 2006 featured three unusual instances where incumbents, having won their primaries, were forced by scandals to withdraw from the general election campaign. Representative Tom DeLay (R-TX) had soundly defeated three opponents in his primary with 62 percent of the vote, despite mounting legal troubles. In September 2005, a Texas grand jury had indicted DeLay of money laundering and state campaign finance violations; the charges stemmed from DeLay's alleged illegal funneling of corporate money into 2002 state legislative races, after which Republicans controlled the Texas house, senate, and governorship. Subsequently, the state legislature undertook an unprecedented second round of redistricting, which dramatically increased the number of Republicans in the Texas delegation to the US House. After his indictment, DeLay was stripped of his position as House majority leader. Shortly after winning his primary, he resigned from the House in April 2006, after his deputy chief of staff pleaded guilty to corruption charges following a federal investigation of "super lobbyist" Jack Abramoff, whom DeLay had called "one of my closest and dearest friends." Abramoff's clients had funneled over $1 million into DeLay's nonprofit organization, the US Family Network.[24] In 2009, DeLay appeared as a contestant on *Dancing With the Stars,* but withdrew after three episodes due to stress fractures in his feet. In January 2011, he was sentenced to three years in prison for the 2002 money-laundering scheme.[25] The Abramoff scandal also ended the political career of Representative Bob Ney (R-OH). In September 2006, Ney reached a plea agreement with the Justice Department over his involvement with Abramoff. Ney admitted to accepting gifts from Abramoff amounting to over $170,000, including a golf trip to Scotland and lavish meals at restaurants owned by Abramoff. In exchange, Abramoff asked Ney to amend the 2002 election reform bill in ways that would benefit his clients. Ney also traveled to London twice to meet with a businessman who hoped Ney could ease the embargo on the sale of US aircraft to Iran. Ney was given thousands of dollars in chips to spend at London casinos and then lied on customs forms about how much money he was bringing back into the United States. He was sentenced to thirty months in prison, community service, and a $6,000 fine.[26] Two weeks after Ney's plea agreement made headlines, six-term representative Mark Foley (R-FL) announced his resignation after it became public that he had sent suggestive e-mails to at least one sixteen-year-old high school boy participating in the House page program. Ironically, Foley had been the author of the sexual-predator provisions of the Adam Walsh Child Protection and Safety Act, signed by President George W. Bush a few months earlier.[27]

Rather than face reelection, most incumbents do resign after a scandal. For example, a series of recent sex scandals led to the resignation of three New York representatives. In March 2010, Representative Eric Massa (D-NY), who earned the nickname "Representative Tickle," announced that he would not seek reelection due to a "cancer scare." A few days later, he announced his immediate resignation when it became public that he was being investigated by the House Ethics Committee for sexually harassing a male staffer.[28] Massa appeared on Fox News's *Glenn Beck* and described the "tickle fights" he'd had with his staff. When Beck asked him about the

Ethics Committee investigation, Massa said, "Now they are saying I groped a male staffer. . . . Yeah, I did. Not only did I grope him. I tickled him until he couldn't breathe, and then four guys jumped on top of me. It was my 50th birthday. . . . You can take anything out of context."[29] Less than a year later, in February 2011, Representative Chris Lee (R-NY) resigned only four hours after Gawker.com revealed that Lee had sent a series of e-mails and a shirtless photo of himself to a woman, not his wife, whom he had met through Craig's List.[30] And four months after that, Representative Anthony Weiner (D-NY) called a press conference claiming that a hacker had broken into his Twitter account and posted an inappropriate photo, but for over a week he refused to confirm or deny that the photo was of him. As more photos were discovered and more women came forward claiming that Weiner had engaged in phone sex and "sexting" with them, Weiner still denied any wrongdoing. Three weeks later, he announced his resignation. During the scandal, it was also revealed that Weiner's wife, Huma Abedin, a top aide to Secretary of State Hillary Clinton, was pregnant.[31]

In many cases, however, scandal has remarkably little effect on incumbents. Representative Jim Moran (D-VA), for example, has long had a reputation for being controversial. In 1995, Moran had to apologize to Representative Randy Cunningham (R-CA) after he shoved him off the House floor and into a cloakroom.[32] In a bizarre incident in 2000, Moran accused an eight-year-old black boy of approaching him in a school parking lot with a gun and trying to steal his car. There was no evidence the boy had any kind of weapon, and his parents filed a formal complaint with police against Moran for harassing their son.[33] In 2002, with over two dozen credit cards and $700,000 worth of debt, Moran received a home-refinancing loan from MBNA, the largest loan the company made that year, at a lower interest rate than industry standards suggested. Four days later, Moran cosponsored a bankruptcy bill on which MBNA spent millions in lobbying expenses. Even more incredible, Moran gave a speech on the House floor in support of the bankruptcy bill, stating, "Some people are taking these credit cards in, they sign up, they max it out, whatever they can charge. . . . They pile up debt, and then they get themselves relieved from paying off their debt, and oftentimes they can go right back to doing it all over again. It needs to be fixed."[34] At an antiwar event in 2003, Moran blamed the Jewish community for US involvement in Iraq.[35] At a "get out the vote" rally for Virginia Democratic candidates in 2009, he compared the Republican ticket to Islamic extremists, claiming, "I mean, if the Republicans were running in Afghanistan, they'd be running on the Taliban ticket as far as I can see."[36] Despite all this, Moran had been reelected eight times with more than 60 percent of the vote.

Beyond Moran, "one of the most colorful figures" to serve in Congress was former nine-term Democratic representative Jim Traficant from Ohio, well known for his colorful suits and bad hairpiece.[37] He once voted for Republican representative Dennis Hastert for speaker of the House; in response, Democratic Party leaders refused to give Traficant any committee assignments.[38] In 2000, despite an investigation for violating tax laws and accepting illegal gifts, he cruised to reelection, winning 69 percent of the vote. Shortly afterward he was indicted on ten counts of bribery, tax evasion, and obstruction of justice.[39] During the trial, he represented himself. He admitted he took money from mobsters, but claimed he did it to get evidence against them, and argued that the investigation of him was a "government vendetta."[40] After he was convicted in 2001 on all ten counts, he refused to resign his House seat and ran for reelection in 2002 as an Independent; he vowed to become the first person elected to Congress from a prison cell.[41] Even in jail, he received 15 percent of the vote and had a 30 percent approval rating.[42]

In 2006, Republicans were not the only ones dealing with corruption issues. In its bribery investigation of Representative William Jefferson (D-LA), in May 2006, the FBI revealed that agents had found nearly $100,000 in "cold hard cash" in Jefferson's freezer and then raided his Washington, D.C., office. The money, given to Jefferson by a business associate (an FBI informant), was intended to be used to bribe the vice president of Nigeria to secure a telecommunications deal in which Jefferson had a stake. During a press conference, Jefferson maintained that he had done nothing wrong and blasted the FBI for "an outrageous intrusion into separation of powers" when they had searched his office.[43] Jefferson managed to hold on to his House seat that fall, defeating eight Democrats and three Republicans. However, in 2008, Jefferson won the Democratic primary but was narrowly defeated in the general election, in what was considered a major upset, by Republican Joseph Cao, who became the first Vietnamese American elected to Congress and the first Republican to represent Louisiana's Second District since 1891. Jefferson was convicted in 2009 and sentenced to thirteen years in prison, the longest sentence ever given to a member of Congress for corruption charges.[44]

Representative Charlie Rangel (D-NY), the chair of the powerful House Ways and Means Committee, was stripped of his position as chair and censured by the House for a variety of ethics violations and still held on to his seat. Censure is among the most serious punishments that can be given to a House member, second only to expulsion, and had not been used in almost three decades. The scandal involving Rangel first became public in July 2008, when the *Washington Post* reported that Rangel had been using his congressional letterhead to solicit donations from corporate leaders, including Donald Trump, whose companies would be affected by legislation that passed through the Ways and Means Committee. The donations were to support the building of the Charles B. Rangel Center for Public Service at the City College of New York in his district. Rangel had also secured earmarks and federal loans totaling nearly $2.7 million for the project.[45] It was also revealed that Rangel had failed to pay taxes on income he had earned from rental property he owned in the Dominican Republic. Rangel blamed his wife for "inadvertent bookkeeping oversights" and the "cultural and language barriers" created by doing business in a foreign country.[46] In September 2008, the House Ethics Committee announced that it would begin an investigation, which clearly had no impact on his reelection campaign.[47] Rangel easily won a twentieth term with 90 percent of the vote. He remained defiant throughout the two-year investigation and dared the Ethics Committee to "fire your best shot."[48] He refused to formally give up his position as Ways and Means chair and, in March 2010, instead said he would take a temporary "leave of absence" as chair until the investigation concluded.[49] He was reelected in 2010 with well over 80 percent of the vote. A few weeks after the election, the Ethics Committee eventually found Rangel guilty of eleven violations of House rules.[50]

It is interesting to note that all of these examples involve male politicians. This is not to say that women have not been involved in scandals. For example, most recently, in August 2010, the House Ethics Committee released a report regarding its investigation of Representative Maxine Waters (D-CA) and her involvement in securing $12 million in funds from the Troubled Asset Relief Fund for OneUnited Bank. Waters's husband, Sidney, was on the board of directors of the bank and owned several hundred thousand dollars of stock in the bank. The Ethics Committee concluded in its report that Waters had "probably violated House conflict-of-interest rules."[51] Waters was easily reelected with 79 percent of the vote. During the 2008 campaign for governor in South Carolina, Nikki Haley, who had been married for thirteen years, was accused of having "inappropriate sexual relationships" with two men. Haley unequivocally denied the allegations. One of the men, after calling her a liar, endorsed her in his blog.[52] Haley won the election, becoming South Carolina's first female governor. While the evidence is anecdotal, it does appear that female politicians are much less likely to become involved in scandals, especially those involving sexual impropriety. As Representative Candice Miller (R-MI) explained, "Every time one of these sex scandals goes, we just look at each other, like, 'What is it with these guys? Don't they think they're going to get caught?'"[53]

■ Open Seat Elections to the House and Senate

Given the tremendous odds against defeating an incumbent, it would appear that the primary opportunity for turnover is open seats. And there is some evidence that women are more likely to run in open seats and win.[54] In fact, the election to draw the most women candidates was a 1996 Democratic primary for Maryland's Seventh District, a safe, Democratic, black-majority district that covered large sections of Baltimore. Representative Kweisi Mfume (D-MD) resigned in February to become the head of the National Association for the Advancement of Colored People (NAACP), and the state decided to combine the primaries for the special and general elections. The stampede of candidates included five Republicans and twenty-seven Democrats. Six of the Democrats were women. Elijah Cummings, the speaker pro tem of the Maryland house of representatives, was the strongest candidate and locked up the primary with 37 percent of the vote. His closest competitor was Reverend Frank Reid, from a large African American church. State senator Delores Kelley came in third, with 10 percent of the vote.[55] Kelley, also African American, had been in the state legislature since 1991. After her congressional-primary loss in 1996, she held on to her state senate seat and held several leadership positions.[56] The winner of the Republican primary was Kenneth Kondner, a dental technician. After the primary, Cummings beat Kondner in the special election and then again in the regularly scheduled general election in November.

As Figure 3.2 shows, the number of open House seats has fluctuated substantially over the fifty-four years of our analysis. The most prominent feature of this figure is the spike in open House seats in 1992, the election cycle that produced the dramatic increase in the number of women running and winning election to Congress. The reapportionment based upon the 1990 US Census reallocated nineteen House seats from states losing population in the Northeast and Midwest to states gaining population in the South and West.[57] The process of redrawing congressional district lines typically induces some incumbents to retire rather than face reelection in a district with a substantial proportion of new constituents. As a result, the average number of open House seats in elections immediately after redistricting was sixty-three, while the average number of open House seats in the following four election cycles, when the lines were fixed, was forty.

Figure 3.2 Open Seats in Elections to the US House and Senate, 1956–2010

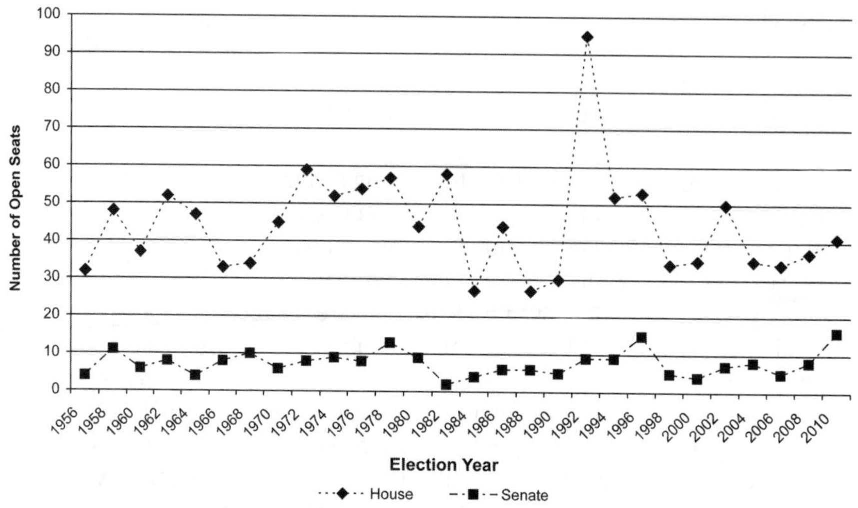

Source: Data compiled by the authors.
Note: House average 44.5, Senate average 7.6.

There were, however, additional factors at work in 1992 that brought the number of open seats to ninety-five. It was the last year that members of Congress could take advantage of a loophole in campaign finance regulations allowing them to convert leftover campaign funds to personal use; twenty representatives were eligible to take over $500,000 with them if they retired that year.[58] The House check-writing scandal also contributed to creating the unusually high number of open seats. In 1991, the General Accounting Office discovered that the House bank, run by the sergeant-at-arms, reported 8,331 bounced checks. The bank covered the checks of 269 representatives with no penalties or interest.[59] Many of the worst offenders, such as Representative Dennis Hertel (D-MI), who had 547 overdrafts, decided to retire.[60]

Consequently, the "Year of the Woman" was largely a function of women taking advantage of this remarkable number of opportunities.[61] It was "the perfect storm," an election cycle that featured a unique combination of factors: a campaign environment that favored women candidates, a mobilizing event in the Thomas-Hill hearings, and an unusually high number of open seats. Consequently, it is unlikely that anything like the increases in women's success that happened in 1992 will occur again. For example, the anticipation of a wave election often prompts some incumbents of the disadvantaged party to retire rather than face electoral defeat.

As Figure 3.2 shows, however, the numbers of open seats in the three wave elections of 2006 (thirty-four), 2008 (thirty-seven), and 2010 (forty-one) were not, by historical standards, particularly large.

While the number of open seats in the House fluctuates from election to election, the number of open Senate seats has remained relatively stable over the past fifty years at an average of just over seven. The peak in open Senate seats actually occurred not in 1992, but in 1996 and 2010, when the number reached fifteen. Of the twenty-two women initially elected to the Senate during this period, fifteen, or 68 percent, were elected in open seats. Between 1956 and 2010, seven of seventy-six women who challenged Senate incumbents won their elections, a success rate of 9 percent. Fifteen of thirty-seven women running in open seat races were victorious, a success rate of 41 percent. While open seats are clearly the primary avenue to the Senate for women, nearly 60 percent of those women who win their nominations are defeated in general election contests for open seats. For example, in the 2004 Florida open seat race for the Senate, Betty Castor ran against Republican Mel Martinez, the former secretary of Housing and Urban Development (HUD). Martinez ran an ad insinuating that Castor was against the "war on terror." He attacked her for refusing to suspend Professor Sami al-Arian while she was president of the University of South Florida. Al-Arian was suspected of having ties to Islamic Jihad and was accused of financing terrorism. The Florida Leadership Council, a PAC, attacked Castor's handling of al-Arian in a newspaper ad asking, "Who would Osama bin Laden prefer?"[62] Castor countered with her own ads, calling Martinez "unprincipled and nasty."[63] She attacked him for authorizing federal grants for nursing homes to refurbish rooms with La-Z-Boy furniture while he was secretary of HUD; after Martinez left HUD, he became a member of La-Z-Boy's board of directors.[64] Martinez won with 49 percent of the vote to Castor's 48 percent, becoming the first Cuban American to be elected to the Senate and the first Hispanic senator to serve since 1977.[65] Castor's daughter, Kathy, successfully ran for the House in 2006.

Ultimately, our analysis thus far provides a great deal of evidence that there is not much genuine competition in US congressional elections. Incumbents, especially in the House, have very little opposition and are virtually invincible. As former representative Clem Miller (D-CA) explained, "Few die and none resign."[66]

▩ The Rise of Careerism

It is important to keep in mind, however, that the pursuit of long-term congressional careers is a twentieth-century phenomenon. High reelection

rates and low retirement rates are associated with the development of professionalized legislatures.[67] Even today, many state legislatures, for example, meet only periodically for short sessions and provide, at best, a modest
salary for members. For example, the Texas legislature meets every other
year for 140 days and pays only $7,200 per year.[68] Of necessity, Texas leg-
islators have other jobs. In New Hampshire, an amendment in the state
constitution from 1889 limits the salary of members of the state house of
representatives to $200.[69] This amendment actually reduced the salary
from $250, set in 1784. In contrast, for the 112th Congress (2011 session),
rank-and-file House members and Senators earned $174,000 annually.[70]

In contrast to "amateur" or "citizen" legislatures, where membership
turnover is high, professionalized bodies have a variety of identifiable
characteristics that further the careerist aspirations of their members.[71]
There is a division of labor through a committee system with fixed juris-
dictions. In addition, there are formal rules and informal norms that govern member behavior. Within committees, for example, the norm of
specialization encourages the development of substantive expertise. Position in the committee hierarchy is determined largely by seniority. Given
this, the importance of continuous service becomes obvious: influence in
the policymaking process and prestige among colleagues are among the
payoffs for the successful careerist. Reelection becomes the most immediate goal, and a necessary condition, for long-term service. Thus the mind-
set of the careerist "is not just how to win next time, but how to win
consistently."[72] Incumbents run for reelection over and over because they
want to. For the first hundred years of Congress, however, most members
did not want to run for reelection.

Figure 3.3 presents, for the years from 1800 to 1992, the proportion of
House members who retired after one or two terms and the proportion of
House members who served six or more terms.[73] There are three distinct
eras: a period characterized by short careers in the House from 1800 to
1860, a transition era between 1862 and 1914, and a period of substantial
growth in careerism beginning in 1916. From 1800 to 1860, nearly one-
fourth of all members retired from the House after serving one or two
terms; only 6 percent served for six or more terms. During these years, it
was understandable why long careers were rare. First, there were the physical conditions. The city of Washington, D.C., was not a pleasant place. It
was hot, humid, and undeveloped, and "epidemics of fever were
chronic."[74] Congress itself could be equally unpleasant—crowded, noisy,
smelly, and occasionally violent. One of the most notorious examples was
in 1856, when Representative Preston Brooks (D-SC) beat Senator Charles
Sumner (R-MA) senseless with a cane on the Senate floor because of their

differing views on the issue of slavery.[75] Duels were not uncommon.[76] There were few social or cultural diversions in the city, no museums or monuments, and cows grazed in front of the White House.[77] In fact, the presence of politicians in Washington seemed to act "as a magnet for society's idle and society's unwanted: people sick in mind or body, imagining conspiracies against them."[78]

Second, long-term service was not pursued largely because it removed most members from both their private occupations and their homes. A political career meant "estrangement from wives and children" and potentially "financial ruin."[79] To reduce this separation from family and career, as well as to escape the hot summers in the capital city, Congress adapted its work schedule to the planting and harvest cycle. For example, the 7th Congress, elected in 1800, did not convene until December 7, 1801, and adjourned in time for the planting season on May 3, 1802. The last congressional session before the onset of the Civil War, the second session of the 36th Congress, began on December 3, 1860, and ended on March 3, 1861.[80]

Third, in the later part of this era, the rise of strong party organizations actually discouraged careerism in the House. Nominations to run for the House were a product of local party conventions, and in many areas of the country, parties adopted a practice of office rotation to prevent infighting.[81] In 1846, for example, Abraham Lincoln was nominated by the Whig Party

Figure 3.3 Careerism in the US House, 1800–1992

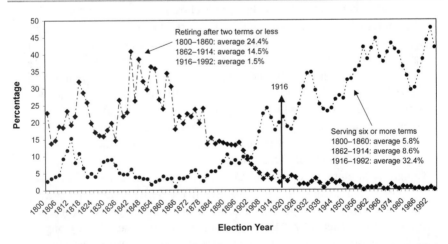

Source: Compiled by the authors from Elaine Swift, Robert Brookshire, David Canon, Evelyn Fink, and John Hibbing, comps., *Database of Congressional Historical Statistics,* Study no. 3371 (Ann Arbor, MI: Interuniversity Consortium for Political Research, 2004).

convention in the Seventh District of Illinois after the incumbent of his party declined renomination. After serving for one term, Lincoln stepped aside and ended his career in the House.[82]

The post–Civil War years were an era of transition. From 1862 to 1914, there was a noteworthy decline in early retirements, dropping from a high of 31 percent to a low of 6 percent. On average, the retirement rate declined from 24 percent in the prior era to 14 percent. The proportion of members serving lengthy careers in the House increased as well. Initially, the increase was gradual, from 1 percent in 1864 to 10 percent in 1900, and then became more rapid, peaking at 24 percent in 1910. Emerging national issues, coupled with the legislative agenda forwarded by Presidents Theodore Roosevelt and Woodrow Wilson, made Congress a "more authoritative locus of public policy."[83] As a result, the job of a congressman "became more important and probably more prestigious, and the hardships became more endurable."[84] The installation of air conditioning in the Capitol in the 1930s is often credited with not only making sessions of Congress more comfortable but also actually prolonging them.[85]

In addition, two Progressive-era reforms made it easier for incumbents to pursue a career. First, the direct primary, adopted by numerous states between 1905 and 1910, reduced the influence of local party elites in the selection of candidates for the House.[86] Second, the introduction of the Australian ballot paved the way for candidate-centered campaigning and the cultivation of a "personal vote." Under the old system, the "party strip ballot" was a single sheet of paper, often produced and distributed by the local party, that provided only the party's chosen candidate for each office. The names of rival candidates within the party were not included. In many states, voters simply deposited the "party strip" in the ballot box. The character of these ballots not only encouraged straight-ticket voting, but also "limited the relevance of any individual candidate's personal reputation for the voter's choice."[87] In contrast, the Australian ballot listed all candidates running for each office; while a straight-ticket option was often maintained, voters now had the ability to express their preference office-by-office.[88] Between 1888 and 1910, forty-three of the forty-eight states adopted the Australian ballot.[89] Both of these changes helped to open a path to the US Congress for entrepreneurial and careerist-oriented candidates.

The last era, from 1916 onward, was marked by substantial growth in careerism. On average, nearly one-third of the House membership served for six or more terms. As Figure 3.3 shows, during the 102nd Congress (1993 session), nearly half the members, 48 percent, were long-term incumbents; the average proportion of members retiring after one or two terms dropped below 2 percent. In the 112th Congress (2011 session), the average length of service for House members was just under five terms.[90]

In fact, the 112th Congress was one of the oldest in the history of both the Senate and the House; the average age in the Senate was sixty-two, and the average age in the House was fifty-seven.[91] Senator Strom Thurmond (R-SC) holds the record as the oldest person to serve. He retired at the age of 100 in January 2003, after forty-eight years in Congress; he died a few months later.[92] Representative John Dingell (D-MI) currently holds the record for longest consecutive service in the House, fifty-five years, beginning in 1955; he was elected to his twenty-ninth term in 2010.[93] The longest-serving woman is Edith Nourse Rogers (R-MA), who was a House member for thirty-six years after being elected in 1925. Her time as a field hospital inspector during World War I and Red Cross volunteer working with veterans had a profound effect on her. During her congressional career, she was a champion for men and women in the armed services and created the Women's Army Corps and sponsored the GI Bill of Rights. She eventually rose to the position of chair of the House Veterans' Affairs Committee in 1947. In September 1960, at the age of seventy-nine, she died two days before the Republican primary; her name was on the ballot unopposed.[94] Representative Cardiss Collins (D-IL) served for nearly twenty-four years, from 1973 to 1997, and is the longest-serving woman of color. For ten years, she was the only African American woman in Congress. Known for her "low-key style" and preference for working behind the scenes, she fought for women's rights and civil rights, introducing the first-ever mammogram bill, leading an investigation of the funding of college sports teams for men and women, and pushing the Federal Communications Commission to give more broadcasting licenses to women and minorities.[95] In contrast to the first hundred years of congressional history, individuals retiring after a short period of service have become a rarity.

In some respects, women in Congress have nearly caught up to their male counterparts. In the 112th Congress (2011 session), there were eighty men, 22 percent, who served for ten or more terms. Fourteen women, 19 percent, served ten or more terms. The most senior woman, Representative Marcy Kaptur (D-OH), was first elected in 1982 and had served fifteen consecutive terms. However, there are twenty-two men who had more seniority than she had. In fact, there were six men who served more than twenty consecutive terms.[96] As Table 3.3 shows, in the history of Congress only twenty-five women, 10 percent of all women who ever served in the House, have accumulated ten or more terms of service. Over half of the women who have such lengthy careers are members of the current House.

Recognizing the development of a career-oriented membership is essential for understanding the context in which women emerged as candidates and officeholders. The timing of this development is of particular importance. Figure 3.3 shows that after the election of 1900, the proportion of members serving six or more terms in the House first exceeded the proportion serving two terms or less, but just barely, by 10 percent to 9 percent. Following the election of 1916, when Jeannette Rankin (R-MT) became the first woman elected to the House, the proportion of House members serving six or more terms had grown to 20 percent, while the proportion serving two terms or less dropped to just 2 percent. After Rankin's breakthrough election, the development of careerism in the House would continue to accelerate. In 1917, only twenty-six men, 6 percent, had served for ten or more terms in the House. In 1971, just before the number of women in Congress began to rise, eighty-seven men, 20 percent, had served for ten or more terms.[97]

Thus the movement of women into the electoral arena began in an era when careerism in the House was in its early stages. In the early part of the

Table 3.3   Women Who Served Ten or More Terms in the US House

	Year First Elected	Terms
Mary Teresa Norton (D-NJ)	1924	13
Edith Nourse Rogers (R-MA)	1925	18
Frances Bolton (R-OH)	1940	15
Leonor Sullivan (D-MO)	1952	12
Edith Green (D-OR)	1954	10
Martha Griffiths (D-MI)	1954	10
Patricia Schroeder (D-CO)	1972	12
Cardiss Collins (D-IL)	1972	12
Marilyn Lloyd (D-MD)	1974	10
Margaret Roukema (R-NJ)	1980	11
Nancy Johnson (R-CT)	1982	12
Marcy Kaptur (D-OH)	1982	15[a]
Louise Slaughter (D-NY)	1986	13[a]
Nancy Pelosi (D-CA)	1987	13[a]
Nita Lowey (D-NY)	1988	12[a]
Ileana Ros-Lehtinen (R-FL)	1989	12[a]
Rosa DeLauro (D-CT)	1990	11[a]
Maxine Waters (D-CA)	1990	11[a]
Corrine Brown (D-FL)	1992	10[a]
Anna Eshoo (D-CA)	1992	10[a]
Eddie Bernice Johnson (D-TX)	1992	10[a]
Carolyn Maloney (D-NY)	1992	10[a]
Lucille Roybal-Allard (D-CA)	1992	10[a]
Nydia Velazquez (D-NY)	1992	10[a]
Lynn Woolsey (D-CA)	1992	10[a]

Source: Data compiled by the authors.
Note: a. Currently serving in the 112th Congress (2011 session).

twentieth century, incumbency advantages were developing just as the first women were running for Congress and winning. Six decades later, when women finally began entering the electoral arena in noticeable numbers, opportunities for success were scarce.[98]

The Importance of Seniority in the Contemporary Congress

This growth in careerism and incumbency has had a substantial impact on how the modern Congress operates. It has influenced the structure of the committee system,[99] the committee assignments sought by members,[100] the wave of internal reforms adopted by the House in the 1970s,[101] how members strategically allocate their time, and the way members campaign for reelection.[102] Entry into the leadership structure of Congress, particularly in the House, depends upon longevity and seniority. This is especially true within the committee system, where the key positions—chairs and ranking members—are based largely upon continuous service on committees and subcommittees. As Representative Chellie Pingree (D-ME) explained, "Being a freshman Member of Congress is like being a freshman in high school. You hope the seniors notice you."[103]

Until very recently, women have barely been represented in the leadership hierarchy. In fact, it was not until the 108th Congress (2004 session) that there was at least one woman on every committee.[104] In the history of Congress, only twenty-eight women have chaired committees, eighteen in the House and ten in the Senate.[105] The first was Representative Mae Ella Nolan (R-CA), who chaired the House Committee on Expenditures in the Post Office Department from 1923 to 1925. As the first woman committee chair—and as the first woman to take over her husband's seat after his death—Nolan was bombarded by media attention. The press was particularly merciless about her figure; at least one story reported that she had taken up golf to lose weight.[106]

When the Democrats took over the House after the 2006 election and Representative Nancy Pelosi (D-CA) became speaker, the 110th Congress (2007 session) actually saw a substantial increase in the number of women in leadership positions.[107] Four women chaired committees in the House, a record number, after a decade with no female committee chairs. Fourteen women chaired subcommittees. Four women served as deputy majority whips, and a woman served as the chair of the Democratic Steering Committee. On the Republican side, seven women were ranking members on subcommittees, and Representative Kay Granger (R-TX) served as vice chair of the Republican Conference.[108] The value of lengthy careers becomes obvious when looking at the length of service among those in leadership positions in the 110th Congress. Among all twenty-two chairs of the standing House committees, the average number of terms served was fourteen. Among the Republicans who were ranking members on full committees, the average length of service was ten terms. The average length of service among the four women committee chairs was eight terms. Among the fourteen Democratic women who chaired subcommittees, the average was six terms. Among the seven Republican women who were ranking members of subcommittees, the average length of service was four terms. All of this suggests that the "threshold" for moving into the leadership structure is roughly five terms, or ten years of service.

In the 111th Congress (2010 session), five Democratic women chaired House committees. Because committee chairs are a function of majority-party control, after the Republicans took over the House the number of women in leadership positions declined. Only one woman, Representative Ileana Ros-Lehtinen (R-FL), served as chair of the House Foreign Affairs committee.[109] In the 112th Congress (2011 session), there were only half as many Republican women compared to Democratic women overall, and very few Republican women had a great deal of seniority. In fact, as Table 3.3 shows, Representative Ros-Lehtinen was the only Republican woman who served ten or more terms; she was the most senior Republican woman in the House.

Conclusion

One of the most compelling explanations for the lack of women in Congress is the power of incumbency.[110] For both genders, crossing the threshold from challenger to officeholder is extremely difficult. Thus, women have a hard time winning seats in Congress not because they are women, but because of incumbency—and most incumbents are men. Since the 1950s, over 95 percent of incumbents seeking reelection have been successful. It is important to keep in mind, however, that long congressional careers, especially in the House, are a twentieth-century phenomenon. In fact, it is quite striking that careerism peaked at almost exactly the same time that women first began running for Congress in measurable numbers. Just as women were entering the political arena, success in that arena became more difficult. As a result, the phenomenon of incumbents seeking and winning reelection over the long term was firmly entrenched well before traditional social attitudes and gender stereotypes began to change in the 1970s.

There is no doubt that incumbency plays a fundamental role in candidate strategy; the likelihood of success even influences the decision to become a candidate.[111] Today, women do not typically offer themselves up as "sacrificial lambs"—running without any hope of winning—any more often than men do.[112] Logically, then, open seats are thought to be the main avenue of access for women. The problem with open seats, of course, is that there are so few of them in a given election cycle. As a result, if women wait for an opportunity to run in an open seat, they may be waiting for a long time. If the average incumbent is now serving five terms, that means the seat is open once every decade. As this chapter has shown, careerism and the power of incumbency are the foundations for understanding why the integration of women into Congress over the past century is a case of "arrested development." But, as the rest of our analysis will explore, this arrested development is not merely a function of incumbency. Several other factors, often more subtle, are at work.

■ Notes

1. For 1940 to 1970, the work force data were obtained from *Historical Statistics of the United States,* p. 133. Data for subsequent years were gathered from relevant editions of the *Statistical Abstract of the United States.* The proportion of the law degrees awarded to women is reported by the National Center for Education Statistics, "Table 279: Degrees Conferred." Our measure of public opinion is based upon a question regularly included in the American National Election Surveys and can be found at http://electionstudies.org//nesguide/toptable/tab4c_1.htm. Respondents are given a 7-point scale to respond to the following question: "Some people feel that women should have an equal role with men in running business, industry, and government. Others feel that women's place is in the home. Where would you place yourself on this scale or haven't you thought much about it?" On the scale, positions 1, 2, and 3 represent agreement with the "equal role" while positions 5, 6, and 7 indicate agreement with "women's place is in the home." Figure 3.1 reports the proportion of respondents placing themselves at positions 1, 2, or 3.

2. Our characterization of this pattern is based upon the classifications of change presented in Carmines and Stimson, *Issue Evolution,* pp. 138–144. See also Steinhorn, *The Greater Generation.*

3. Carmines and Stimson, *Issue Evolution,* p. 139.

4. See Epstein, *Women in Law.*

5. Jaschik, "For First Time, More Women Than Men Earn PhD"; National Center for Education Statistics, "Table 279: Degrees Conferred." Unfortunately, only projected statistics were available for 2010, so we use the actual numbers for 2008 here.

6. See, for example, Carson, Engstrom, and Roberts, "Candidate Quality, the Personal Vote, and the Incumbency Advantage in Congress"; Herrnson, *Congressional Elections;* Jacobson, *The Politics of Congressional Elections.*

7. Herrnson, *Congressional Elections,* p. 216.

8. Ibid., pp. 228–229.

9. Sidlow, *Challenging the Incumbent.*

10. Herrnson, *Congressional Elections,* p. 228.

11. Davidson, Oleszek, and Lee, *Congress and Its Members,* p. 147.

12. Ibid., p. 148.

13. Davidson and Oleszek, *Congress and Its Members,* p. 69.

14. Jacobson, *The Politics of Congressional Elections,* pp. 67–74; Stanley and Niemi, *Vital Statistics on American Politics, 2009–2010,* pp. 98–100.

15. "2010 Overview: Incumbent Advantage."

16. "Dingell, John D."

17. Gaddie, "The Texas Redistricting," pp. 19–24.

18. Ibid., p. 24.

19. See Garrett, *Campaign Crises,* for an analysis of how candidates and their campaign staffs handle crises.

20. Lengel and Dvorak, "Condit Offers Long-Awaited Comment Tonight," p. A18.

21. See http://nationaljournal.com/pubs/almanac/2004/people/ca/rep_ca18.htm (accessed July 15, 2005).

22. Lengel, "Discovery May Alter Questions for Condit," p. A22.

23. At the time of his trial for Levy's disappearance, Guandique was already in prison for attacking several female joggers in Rock Creek Park; "Chandra Levy's Killer Gets 60 Years."

24. Smith, "DeLay Indicted in Texas Finance Probe"; Smith, "The Delay-Abramoff Money Trail"; Weisman and Cillizza, "DeLay to Resign from Congress."

25. McKinley, "DeLay Sentenced to 3 Years in Conspiracy and Money-Laundering Case."

26. Schmidt and Grimaldi, "Ney Sentenced to 30 Months in Prison for Abramoff Deals"; Shenon, "Lawmaker Admits He Took Illegal Gifts."

27. Babington and Weisman, "Rep. Foley Quits in Page Scandal."

28. Bresnahan and Thrush, "Rep. Eric Massa to Resign."

29. Hernandez, "Ex-Congressman Describes Tickle Fights with Aides."

30. Sherman and Bresnahan, "Rep. Chris Lee Resigns over Suggestive Photo."

31. Fahrenthold and Kane, "Rep. Anthony Weiner Resigns."

32. Geraghty, "Moranic Record."

33. O'Hanlon and Davis, "Parents File Complaint Against Va.'s Moran."

34. Becker and Hsu, "Credit Firm Gave Moran Favorable Loan Deal," p. A1.

35. Jenkins and Melton, "Contrite, Combatative Moran on the Ropes," A1.

36. Gardner, "Jim Moran Calls GOP the 'Taliban Ticket.'"

37. "Traficant, James A., Jr."

38. Ibid.

39. Ibid.

40. Ibid.; Patrick, "Traficant Refuses to Go Quietly Despite Calls for His Resignation," p. 962.

41. Torry, "From His Cell, Traficant Still a Force in Election," p. 1A.

42. Ibid.

43. Markon, "Ex-Rep. Jefferson (D-La) Gets 13 Years in Freezer Cash Case"; Milbank, "So $90,000 Was in the Freezer."

44. Markon, "Ex-Rep. Jefferson (D-La) Gets 13 Years in Freezer Cash Case."

45. Lee, "Rangel's Pet Cause Bears His Own Name."

46. Kocieniewski, "Congressman Pays Back Tax on Dominican Republic Villa."

47. Kocieniewski, "House Ethics Committee Votes to Begin an Inquiry on Rangel."

48. Kane, "Charlie Rangel Censure Recommended by House Ethics Committee."

49. Hulse and Herszenhorn, "Rangel Steps Aside from Post During Ethics Inquiry."

50. Kane, "Charlie Rangel Censure Recommended by House Ethics Committee."

51. Kane and Pershing, "Rep. Maxine Waters of California Probably Broke Ethics Rules."

52. Condon, "Haley Endorsed by Blogger Who Claimed Affair with Her."

53. Stolberg, "When It Comes to Scandal, Girls Won't Be Boys."

54. See, for example, Bernstein, "Might Women Have the Edge in Open-Seat House Primaries?"; Burrell, "Women Candidates in Open-Seat Primaries for the US House"; Mueller and Poole, "A New Year of the Woman?"

55. "New Member Profile: Elijah E. Cummings," p. 1070.

56. "Maryland Senate: Delores Goodwin Kelley."

57. *CQ's Guide to 1990 Congressional Redistricting,* p. 1.

58. Hook, "Will the Flood of Retirements Arrive in 1992?" p. 72.

59. Kuntz, "Uproar over Bank Scandal Goads House to Cut Perks," p. 2841.

60. Ibid.; Kuntz, "Overdrafts Were a Potent Charge," p. 3575.

61. Berch, "The 'Year of the Woman' in Context"; Burrell, *A Woman's Place Is In the House;* Carroll, *Women as Candidates in American Politics;* Chaney and Sinclair, "Women and the 1992 House Elections"; Cook and Wilcox, "Women Voters in the Year of the Woman"; Duerst-Lahti, "The Bottleneck: Women Becoming Candidates"; Gaddie and Bullock, "Congressional Elections and the Year of the Woman"; Wilcox, "Why Was 1992 the 'Year of the Woman'?"

62. March and Epstein, "Bile Flows As Tight Senate Race Heads to End," p. 1.

63. Rutenberg, "An Idea, with 4 Words," p. 15.

64. Bousquet and Kumar, "Castor, Martinez Keep Senate Race Attacks Coming," p. 5B.

65. Jones and Gedalius, "Martinez 'Humbled to Be' US Senator," p. 5.

66. Miller, *Member of the House,* p. 93.

67. Katz and Sala, "Careerism, Committee Assignments, and the Electoral Connection"; Kernell, "Toward Understanding 19th Century Congressional Careers"; Price, "Congress and the Evolution of Legislative Professionalism"; Polsby, "The Institutionalization of the US House of Representatives."

68. "Texas Politics."

69. *State Constitution of New Hampshire,* Article 15 (as amended), www.nh.gov/constitution/house.html (accessed July 7, 2011).

70. Brudnick, "Congressional Salaries and Allowances."

71. There is evidence that until the 1970s, women were more likely to serve in part-time, less professionalized legislatures; Hill, "Political Culture and Female Representation."

72. Fenno, *Congress at the Grassroots,* p. 8.

73. In constructing this figure, we relied upon Swift et al., *Database of Congressional Historical Statistics.* The 6th Congress, in 1800, was the first to convene in Washington, D.C. Here, our data end in 1992 because this was the last year provided by the Swift et al. dataset.

74. Young, *The Washington Community,* p. 42. See also "The Battle for America's Front Yard," p. 70.

75. Davidson and Oleszek, *Congress and Its Members,* 5th ed., p. 32.

76. Freeman, *Affairs of Honor.*

77. "The Battle for America's Front Yard," p. 70.

78. Young, *The Washington Community,* p. 25.

79. Ibid., pp. 52–53.

80. Ibid.

81. Struble, "House Turnover and the Principle of Rotation." See also Kernell, "Toward Understanding 19th Century Congressional Careers," pp. 685–688.

82. Struble, "House Turnover and the Principle of Rotation." pp. 659–660.

83. Kernell, "Toward Understanding 19th Century Congressional Careers," p. 674.

84. Ibid.

85. Davidson and Oleszek, *Congress and Its Members,* 9th ed., p. 34.

86. Brady, Buckley, and Rivers, "The Roots of Careerism in the US House of Representatives."

87. Katz and Sala, "Careerism, Committee Assignments, and the Electoral Connection," p. 22.

88. See, for example, Cain, Ferejohn, and Fiorina, *The Personal Vote;* Rusk, "The Effect of the Australian Ballot on Split Ticket Voting."

89. Katz and Sala, "Careerism, Committee Assignments, and the Electoral Connection," p. 25.

90. Manning, *Membership of the 112th Congress,* p. 5.

91. Ibid., pp. 1–2.

92. "Thurmond, James Strom."

93. Manning, *Membership of the 112th Congress,* p. 8. The longest-serving member of Congress in history is Senator Robert Byrd (D-WV), who was first elected to the House in 1952, served three terms, and then ran for the Senate in 1958. He died in June 2010 after being elected to his ninth term; "Byrd, Robert Carlyle."

94. *Women in Congress,* pp. 70–74; Foerstel, *Biographical Dictionary of Congressional Women,* p. 234.

95. Foerstel, *Biographical Dictionary of Congressional Women,* pp. 65–66.

96. Haas, "Seniority List."

97. Bullock, "House Careerists."

98. See also Andersen and Thorson, "Congressional Turnover and the Election of Women"; Darcy and Choike, "A Formal Analysis of Legislative Turnover."

99. Polsby, "The Institutionalization of the US House of Representatives."

100. Deering and Smith, *Committees in Congress;* Fenno, *Congressmen in Committees;* Katz and Sala, "Careerism, Committee Assignments, and the Electoral Connection."

101. Ornstein, *Congress in Change.*

102. Druckman, Kifer, and Parkin, "Campaign Communications in US Congressional Elections"; Fenno, *Congress at the Grassroots;* Fiorina, *Congress: Key-*

stone of the Washington Establishment; Mayhew, *Congress: The Electoral Connection.*

103. Speech at Running Start's Young Women's Political Leadership Conference, Washington, D.C., July 21, 2010.

104. Hardy and McCurdy, "Representational Threshold."

105. "Women Who Have Chaired Congressional Committees." The count of female chairs includes standing, select, and joint committees. See also McCurdy, "The Institutional Role of Women Serving in Congress."

106. *Women in Congress,* p. 58.

107. Rosenthal, "Climbing Higher"; "Special Report: CQ's Guide to the Committees."

108. "Special Report: CQ's Guide to the Committees."

109. "Women Who Have Chaired Congressional Committees."

110. See, for example, Burrell, *A Woman's Place Is In the House;* Carroll, *Women as Candidates in American Politics;* Darcy, Welch, and Clark, *Women, Elections, and Representation;* Palmer and Simon, "Breaking the Logjam."

111. See, for example, Cooperman and Oppenheimer, "The Gender Gap in the House of Representatives"; Palmer and Simon, "Breaking the Logjam"; Rule, "Why Women Don't Run."

112. Darcy, Welch, and Clark, *Women, Elections, and Representation;* Fox, *Gender Dynamics in Congressional Elections;* Gertzog and Simard, "Women and 'Hopeless' Congressional Candidacies." But see Deber, "The Fault Dear Brutus"; Jennings and Thomas, "Men and Women in Party Elites"; Lamson, *Few Are Chosen;* Seligman, "Political Recruitment and Party Structure."

FOUR

Keeping It In the Family:
Widows, Daughters, and Mothers

Why does anyone, male or female, decide to run for political office? Their personal life is fair game for the press. They have to ask people for money and, in some instances, may have to go into a great deal of personal debt. There are emotional costs as well. Campaigns are grueling, often focused on the personal and trivial, and potentially humiliating. And after all that is the risk of losing. Representative Lynn Martin (R-IL) successfully ran for the House in 1980, but her very first race for public office was actually in the eighth grade for class president. She lost by one vote—her own. She voted for her boyfriend; he voted for himself. After the election, they broke up.[1] In Tar Heel, North Carolina, no one registered for any of the small town's 2011 public offices, leaving the entire city with no candidates. Outgoing mayor Ricky Martin said he was "not surprised. . . . Even in a town of 117, it's hard work with little compensation."[2]

As suggested in the previous chapter, running for the US House of Representatives can be especially daunting. The overwhelming majority of the opportunities to run are found in districts with sitting incumbents. The typical challenger faces substantial disadvantages in name recognition, and raising money is extremely difficult. Political action committees (PACs) give incumbents seven times more money.[3] Between 1972 and 2006, there were 3,027 challengers who spent less than $100,000, and only one of those successfully defeated an incumbent.[4] Since the 1950s, the probability of a challenger winning has been 0.05. These barriers are almost insurmountable.

There is, however, one factor that has helped many aspiring candidates find their way around them: their family name. In this chapter, we explore the role of family in the pursuit of public office. Many of the early women who successfully ran for the House benefited from their last names. They were the widows of members of Congress, running for and winning special elections to fill their deceased husbands' seats. Until the 1970s, given cultural expectations and traditional attitudes toward women's roles, these widows were stereotyped as "reluctant placeholders": someone the party could recruit to temporarily hold a seat and capitalize on the familiar last name to win the special election. The presumption was that after finishing her deceased husband's term, she would gracefully and willingly step aside, after a "real" replacement was found. This stereotype, however, did not match reality. Many congressional widows were well-known, politically experienced, popular in their own right, and went on to long and successful House careers. Being a widow bestowed many of the advantages of incumbency, including name recognition, a ready-made staff, access to donors, and knowledge of the district. The "widow connection" is not, however, the only familial relationship among female members of Congress. In fact, multiple family connections among the women—and men—in Congress are not uncommon. There is a long history of fathers and daughters, fathers and sons, and mothers and sons.

As cultural expectations have changed, the role of family has changed for female candidates. Over the past hundred years, female candidates have transitioned from widows to mothers; as the widow route has become less frequent, the role of mother has gradually gained more acceptance. Because women are still the primary caregivers for children, women typically wait until their children are grown and thus are older than men when they run for office the first time. Voters still question whether women with young children will have enough time to devote to the demands of public office. However, while there are very few young women who have served in Congress, there are now many examples of women who have successfully combined politics and parenthood. But because so much of what determines power and influence in the House is based on seniority, there are ramifications for those who wait to run.

Having a Famous Family Name

Studies of political ambition and the choice to run for office often look at factors such as the competitiveness of the race, the characteristics of the district or state, the costs associated with running (both personal and financial), and the role of parties.[5] It is actually quite difficult to find systematic analyses of the role of family connections among those who run for office.[6] While the United States clearly has "political family dynasties," such as the Kennedys and Bushes, most Americans would probably find the idea of inheriting a political office as something distinctly "un-American" and a throwback to the days before the United States rejected the British monarchy. But there is a great deal of research that shows the importance of the family in political socialization. If parents consider themselves Republicans, then so will their children; if they call themselves Independents, so will their children. If parents are interested in politics and public affairs, then so are their children. If parents vote, so will their children.[7] When Representative Chellie Pingree (D-ME) ran for state legislature in the 1990s, she took her daughter, Hannah, with her on the campaign trail. Her daughter eventually became the speaker of the Maine house of representatives at the age of thirty-three.[8] As one study put it, "Engaged parents tend to raise engaged children,"[9] and there is evidence that this is true across race, income, and education levels.[10]

In light of these findings, it seems logical to expect that one of the best predictors of whether someone will run for office is if they come from a political family.[11] For example, a member of the Dingell family has occupied the seat representing the Fifteenth District of Michigan for over seventy-five years. John Dingell (D-MI) was first elected to the House in 1932 and served until he died in 1955.[12] His son, John Dingell Jr. (D-MI), won his seat and was reelected to his twenty-ninth term in 2010.[13] At least one American political family can trace its roots back to the colonial era. Frederick Frelinghuysen was born in New Jersey in 1753, fought in the Revolutionary War, served in the Continental Congress, and was a member of the New Jersey convention to ratify the US Constitution. He served in the US Senate from 1793 to 1796.[14] His son, Theodore Frelinghuysen, was captain of the Volunteer Militia in the War of 1812 and served as New Jersey attorney general. He won election to the US Senate in 1829.[15] His nephew, whom he actually adopted as his son, Frederick Theodore (R-NJ), was a member of a peace convention to prevent the Civil War in 1861, and also served as New Jersey attorney general. He served two nonconsecutive terms in the US Senate, from 1866 to 1869 and 1871 to 1877.[16] Joseph Sherman Frelinghuysen (R-NJ), the great-grandson of Frederick and cousin of Frederick Theodore, served in the Spanish American War and was elected to the US Senate for one term in 1917.[17] Peter Hood Ballantine Frelinghuysen (R-NJ), the great-great-great-grandson of Frederick and great-great-nephew of Theodore, served in the Office of Naval Intelligence during World War II, and then broke family tradition and served in the US House from 1953 to 1975.[18] Rodney Frelinghuysen (R-NJ), Peter's son, was a member of the New Jersey state assembly and won election to the US House in 1994; he was reelected for the eighth time in 2010.[19]

The Frelinghuysen and Dingell families, while unmatched in political longevity, are not alone. One study of Congress found that in the early years of the republic, almost a quarter of the men who served were the sons, grandsons, nephews, brothers, or first cousins of other members, but that this had declined to just 5 percent by 1960.[20] However, a survey of state legislators in four states in the 1950s suggested that between 41 and 59 percent of them had relatives in politics.[21] Wikipedia lists hundreds of American political families, from the Adamses to the Udalls and the Washingtons.[22]

Husbands and Wives

Until relatively recently, family connections did play a very direct role in the lives of many of the women who served in Congress. As Table 4.1 shows, 41 of the 239 women who served in the House, or 18 percent, won seats that were held by their husbands; 38 of these women immediately succeeded their husbands. Representative Ruth Hanna McCormick (R-IL) won the seat held by her husband four years after his death. Representative Leonor Sullivan (D-MO) could not convince Democratic Party leaders to nominate her to run in the special election after her husband's death in 1951. They told her, "We don't have anything against you. We just want to win."[23] The candidate they nominated lost. A year later she defeated seven other candidates in the Democratic primary and won the general election with 65 percent of the vote. Representative Niki Tsongas (D-MA) won her husband's seat almost thirty years after his service in the House. Paul Tsongas (D-MA) had been a representative from Massachusetts's Fifth District from 1974 until 1979. Niki and Paul actually met when she was in high school and he was an intern for the then–Fifth District representative, Brad Morse. Paul ran for the Senate in 1978, but did not seek a second term after he was diagnosed with cancer. After a successful bone marrow transplant, he ran for president in 1992. He died in 1997.[24] Niki successfully ran in a special election in 2007 for the same House seat her husband held in the 1970s.

In two more instances, women successfully replaced their husbands on the ballot after they died during their initial run for the House. Charlotte Reid (R-IL), who had a career as a singer on a popular radio show in the 1930s, was married to Frank Reid Jr., an attorney from Aurora, Illinois. In 1962, Frank was nominated by the state Republican Party to run for an open House seat, but he died of a heart attack in August. Party leaders convinced Charlotte to take over the campaign. She won with 60 percent of the vote.[25] In 1974, Marilyn Lloyd (D-TN) took over her husband Mort's House campaign. A few weeks after he had won the Democratic nomination, he was killed in a plane crash. Her supporters wore buttons from her husband's campaign with black tape over Mort's name, so they would read

Table 4.1 Women Who Succeeded Their Husbands in the US House

	Service Begins	Service Ends
Mae Ella Nolan (R-CA)	1/23/1923	3/3/1925
Florence Kahn (R-CA)	5/4/1925	1/3/1937
Edith Nourse Rogers (R-MA)	1/30/1925	9/10/1960
Katherine Langley (R-KY)	3/4/1926	3/3/1931
Pearl Oldfield (D-AR)	1/11/1929	3/3/1931
Ruth Hanna McCormick (R-IL)[a]	3/4/1929	3/3/1931
Effigene Wingo (D-AR)	4/4/1930	3/3/1933
Willa McCord Eslick (D-TN)	12/5/1932	3/3/1933
Marian Clarke (R-NY)	12/28/1933	1/3/1935
Elizabeth Gasque (D-SC)	1/13/1938	1/3/1939
Florence Gibbs (D-GA)	1/3/1940	1/3/1941
Clara McMillan (D-SC)	1/3/1940	1/3/1941
Margaret Chase Smith (R-ME)	1/3/1940	1/3/1949
Frances Bolton (R-OH)	1/27/1940	1/3/1969
Katharine Byron (D-MD)	1/11/1941	1/3/1943
Veronica Boland (D-PA)	1/19/1942	1/3/1943
Willa Fulmer (D-SC)	1/16/1944	1/3/1945
Marguerite Church (R-IL)	1/3/1951	1/3/1963
Maude Kee (D-WV)	7/26/1951	1/3/1963
Vera Buchanan (D-PA)	8/1/1951	11/26/1955
Leonor Sullivan (D-MO)[a]	1/3/1953	1/3/1977
Kathryn Granahan (D-PA)	11/6/1956	1/3/1963
Edna Simpson (R-IL)	1/3/1959	1/3/1961
Catherine Norrell (D-AR)	4/18/1961	1/3/1963
Louise Reece (R-TN)	5/16/1961	1/3/1963
Corrine Riley (D-SC)	4/10/1962	1/3/1963
Irene Baker (R-TN)	3/10/1964	1/3/1965
Lera Thomas (D-TX)	3/26/1966	1/3/1967
Elizabeth Andrews (D-AL)	4/4/1971	1/3/1973
Corrine (Lindy) Boggs (D-LA)	3/20/1973	1/3/1991
Cardiss Collins (D-IL)	6/5/1973	1/3/1997
Shirley Pettis (R-CA)	4/29/1975	1/3/1979
Beverly Byron (D-MD)	1/3/1979	1/3/1993
Jean Ashbrook (R-OH)	7/12/1982	1/3/1983
Sala Burton (D-CA)	1/21/1983	2/1/1987
Catherine Long (D-LA)	4/4/1985	1/3/1987
Jo Ann Emerson (R-MO)	11/5/1997	Currently serving
Lois Capps (D-CA)	3/17/1998	Currently serving
Mary Bono Mack (R-CA)	4/21/1998	Currently serving
Doris Matsui (D-CA)	3/3/2005	Currently serving
Niki Tsongas (D-MA)[a]	10/16/2007	Currently serving

Source: Data compiled by the authors.
Note: a. Did not directly succeed husband.

"Lloyd for Congress." She defeated a two-term incumbent with 51 percent of the vote.[26]

Of these forty-three women, all but one were widows, winning election after their husbands' deaths. Representative Katherine Langley (R-KY) is the exception. She is the only woman to succeed her husband while he was still alive: he was in jail. Katherine was the daughter of Representative James Gudger (D-NC) and the wife of Representative "Pork Barrel John" Langley, a Kentucky Republican first elected in 1906. John and his father-in-law served together as members of the House during the 62nd and 63rd Congresses (1911–1915).[27] In 1924, Congressman Langley was tried and convicted of "conspiring illegally to transport and sell liquor."[28] He attempted to bribe a Prohibition officer. While his case was under appeal in November 1924, he was reelected to his tenth term in the House. He had to resign his seat in January 1926, and was subsequently jailed at the federal penitentiary in Atlanta. In the election that followed, with John's support, Katherine won the seat with 58 percent of the vote. In a letter from prison, John appealed to family values, urging voters to "send my wife, the mother of our three children, to Washington . . . she knows better than anyone else my unfinished plans."[29] As secretary to her husband throughout his career, Katherine was quite familiar with the ways of Washington. However, the response to Katherine among the "Washington elite" was less than favorable. Evidently, polite society regarded the election of a convicted felon's spouse as "gauche."[30] President Calvin Coolidge, at Katherine's urging, issued a grant of clemency to her husband; his release was subject to the condition that he would not seek election to any public office. In 1929, a less-than-grateful John declared himself a candidate for his former seat. Katherine, however, refused to give up her seat "for John or anyone else."[31] While John ultimately decided not to run, historical accounts refer to a "family feud" and "marital spat" that ultimately led to her 1930 defeat by Democrat Andrew Jackson May, the same candidate she had defeated twice before. Little is known about what transpired between Katherine and John after her loss, but they were buried in separate cemeteries.[32]

The "widow route" was far more common for female candidates in the first half of the twentieth century. Prior to World War II, fourteen of the twenty-eight women who were elected to the House, 50 percent, succeeded their spouses. Between 1942 and 1971, the proportion of widows among those women elected to the House dropped to fourteen of forty-three, 33 percent. Of the 173 women elected to the House between 1972 and 2010, only twelve, 7 percent, were widows. After the 2010 election, five of the seventy-two female House members were serving in seats held by their deceased husbands: Representatives Jo Ann Emerson (R-MO), Lois Capps (D-CA), Mary Bono Mack (R-CA), Doris Matsui (D-CA), and Niki Tsongas (D-MA).

However, as late as the 1970s, much of the attention devoted to women in Congress focused on the widow connection, which was characterized as the primary route to the House and the Senate for women.[33] The prevailing wisdom, particularly in the press, was that women who served in Congress got there "over their husband's dead bodies."[34] In fact, there emerged a "widow stereotype" that included a common storyline describing the widow's journey to elective office: after a member of Congress died, party leaders would recruit the grieving, uncertain widow to capitalize on public sympathy, ensure that the party held the seat in the interim, help the party avoid internal disputes, and provide time to recruit a "real" replacement.[35] In many cases, the understanding, whether explicit or implicit, was that the widow would not try to retain the seat during the next election cycle. Representative Frances Bolton (R-OH) noted that the party supported her because "they were sure I would get tired of politics in a few months and flit on to something else."[36] In fact, the stereotype of these early women was the "bereaved widow" who was a "reluctant placeholder" for a deceased husband.[37] Even women who were not "congressional widows" and won election in their own right were often lumped into this category.

A vivid example of the stereotype was, in fact, the very first congressional widow, Mae Ella Nolan (R-CA). In 1922, Representative John Nolan, chair of the House Labor Committee, died shortly after his fifth reelection to the House. Civic leaders convinced Mae to run in the special election held to fill his seat; she defeated six men in the primary. She saw herself as a stand-in for her husband, explaining, "I owe it to the memory of my husband to carry on his work. . . . His minimum-wage bill, child labor laws and national education bills all need to be in the hands of someone who knew him and his plans intimately. No one better knows than I do his legislative agenda."[38] She served on the House Labor Committee, a committee that was chaired by her husband. After completing the two-year term, Mae declared that she would not seek reelection, explaining that "politics is entirely too masculine to have any attraction for feminine responsibilities."[39] Nolan was not alone among the widows to express her distaste for political life. After serving less than one term in 1929, Representative Pearl Oldfield (D-AR) announced that she would "gladly retire to where women belong—in the home."[40] Similarly, Representative Florence Gibbs (D-GA) left the House after three months because the job was not "to her liking."[41]

Such examples notwithstanding, the problem with the "widow stereotype" is that it rests on several tenuous assumptions. First, it creates the impression that the widow-as-successor is the most common method of filling vacancies. But if one looks at the number of incumbents who died in office, very few wives succeeded their husbands. From 1917 to 1976, for example, 487 members died in office, and widows were the successors only thirty-two times, or 7 percent.[42] Another assumption of the stereotype is that widows were "given" the seats vacated by their dead husbands. This is simply inaccurate. Although vacant Senate seats can be filled by appointment, vacant House seats must be filled through special elections. Many widows who served in the House faced substantial competition in special primary and general elections; there were several widows who ran for their husbands' seats and were defeated.[43]

Photo courtesy of the Library of Congress

Representative Pearl Oldfield (D-AR) had one of the shorter House careers among congressional widows, from November 11, 1929, until March 3, 1931.

In addition, almost half of all congressional widows worked with or for their husbands when their husbands served in the House, and almost a third had political experience independent of their husbands.[44] For example, Sala Burton was married to Representative Phillip Burton (D-CA), a powerful House member and leader of the liberal wing of the Democratic Party in the 1970s and early 1980s. His brother, John Burton (D-CA), also served as a House member from a neighboring district. Although Sala was never formally on his congressional staff, Phillip called her his "political partner," and she was an integral part of his thirty-year political career.[45] Pansy Ponzio, a member of the local Democratic Party, explained that "she knew just about as much about the office and the constituents and the people who live in San Francisco as he did."[46] Phillip and Sala met at a Young Democrats convention in 1950. When her husband was a member of the California state legislature, she organized the California Democratic Council and then served as its vice president. She also served on the San Francisco Fair Housing Committee, was a member of the state Democratic Party Steering Committee, and chaired the Democratic Women's Forum. After Phillip became a member of Congress, she served on the boards of the National Security Committee, the National Council on Soviet Jewry, and the Women's National Democratic Club.[47] She was also the president of the Democratic Wives of the House and Senate and a delegate to four Democratic presidential conventions.[48] While serving his tenth term, Phillip died of an embolism in April 1983. Eight days after his death, Sala announced that she would run for his seat and defeated ten other candidates in the special election with 57 percent of the vote.[49] Within days of her victory, she announced that she would run for reelection in 1984.[50] She ran again in 1986 and won, but unfortunately was diagnosed with cancer and died shortly after being sworn in for her third term.[51] Because of the independent political experience gained while her husband was alive, she easily won the support of party leaders, knew how to campaign, and became a successful member of Congress in her own right. Before she died in February 1987, she encouraged Nancy Pelosi to run for her seat and formally endorsed her. Pelosi had worked on both Sala's and Phillip's campaigns and won the special election with 63 percent of the vote. Representative Pelosi (D-CA) thus became the first woman to win a House seat after the death of another woman.

More important, as Table 4.1 illustrates, many widows did not step down after their initial terms expired. The average length of service among widows who sought reelection to the House is seven terms. Twelve widows served for over ten years in the House. Representative Edith Nourse Rogers (R-MA), the longest-serving woman in congressional history (1925–1960), took over her husband's seat after he died of cancer. She announced her candidacy a week after his death and won the special election with 87 percent of the vote. In a swing district that was nearly evenly divided between Republicans and Democrats, Rogers consistently won with huge margins.[52] Representative Leonor Sullivan (D-MO) served for twenty-three years (1952–1975) and became a well-known advocate of consumer protection, chairing the Banking and Currency Subcommittee on the Consumer Affairs Committee and chairing the Merchant Marine and Fisheries Committee.[53]

Cardiss Collins (D-IL), the longest-serving woman of color, served for nearly twenty-four years (1973–1997) and is the only African American woman to have taken the widow route.[54] After graduating from high school, Collins worked in a mattress factory and as a stenographer for a carnival equipment factory. Going to school at night, she got a degree in business at Northwestern University. Her first foray into politics was serving as a committee woman for the Democratic Party in Chicago. After she married George Collins, she worked on his campaigns for alderman and for the House. Shortly after he had been elected to his second term, in 1972, George was killed in a plane crash near Midway Airport. Initially, Cardiss "never gave politics a thought" for herself, but she changed her mind.[55] With the backing of Mayor Richard Daley, she became the first African American woman elected from Illinois, winning 92 percent of the vote.

As widows, women do have substantial electoral advantages. These include inherited name recognition, familiarity with potential donors, and a ready-made staff. Many of them worked on their husbands' campaigns and, as a result, knew their districts well. Representative Corrine "Lindy" Boggs (D-LA) is another noteworthy example. She was first elected to the House in 1973 after her husband, Majority Leader Hale Boggs, disappeared in a plane crash in Alaska. After a two-month search for the plane, the House declared the seat vacant, and Lindy won the seat with 81 percent of the vote in the special election. Her political career, however, had begun well before that. Her grandfather was a state legislator, and her cousin was the mayor of New Orleans. For twenty-five years, she served as her husband's campaign manager and worked in his congressional office in Washington, D.C. She also chaired the inaugural ball committees for John F. Kennedy and Lyndon Johnson. Boggs served in the House for almost two decades, retiring in 1991.[56] In fact, most congressional widows were as politically inclined as their husbands and had access to resources and advantages similar to those enjoyed by incumbents.[57] In essence, being a widow confers many of the advantages of incumbency.

Similar trends can be seen among Senate widows. Of the fourteen women appointed to the Senate, seven were widows, as shown in Table

4.2. Four did not seek service beyond their initial appointment: Jocelyn Burdick (D-ND), Vera Bushfield (R-SD), Muriel Humphrey (D-MN), and Rose Long (D-LA). Long's husband, the notorious former governor of Louisiana, Huey Long, was assassinated after serving in the Senate for only three years. Rose was not the first choice of Governor O. K. Allen, but the governor died before he could make the appointment. Allen's successor selected Rose to avoid infighting in the Democratic Party.[58]

Three widows attempted to retain their seats and ran in the special elections to complete the remainder of their terms. Only one, Senator Hattie Caraway (D-AR), was successful; after her initial appointment in 1931, she was reelected twice. The other two were not successful. Maryon Allen (D-AL) was initially appointed by Governor George Wallace to the Senate in June 1978 after the death of her husband, Senator James Allen. While it was assumed she would not try to keep the seat, she decided that she would run in the special election that fall to fill the remaining two years of her husband's term.[59] She lost the primary. Her defeat is partially attributed to an interview she did for the style section of the *Washington Post* that ran in July. The article described her as a "small, fragile, delicate-looking . . . southern lady," and also noted that she was "startlingly honest." In the interview, Allen said, "I learned one thing in politics. The hardest thing to do is keep your mouth shut. I never have before. Sometimes I just want to

Table 4.2 Women Who Were Appointed to the US Senate

	Service Begins	Service Ends	Family Connection
Rebecca Felton (D-GA)	11/21/1922	11/22/1922	Husband was House member
Hattie Caraway (D-AR)	12/8/1931	1/2/1945	Widow
Rose Long (D-LA)	2/10/1936	1/2/1937	Widow
Dixie Graves (D-AL)	8/20/1937	1/10/1938	Husband was governor
Vera Bushfield (R-SD)	10/6/1948	12/27/1948	Widow
Eva Bowring (R-NE)	4/26/1954	11/7/1954	Husband was state legislator
Elaine Edwards (D-LA)	8/7/1972	11/13/1972	Husband was governor
Muriel Humphrey (D-MN)	2/6/1978	11/13/1978	Widow
Maryon Allen (D-AL)	6/12/1978	11/7/1978	Widow
Jocelyn Burdick (D-ND)	9/16/1992	12/14/1992	Widow
Sheila Frahm (R-KS)	6/11/1996	11/8/1996	None
Jean Carnahan (D-MO)	1/3/2001	11/23/2002	Widow
Lisa Murkowski (R-AK)	12/20/2002	Currently serving	Father was governor
Kirsten Gillibrand (D-NY)	1/27/2009	Currently serving	Father was lobbyist, grandmother active in Albany politics

Source: Data compiled by the authors.

scream at some of these people and say 'you goddam idiot.'" Halfway through the interview, Allen asked to borrow a mirror to retouch her lipstick and said that "without a mirror I always end up with lipstick halfway up my nostril." She called the management style of the Carter administration "dumb," noted that conservative activist Phyllis Schlafly was "about as feminine as a sidewalk drill," and described the chief justice of the Alabama supreme court, Howell Heflin, as "cuter than Warren Burger," and Robert Byrd, then–majority leader of the Senate, as "just a little power nuts and everybody knows it."[60]

The other widow who pursued reelection, Senator Jean Carnahan (D-MO), became senator after "one of the most unusual elections in US history."[61] Mel Carnahan, the Democratic candidate and governor of Missouri, was killed in a plane crash three weeks before the November election of 2000. It was too late to remove his name from the ballot. Democratic Party leaders convinced Jean to accept the lieutenant governor's appointment if Mel won. He did, making him the first deceased candidate to win a Senate election.[62] He defeated incumbent Republican senator John Ashcroft, who was later appointed attorney general by President George W. Bush. Two years later, when Jean had to run in a special election to complete the remainder of the term, she was defeated by Republican representative Jim Talent.

One additional woman, Maurine Neuberger (D-OR), obtained her late husband's Senate seat, but was not appointed to complete the remaining nine months of his 1960 term. Instead, the governor chose state supreme court justice Hall Stoner Lusk, who agreed to resign after serving the nine months. Because of the timing of her husband's death, Maurine simultaneously ran in both a special election to serve out the remaining two months of her husband's 1960 term and the general election for the full term that began in January 1961. Maurine and her husband, Richard, were a 1950s version of the political "power couple." Maurine was the manager of her husband's successful campaign for the Oregon senate in 1948. Two years later, she was elected to the state house of representatives. In 1954, she managed her husband's successful campaign for the US Senate and left the Oregon legislature to work in his Washington, D.C., office. Following his election to the Senate, Richard wrote an article for *Harper's* titled "My Wife Put Me in the Senate."[63] When asked if she would run for Congress in 1956, she replied, "One member of Congress in the family is enough."[64] After her husband's death from a brain hemorrhage, she explained that "I couldn't think of anything except going back to Washington and getting Muffet, our cat, closing the office, and moving out of our apartment."[65] She eventually reconsidered and "began to realize I was probably as qualified as any other candidate. And, above all, I knew that Dick would have wanted me to run."[66] She won with 55 percent of the vote.[67] Neuberger did not seek reelection in 1966.

Of the remaining seven women who were appointed to the Senate, two benefited from having husbands who were alive, both of them governors. Dixie Graves (D-AL) was appointed by her husband, Alabama governor Bibb Graves, to complete the term of Senator Hugo Black, who resigned from his Senate seat in 1937 to become an associate justice on the US Supreme Court.[68] Elaine Edwards (D-LA) was appointed by her husband, Louisiana governor Edwin Edwards, after the death of Senator Allen Ellender (D-LA) in 1972. Edwin explained that he chose Elaine as a "'meaningful symbolic gesture' against decades of discrimination against women in politics."[69] Appointing her also helped him avoid a potentially nasty family feud; two of his brothers were interested in running for the seat. Elaine and Edwin actually divorced in 1989 after forty years of marriage.[70]

There has not, as of yet, been a congressional widower, although two husbands have tried. Representative Patsy Mink (D-HI) died on September 28, 2002, a week after easily winning her primary, but two days after the deadline to replace her name on the ballot. She actually won the general election posthumously. At the end of November, a special election was held for the remaining five weeks of her term, with Democrat Ed Case as the victor. Another special election had to be held to fill her two-year term, and Mink's widower, John, ran in a field of forty-three candidates. Case, however, held on to the seat.[71] Representative Jo Ann Davis (R-VA), first elected in 2000, died in 2007 after a two-year battle with breast cancer.[72] Her husband, Chuck, a firefighter, expressed interest in the seat.[73] Rather than holding a primary, the Republicans held a convention and selected Rob Wittman, a state legislator, who won the general election with 62 percent of the vote.

Aside from gaining a congressional seat from a spouse, eleven female members have gained congressional spouses: they married male members of Congress. As shown in Table 4.3, three women married men and served in Congress with them: in 1975, Representative Martha Keys (D-KS) married Representative Andrew Jacobs (D-IN), the son of a former House member; in 1994, Representative Susan Molinari (R-NY), the daughter of a former House member, married Representative Bill Paxon (R-NY)—he actually proposed to her on the House floor;[74] and in 2007, Representative Mary Bono (R-CA) married Representative Connie Mack IV (R-FL), the son of a former senator.[75]

Representative Ruth Hanna McCormick (R-IL) was married to two members of Congress. As the daughter of Senator Mark Hanna, at the age

Table 4.3 Congressional Women Who Married Members of Congress

	Her Dates of Service	Married	His Dates of Service	Year of Marriage
Served together while married				
Rep. Martha Keys (D-KS)	1975–1978	Rep. Andrew Jacobs (D-IN)[a]	1965–1996	1975
Rep. Susan Molinari (R-NY)[a]	1990–1997	Rep. Bill Paxon (R-NY)	1989–1998	1994
Rep. Mary Bono Mack (R-CA)	1997–present	Rep. Connie Mack IV (R-FL)[b]	2005–present	2007
Served together but not while married				
Rep. Ruth Hanna McCormick (R-IL)[b]	1929–1930	Rep. Albert Simms (R-NM)	1929–1930	1932
Sen. Nancy Landon Kassebaum (R-KS)	1977–1996	Sen. Howard Baker Jr. (R-TN)[a]	1967–1984	1996
Rep. Olympia Snowe (R-ME)[c]	1979–1994	Rep. John McKernan (R-ME)	1983–1986	1989
Rep. Stephanie Herseth Sandlin (D-SD)	2003–2011	Rep. Max Sandlin (D-TX)	1997–2004	2007
Did not serve together				
Sen. Rebecca Latimer Felton (D-GA)	1922	Rep. William Felton (D-GA)	1875–1881	1853
Rep. Ruth Hanna McCormick (R-IL)[b]	1929–1930	Rep. Medill McCormick (R-IL)[c]	1917–1918	1903
Rep. Emily Taft Douglas (D-IL)	1945–1946	Sen. Paul Douglas (D-IL)	1949–1967	1931
Rep. Marjorie Margolies-Mezvinsky (D-PA)	1993–1994	Rep. Ed Mezvinsky (D-IA)	1973–1976	1975
Sen. Elizabeth Dole (R-NC)	2003–2008	Sen. Bob Dole (R-KS)	1969–1996	1975

Sources: *Women in Congress, 1917–2006*, Office of the Clerk of the US House of Representatives (Washington, DC: US Government Printing Office, 2006); *Biographical Directory of the United States Congress*, http://bioguide.congress.gov.

Notes: a. Daughter or son of a representative.
b. Daughter or son of a senator.
c. Also served in the Senate.

of seventeen, she accompanied her father on the campaign trail in 1897 when he ran in a special election for a vacated Senate seat and later when he was William McKinley's presidential campaign manager. After her father's successful Senate campaign, she went with him to Washington, D.C., and worked as his secretary. In 1903, she married Medill McCormick, publisher of the *Chicago Tribune*. After Medill was elected to the state legislature in 1912, Ruth successfully lobbied for the passage of the Illinois Equal Suffrage Act, which gave women the vote in city and presidential elections. Medill was elected to the US House in 1916 and then successfully ran for the Senate in 1918. However, when he was up for reelection, he lost the Republican nomination to Charles Deneen and committed suicide. Ruth was convinced that one reason for her husband's defeat was low turnout among Republican women. In response, she created a statewide network of Republican women's clubs, which she would later rely on during her own campaign. In 1928, she ran for one of Illinois's at-large House seats; she traveled over 34,000 miles, made hundreds of speeches, and defeated nine other candidates. In 1930, she ran for the Senate. She easily defeated Deneen in the primary. In the general election, she faced Democrat James Hamilton Lewis, the candidate whom Medill had defeated in his initial Senate run. During the campaign, Ruth had to appear before a Senate committee that was investigating allegations regarding her primary expenditures. She revealed that she had spent over $250,000 to defeat Deneen, ten times what he had spent. While the Senate dropped its investigation, she never recovered from the public backlash due to the growing economic depression and rising unemployment. She lost with only 31 percent of the vote. But this was not the end of her involvement in politics. In 1932, she married former House member Albert Gallatin Simms (R-NM) and ran two newspapers and a radio station. In 1940, beginning much like where she started, she managed Thomas Dewey's presidential campaign.[76]

Fathers and Daughters, Mothers and Sons

Having a well-placed husband is not the only family connection among female members of Congress. In fact, as Table 4.3 also suggests, multiple family connections among the men and women in Congress are not uncommon; among these twelve congressional couples are five children of members. For example, Senator Howard Baker Jr. (R-TN), husband of Senator Nancy Kassebaum (R-KS), was the son of Representative Howard Baker (R-TN) and the stepson of Representative Irene Bailey Baker (R-TN); Irene won her husband's seat after his sudden death from a heart attack in January 1964. Kassebaum was actually Senator Baker's second wife. His first wife, Joy, who died of cancer, was the daughter of Senator Everett Dirksen.

Fourteen women in Congress had famous political fathers, as shown in Table 4.4.[77] Two of these women were the daughters of presidential candidates. Senator Nancy Kassebaum was the daughter of Kansas governor Alf Landon, who ran unsuccessfully as the Republican nominee for president in 1936.[78] Representative Ruth Bryan Owen (D-FL) was the daughter of three-time presidential nominee and former secretary of state William Jennings Bryan. At the age of twenty-three, she served as secretary to her father during his unsuccessful 1908 presidential campaign against Republican William Howard Taft. Following the divorce from her first husband, she became a "single mom" and supported her family as a lecturer and newspaper writer. She later married Reginald Owen, a former British military officer. Because of Reginald's illness, they moved to Florida and lived with her parents. Following her father's death in 1925, Owen began her own political career and ran for the House. She narrowly lost the Democratic primary to incumbent William Sears in 1926. After her husband's death in 1927, Ruth again announced her candidacy, defeated Sears to win the primary in 1928, and then went on to an easy victory in the general election, defeating Republican William Lawson by a wide margin, 65 to 35 percent. Lawson, however, challenged the election, arguing that she had forfeited her citizenship and eligibility to run for the House when she married a British citizen. The House upheld her election. Owen was reelected in 1930 and, during her time in the House, served on the Foreign Relations Committee and was an advocate of pensions for mothers, a program later included in the legislation that created the Social Security system. Owen was defeated in the 1932 Democratic primary, where her opponent, J. Mark Wilcox, attacked her for supporting Prohibition.[79]

Eleven female House members had fathers who served in Congress, including former speaker of the House Nancy Pelosi (D-CA). Three of these women immediately succeeded their fathers: Representatives Winnifred Huck (R-IL), Susan Molinari (R-NY), and Lucille Roybal-Allard (D-CA).[80]

One woman, Senator Lisa Murkowski (R-AK), assumed her father's Senate seat under a rather unique set of circumstances. Frank Murkowski (R-AK) had served in the Senate since 1980, and in 2002 decided to run for governor of Alaska and won. In December 2002, now serving as governor, he appointed his daughter, a two-term state legislator, to complete his Senate term. In 2004, to retain the seat, Lisa easily won the Republican primary against three men, but faced a former Democratic governor, Tony Knowles, in the general election. Knowles made nepotism one of

Representative Ruth Bryan Owen (D-FL), the daughter of three-time presidential nominee William Jennings Bryan, and Representative Ruth Hanna McCormick (R-IL), the daughter of Senator Mark Hanna and wife of two House members, served together from 1929 to 1931.

Table 4.4 Congressional Women with Prominent Political Fathers

	Her Dates of Service	Father	His Dates of Service
Daughters of presidential candidates			
Rep. Ruth Bryan Owen (D-FL)	1929–1933	Rep. William Jennings Bryan (D-NE)	1896, 1900, 1908
Sen. Nancy Kassebaum (R-KS)	1978–1997	Gov. Alf Landon (R-KS)	1936
Daughters who directly succeeded their fathers			
Rep. Winnifred Huck (R-IL)	1922–1923	Rep. William Mason (R-IL)	1887–1890, 1917–1922[a]
Rep. Susan Molinari (R-NY)	1990–1997	Rep. Guy Molinari (R-NY)	1981–1990
Rep. Lucille Roybal-Allard (D-CA)	1993–present	Rep. Edward Roybal (D-CA)	1963–1993
Sen. Lisa Murkokwsi (R-AL)	2002–present	Sen. Frank Murkowski (R-AL)	1981–2002
Daughters who did not directly succeed their fathers			
Rep. Katherine Langley (R-KY)	1927–1931	Rep. James Gudger Jr. (D-NC)	1903–1914
Rep. Ruth Hanna McCormick (R-IL)	1929–1931	Sen. Mark Hanna (R-OH)	1899–1904
Rep. Ruth Bryan Owen (D-FL)	1929–1933	Rep. William Jennings Bryan (D-NE)	1891–1894
Rep. Claire Boothe Luce (R-CT)	1943–1947	Rep. Elmer Austin (R-CT)	1939–1941
Rep. Louise Reece (R-TN)	1961–1963	Sen. Guy Goff (R-WV)	1925–1930
Rep. Elizabeth Patterson (D-SC)	1987–1993	Sen. Olin Johnston (D-SC)	1945–1966
Rep. Nancy Pelosi (D-CA)	1987–present	Rep. Thomas D'Alesandro (D-MD)	1939–1947
Rep. Shelly Moore Capito (R-WV)	2001–present	Rep. Arch Moore (R-WV)	1957–1968

Source: Women in Congress, 1917–2006, Office of the Clerk of the US House of Representatives (Washington, DC: US Government Printing Office, 2006), updated by the authors.

Note: a. Mason served in the Senate from 1897 to 1902.

the primary themes of his campaign and also attacked her for giving a $6.5 billion tax break to Exxon Mobil. Murkowski countered by pointing out that the $6.5 billion figure had been "made up" by the Knowles campaign and that the legislation she supported would bring jobs to Alaska. During one of their televised debates, the candidates were asked to name something they liked about each other. Knowles said, "Senator Murkowski is a good person with a great family." Senator Murkowski said that her sons really liked his black Labradors.[81] She defeated Knowles 49 to 45 percent, proclaiming, "Alaska girls kick ass."[82] Murkowski's 2010 reelection campaign was actually quite extraordinary and was called "one of the biggest political upsets in Alaska history."[83] She lost the Republican primary to a virtually unknown candidate with no prior political experience, Fairbanks attorney Joe Miller. Miller had the backing of the Tea Party and had been endorsed by former Alaska governor and 2008 vice presidential candidate Sarah Palin. Palin had actually defeated incumbent Frank Murkowski in the Republican gubernatorial primary in 2006, and the feud between the two families was "legendary." After Lisa Murkowski conceded the primary to Miller, she refused to endorse him and decided to run as a write-in candidate in the general election. Miller was the frontrunner for most of the campaign, until he made a variety of gaffes. In one incident, his private security guards handcuffed a reporter who tried to ask him a question at a campaign event.[84] On election day, Murkowski appeared to be in the lead, but it took two months before the election was certified, making her the first successful write-in candidate for the Senate since 1954.[85]

There have, of course, been men who benefited from the political connections of their mothers. As Table 4.5 shows, five women in the House and two women in the Senate had sons who served in Congress. Two women had their sons take over their seats. The first, Representative Maude Kee (D-WV), a widow who succeeded her husband, was succeeded by her son, Representative James Kee (D-WV). In 1964, Maude decided to retire after eight terms in the House. James had been her administrative assistant and easily won her seat with 70 percent of the vote.[86] The second, Representative Carrie Meek (D-FL), was succeeded by her son, Representative Kendrick Meek (D-FL). At the age of seventy-two, Carrie retired after serving six terms. Kendrick served in the Florida senate before winning her seat in 2002. The sons of the remaining members served after their mothers left the House, with one exception. Representative Frances Bolton (R-OH), one of the richest women in the United States and heir to the Standard Oil fortune, actually served with her son, Representative Oliver Bolton (R-OH), for seven years.[87]

Table 4.5   Congressional Women Whose Sons Served in Congress

	Her Dates of Service	Son	His Dates of Service
Served with son			
Rep. Frances Bolton (R-OH)	1940–1969	Rep. Oliver Bolton (R-OH)	1953–1957, 1963–1965
Directly succeeded by son			
Rep. Maude Kee (D-WV)	1951–1965	Rep. James Kee (D-WV)	1965–1973
Rep. Carrie Meek (D-FL)	1993–2003	Rep. Kendrick Meek (D-FL)	2003–2011
Son served later			
Sen. Rose McConnell Long (D-LA)	1936–1937	Sen. Russell Long (D-LA)	1948–1987
Rep. Katharine Byron (D-MD)	1941–1943	Rep. Goodloe Byron (D-MD)	1971–1978
Rep. Irene Baker (R-TN)	1964–1965	Sen. Howard Baker (R-TN)[a]	1967–1985
Sen. Jean Carnahan (D-MO)	2001–2003	Rep. Russ Carnahan (D-MO)	2005–present

Source: Women in Congress, 1917–2006, Office of the Clerk of the US House of Representatives (Washington, DC: US Government Printing Office, 2006), updated by the authors.
   Note: a. Stepson.

There have been three instances of sons serving simultaneously with their fathers. Henry Dodge (D-WI) was a delegate to the Senate representing the Territory of Wisconsin from 1841 to 1844, and was then appointed governor of the territory. When Wisconsin became a state, he was elected one of its first two senators and served from 1848 to 1857. His son, Augustus Dodge (D-IA), was first elected in 1839 as a delegate to the Senate for the Territory of Iowa. When Iowa became a state, Augustus became one of its first two senators and served from 1847 to 1854.[88] Senator Ted Kennedy (D-MA) overlapped with his son, Representative Patrick Kennedy (D-RI), for fourteen years. Patrick would be the last of the Kennedys to serve in Congress, ending one of the most famous family dynasties in US history, spanning over a hundred years. Patrick's great-grandfather, Representative John Fitzgerald (D-MA), served in the House from 1895 to 1900 and again from 1919 to 1920. Ted first ran for the Senate in a special election in 1960, after his brother John was elected president. Ted was reelected to the Senate eight times. He died of a brain tumor in 2009. Patrick served in the House from 1995 until 2010. Ted also served in the Senate with his other brother, Robert (D-NY), from 1965 until 1968; Robert was assassinated while campaigning for president in 1968. Robert's son Joseph P. Kennedy (D-MA) also pursued a political career, but served much later in the House, from 1987 to 1998.[89] The final father-and-son team to serve together were Ron and Rand Paul. Representative Ron Paul (R-TX), a perennial presidential candidate, has served off and on in the House since 1974 and was elected to his twelfth term in 2010. That same year, his son, Tea Party favorite Rand Paul (R-KY), was elected to the Senate.[90]

There has been one grandson who followed his grandmother. In 2007, Representative Julia Carson (D-IN), while being treated for a leg infection, was diagnosed with lung cancer. She died shortly thereafter. Her grandson, Andre Carson, won the special election to fill her seat, becoming the second Muslim to serve in Congress after Representative Keith Ellison (D-MN).[91]

In May 2007, the first daughter to run for her mother's seat announced her candidacy. Representative Juanita Millender-McDonald (D-CA) died of cancer in April. Her daughter, Valerie McDonald, announced she would run for her mother's seat. Although she had never run for office before, she helped her mother for years as an "informal adviser" and explained that her mother had often encouraged her to run for the seat after she retired.[92] In a crowded primary with eleven Democrats, five of whom were women, McDonald came in a distant third with 9 percent of the vote, behind former state representative Laura Richardson, who won the primary with 37 percent and went on to win the general election.[93]

In the history of Congress, there have been two sisters who served together, Representatives Loretta Sanchez (D-CA), who was first elected to the House in 1996, and Linda Sanchez (D-CA), who was first elected in 2002; both were still serving in the 112th Congress (2011 session). Loretta has commented that Linda is "definitely the more liberal one" and the funnier one. Linda has appeared at charity fundraisers at the DC Improv, a professional comedy club.[94] Also in the 112th Congress, two brothers served together, Senator Carl Levin (D-MI) and Representative Sandy Levin (D-MI).[95] Remarkably, in the late nineteenth century, the Washburn family produced four brothers who all served in Congress, three of them at the same time. Cadwallader Washburn (R-WI) served in the House from 1855 to 1860 and then again from 1867 to 1870, overlapping with Israel Washburn (Whig-ME), who served in the House from 1851 to 1860, and Elihu Washburne (R-IL), who added an "e" to his last name and served in the House from 1853 to 1870. William Drew Washburn (R-MN), the youngest brother, served in the House from 1879 to 1884 and in the Senate from 1889 to 1894.[96]

▨ Having a Family

For much of the twentieth century, the widow stereotype played a prominent role in the way women who ran for and held public office at the national level were portrayed. However, while being a widow did give these women many of the advantages of incumbency, many of the assumptions behind the stereotype were simply not true. And since 1972, the widow route to Congress has become quite rare. In fact, instead of gaining a House seat from a dead husband, it is now about as common for female members to gain a husband from the House. As cultural expectations have changed, the nature of family connections for female candidates—and the role of their families—have changed as well.

Surveys of potential candidates have shown that when women consider running for office, one of the biggest factors that influences their decision is their family situation, particularly if they have young children. For example, the Citizen Political Ambition Study (CPAS), conducted in 2002 and 2008, surveyed approximately 3,000 people in the three fields that tend to produce the most candidates for public office: law, business, and education. Among the survey respondents who came from two-income families, women were twelve times more likely than their spouses to be responsible for housework and ten times more likely to be responsible for childcare.[97] Interviews with a random sample of 100 women who completed the survey found that 65 percent of them agreed that "children made seeking office a much more difficult endeavor for women than for men."[98] For many women, entering the political arena is "an option only after the child-care duties abate."[99] The 2008 Center for American Women and Politics (CAWP) Recruitment Study surveyed almost 1,300 state legislators across the country and found that 57 percent of the women who responded rated "my children being old enough" as a very important factor in their decision to run for state legislature. Only 42 percent of men rated this factor as very important. Only 3 percent of female legislators had children under the age of six. As one woman put it, "a wife seldom has a stay-at-home wife."[100]

For example, Senator Lisa Murkowski's (R-AK) political career began when she served as a local Republican Party leader in her home state of Alaska. When her state representative announced his retirement, he asked her to recruit someone to take his place. As she was making phone calls to prospective candidates, she realized that she was just as qualified as anyone to run for the seat. But she waited for a long time to talk to her husband about this; she had two young sons, ages six and eight, and was worried about the impact that running and serving would have on her family. When she finally did discuss it with her husband, he said, "I can take care of the kids while you are in Juneau." Murkowski remarked that, "at that moment, I knew I had married well."[101] Former speaker of the House Nancy Pelosi (D-CA) often talks about her initial reluctance to run for office. She eventually had a discussion with her daughter, Alexandra, and said to her, "Mom has an opportunity to run for Congress. . . . You have one more year of high school. If you don't think that's a good idea, then don't worry about it because I'm not invested into this." Alexandra's response: "Mother, get a life."[102]

As Table 4.6 shows, only eight women gave birth while serving in Congress. The first was Representative Yvonne Brathwaite Burke (D-CA), elected in 1972, who gave birth during her first congressional term in November 1973. The next birth would not occur until 1995. In 1992, Enid Greene (R-UT) ran for Congress for the first time and narrowly lost in an open seat race against Democrat Karen Shepherd. During the campaign, given the conservative constituency, Shepherd ran as a moderate, reform-oriented Democrat and emphasized that "she was a wife and mother while Greene was single."[103] The campaign of 1994 featured a rematch with Greene, now wed to Joseph Waldholtz, her campaign manager. Running under her married name, Waldholtz exploited the vulnerabilities of Shepherd as a first-term incumbent, particularly her vote for the Clinton tax increase of 1993.[104] This time, Waldholtz won. Shortly after her swearing-in, she appeared to be a rising Republican star and was awarded a seat on the prestigious House Rules Committee. In March 1995, she announced that she was pregnant. Later that year, her political career collapsed. Her husband had embezzled $4 million from her father through a phony real estate scheme.[105] A large portion of this money had been funneled into Waldholtz's campaign. In March 1996, at the behest of Republican leaders, Waldholtz announced that she would not seek a second term in the House.[106] On June 6, 1996, Joseph Waldholtz pleaded guilty in federal district court to numerous tax, campaign, and banking violations.[107] Enid divorced him the same day. Subsequent investigations cleared her of any legal wrongdoing.[108] As her attorney explained, "She trusted her husband. . . . A lot of people trust their spouses."[109]

In 1996, Representative Susan Molinari (R-NY) and her husband, Representative Bill Paxon (R-NY), had a child while they were both serv-

Table 4.6 Women Who Gave Birth While Serving in Congress

	Dates of Service	Year Child Was Born
Rep. Yvonne Brathwaite Burke (D-CA)	1973–1979	1973
Rep. Enid Greene Waldholtz (R-UT)	1995–1997	1995
Rep. Susan Molinari (R-NY)	1990–1997	1996
Rep. Blanche Lambert Lincoln (D-AR)	1995–1997	1996
Rep. Cathy McMorris Rodgers (D-WA)	2005–present	2007, 2010
Rep. Kirsten Gillibrand (D-NY)	2007–2009	2008
Rep. Stephanie Herseth Sandlin (D-SD)	2004–2011	2008
Rep. Linda Sanchez (D-CA)	2003–present	2009

Source: Data compiled by the authors.

ing in the House.[110] Also in 1996, Blanche Lambert Lincoln (D-AR), while she was a House member, became pregnant with twins, and decided not to seek reelection. She successfully ran for the Senate two years later. In 2006, Representative Cathy McMorris Rodgers (R-WA) learned she was pregnant while she was campaigning for her second term. After winning reelection, she had a boy in April 2007, noting that "one of the positives about this job is you do have a flexible schedule. . . . Also, I have a spouse. He's excited about being a caregiver."[111] She and her husband had their second child in 2010.

Women who do run for Congress while they have children have often had to deal with criticism that their male colleagues with young children do not have to face. For example, in her 1964 House campaign, Patsy Mink was accused of "abandoning her children."[112] In 1971, when Barbara Boxer ran in her first race for county supervisor at the age of thirty-two, she sought the advice of her next-door neighbor, who said, "I don't think you should do this. Your kids are young and it doesn't seem right."[113] In 1972, Pat Schroeder (D-CO), during her first campaign, was constantly asked how she could run for Congress while having two young children. Frustrated at the press for ignoring her position on the Vietnam War and instead focusing on her parenting skills, she finally told one reporter, "Jim and I get up very early—about 6 A.M. We bathe and dress the children and give them a wonderful breakfast. Then we put them in the freezer, leave for work and when we come home we defrost them. And we all have a wonderful dinner together."[114] In the spring of 1998, Mary Bono (R-CA), who had two children, ages seven and nine, ran for her husband's seat in a special election against Ralph Waite, the actor who played "Pa" on *The Waltons.* Representative Sonny Bono (R-CA), former mayor of Palm Springs and costar of *The Sonny and Cher Show,* had been killed in a ski accident. A week before the election, Mary's mother-in-law, Jean Bono, wrote a letter to the editor of the *Riverside Press Enterprise,* stating, "Sonny Bono cannot rest in peace. . . . It would disturb him greatly that, if you hired her for the job, his children would essentially become orphans open to abuse by strangers."[115] Mary's thirty-nine-year-old stepdaughter, Christy, responded that Mary would probably be a better representative than her father.[116]

There is, however, evidence that these attitudes about the compatibility of motherhood and public office are changing, at least among candidates.[117] Representative Shelley Berkley (D-NV) was thirty when she was deciding between running for the state assembly and taking time off to have children. She assumed that she would have to choose between one or the other. Her mother told her to "do both."[118] Representative Debbie

Wasserman Schultz (D-FL) first ran for the Florida state legislature at the age of twenty-six in 1992. While in office, she gave birth to twins. When she learned that Representative Peter Deutsch's seat was going to be open in 2004, she decided to run for Congress. In August 2003, she had a baby girl, Shelby, whom she took on the campaign trail with her. At one point during her campaign, she brought Shelby with her to a lunch meeting with Susannah Shakow, president of the Women Under Forty Political Action Committee. As Shakow explained:

> We met at this really nice restaurant in downtown Washington to talk about how our PAC could help her. She came with her finance director, her campaign manager, and her three-month-old baby. I told a lot of people about that meeting. Some people were shocked that she would bring her baby along to meetings where she was trying to present herself as a serious candidate. But most people I talked to thought it was great that she brought her child. Young women who have children too often feel pressure to hide that fact when they are doing business. Debbie is a role model for proving that a woman can be professional and a mother at the same time.[119]

Many women no longer feel that a political career and raising a family are mutually exclusive. Senator Mary Landrieu (D-LA) said:

> It breaks my heart when I meet older women who once made a choice between career and a family. There was a time, not long ago, when many women had to make that choice. Now these women are retired, and they have no children, no grandchildren. In some cases, not all, they were forced to sacrifice one great joy for another. It just doesn't seem right. I want to make sure that picture is changed for good. If I can do it, other women can.[120]

As Representative Wasserman Schultz explained, "It's important to have moms in Congress. . . . I want to show other young women that it can be done."[121]

As Table 4.6 shows, five of the births to women serving in Congress, over half, have occurred since 2007. Representative Kirsten Gillibrand (D-NY) had her child in 2008, before she was appointed to the Senate to fill the vacancy created when President Barack Obama nominated Senator Hillary Clinton (D-NY) to be secretary of state. Gillibrand said the recent "baby boom" is "exciting. . . . I think it's good for Congress."[122] As Representative Stephanie Herseth Sandlin explained, "Our approach to policies that were important to us before become[s] even more important, whether it's early childhood development and how you fund it, . . . quality child-care, child nutrition, [or] prenatal care."[123]

While candidates may be becoming more comfortable with mother-hood, there is still some ambivalence among voters regarding female can-didates and their status as parents. In her 2008 vice presidential campaign, Sarah Palin played up her large family and motherhood and encountered both cheers and jeers.[124] In a 2010 study, 300 college students were shown a photo of a mock candidate for governor and an excerpt from a political speech and were then asked about their evaluation of the candidate's quali-fications.[125] While the speech remained the same, the photos varied the gen-der and parental status of the candidate and the ages of the children. With regard to whether the candidate would have the time to devote to being gov-ernor, the students judged female candidates with young children as the most disadvantaged. Male candidates, regardless of their parental status, were perceived to have more time to commit to the job than all female can-didates. The results suggest that voters might still perceive "more of a con-flict for female candidates between their families and politics than they do for male candidates."[126] As Representative Wasserman Schultz (D-FL) ex-plained, however, having young children can, in some situations, be a major advantage. She noted that when she brings her six-year-old with her to town hall meetings, "People are nicer and don't attack you."[127]

Because they typically wait until their children have grown, women do tend to be older than men when they first run for office.[128] Among all women to serve in the House between 1917 and 2011, the average age when they first ran for office was forty-nine. While attitudes about moth-ers and children on the campaign trail are changing, the election of young women to congressional offices is still quite uncommon. As Table 4.7 shows, only forty-one women under forty years old have served in the House. All but nine have been elected since 1972. Eight have been women of color. Only one woman under the age of forty has been elected to the Senate: Blanche Lambert Lincoln (D-AR) ran in 1998 at the age of thirty-eight, after having successfully run for the House in 1992 at the age of thirty-two. The first woman to serve in Congress, Representative Jeannette Rankin (R-MT), ran at the relatively young age of thirty-six. The youngest woman to serve in the House is Representative Elizabeth Holtzman (D-NY), elected at the age of thirty-one.[129] Among the ninety-four newly elected members of the House in the 112th Congress (2011 session), thir-teen of the men were under forty, but only three women were.[130]

In 2010, South Dakota's at-large House district featured the first gen-eral election in history with two women under forty. Stephanie Herseth Sandlin's first attempt at running for Congress was in 2002, when she ran for South Dakota's open at-large seat at the age of thirty-one as a moder-

Table 4.7   Women Under Forty Years Old Who Served in the US House

	Age When First Elected to the House	Dates of Service
Jeannette Rankin (R-MT)	36	1917–1919, 1941–1943
Mae Ella Nolan (R-CA)	36	1923–1925
Katherine Langley (R-KY)	38	1926–1931
Kathryn O'Laughlin McCarthy (D-KS)	38	1929–1931
Katharine Byron (D-MD)	37	1941–1943
Clare Boothe Luce (R-CT)	39	1943–1947
Winnifred Stanley (R-NY)	33	1943–1945
Patsy Mink (D-HI)	36	1965–1977, 1990–2002
Margaret Heckler (R-MA)	35	1967–1983
Elizabeth Holtzman (D-NY)	31	1973–1981
Barbara Jordan (D-TX)	36	1973–1979
Patricia Schroeder (D-CO)	32	1973–1997
Mary Rose Oakar (D-OH)	36	1977–1993
Olympia Snowe (R-ME)	31	1979–1995
Claudine Schneider (R-RI)	33	1981–1991
Marcy Kaptur (D-OH)	36	1983–present
Jill Long (D-IN)	37	1989–1995
Ileana Ros-Lehtinen (R-FL)	37	1989–present
Susan Molinari (R-NY)	31	1990–1997
Blanche Lincoln (D-AR)	32	1993–1997
Cynthia McKinney (D-GA)	37	1993–2003, 2005–2007
Nydia Velazquez (D-NY)	39	1993–2005
Maria Cantwell (D-WA)	34	1993–1995
Enid Greene Waldholtz (R-UT)	36	1995–1997
Lynn Rivers (D-MI)	37	1995–2005
Linda Smith (R-WA)	34	1995–1999
Loretta Sanchez (D-CA)	36	1997–present
Diana DeGette (D-CO)	39	1997–present
Mary Bono Mack (R-CA)	36	1999–present
Heather Wilson (R-NM)	37	1999–2009
Tammy Baldwin (D-WI)	36	1999–present
Melissa Hart (R-PA)	38	2001–2007
Linda Sanchez (D-CA)	34	2003–present
Stephanie Herseth Sandlin (D-SD)	33	2004–2011
Cathy McMorris Rodgers (R-WA)	33	2005–present
Debbie Wasserman Schultz (D-FL)	37	2005–present
Gabrielle Giffords (D-AZ)	36	2007–present
Kirsten Gillibrand (D-NY)	39	2007–2009
Jaime Herrera Beutler (R-WA)	32	2011–present
Kristi Noem (R-SD)	39	2011–present
Martha Roby (R-AL)	34	2011–present

Source: Data compiled by the authors.

ate Democrat. Her opponent was Republican Bill Janklow, the state's "larger than life" former governor, a fixture in South Dakota politics for over thirty years. As attorney general in 1975, he charged into the capitol with an automatic rifle during a hostage situation. After Jerry Brown, governor of California, refused to extradite Dennis Banks, a prominent member of the American Indian Movement, Janklow said he would pardon criminals in South Dakota if they agreed to move to California.[131] Janklow defeated Herseth Sandlin with 53 percent of the vote, but a few months later he ran a stop sign at over seventy miles per hour and killed a motorcyclist. Janklow had a reputation for speeding; he had been stopped by police at least sixteen other times since 1994.[132] After Janklow's manslaughter conviction, Herseth Sandlin ran again in the special election held in June 2004, defeating Larry Diedrich, a state legislator. Five months later, she defended her seat and defeated Diedrich again with 53 percent of the vote. In her 2010 reelection campaign, thirty-nine-year-old Herseth Sandlin faced thirty-nine-year-old Republican Kristi Noem. While stating that she "wanted no part" in the comparison, Noem had been labeled the "South Dakota Sarah Palin." As a former state legislator and rancher, she played up the fact that she was a mother of three and an avid elk hunter.[133] In the largely Republican state in a terrible year for Democrats, Noem won with 51 percent of the vote.

The importance of starting young becomes particularly apparent given that thirteen of the last twenty presidents first ran for elective office before they reached the age of thirty-five. Teddy Roosevelt was twenty-four when he first ran for state assembly in New York, Lyndon Johnson was twenty-nine when he first ran for the US House, and Barack Obama was thirty-five when he ran for the Illinois state senate.[134] As suggested in Chapter 3, there are particular consequences to running for Congress later in life, given the importance of seniority in obtaining leadership positions. Eight of the thirteen women first elected under the age of forty who served in the 112th Congress (2011 session) held leadership positions. Representative Ileana Ros-Lehtinen (R-FL) served as the chair of the House Foreign Affairs Committee, and Representative Mary Bono Mack (R-CA) was the chair of the Subcommittee on Commerce, Manufacturing, and Trade of the House Energy and Commerce Committee. Representative Linda Sanchez (D-CA) was the ranking member on the House Ethics Committee. Three Democratic women were ranking members on House subcommittees.[135] Representative Cathy McMorris Rodgers (R-WA) served as the vice chair of the Republican Conference.[136] Representative Diana DeGette (D-CO) served as deputy minority whip,[137] along with Representative Debbie Wasserman Schultz (D-FL), who also served as vice chair of the Democratic Steering and Policy Committee.[138] Three of the five who did not have leadership

Photo by Barbara Palmer

Representative Stephanie Herseth Sandlin (D-SD) first ran for the House in 2002 at the age of thirty-one.

roles were elected in 2010. If these three are taken out of the equation, 80 percent of the women who ran when they were in their thirties held leadership positions.

■ Conclusion

In the early nineteenth century, almost a quarter of the men who served in Congress were the sons, brothers, grandsons, nephews, or first cousins of other members, but by 1960 this proportion had declined to just 5 percent.[139] By comparison, from 1916 to 1972, most of the twentieth century, almost half of the women who served in the House were the daughters, sisters, or widows of other members, a proportion that declined to 13 percent by the 112th Congress. Family is thus a source of both continuity and change in electoral politics. It is a source of continuity in that the "family name" has been an important political resource throughout US history; while it may be declining, it serves as a form of "political inheritance" and bequeaths upon family members a variety of electoral advantages. As the daughter of two House members, Representatives Hale Boggs (D-LA) and Corrine "Lindy" Boggs (D-LA), journalist Cokie Roberts explained, "Politics is our family business."[140] Jo Ann Emerson (R-MO) ran for Congress when her husband, Representative Bill Emerson (R-MO), died of lung cancer in 1996. Her father worked with the Republican National Committee and her mother was a lobbyist. She grew up living next door to the Boggs family. Cokie was her babysitter.[141] Just as they hand down their family name, parents hand down their passion for politics. Fathers pass it down to their daughters. Mothers pass it down to their sons.

Expectations about women's "proper" roles within the family, however, have changed. For most of the twentieth century, women were to devote themselves to family, while politics was regarded as a realm reserved to men. The "widow route," however, provided a substantial number of women the opportunity to defy prevailing cultural norms and demonstrate that they were as qualified and ambitious as men, both as candidates and as policymakers. It also gave these women substantial advantages, much like those enjoyed by incumbents. Since the 1970s, much has changed. Today, the widow route is only rarely used. Moreover, in recent decades, there have been more young women winning election to the House, and several have demonstrated that it is possible to give equal justice to pursuing a career in the House as well as beginning and raising a family. Combining parenthood and politics is becoming more acceptable for women.

■ **Notes**

1. Clift and Brazaitis, *Madam President,* 1st ed., p. 70.
2. "Tar Heel, NC Has Election, but No One Bothers to Run."
3. Jacobson, *The Politics of Congressional Elections,* 7th ed., pp. 67–74; Stanley and Niemi, *Vital Statistics on American Politics, 2009–2010,* pp. 98–100.
4. Jacobson, *The Politics of Congressional Elections,* 7th ed., p. 46.
5. See, for example, Andolina et al., "Habits from Home, Lessons from School"; Canon, *Actors, Athletes, and Astronauts;* Fowler and McClure, *Political Ambition;* Kazee, *Who Runs for Congress?;* Rohde, "Risk-Bearing and Progres-

sive Ambition"; Schlesinger, *Ambition and Politics;* Williams and Lascher, *Ambition and Beyond.*

6. There appear to be only two comprehensive studies of family relationships in US politics that cover US history through the 1960s: Clubok, Wilensky, and Berghorn, "Family Relationships, Congressional Recruitment, and Political Modernization," and Hess, *America's Political Dynasties.*

7. Burns, Schlozman, and Verba, *Private Roots of Public Action;* Jennings and Niemi, *Generations and Politics;* Jennings, Stoker, and Bowers, "Politics Across Generations."

8. Speech at Running Start's Young Women's Political Leadership Conference, Washington, D.C., July 21, 2010.

9. Andolina et al., "Habits from Home, Lessons from School," p. 279.

10. McIntosh, Hart, and Youniss, "The Influence of Family Political Discussion on Youth Civic Engagement."

11. See, for example, Flanigan and Zingale, *Political Behavior of the American Electorate;* Lawless and Fox, *It Still Takes a Candidate.*

12. "Dingell, John David."

13. "Dingell, John David, Jr."

14. "Frelinghuysen, Frederick."

15. "Frelinghuysen, Theodore."

16. "Frelinghuysen, Frederick Theodore."

17. "Frelinghuysen, Joseph Sherman."

18. "Frelinghuysen, Peter Hood Ballantine."

19. "Frelinghuysen, Rodney."

20. This study collected data on all members of the House and Senate and those who served as delegates from territories in the 1st Congress (1789–1791) through the 86th Congress (1959–1961), and counted all members who were sons, grandsons, nephews, brothers, or first cousins; Clubok, Wilensky and Berghorn, "Family Relationships, Congressional Recruitment, and Political Modernization."

21. Eulau, "The Political Socialization of American State Legislators."

22. See http://en.wikipedia.org/wiki/List_of_United_States_political_families (accessed August 10, 2011); see also Hess, *America's Political Dynasties;* Hess, "America's Top Dynasty?"

23. *Women in Congress,* p. 307.

24. "Niki Tsongas, Long Bio."

25. *Women in Congress,* p. 416.

26. Ibid., p. 523.

27. Foerstel, *Biographical Dictionary of Congressional Women,* pp. 155–156.

28. Chamberlin, *A Minority of Members,* p. 63.

29. Ibid., p. 64.

30. Ibid., pp. 63–65.

31. Ibid., p. 65.

32. John Langley died on January 17, 1932, and was buried in Langley Cemetery in Middle Creek, Kentucky. Katherine Langley died on August 15, 1948, and was buried in Johnson Memorial Cemetery in Pikeville, Kentucky; *Biographical Directory of the American Congress,* p. 1262.

33. See, for example, Amundson, *The Silenced Majority;* Bullock and Heys, "Recruitment of Women for Congress"; Gertzog, "The Matrimonial Connection"; Gertzog, *Congressional Women;* Gruberg, *Women in Politics;* Kirkpatrick, *Politi-*

cal Woman; Solowiej and Brunell, "The Entrance of Women to the US Congress"; Tolchin and Tolchin, *Clout;* Werner, "Women in Congress."

34. Kincaid, "Over His Dead Body," p. 96.

35. Ibid., p. 97.

36. Foerstel, *Biographical Dictionary of Congressional Women,* p. 30.

37. Kincaid, "Over His Dead Body."

38. *Women in Congress,* p. 56.

39. Foerstel, *Biographical Dictionary of Congressional Women,* p. 203.

40. Ibid., p. 212.

41. Ibid., p. 98.

42. Kincaid, "Over His Dead Body," p. 97. See also Gertzog, "The Matrimonial Connection"; Gertzog, *Congressional Women.*

43. Kincaid, "Over His Dead Body," p. 101. There is no source that systematically gathers and presents data on these special elections. Additionally, as one goes back in time, information on these elections becomes increasingly sparse. As a result, it would be very difficult to determine the number of special elections in which the widow unsuccessfully sought to replace her husband.

44. For a statistical analysis of careerism among widows elected to the House, see Palmer and Simon, "Political Ambition and Women in the US House of Representatives."

45. Dickenson and Taylor, "Widow of Burton Will Seek Election to His House Seat," p. A7.

46. Turner, "Burton's Widow Among 4 Considering Race for Congress Seat," p. A12.

47. Gamarekian, "'The Popular Burton' and Her Mission," p. A10.

48. Foerstel, *Biographical Dictionary of Congressional Women,* p. 43.

49. Gamarekian, "'The Popular Burton' and Her Mission," p. A10.

50. "Widow of Rep. Burton Is Elected in California Congressional Race," p. A16.

51. Foerstel, *Biographical Dictionary of Congressional Women,* p. 43.

52. *Women in Congress,* pp. 70–72.

53. Foerstel, *Biographical Dictionary of Congressional Women,* pp. 263–264.

54. See Hardy-Fanta, *Latina Politics, Latino Politics;* Moncrief, Thompson, and Schuhmann, "Gender, Race, and the State Legislature"; Prestage, "Black Women State Legislators"; Prestage, "The Case of African American Women and Politics."

55. *Women in Congress,* p. 507.

56. Foerstel, *Biographical Dictionary of Congressional Women,* p. 8.

57. Darcy, Welch, and Clark, *Women, Elections, and Representation,* pp. 91–92.

58. Foerstel, *Biographical Dictionary of Congressional Women,* p. 163.

59. Ibid., p. 21.

60. Quinn, "Maryon Allen," p. K1.

61. "Carnahan, Jean."

62. Ibid.

63. Foerstel, *Biographical Dictionary of Congressional Women,* pp. 201–203.

64. *Women in Congress,* p. 399.

65. Ibid., p. 400.

66. Ibid.

67. Ibid.

68. Foerstel, *Biographical Dictionary of Congressional Women,* p. 102.

69. *Women in Congress,* p. 467.

70. Ibid., p. 468.

71. Reyes, "Case Wins Hawaii's 2nd Congressional District."

72. "Jo Ann Davis Dies at 57."

73. "Jo Ann Davis' Husband May Seek Her Congressional Seat."

74. Women in Congress, p. 674.

75. "Reps. Connie Mack, Mary Bono Wed."

76. *Women in Congress,* pp. 84–87.

77. Unfortunately, there are no easily available data on the number of fathers and sons who have served in Congress, particularly for those who have served in recent years.

78. *Women in Congress,* p. 577.

79. Foerstel, *Biographical Dictionary of Congressional Women,* pp. 213–214; Gillon, *That's Not What We Meant to Do,* pp. 43–46.

80. "Familial Connections of Women Representatives and Senators in Congress."

81. Tsong and Cockerham, "ANWR, Tax Issue Separate Debaters," p. A1.

82. Mauer, Tsong, and Dobbyn, "Murkowski Up," p. A1.

83. Cockerham, "Murkowski Concedes GOP Senate Race to Miller."

84. Somashekhar, "In Alaska's Senate Race, Murkowsi's Write-In Bid Bears Fruit."

85. "Alaska Certifies Sen. Murkowski's Re-elections."

86. *Women in Congress,* p. 295.

87. Ibid., p. 191.

88. "Rand, Ron Paul Make History"; "Dodge, Henry"; "Dodge, Augustus."

89. "Kennedy, Edward Moore (Ted)"; "Kennedy, Patrick Joseph"; "Kennedy, Robert Francis."

90. "Paul, Ronald Ernest"; "Paul, Rand"; "Rand, Ron Paul Make History."

91. "Andre Carson Wins Special Election."

92. Maddaus, "Congress a Family Affair?"

93. "Special Election Results."

94. Barone and McCutcheon, *Almanac of American Politics, 2012,* p. 242.

95. Groer, "Congress as a Family Business." Unfortunately, there are no easily available comprehensive lists of all of the brothers who have served in Congress. We do know of two more pairs of brothers who have served recently. Representative Mario Diaz-Balart (R-FL) served in the House from 1992 to 2010. His brother, Representative Lincoln Diaz-Balart (R-FL), was first elected in 2002 and was elected to his fifth term in 2010. Senator Ken Salazar (D-CO) served one term from 2004 to 2010, which coincided with the three terms that his brother, John Salazar (D-CO), served in the House.

96. Groer, "Congress as a Family Business"; "Washburn, Cadwallader Colden"; "Washburn, Israel, Jr."; "Washburne, Elihu Benjamin"; "Washburn, William Drew."

97. Lawless and Fox, *It Still Takes a Candidate,* p. 74.

98. Ibid., p. 80.

99. Ibid., p. 82.

100. Sanbonmatsu, Carroll, and Walsh, *Poised to Run,* pp. 24–25. See also Fulton et al., "The Sense of a Woman"; Sapiro, *The Political Integration of Women.*

101. Speech at Running Start's Young Women's Political Leadership Conference, Washington, D.C., July 20, 2011.

102. Peters and Rosenthal, *Speaker Nancy Pelosi and the New American Politics*, p. 201.

103. Barone and Ujifusa, *Almanac of American Politics, 1994*, p. 1289.

104. Ibid., *1996*, p. 1350.

105. Ibid., *1998*, p. 1422; Foerstel, *Biographical Dictionary of Congressional Women*, pp. 106–107.

106. Barone and Ujifusa, *Almanac of American Politics, 1998*, p. 1422.

107. Roddy, "Admission of Guilt," p. A6.

108. Foerstel, *Biographical Dictionary of Congressional Women*, p. 107.

109. Roddy, "Admission of Guilt," p. A6.

110. Foerstel, *Biographical Dictionary of Congressional Women*, p. 193.

111. "Congresswoman Balances Bills with Birth."

112. Foerstel and Foerstel, *Climbing the Hill*, p. 113.

113. Boxer, *Strangers in the Senate*, p. 83.

114. Foerstel and Foerstel, *Climbing the Hill*, p. 114.

115. Henry, "Bono's Mother Doesn't Want His Widow Elected," p. A1.

116. Henry, "Phone Call Discouraged Election Run," p. B1.

117. Witt, Paget, and Matthews, *Running As a Woman*.

118. Author interview, March 20, 2002.

119. Author interview, November 14, 2004.

120. Mikulski et al., *Nine and Counting*, p. 25.

121. Cohen, "Member Moms," pp. 14–19.

122. Bash, "What's New on Capitol Hill?"

123. Ibid.

124. See, for example, Kornblut, *Notes from the Cracked Ceiling;* Traister, *Big Girls Don't Cry.*

125. Stalsburg, "Voting for Mom."

126. Ibid., p. 390.

127. Speech at Running Start's Young Women's Political Leadership Conference, Washington, D.C., July 21, 2010.

128. See Bernstein, "Why Are There So Few Women in the House?"; Burrell, *A Woman's Place Is In the House;* Burrell, "The Political Opportunity of Women Candidates for the US House of Representatives in 1984"; Carroll, "Political Elites and Sex Differences in Political Ambition"; Diamond, *Sex Roles in the State House;* Gertzog, "The Matrimonial Connection"; Kirkpatrick, *Political Woman;* Mandel, *In the Running;* Sanbonmatsu, Carroll, and Walsh, *Poised to Run;* Sapiro, "Private Costs of Public Commitments or Public Costs of Private Commitments?". But see Dolan and Ford, "Change and Continuity Among Women State Legislators."

129. There have been two other women who were elected at age thirty-one, Susan Molinari (R-NY) and Olympia Snowe (R-ME), but both were a few months older. Molinari served as the youngest member of New York's city council at the age of twenty-six and ran for the US House seat vacated by her father in 1990. Snowe, who first ran for the state legislature in 1973 at the age of twenty-six, now serves in the US Senate. If Tulsi Gabbard wins election to Hawaii's Second District seat, Holtzman would still be the youngest female House member by four months.

130. "New Member Pictorial Directory."

131. deFiebre, "Janklow Case," p. 1B.

132. "Janklow Trial Begins."

133. Karl, "In South Dakota: Another Sarah Palin?"

134. Mandel and Kleeman, *Political Generation Next,* p. 7. Updated by the authors.

135. Representative Loretta Sanchez (D-CA) was the ranking member on the Strategic Forces Subcommittee of the House Armed Services Committee; Representative Diana DeGette (D-CO) was the ranking member on the Subcommittee on Oversight and Investigations of the House Energy and Commerce Committee; and Representative Gabrielle Giffords (D-AZ) was the ranking member on the Subcommittee on Space and Aeronautics of the House Science, Space, and Technology Committee; Haas, "List of Standing Committees."

136. "Republican Leadership."

137. "Biography," Chief Deputy Whip Diana DeGette.

138. "Biography," Congresswoman Debbie Wasserman Schultz.

139. Clubok, Wilensky, and Berghorn, "Family Relationships, Congressional Recruitment, and Political Modernization."

140. "Women's History Month."

141. Foerstel, *Biographical Dictionary of Congressional Women,* p. 80.

FIVE

Women as Targets: Understanding the Competitive Environment

What happens when a woman overcomes political and cultural barriers, wins a seat in Congress, and becomes an incumbent herself? Does she reap the same benefits of incumbency that men do? Or do gender and incumbency interact to create a different playing field?

There are examples that suggest that the road to reelection may be more perilous for women. For example, in 1986, after serving five terms in the House, Barbara Mikulski (D-MD) won an open Senate seat, defeating Republican Linda Chavez with 61 percent of the vote. This race was only the second time in history that two female candidates faced off in a general election for the Senate. Despite the fact that Mikulski won her Senate seat by a margin conventionally considered safe, in her reelection campaign of 1992, fifteen Republicans ran in the opposition primary, including two women. Even more astonishing was that six candidates, all male, challenged her in the Democratic primary. She won the primary easily with 77 percent of the vote, and then went on to trounce Republican Alan Keyes in the general election with 71 percent of the vote. But even that performance was not sufficient to scare off competition. In 1998, ten male Republicans fought for the nomination, and two candidates, one man and one woman, challenged her in the Democratic contest. Mikulski won her primary with 84 percent of the vote and won the general election with 71 percent of the vote. Finally, in 2004, "her electoral strength [was] finally beginning to sink in"; she ran uncontested in her own primary, and only one Republican, a little-known state senator, threw his hat in the ring to challenge her.[1] Her electoral strength did not, however, sink in for very long, because 2010 was another free-for-all: three men and three women challenged Mikulski in her own primary and eleven men ran in the Republican primary. Her Democratic challengers averaged only 3 percent of the vote, and Mikulski cruised through the general election with 63 percent of the vote. Clearly, the history of Mikulski's reelection efforts challenge the conventional wisdom that incumbency discourages opposition.

In this chapter, we explore the impact of incumbency and the competitive environment on the electoral fortunes of women. For the most part, because of the near invincibility of incumbents and the fact that most incumbents are male, it has been assumed that open seats are the primary avenue of entry for women into the House.[2] As a result, there has been very little analysis of female incumbents and their success rates.[3] It turns out that female incumbents do have slightly higher reelection rates than male incumbents. In addition, female incumbents win with higher margins than their male counterparts. It would thus appear that women have achieved parity in the electoral arena.

However, when we look beneath the surface, it turns out that female incumbents face a more competitive environment. They are much more likely to be challenged in their own party's primary, and candidates "come out of the woodwork" to run in the opposition-party primary. Male incumbents are more likely to run uncontested and get a "free pass," with no competition in their own primary and the opposition party simply conceding and not bothering to run any candidates at all. In addition, female incumbents are more likely to face female challengers. These results lead us to conclude that female incumbents have a "hidden influence." While on the surface women win reelection at rates comparable to those of men, they have to work harder to retain their seats. Their presence also encourages other women to run.

▪ When Women Run Against Women

The first time two women faced each other as opponents in a general election was a House race in 1934, when Democrat Caroline O'Day ran against Republican Natalie Couch for New York's at-large open seat. O'Day was active in Democratic Party politics and was selected as a delegate to each Democratic National Convention between 1924 and 1936. She also worked with Jeannette Rankin, lobbying to give women the right to vote in New York in 1917. Her electoral success in 1934 is attributed to her friendship with Eleanor Roosevelt, who campaigned for her—the first time a first lady campaigned for anyone.[4] In each of her three reelection bids, the Republicans nominated a woman to oppose her.

The first time two women ran against each other in a general election for the Senate was in 1960, when incumbent senator Margaret Chase Smith (R-ME) defeated Democrat Lucia Cormier. Cormier served six terms in the Maine house of representatives and was the Democratic floor leader.

During the campaign, Cormier and Smith participated in one of the first televised political debates, the same year as the debate between John F. Kennedy and Richard Nixon. Cormier spent $20,000 in the effort to oust Smith, who spent only $5,000. Smith won with 62 percent of the vote, the highest vote total of any Republican Senate candidate that year. The race made the cover of *Time* magazine.[5]

Because there have been so few instances in which women have found themselves running against other women candidates, there is very little analysis of this phenomenon.[6] Between 1956 and 2010, only 2 percent of all primary and general election races for Congress featured multiple women candidates.[7] From 1916 to 2010, there were 141 general elections featuring two female candidates. As Table 5.1 shows, nine of these races were for the Senate. All but one of these Senate races occurred since 1972. Eight of the nine races involved female Senate incumbents, and seven of these incumbents won reelection. Senator Elizabeth Dole (R-NC) is the only female incumbent senator to be defeated by another woman. In 2008, Dole was one of the most well-known names in the Senate, having served as secretary of transportation for President Ronald Reagan and secretary of labor for President George H. W. Bush, having helped her husband, Senator Bob Dole (R-KS), run for president in 1996, and having run for president in her own right in 2000. Her Senate reelection campaign in 2008 turned into one of the nastier ones that year. In the final week of the campaign against Democrat Kay Hagan, a former state senator, Dole ran an ad that called Hagan "godless" and said she "secretly" took "godless money" from a political action committee (PAC) that advocated for the rights of atheists. The ad backfired, and Hagan threatened to sue Dole for libel and defamation.[8] Hagan defeated Dole with 54 percent of the vote.

Table 5.1 General Elections for the US Senate with Two Female Candidates

	State	Winner	Status	Opponent
1960	ME	Margaret Chase Smith (R)	Incumbent	Lucia Cormier (D)
1986	MD	Barbara Mikulski (D)	Open seat	Linda Chavez (R)
1998	WA	Patty Murray (D)	Incumbent	Linda Smith (R)
2002	LA	Mary Landrieu (D)	Incumbent	Suzanne Terrell (R)
2002	ME	Susan Collins (R)	Incumbent	Chellie Pingree (D)
2006	TX	Kay Bailey Hutchison (R)	Incumbent	Barbara Radnofsky (D)
2006	ME	Olympia Snowe (R)	Incumbent	Jean Bright (D)
2008	NC	Kay Hagan (D)	Challenger	Elizabeth Dole (R)
2010	CA	Barbara Boxer (D)	Incumbent	Carly Fiorina (R)

Source: Data compiled by the authors.

Between 1956 and 2010, only 4 percent of the contested Senate primaries featured multiple women candidates. One of these was for an open Senate seat in New York in 1992. The New York Democratic primary featured two male candidates, Robert Abrams, the state attorney general, and Al Sharpton, the flamboyant boxing promoter and preacher, along with two female candidates, Elizabeth Holtzman, the youngest woman to serve in the House, and Geraldine Ferraro, a former member of the House and vice presidential candidate. Ferraro and Holtzman targeted their campaigns almost exclusively against each other, and the race became known as "the mother of all cat fights."[9] About a month before the primary, when Ferraro had a commanding lead in the polls, the *Village Voice* ran a story titled "Gerry and the Mob." The article claimed that she and her husband had ties to twenty-four Mafia figures. For example, two of Ferraro's campaign supporters were named "One-Eyed Charlie" and "Billy the Butcher."[10] Part of the story focused on an incident that occurred during her 1984 vice presidential campaign, when it was revealed that Ferraro's husband had rented space to a child pornographer with mob ties. She pledged to evict the tenant, but he remained in the building for three more years. Holtzman's attack ads became some of the most memorable of the campaign, with one of them stating, "Questions Gerry Ferraro won't answer: collecting $340,000 from a child pornographer—after promising not to."[11] Ultimately, Abrams narrowly won the primary, but was defeated by Republican Alfonse D'Amato in the general election.

The vast majority of House races with two female candidates have also occurred relatively recently. From 1916 to 1970, there were a mere ten general House elections with a Democratic woman running against a Republican woman, and four of these involved Representative O'Day (D-NY). Since 1972, there have been 122 general House elections with two women candidates. Surprisingly, as Table 5.2 shows, even since 1972 there has not been a slow and steady increase in these numbers. During the 1970s and 1980s, the average number of general elections with two women candidates was two. In 1992, the number jumped to five. Since 1994, the number of House races with two women candidates has fluctuated from a minimum of four in 1996 to a maximum of fourteen in 1998. Since 2000, however, the number has leveled off at around ten contests in each election cycle. Over the past decade, the number of House races featuring two women has stalled. In general elections for the House and Senate, races with women as major party nominees are still a rarity.

Table 5.2 also reveals that the vast majority of female House candidates who face a female opponent in the general election are incumbents. Of the races since 1972 featuring two women in the general election, 86 percent have been elections with female incumbents facing female challengers. In fact, a substantial majority of female incumbents have been challenged by a woman more than once. Of the ninety-eight House races with a female incumbent facing a female challenger, sixty-five, or 66 percent, involved female incumbents who were challenged by women at least twice. The leader here is Representative Pat Schroeder (D-CO), who during her career faced a female Republican in five of her reelection races. Representatives Jane Harman (D-CA) and Nancy Johnson (R-CT) faced female opponents four times. Nine female incumbents, including Representatives Jennifer Dunn (R-WA), Cynthia McKinney (D-GA), Patsy Mink (D-HI), and Nancy Pelosi (D-CA), faced female challengers three times. Nineteen more have run against women twice. This reveals, then, that the actual pool of women who have run against other women is quite small. These numbers also suggest that female incumbents seeking reelection

Table 5.2 General Elections for the US House with Two Female Candidates, 1972–2010

	Female Incumbent Defeats Female Challenger	Female Challenger Defeats Female Incumbent	Open Seats	Total
1972	2	0	0	2
1974	3	0	0	3
1976	1	0	0	1
1978	2	0	0	2
1980	2	0	0	2
1982	1	0	2	3[a]
1984	2	0	0	2
1986	3	0	1	4[a]
1988	3	0	0	3
1990	2	0	0	2
1992	1	0	4	5
1994	9	2	0	11
1996	3	0	1	4
1998	13	0	1	14
2000	10	0	1	11
2002	8	1	2	11
2004	8	0	3	11
2006	8	0	1	9
2008	9	2	1	12
2010	8	2	0	10
Total	98	7	17	122

Source: Data compiled by the authors.
Note: a. Count includes a special election.

may encourage aspiring women within the opposition party to defy the power of incumbency and launch a run for the House.

Not surprisingly, the female incumbents in Table 5.2 have a 93 percent success rate. Only seven female challengers have ever defeated a female incumbent. In addition, very few open House seats have featured two women candidates. Since 1972, there have been only seventeen. In fact, prior to 1982, there was never an open seat House race with two women candidates in the general election. One of the 1982 races featured Republican Barbara Vucanovich, a former speed-reading school owner, and Democrat Mary Gojack, a state senator, in a race for Nevada's Second District, which covered nearly the entire state. While Gojack began the campaign with more name recognition due to her unsuccessful bid for the US Senate two years prior, President Ronald Reagan stumped for Vucanovich during a campaign stop in Reno. Vucanovich, who was sixty-one years old and had fifteen grandchildren, turned out to be a good match for the conservative, mostly rural district and won with 56 percent of the vote.[12] She retired after serving seven terms. The other race in 1982 was actually a special election in January for Connecticut's First District, to fill the open seat created by the death of Representative William Cotter (D-CT). Democrat Barbara Kennelly came from a prominent Connecticut political family. Her father, John Bailey, served as chair of the Democratic National Committee and was credited with getting John F. Kennedy elected president. Kennelly served on the city of Hartford's court of common council and as secretary of state. Her opponent in 1982 was Hartford's former mayor, Republican Ann Uccello. Kennelly, a master fundraiser, outspent Uccello three to one and won with 59 percent of the vote. During her sixteen-year career, Kennelly worked hard to break down barriers within the male power structure in the Democratic Party. She even learned to play golf in order to "mingle" with her overwhelmingly male colleagues. It all paid off, and she became the most powerful woman in the House. She was the first woman to serve on the Permanent Select Committee on Intelligence and the first female chief deputy majority whip, and was elected vice chair of the Democratic Caucus.[13]

■ "Equality" in the Electoral Arena

Although women are less likely to consider running for office or to be encouraged to run, when women do run they are as likely to win as men.[14] Women who challenge incumbents are not any more likely to win (or lose) than men who challenge incumbents. As Table 5.3 shows, female incumbents are reelected at slightly higher rates than male incumbents; their overall rate is 95.1 percent, compared to 94.9 percent for men. The table also shows that there has been little variation in these reelection rates over the redistricting periods in the past fifty years. The largest difference was from 1982 to 1990, when female incumbents had a perfect track record, winning all 101 of their reelection campaigns. During this time, sixty-five male incumbents lost. In 2004, female incumbents also had a perfect record; all fifty-seven female House incumbents won, as did all five female incumbents in the Senate. Eight male House incumbents lost. In the three "wave elections" of 2006, 2008, and 2010, the victory rates of male (92 percent) and female (91 percent) incumbents were virtually identical. Thus, as far as winning reelection is concerned, female incumbents have reached electoral parity with men.

Moreover, female incumbents tend to win with larger electoral margins. From 1956 to 2010, slightly more female incumbents earned the status of a "safe seat" and were likely to win with larger shares of the

Table 5.3   Reelection Rates for Male and Female House Incumbents, by Redistricting Period, 1956–2010 (percentages)

	Reelection Rates for Male Incumbents	Reelection Rates for Female Incumbents	Male Incumbents Reelected with Safe Margin	Female Incumbents Reelected with Safe Margin
1956–1960	93.6	93.2	78.9	86.4
1962–1970	94.1	95.9	83.6	95.9
1972–1980	94.3	95.6	85.0	91.2
1982–1990	96.4	100.0	89.3	95.0
1992–2000	95.8	94.4	87.0	83.3
2002–2010	94.8	93.9	88.5	88.1
Overall	94.9	95.1	85.8	90.1

	Average Two-Party Vote for Male Incumbents	Average Two-Party Vote for Female Incumbents
1956–1960	61.0	61.7
1962–1970	63.0	67.4
1972–1980	65.1	71.4
1982–1990	66.1	68.8
1992–2000	64.7	66.4
2002–2010	65.2	67.0
Overall	64.4	67.2

Source: Data compiled by the authors.

two-party vote than their male counterparts.[15] On average, female incumbents won 67 percent of the vote, 3 points higher than male incumbents, who won 64 percent of the vote. In every redistricting period, women won more of the two-party vote share than men. During the 1970s, this difference was 6 points.

This suggests that there is a level playing field for male and female candidates, at least in terms of outcomes. Female incumbents actually do a little better in terms of reelection rates. They are more likely to come from a safe seat and win by a larger margin. But what does the broader competitive arena look like?

■ Understanding the Competitive Environment

Despite the parity in electoral success, campaigns with female candidates are different from those where only men compete for nomination and election. In particular, there are differences in how the media cover the campaigns of female candidates, how voters perceive and evaluate male and female candidates, and how candidates formulate campaign strategy.

Media Coverage

Study after study shows that media coverage of campaigns varies substantially depending on the gender of the candidate. Press secretaries for female members of Congress consistently report that the media tend to stress that their bosses are women first and representatives second. As one press secretary put it, "The next time [our local paper] puts together a story that doesn't mention she's a mom with young children, it will be a first."[16] In contrast, press secretaries for male members of Congress generally complain about the way the media cover issues and legislation sponsored by their representatives. News stories about women are still substantially more likely to mention marital status and age compared to news stories about men.[17] Women who run for higher-level office, such as senator, governor, or even president, actually receive less media coverage than their male counterparts.[18] And when they do receive coverage, the content tends to reinforce sex-role stereotypes and traditional attitudes about women's roles.[19] In fact, media coverage is often "the bane of the political woman's existence."[20] As Representative Susan Molinari (R-NY) explained, "There I'd be, in a war zone in Bosnia, and some reporter—usually female— would comment on how I was dressed, then turn to my male colleague for answers to questions of substance."[21]

In fact, media coverage of women in elective office does not appear to have changed much over the past hundred years. Beginning with the first woman to serve in Congress, female candidates have always complained about the "soft news" focus in which their wardrobe, hairstyles, femininity, and family relationships receive more emphasis than their political experience or issue positions.[22] Even the first woman to serve in Congress, Representative Jeannette Rankin (R-MT), was frustrated by her media coverage. She was constantly asked about her wardrobe and often portrayed as "a lady about to faint."[23] Once, when an *Associated Press* reporter appeared in her office, she told him to "go to hell."[24] The woman who followed Rankin in 1921, Representative Alice Robertson (R-OK), though very different from her predecessor, was lambasted by the press. Robertson was an ardent antisuffragist and made it very clear that, unlike Rankin, she would have voted for the United States to enter World War I. The press, however, went well beyond comparing their policy positions. The *New York Times,* for example, wrote, "She is no tender Miss Rankin. . . . [She] never wore a pair of silk stockings and won't wear high-heeled shoes."[25]

Even today, examples of sexist commentary in the media are not hard to find. In 2007, an article titled "Hillary Clinton's Tentative Dip Into New Neckline Territory" appeared in the style section of the *Washington Post.* The article began:

> There was cleavage on display Wednesday afternoon on C-SPAN2. It belonged to Senator Hillary Clinton. She was talking on the Senate floor about the burdensome cost of higher education. She was wearing a rose-colored blazer over a black top. The neckline sat low on her chest and had a subtle V-shape. The cleavage registered after only a quick glance. No scrunch-faced scrutiny was necessary. There wasn't an unseemly amount of cleavage showing, but there it was. Undeniable. . . . There was the sense that you were catching a surreptitious glimpse at something private. You were intruding—being a voyeur.[26]

The article caused a firestorm on political blogs. Clinton, however, used the discussion as an opportunity to raise money for her presidential campaign, sending an e-mail to supporters with the subject line "Cleavage."[27] In 2009, after she secured funding for Medicaid financing for her state, Fox News's talk show host Glenn Beck called Senator Mary Landrieu (D-LA) a "high-class prostitute." Rush Limbaugh countered, arguing that she was "the most expensive prostitute in the history of prostitutes."[28] The *Washington Post* referred to the 2010 South Dakota House race between incumbent Democratic representative Stephanie Herseth Sandlin and Republican state representative Kristi Noem as the "Battle of the

Photo courtesy of the Library of Congress

Representative Alice Robertson (R-OK), the second woman to serve in Congress, was plagued by press coverage focusing on her appearance.

Babes." Herseth Sandlin was described as "South Dakota's princess . . . a pretty, perky prairie girl who can do no wrong." Noem's coverage included a description of her three kids "storming in and out for dinner" from her "farmhouse kitchen."[29]

Without doubt, both male and female candidates face a new "media reality" with the growing reach of blogs, Twitter, Facebook, and other new media.[30] Some of the worst examples of sexism toward female candidates can be found in these new media outlets.[31] For example, during Christine O'Donnell's 2010 campaign for the Senate in Delaware, Gawker.com posted an anonymous story claiming that she had showed up in a ladybug costume at the author's apartment on Halloween in 2007. The author described a drunk O'Donnell as "aggressive. . . . I won't get into the nitty gritty details of what happened between the sheets that evening. But I will say that it wasn't half as exciting as I'd been hoping it would be. She made it seem like she'd never had sex in her life, which seemed pretty improbable for a woman her age." The article received almost 600,000 hits and 100,000 "likes" on Facebook.[32] As Eleanor Roosevelt put it, "If you're going to be a woman in public life, you've got to have skin as thick as a rhinoceros."[33]

Women who cry—or even allegedly cry—cause a media frenzy. When Rankin cast her vote against World War I in 1917, the front page of the *New York Times* ran a headline that read, "Miss Rankin, Sobbing, Votes No."[34] While Rankin's biographer noted that as she read her sixteen-word statement on the House floor, "tears wandered down her cheeks,"[35] the *New York Times* reported that she "sank back to her seat . . . pressed her hands to her eyes, threw her head back and sobbed,"[36] which was patently false. Moreover, the paper neglected to mention that many of the male members, regardless of how they voted, were also weeping.

Fast-forward seventy years later. In September 1987, Representative Pat Schroeder (D-CO) held a press conference in Denver announcing that she was dropping out of the Democratic presidential primary. When she came to the part of her speech when she said she would no longer be running, tears momentarily ran down her face. The photo of her crying has become one of the most famous in presidential politics.[37] As Schroeder put it, "Those seventeen seconds were treated like a total breakdown."[38] Her tears were the subject of weeks of media coverage and debate. In fact, she noted that even after all of her years of service in Congress, "Anytime I go to any city to talk, that's the first piece of film the TV stations pull out. They've just decided that's the only thing I've ever done that counted."[39]

Even in the twenty-first century, a woman candidate crying is big news. In 2002, when Governor Jane Swift (R-MA) announced she would not run for reelection, the front page of the *Massachusetts Telegram and Gazette* featured a photo of her wiping a tear from her eye. During her entire press conference, which lasted over thirty minutes, Swift teared up for about

DEBATE LASTED 16 1/2 HOURS

One Hundred Speeches Were Made—Miss Rankin, Sobbing, Votes No.

ALL AMENDMENTS BEATEN

Resolution Will Take Effect This Afternoon with the President's Signature.

KITCHIN WITH PACIFISTS

Accession of the Floor Leader Added Others to the Anti-War Faction.

Special to The New York Times.
WASHINGTON, Friday, April 6. At 3:12 o'clock this morning the House of Representatives by the overwhelming vote of 373 to 50 adopted the resolution that meant war between the Government and the people of the United States and the Imperial German Government. . . .

Miss Rankin Votes "No."

Miss Jeanette Rankin, the woman Representative from Montana, had been absent from the House most of the evening, but took her accustomed place while the roll call was in progress. When her name was called she sat silent. "Miss Rankin," repeated the clerk. Still no answer. The clerk went on with his droning, and floor and galleries buzzed.

On the second roll call, Miss Rankin's name was again called. She sat silent as before. The eyes of the galleries were turned on her. For a moment there was breathless silence. Then Miss Rankin rose. In a voice that broke a bit but could be heard all over the still chamber she said:

"I want to stand by my country, but I cannot vote for war. I vote no." The "No" was scarcely audible.

And the maiden speech of the first woman Congressman ended in a sob. She was deeply moved and big tears were in her eyes.

Source: New York Times, April 6, 1917, p. 1.

thirty seconds as she was thanking her staff, yet that was the photo the paper ran above the fold. Even the *Boston Globe* referred to the event as her "tearful State House news conference."[40] Swift said she dropped out because of the challenge she would face in the Republican primary from Mitt Romney, former head of the Salt Lake City Olympic Committee. Swift gained national attention as the first woman to give birth while governor and was dogged by bad press during much of her term. When she decided not to run for reelection, citing family reasons, Massachusetts's *Lowell Sun* ran a front-page story titled "Swift Sent Women a Bad Message."[41]

During her 2008 presidential campaign, Hillary Clinton may have actually been helped by media coverage of her "crying." After she finished a disappointing third behind Barack Obama and John Edwards in the Iowa caucuses, she was at a campaign stop at a coffee shop in New Hampshire a few days before the primary, where the polls were predicting another Obama victory. At the coffee shop were sixteen undecided voters, mostly women, and over a hundred journalists. After Clinton talked for over an hour giving detailed policy positions, one of the women wanted to know how the campaign was affecting Clinton personally, asking, "How did you get out the door every day?"[42] Clinton replied, "I couldn't do it if I just didn't passionately believe it was the right thing to do. I have [had] so many opportunities from this country. I just don't want to see us fall backwards. This is very personal for me—it's not just political, it's not just public."[43] As she said this, her voice quivered and her eyes did well up with tears. The media storm that followed in blogs, editorials, and cable news talk shows lambasted Clinton, with some suggesting that the entire thing was a political ploy.[44] Maureen Dowd, a columnist for the *New York Times,* wrote an editorial with a headline asking, "Can Hillary Cry Her Way Back to the White House?" Dowd noted that after watching the footage of Clinton at the coffee shop, one reporter joked, "That crying really seemed genuine. I'll bet she spent hours thinking about it beforehand."[45] The criticism of Clinton in the media appeared to swing women voters over to her side, and she won the primary. At her victory celebration, even Clinton herself acknowledged that this moment during the campaign had helped her, stating, "Over the last week, I listened to you, and in the process I found my own voice. I felt like we all spoke from our hearts, and I'm so glad that you responded."[46]

Of course, there is a long list of male politicians who have cried. With the help of friends and constituents, Representative Schroeder created a "sob sister file." It includes the story of George Washington's farewell meeting with his Revolutionary War generals, who all cried around the dinner table. Her file also includes President George H. W. Bush, Russian leader Mikhail Gorbachev, Lieutenant-Colonel Oliver North, General Norman Schwarzkopf, President Ronald Reagan, Chile's General Augusto Pinochet, Senator John Sununu, and several male professional athletes.[47] One of the more famous examples is Edmund Muskie's 1972 Democratic presidential campaign. In late February, a week before the New Hampshire primary, Muskie was leading in the polls by a two-to-one margin, and was considered the man to beat. New Hampshire's *Manchester Union Leader* then published stories attacking his wife and accusing him of racial slurs against New Hampshire's French Canadian population. Muskie appeared live on the *CBS Evening News* to respond to the charges. Anchor Roger Mudd opened the story, stating, "Senator Edmund Muskie today denounced William Loeb, the conservative publisher of the Manchester, New Hampshire, *Union Leader,* as a 'liar' and a 'gutless coward,'" and then cut to Muskie, who was standing on a flatbed truck in front of the paper's offices as the snow fell, crying, his voice breaking, barely able to speak. Muskie later explained that the moment "changed people's minds about me. . . . They were looking for a strong, steady man, and here I was weak." He won the primary, but only by 9 points. In the wake of this episode, Muskie's campaign floundered. He came in fourth in the next primary in Florida, and by the end of April had dropped out of the race.[48]

More recently, Speaker of the House John Boehner (R-OH) earned the nickname "Weeper of the House." On election night in November 2010, in the speech he gave after learning of the Republican takeover of the House, Boehner choked up several times.[49] A month later, Boehner broke down twice during an interview on *60 Minutes* with Leslie Stahl. As Stahl explained, "It's full bore crying. It's not just little tears . . . and he does it a lot."[50] Shortly after he became speaker, Boehner teared up during the 2011 State of the Union speech, after Obama noted, "someone who began sweeping the floors of his father's Cincinnati bar can preside as Speaker of the House."[51] In April, *ABC News* reported that he cried during a closed-door meeting with House Republicans about the budget negotiations and possible government shutdown.[52] The magazine *Washingtonian* noted that "'John Boehner crying' is now the third-most popular search for his name on Google, ahead of 'John Boehner smoking' and 'John Boehner tan.'"[53]

Over the past century, while cultural attitudes about women running for office have changed substantially, and while more and more women have run for political office, it seems that media coverage of women candidates has remained remarkably constant. Even today, when female candidates win at rates equal to those of their male counterparts, the media still reinforce sex-role stereotypes and portray them in a way that can disadvantage their campaigns. In other words, they do not receive equal treatment by the press. Consequently, in order to achieve equal rates of success compared to men, female candidates may have to work harder to counteract the stereotypes and sexism typically found in their media coverage.

Voter Perceptions

Despite the media's remarkable consistency over the past century with regard to the treatment of female politicians, there has been a substantial change in the attitudes of voters about the appropriateness of women seeking political office. As Senator Barbara Boxer (D-CA) explained, "In 1972 you never mentioned being a woman. You never brought it up, and you hoped nobody noticed."[54] Today, however, the vast majority of American voters no longer see being a member of Congress as a "man's job."[55] In fact, in states such as Arizona, California, and Maine, places where women have held high-level political office for quite some time, voters largely perceive few differences between the men and women who run.[56]

Generally, however, male and female candidates are still often seen as having different leadership traits, some of which benefit women. Men are seen as more assertive, aggressive, and self-confident, while women are viewed as being more compassionate, trustworthy, and willing to compromise.[57] A survey by the Pew Research Center in 2008 found that women were also seen as more intelligent and creative.[58] "Likability" also appears to be a much bigger factor in determining the success of female candidates than male candidates, but female candidates are also presumed to be better at connecting with voters.[59] Interestingly, while the media often go into a frenzy when female candidates shed a tear, voters see things differently; a recent study showed that when candidates cried, they were all viewed as more empathetic and honest, regardless of gender.[60]

Voters also make assumptions about candidates based on their gender, particularly with regard to "issue ownership"—the issues on which candidates are viewed as more competent.[61] Women candidates are typically seen as more competent on issues such as education, healthcare, civil rights, the environment, and welfare, while men are seen as more competent on issues such as taxes, budgets, crime, national defense, and foreign policy.[62]

Voter perceptions of a particular candidate's ideology are also strongly related to the gender of that candidate. Compassion issues such as education, healthcare, and welfare are largely associated with the Democratic Party and liberal policy positions. In contrast, the Republican Party is generally considered more competent to deal with issues like taxes, national defense, and crime.[63] These general party associations interact with gender: female Democrats are perceived as more liberal than they actually are, and female Republicans are perceived as less conservative than they actually are.[64] As a result, female Republican candidates are held to a higher standard by voters in Republican primaries in proving their ideological credentials.[65]

Thus, like political-party labels, the gender of the candidate acts as a cue for voters.[66] Just knowing this small bit of information, voters "make inferences about a candidate's issue positions, policy competencies, ideological leanings, and character traits."[67] Gender provides a shortcut that helps voters "estimate the views of candidates."[68] Because a woman running for office, especially a statewide office, is still a rare event, voters are more likely to rely on gender as a cue.[69] Gender cues are especially salient when women are a "novelty," such as in a primary election with a woman candidate running against several male competitors.[70] Thus, gender and party interact and have an impact on voter perceptions of a candidate's issue positions, leadership traits, and ideology.

Campaign Strategy

All of this suggests that successful female candidates must adapt their campaign strategies to account for gender stereotypes about their character traits, issue competence, and ideology, as well as for media coverage that reinforces sex-role stereotypes.[71] In essence, women face particular challenges in their "presentation of self."[72] According to Richard Fenno's classic work *Home Style: House Members in Their Districts,* this is the fundamental act of campaigning, in which candidates place themselves in the "immediate physical presence of others" and "make a presentation of themselves."[73] More simply put: candidates have to cultivate their images. The presentation of self is both verbal and nonverbal. The nonverbal is critical, particularly for women, since it may enhance or undermine the credibility given to verbal presentations and the level of trust that audiences place in the candidate. For example, in her first unsuccessful campaign for the Senate in 1974, Barbara Mikulski realized that "one of my problems is that I don't fit the image of a US senator. You know, an Ivy-League-looking male, over 50 and over six feet tall." Instead, she was a "round, short, fuzzy-haired Polish woman from Southeast Baltimore." So as part of her campaign, she went on a diet. She said, "It showed people I could keep my mouth shut. . . . But it also showed them that when I make up my mind to do something, I can follow a goal."[74]

It is from this presentation of self that voters make judgments about candidates. For the woman who seeks elective office, the challenge is to "craft a message and a public persona" establishing that "she can be as clear and independent a decision maker as any man, but more caring and trustworthy."[75] For example, the success of Representative Debbie Wasserman Schultz (D-FL), who became chair of the Democratic National Committee in 2011, has been attributed to her "uncanny knack for being both disarming and aggressive in the same conversation."[76] Based on pre- and postelection polls of registered voters in 2010, the Barbara Lee Foundation created a campaign guide, "Turning Point, 2010," for women interested in running for office. The analysis revealed that "voters continue to set a higher bar for women candidates than for their male counterparts." It suggested that female candidates need to show that they are "honest and ethical," that they "connect with people" and "reference family." At the same time, however, they need to "display toughness" and should not be "a goody-two-shoes."[77]

The campaign guide also noted that female candidates are punished more harshly by voters for going negative; in fact, "negative campaigning undercuts all gender advantages for women candidates. . . . Critiquing an opponent's record, priorities, or decisions without being seen as negative is an extraordinary challenge for women candidates and their campaign teams."[78] Moreover, a 2010 study using hypothetical candidates found that when female candidates were attacked with even mildly sexist language, it had a substantial effect on voter perceptions: after hearing a female candidate being called "mean girl" or "ice queen," 70 percent of potential voters said they would be less likely to vote for her. While attacks based on a female candidate's issue positions also affect voter perceptions, sexist attacks are the most "effective" at reducing her support.[79] Thus "the woman candidate has to maintain . . . a political above-it-all demeanor expected of a lady, all the while beating her opponents in what sometimes seems the closest thing to blood sport that is still legal."[80]

Women candidates must also account for the "political mood" or temper of the times, both nationally and locally, in formulating their campaign messages and issue agendas. There are two important ways that political mood can affect women's success. The first pertains to the problems and issues deemed most important by their constituency and the degree to which these concerns mesh with voter perceptions of issue competency. If the focus rests on compassion issues, as it did in 1992, female candidates will be advantaged. In such circumstances, when women candidates use sex-role expectations to their advantage, run on compassion issues, and target women voters, they are substantially more likely to win. The quintessential example is Patty Murray (D-WA), who ran as the "mom in tennis shoes."[81] To the extent that the political mood and agenda focus on budgets and economic policy or foreign and defense policy, as they did in 2002, women must formulate strategies to weaken the stereotypes and establish perceptions of issue competency on these traditional male issues. Second, there are times when the political mood is especially restive toward "politics as usual" and incumbents. Women can take advantage of being perceived as more honest during election cycles when events and scandals call into question the trustworthiness of politicians, which became a major theme in 2006. Thus the campaign strategies employed by female candidates must take these factors into consideration. If they do not, female candidates could be substantially disadvantaged at the polls.

Implications for the Competitive Environment

These three factors—media coverage, gender stereotypes, and campaign strategy—suggest important implications for the electoral competition that women might face and lead us to draw several conclusions. Female candidates, including female incumbents, might be perceived by potential opponents as more vulnerable in the electoral arena than male candidates.[82] Despite the increasing presence of women in the electoral arena, a female nominee or incumbent remains a novelty. From 2002 to 2010, a woman won the Democratic nomination for the House at least once in 180 of the 435 congressional districts, 41 percent of all districts; voters in the remaining 255 districts, 59 percent, never saw a female Democratic nominee. In other words, during the five election cycles in the redistricting period, there were no female Democratic candidates in a general election in well over half of all districts. The nomination of a female Republican is even more of a rare event. For the same period, there were female Republican nominees in only 117 districts, 27 percent of all districts, and no female nominees in 318 districts, 73 percent. This is particularly important because reliance on gender stereotypes is stronger in exactly these circumstances, when candidates are perceived as novelties.[83]

A second implication is more positive. Conceivably, women candidates may foster competition in a different way, as role models for other women. In states with competitive female candidates, women are more likely to discuss politics, have higher levels of political knowledge, and feel politically efficacious; viable women candidates "represent symbolic and substantive cues to women citizens that increase their political engagement."[84] Research suggests that a female candidate may stimulate more voter participation among women.[85] The logical extension of this is that successful women candidates inspire other women to run. Beyond the role-model effect, however, deciding to run against another woman can also be a strategic decision.[86] Against the backdrop of gender stereotypes, it is important to consider what the success of a woman winning a House seat signifies. It demonstrates that the female candidate was able to neutralize the stereotypes or make them work to her advantage. Her victory serves as a cue signaling that a woman can overcome the hurdles and compete successfully in that district.

Thus gender stereotypes may work in a number of ways to stimulate competition. The novelty of female candidates may suggest vulnerability. In addition, female candidates as role models may inspire more women to run. A female incumbent may provide a "strategic signal" to other women about the probability of winning a district. Given all of this, do female incumbents face more competition to retain their House seats than their male counterparts? Do female incumbents face more competition from female candidates?

◼ Explaining the Competitive Environment

On the surface, electoral outcomes for the US House do indicate parity between male and female candidates. As Table 5.3 shows, female incumbents actually do slightly better than male incumbents. This does suggest that there is gender equality, at least as far as the final outcome of an election is concerned. We expect, however, given the disparity in press coverage and the way gender can affect voter perceptions and campaign strategies, that female candidates, particularly female incumbents, may be perceived as more vulnerable, and as a result may draw more competition than their male counterparts. In addition, female incumbents may have a "role model" effect and draw more female competition than their male counterparts.

While reelection rates show that there are no differences between male and female incumbents, there are, however, other aspects of the competitive environment that have not been explored. In addition to reelection rates, there are three other indicators of competition: no opponent in the primary, no major party opponent in the general election, and the "free pass," in which the incumbent has no opposition in both primary and general elections. By examining these additional measures of competition, we produce a more complete and nuanced picture of the electoral environment.[87]

Table 5.4 shows, first of all, that female incumbents are less likely to enjoy the luxury of having no opponent.[88] In districts where women stand for reelection, there are slightly more contested primaries: 32 percent of districts compared to 29 percent of districts where men stand for reelection. Female incumbents also have fewer uncontested general elections: 9 percent compared to 16 percent for men. In fact, female incumbents are approximately half as likely to get a "free pass"; while 12 percent of male incumbents face no competition in their primary or general elections, only 6 percent of women are that fortunate.

Table 5.4 reveals substantial partisan differences as well. Among Democratic incumbents, men and women are equally likely to face competition in their primary—35 percent of men and 33 percent of women— but the equality ends there. Democratic female incumbents are substantially more likely to face major party opposition in the general election; the proportion of uncontested general elections for women, 11 per-

Table 5.4   Uncontested Primary and General Elections Among US House Incumbents, 1956–2010

	Male Incumbents	Female Incumbents
All incumbents		
Contested primary election	28.9% (2,870/9,929)	31.7% (245/774)
Uncontested general election	15.9% (1,611/10,116)	9.2%[a] (73/790)
Uncontested primary and general elections	11.8% (1,169/9,929)	6.3%[a] (49/774)
Democratic incumbents		
Contested primary election	35.3% (2,007/5,692)	33.3% (175/526)
Uncontested general election	20.6% (1,183/5,754)	10.9%[a] (58/534)
Uncontested primary and general elections	14.4% (818/5,692)	6.8%[a] (36/526)
Republican incumbents		
Contested primary election	20.4% (863/4,237)	28.2%[a] (70/248)
Uncontested general election	9.8% (428/4,362)	5.9%[a] (15/256)
Uncontested primary and general elections	8.3% (351/4,237)	5.2%[a] (13/248)

Source: Data compiled by the authors.
Note: a. p < 0.05.

cent, is significantly lower than the rate for men, 21 percent. A similar re-sult holds for the "free pass." Only 7 percent of Democratic female in-cumbents avoid competition throughout the election cycle, compared to 14 percent for Democratic males.

It should be noted that, in general, Republican incumbents face a less contentious primary arena than their Democratic counterparts. Democratic incumbents face primary challenges in 35 percent of their primaries, whereas the rate for Republicans is only 20 percent. But the patterns be-tween Republican men and women are different in two ways. First, in con-trast to the parity between men and women in Democratic primaries, female Republican incumbents are more likely to be challenged in a pri-mary than their male counterparts, 28 percent versus 20 percent. Second, there is also a significant difference in the rates of competition that Re-publican incumbents face in the general election, with 10 percent of men running uncontested in the general election and only 6 percent of women running uncontested. In addition, male and female Republican incumbents also differ in the proportions that enjoy a "free pass" and face no competi-tion at either stage: 8 percent of men and only 5 percent of women. Thus, while female Democratic incumbents face more competition in general elections, female Republican incumbents face more competition in their primaries. These results demonstrate that the competitive environment is, in part, a product of an interaction between gender and party.

The relationship between the sex of the incumbent and competition should not be confined to contests within the party. If, as we hypothesize, female incumbents are perceived as vulnerable, then there should be greater competition for the nomination within the opposition party as well. As Table 5.5 shows, competition for the opposition-party nomination is significantly greater in districts with a female incumbent. When a female incumbent is running for reelection, there are contested primaries in the opposition party in 48 percent of the districts. When a male incumbent is running for reelection, there are contested primaries in the opposition party in 42 percent of the districts. For example, in 2006, Representative Melissa Bean, a Democratic incumbent from the Eighth District of Illinois, ran for her second term. She defeated Republican incumbent Phil Crane two years prior with 52 percent of the vote. In her reelection campaign, she ran unopposed in her own primary, but six Republicans, including one woman, ran in the opposition primary. In the general election, she defeated former investment banker David McSweeney with 54 percent of the vote.

This relationship holds for both parties, although competition is more intense in Republican districts. When a female Democrat is the incumbent, 46 percent of Republican primaries are contested, compared to 40 percent of districts where the Democratic incumbent is male. Similarly, when a female Republican holds the House seat, 53 percent of the Democratic nominees are chosen in contested primaries, compared to 45 percent when the incumbent is a Republican male. Together, Tables 5.4 and 5.5 show that fe-

Table 5.5   Contested Primary Elections for the US House Within the Opposition Party, 1956–2010

	Districts with Male Incumbents	Districts with Female Incumbents
All opposition contests in districts where an incumbent seeks reelection	42.1% (3,527/8,385)	47.8%[a] (339/709)
Contested Republican primaries in districts with Democratic incumbent seeking reelection	39.6% (1,786/4,509)	45.5%[a] (215/473)
Contested Democratic primaries in districts with Republican incumbent seeking reelection	44.9% (1,741/3,876)	52.5%[a] (124/236)

Source: Data compiled by the authors.
Note: a. $p < 0.05$.

male incumbents are associated with a more competitive electoral environment; they face more contested races than their male colleagues and, at the same time, foster more contested primary races within the opposition party.

While this suggests that female incumbents face more competition than male incumbents in general, do they draw other women into the campaign? In other words, are women more likely to run against women than men? Table 5.6 reports the proportion of contested primaries in which women challenged an incumbent of their own party and an incumbent of the opposition party. Additionally, to provide a composite picture of female challengers, we combine the first two rows of the table and report the total proportion of women seeking the nomination in districts held by male and female incumbents. The table shows that female incumbents foster additional female candidacies in a district. Among all incumbents, the proportion of female incumbents being challenged by a woman in their own party primary, 17 percent, exceeds the rate at which women challenge male incumbents, 12 percent. This intraparty gender effect is more pronounced among Democrats than Republicans. Female Democrats are challenged by women in 20 percent of contested primaries, while male Democrats are challenged by women in 13 percent of the contests. Among Republicans, the difference is small and not significant. Women challenge female Republicans in 10 percent of the contests, while male incumbents face a female opponent in 11 percent of the contested Republican primaries.

Table 5.6 also reveals that female incumbents seeking reelection influence the gender distribution of candidates seeking the nomination within the opposition party. Women are significantly more likely to seek the nomination of the opposition party in districts with a female incumbent, 22 percent, than in districts with a male incumbent, 12 percent. This relationship holds for both parties. Democratic women are more likely to run in districts held by female Republicans, 23 percent, than in districts held by male Republicans, 16 percent. The difference is larger in districts with Democratic incumbents. The presence of Republican women as candidates is greater in districts held by female Democrats, 21 percent, than in districts held by male Democrats, 9 percent.

Finally, the third row of Table 5.6 presents the aggregate picture of primary elections for the House. The presence of additional female candidates is significantly greater in districts where a female incumbent holds the seat. This relationship holds in districts held by Democrats, 21 versus 10 percent, in those controlled by Republicans, 21 versus 15 percent, and in the aggregate, 21 versus 12 percent. This suggests that female incumbents do provide, as role models or as testaments to the "winability" of the district, a signal that leads other women to run for the seat.

Table 5.6 Female Competition in Contested Primary Elections for the US House, 1956–2010

	All Male Incumbents	All Female Incumbents	Male Democratic Incumbents	Female Democratic Incumbents	Male Republican Incumbents	Female Republican Incumbents
Within incumbent party Incumbent faces a primary challenge from a female candidate	12.1% (348/2,870)	17.1%[a] (42/245)	12.8% (257/2,007)	20.0%[a] (35/175)	10.5% (91/863)	10.0% (7/70)
Within opposition party Female candidate seeks nomination within the opposition party	12.0% (1,202/9,996)	21.9%[a] (170/777)	9.2% (523/5,699)	21.1%[a] (111/527)	15.8% (679/4,297)	23.2%[a] (59/250)
Within incumbent and opposition party (sum of rows 1 and 2) Proportion of elections with a female challenger for the nomination	12.0% (1,550/12,866)	20.7%[a] (212/1,022)	10.1% (780/7,706)	20.8%[a] (146/702)	14.9% (770/5,160)	20.6%[a] (66/320)

Source: Data compiled by the authors.
Note: a. $p < 0.05$.

Moreover, within the opposition, not only do women seek the nomination more frequently in districts held by female incumbents, but they win the nomination more frequently in these districts as well. Table 5.7 presents the percentage of nominations won by female candidates in the opposition party. Across all of these opportunities, the success rate for women in districts with a female incumbent is significantly higher than the rate in districts with male incumbents. The relationship also holds for both Democrats and Republicans. In fact, the Republican difference in success rates, 13 versus 6 percent, is larger than the rate among female Democrats seeking the nomination in Republican-held districts, 16 versus 11 percent. The results in Table 5.7 lend further credence to our earlier observation that the presence of a female incumbent may serve as a signal about the electoral prospects for women in a district. Because more women seek and win nominations in districts with a female incumbent, the presence of a female incumbent is likely to be a salient factor in the strategic decisions women make about where to run.

An additional question that arises is whether the effect of female incumbents on the competitive environment varies with the level of electoral security. Table 5.8 presents seven measures of the electoral environment for "marginal" male and female incumbents. We define a marginal district as one in which the incumbent won with less than 55 percent of the vote in the previous election. There are significant differences between safe fe-

Table 5.7   Women Winning the Nomination of the Opposition Party in US House Districts Where an Incumbent Seeks Reelection, 1956–2010

Opposition Party	Districts Held by Male Incumbent	Districts Held by Female Incumbent
All opposition nominations, Democrat and Republican, in districts where an incumbent seeks reelection	7.9% (807/10,225)	14.1%[a] (112/796)
Democrats running in districts where a Republican incumbent seeks reelection	10.9% (478/4,389)	15.6%[a] (40/256)
Republicans running in districts where a Democratic incumbent seeks reelection	5.6% (329/5,836)	13.3%[a] (72/540)

Source: Data compiled by the authors.
Notes: The cell entries represent the proportion of nomination opportunities won by female candidates, including contested primaries, uncontested primaries, and convention nominations.
   a. $p < 0.05$.

male incumbents and their male counterparts on six of the seven indicators. In districts with female incumbents, there are substantially fewer uncontested general elections, 10 percent versus 18 percent for men, and fewer "free passes," 7 percent versus 13 percent for men. In this sense, women actually enjoy less of the electoral security that is conventionally attributed to holding a safe seat. The table shows that women from safe districts do face, albeit narrowly, more primary challenges, and that a significantly greater proportion of these challenges come from women.

Safe female incumbents also stimulate more competition within the opposition party. There were contested primaries in the opposition party in 45 percent of the districts with safe female incumbents, while there were contested primaries in the opposition party in 39 percent of the districts with safe male incumbents. Safe female incumbents also promote greater

Table 5.8   Electoral Competition for Incumbents Seeking Reelection, 1956–2010

	Safe Male Incumbent	Safe Female Incumbent	Marginal Male Incumbent	Marginal Female Incumbent
Uncontested general election	18.3% (1,576/8,609)	10.4%[a] (71/678)	2.8% (45/1,616)	0.8% (1/118)
Incumbent faces contested primary	29.2% (2,453/8,386)	31.1% (206/662)	27.0% (417/1,543)	34.8%[a] (39/112)
Incumbent not contested in primary or general election	13.2% (1,137/8,609)	7.1%[a] (48/678)	2.0% (32/1,616)	0.8% (1/118)
Incumbent challenged by female in party primary	12.4% (304/2,453)	17.5%[a] (36/206)	10.6% (44/417)	15.4% (6/39)
Contested primary in opposition party	39.2% (2,691/6,863)	44.6%[a] 267/598)	54.9% (836/1,522)	64.9%[a] (72/111)
Female seeks nomination in opposition party	11.4% (960/8,430)	19.9%[a] (132/665)	15.4% (242/1,566)	33.9%[a] (38/112)
Female wins nomination in opposition party	7.7% (660/8,609)	12.8%[a] (87/678)	9.1% (147/1,616)	21.2%[a] (25/118)

Source: Data compiled by the authors.
Note: a. $p < 0.05$.

participation by women within the opposition party. In 20 percent of the districts with safe female incumbents, women ran in the opposition party's primary. This occurred in only 11 percent of the districts with male incumbents. Moreover, women were more likely to win the opposition-party primary in these districts; female candidates in opposition-party primaries won the nomination in 13 percent of the districts with safe female incumbents, while they won in 8 percent of the districts with safe male incumbents. Our analysis suggests, in general elections, not only that safe female incumbents face more competition than safe male incumbents, but also that the competition is more likely to be female.

A remarkable illustration is found in the electoral career of Republican representative Connie Morella. Morella was first elected in 1986 from Maryland's Eighth District, which wraps around the northern half of Washington, D.C. A large proportion of her constituents were federal employees, and the district has always leaned Democratic. As a result, throughout her career, Morella was one of the most liberal Republicans in the House. As Table 5.9 shows, only in 1996 did she face any major competition in her own primary. She was never challenged by a Republican woman. However, there always was a great deal of competition within the Democratic primary. In 1996, for example, there were nine candidates in the Democratic primary, even though Morella won the previous election with over 70 percent of the vote. Several of the challengers in the Democratic primary were women, but none of them ever won the nomination. The level of competition is quite surprising in light of the "safeness" of her district. Despite the fact that Morella was a Republican in a Democratic district, she was quite popular among her constituents. Until 2000, she consistently won reelection with at least 60 percent of the vote. In fact, her average two-party vote for all of her successful reelection campaigns was 65 percent. During the redistricting cycle in the wake of the 2000 US Census, Maryland's state legislature substantially redrew her district, making it even more Democratic. As a result, in 2002, state senator Chris Van Hollen won a four-way primary that included one woman, and then went on to defeat Morella in one of the most expensive and highly contested races of the year.[89] He won with only 52 percent of the vote.

Table 5.8 shows that there have been only forty-eight safe female incumbents who enjoyed a "free pass" and had no competition in their primary or general elections. Twenty-two of these races, 46 percent, occurred during the most recent redistricting period, from 2002 to 2010. Only three of these races involved female Republicans. In both 2002 and 2004, Representative Jo Ann Davis (R-VA) was unopposed in her primaries and faced only token third-party candidates in her general election contests. In

2004, Representative Marsha Blackburn (R-TN) was running for her second term; although the Democratic Party did not field an opponent, she spent over $575,000 on her campaign.[90] Of the nineteen contests where female Democrats enjoyed "free passes," fifteen involved African American and Latina incumbents; all represented majority-minority districts. The average vote for the Democratic presidential candidate in these districts was 75 percent. This suggests that women of color, who tend to come from racially gerrymandered districts, may be more secure electorally than white women. In the aggregate, however, the number of safe female incumbents who face no competition is substantially lower than the number of safe male incumbents.

The environment for marginal female incumbents is even more competitive. As Table 5.8 shows, marginal female incumbents face a significantly higher rate of primary challenges than their male colleagues, 35 percent versus 27 percent. Over the time period of our study, only one marginal female incumbent, Niki Tsongas (D-MA), enjoyed an uncontested primary and general election. Tsongas was first elected to the House in a 2007 special election to replace Martin Meehan, who retired to become chancellor of the University of Massachusetts. To win this seat, she first defeated four Democrats in the primary; in the general election, Tsongas faced Republican Jim Ogonowski, a retired Air Force officer whose brother was the murdered pilot of the first aircraft to hit the World Trade Center on September 11, 2001.[91] Tsongas won the general election with 51 percent of the vote. In 2008, she became the first and only marginal female

Table 5.9 Representative Connie Morella (R-MD) and Her Competition

	Her Primary Opponents	Democratic Primary Opponents	Female Democratic Primary Opponents	Her Vote Total in the General Election (percentage)
1986[a]	2	7	1	52.9
1988	0	5	1	62.7
1990	1	3	0	76.8
1992	0	8	0	72.5
1994	1	5	0	70.3
1996	3	9	2	61.3
1998	1	7	1	60.3
2000	0	5	3	53.1
2002	0	4	1	48.3

Source: Data compiled by the authors.
Note: a. Open seat.

incumbent to earn the "free pass." In contrast, forty-five marginal male incumbents faced no primary competition and thirty-two of these faced no major party competition in the general election.

With respect to competition within the opposition party, Table 5.8 shows there are also substantial differences between men and women from marginal districts. As expected, the data show that marginal districts are more competitive than safe districts in general, but there is a clear gender effect; 65 percent of marginal districts with female incumbents had contested primaries in the opposition party, compared to only 55 percent of the marginal districts with male incumbents. Representative Stephanie Herseth Sandlin (D-SD), for example, who won a special election in the summer of 2004 with only 51 percent of the two-party vote, saw seven male Republicans competing to challenge her reelection in the fall. Moreover, marginal female incumbents were more than twice as likely to draw female candidates into the opposition primary. In 34 percent of the districts with marginal female incumbents, women ran in the opposition primary, compared to 15 percent of the districts with marginal male incumbents. And women were over twice as likely to win the opposition primary in districts with marginal female incumbents. Women won the opposition primary in 21 percent of districts with marginal female incumbents, while they won in only 9 percent of districts with marginal male incumbents. As Table 5.8 reveals, in marginal districts, female incumbents not only stimulate more competition within the opposition party, but also draw more women of the opposition party into the fray.

■ Conclusion

Although historically there is an apparent equality among male and female incumbents with respect to reelection rates and margins of victory, if we look more deeply at the competitive environment, we find significant differences between men and women seeking reelection to the House. While there are variations between the parties, women running for reelection face a more competitive environment than their male counterparts in two ways. First, female incumbents face more competition. They foster more competition in the opposition party's primary. They are less likely to face no competition in the general election. They are also less likely to get the "free pass" and face no opposition in the primary and general elections.

Second, the presence of a female incumbent encourages more women to run. Female incumbents face more challenges from female candidates in primary elections. Within the opposition party in particular, more women run as challengers. Interestingly, it appears that the presence of female in-cumbents actually helps their female opponents. Women running in oppo-sition primaries are more likely to win in districts held by female incumbents. Ultimately, this shows that, despite comparable reelection rates, female incumbents have to work harder than male incumbents to re-tain their seats.

Our results thus reveal that female incumbents have a "hidden influ-ence." Their presence increases the entry and participation of female can-didates in House elections. The more women who serve in the House of Representatives, the more women run. On one hand, this enhances the rep-resentative character of House elections. It also has a secondary and salu-tary effect of increasing awareness and activity among female voters within a district.[92] On the other hand, given where these women are more likely to run—in districts with female incumbents—the overall number of women in the House will not necessarily increase under these circum-stances. Female candidacies are disproportionately concentrated in dis-tricts already represented by women. Once a woman is elected, she faces higher probabilities of being challenged for renomination by a woman and facing a female opponent in the general election. As a result, the increase in competition associated with female incumbents does not trigger changes in the gender composition of the House. While the presence of female in-cumbents encourages more women to run, incumbency continues to act as a barrier, impeding the increase in the number of women who serve in Congress. Despite the gains evidenced by women over time, our results demonstrate that the impact of incumbency is gendered and, consequently, the "playing field" for House elections has yet to become entirely level for male and female incumbents.

▓ Notes

1. Stevens, "The Strength of These Women Shows in Their Numbers."
2. For a discussion of the success of women in open seats see, for example, Bernstein, "Might Women Have the Edge in Open-Seat House Primaries?"; Bur-rell, "Women Candidates in Open-Seat Primaries for the US House"; Hoffman, Palmer, and Gaddie, "Candidate Sex and Congressional Elections."
3. But see Berch, "Women Incumbents, Elite Bias, and Voter Response." Neil Berch found that female incumbents faced better-funded challengers than male in-cumbents.
4. Foerstel, *Biographical Dictionary of Congressional Women,* pp. 210–211.
5. Mills, "Mr. Vacationland and Why We Can't Forget the Lady from Rumford."
6. The little research that does exist provides conflicting findings. Robert Bernstein's analysis of the 1992 and 1994 elections found that a woman had a sub-

stantial edge in winning an open seat primary when she was the lone female candidate running against two or more men; in primaries with multiple women candidates, a woman was less likely to win; Bernstein, "Why Are There So Few Women in the House?" Richard Fox, however, in his assessment of 1992 California congressional races, found just the opposite; in primaries with multiple women candidates, all of the women tended to do better than the men; Fox, *Gender Dynamics in Congressional Elections.* See also Bernstein, "Might Women Have the Edge in Open-Seat House Primaries?"; Burrell, "Women Candidates in Open-Seat Primaries for the US House."

7. Here, it is especially important to note that we are referring only to the two major parties. Prior to the 1950s, many women ran as third-party candidates. See Simon and Palmer, "Women as Third Party Candidates in Elections to the US House of Representatives."

8. A link to the ad is available at "Dole Still Keeping the Faith," www.politico.com/blogs/scorecard/1008/Dole_still_keeping_the_faith.html (accessed September 15, 2011).

9. Foerstel and Foerstel, *Climbing the Hill,* p. 75.

10. Dewar, "NY Senate Primary Gets Muddy Near the Wire," p. A3. See also Frankel, "Anything Goes in NY Primary," p. 10A.

11. Stanley, "In Primary Race for Senate, Ads Are Costly and Caustic," p. 1.

12. *Women in Congress,* pp. 629–630.

13. Ibid., pp. 617–618.

14. Burrell, "Women Candidates in Open-Seat Primaries for the US House"; Burrell, *A Woman's Place Is In the House;* Darcy and Schramm, "When Women Run Against Men"; Darcy, Welch, and Clark, *Women, Elections, and Representation;* Gaddie and Bullock, "Congressional Elections and the Year of the Woman"; Palmer and Simon, "Breaking the Logjam"; Seltzer, Newman, and Leighton, *Sex as a Political Variable;* Welch et al., "The Effect of Candidate Gender on Election Outcomes in State Legislative Races." But see Fox, Lawless, and Feeley, "Gender and the Decision to Run for Office"; Fox and Oxley, "Gender Stereotyping in State Executive Elections."

15. We define a safe seat as winning with 55 percent or more of the two-party vote.

16. Niven and Zilber, "'How Does She Have Time for Kids and Congress?'" p. 154.

17. Bystrom et al., *Gender and Candidate Communication,* p. 179.

18. Bystrom et al., *Gender and Candidate Communication;* Kahn and Goldenberg, "Women Candidates in the News." See also Kropf and Boiney, "The Electoral Glass Ceiling?"; Niven and Zilber, "'How Does She Have Time for Kids and Congress?'"; Norris, "Women Leaders Worldwide."

19. Bystrom, "Advertising, Web Sites, and Media Coverage"; Carroll and Schreiber, "Media Coverage of Women in the 103rd Congress"; Clift and Brazaitis, *Madam President,* 1st and 2nd eds.; Falk, *Women for President;* Fowler and Lawless, "Looking for Sex in All the Wrong Places"; Heldman, Carroll, and Olson, "'She Brought Only a Skirt'"; Iyengar et al., "Running As a Woman"; Kahn, "Characteristics of Press Coverage in Senate and Gubernatorial Elections"; Kahn, *The Political Consequences of Being a Woman;* Niven and Zilber, "'How Does She Have Time for Kids and Congress?'"; Schroeder, *Twenty-four Years of House Work and the Place Is Still a Mess;* Watson and Gordon, *Anticipating Madam President;* Witt,

Paget, and Matthews, *Running As a Woman.* For analyses of media coverage of Hillary Clinton's presidential campaign, see Carroll, "Reflections on Gender and Hillary Clinton's Presidential Campaign"; Deckman and Goldstein, "Style or Substance?"; Kornblut, *Notes from the Cracked Ceiling;* Lawrence and Rose, *Hillary Clinton's Race for the White House;* Miller, Peake, and Boulton, "Testing the *Saturday Night Live* Hypothesis"; Traister, *Big Girls Don't Cry.*

20. Witt, Paget, and Matthews, *Running As a Woman,* p. 184.

21. Molinari, *Representative Mom,* p. 7.

22. Braden, *Women Politicians and the Media;* Bystrom et al., *Gender and Candidate Communication;* Dolan, Deckman, and Swers, *Women and Politics;* Fox, *Gender Dynamics in Congressional Elections;* Jamieson, *Beyond the Double Bind;* Niven and Zilber, "'How Does She Have Time for Kids and Congress?'"; Wilson, *Closing the Leadership Gap.*

23. Witt, Paget, and Matthews, *Running As a Woman,* pp. 184–185. See also Giles, *Flight of the Dove,* p. 83.

24. Witt, Paget, and Matthews, *Running As a Woman,* p. 186.

25. Foerstel, *Biographical Dictionary of Congressional Women,* p. 231.

26. Givhan, "Hillary Clinton's Tentative Dip Into New Neckline Territory."

27. Lewis, "Hillary for President."

28. Alpert, "Critics of Sen. Mary Landrieu Presented As Examples by Sexism Watchdogs."

29. Rucker, "In South Dakota, Democrats' Own 'Mama Grizzly' vs. 'The Next Sarah Palin.'"

30. See, for example, Gulati and Williams, "Communicating with Constituents in 140 Characters or Less"; Haynes and Pitt, "Making an Impression"; Heaney, "Blogging Congress"; Lassen and Brown, "Twitter."

31. For a list of particularly egregious examples, see "Name It, Change It: Awards for the Most Sexist Media Coverage in the 2010 Elections."

32. "I Had a One-Night Stand with Christine O'Donnell."

33. Niven and Zilber, "'How Does She Have Time for Kids and Congress?'" p. 149.

34. "Miss Rankin—Sobbing—Votes No," p. 1.

35. Giles, *Flight of the Dove,* p. 83.

36. "Miss Rankin—Sobbing—Votes No," p. 1.

37. See, for example, Clift and Brazaitis, *Madam President,* 1st ed.; Schroeder, *Twenty-four Years of House Work and the Place Is Still a Mess.*

38. Schroeder, *Twenty-four Years of House Work and the Place Is Still a Mess,* p. 185.

39. Witt, Paget, and Matthews, *Running As a Woman,* p. 205.

40. Phillips, "Shake-Up in the Governor's Race," p. A1.

41. Fenn, "Swift Sent Women a Bad Message."

42. Breslau, "Hillary Tears Up."

43. Healy, "On Eve of Primary, Clinton's Campaign Shows Stress."

44. See, for example, Fox and Friends, "For Crying Out Loud"; Paglia, "Hillary Without Tears."

45. Dowd, "Can Hillary Clinton Cry Her Way Back to the White House?"

46. "Stunner in New Hampshire."

47. Schroeder, *Twenty-four Years of House Work and the Place Is Still a Mess,* p. 186.

48. White, *The Making of the President, 1972*, pp. 84–87.

49. For a video of his speech, see Wing, "John Boehner Tries Not to Cry."

50. "John Boehner: Real Men Do Cry."

51. For the YouTube clip of Boehner's reaction, see "Boehner's Tears."

52. Karl, "John Boehner Cries Amid Government Shutdown Standoff."

53. Gilbert, "Go Ahead—It's Okay to Cry."

54. Boxer, *Strangers in the Senate*, p. 82.

55. See, for example, Dolan, *Voting for Women;* Seltzer, Newman, and Leighton, *Sex as a Political Variable.* This may not, however, be true for presidential candidates; see, for example, Paul and Smith, "Subtle Sexism?"

56. "Turning Point, 2010." See also Bystrom, "Advertising, Web Sites, and Media Coverage."

57. Alexander and Anderson, "Gender as a Factor in the Attribution of Leadership Traits"; Brown, Heighberger, and Shocket, "Gender-Based Differences in Perceptions of Male and Female City Council Candidates"; Burrell, *A Woman's Place Is In the House;* Fridkin and Kenny, "The Role of Gender Stereotypes in US Senate Elections"; Huddy and Terkildsen, "The Consequences of Gender Stereotypes for Women Candidates"; Huddy and Terkildsen, "Gender Stereotypes and the Perception of Male and Female Candidates"; Leeper, "The Impact of Prejudice on Female Candidates"; Niven, "Party Elites and Women Candidates"; Sanbonmatsu, "Gender Stereotypes and Vote Choice"; Taylor, "Women and Political Leadership."

58. Taylor, "Women and Political Leadership."

59. "Turning Point, 2010."

60. Brooks, "Testing the Double Standard for Candidate Emotionality."

61. Fox and Oxley, "Gender Stereotyping in State Executive Elections"; Koch, "Gender Stereotypes and Citizens' Impressions of House Candidates' Ideological Orientations"; Petrocik, "Issue Ownership in Presidential Elections."

62. Alexander and Andersen, "Gender as a Factor in the Attribution of Leadership Traits"; Bystrom et al., *Gender and Candidate Communication;* Carroll, *Women as Candidates in American Politics;* Delli Carpini and Fuchs, "The Year of the Woman?"; Dolan, "Electoral Context, Issues, and Voting for Women in the 1990s"; Huddy and Terkildsen, "The Consequences of Gender Stereotypes for Women Candidates"; Huddy and Terkildsen, "Gender Stereotypes and the Perception of Male and Female Candidates"; Fox and Oxley, "Gender Stereotyping in State Executive Elections"; Kaufman and Petrocik, "The Changing Politics of American Men"; Leeper, "The Impact of Prejudice on Female Candidates"; Sanbonmatsu, "Gender Stereotypes and Vote Choice"; Sanbonmatsu and Dolan, "Do Gender Stereotypes Transcend Party?"; "Turning Point, 2010." But see Dolan, *Voting for Women;* Fridkin and Kenney, "The Role of Gender Stereotypes in US Senate Elections." For a review of this literature, see Swers, "Research on Women in Legislatures."

63. Petrocik, "Issue Ownership in Presidential Elections."

64. Alexander and Anderson, "Gender as a Factor in the Attribution of Leadership Traits"; Huddy and Terkildsen, "Gender Stereotypes and the Perception of Male and Female Candidates"; Koch, "Do Citizens Apply Gender Stereotypes to Infer Candidates' Ideological Orientations?"; Sanbonmatsu and Dolan, "Do Gender Stereotypes Transcend Party?"

65. "Turning Point, 2010." See also King and Matland, "Sex and the Grand Old Party."

66. Atkeson, "Not All Cues Are Created Equal"; King and Matland, "Sex and the Grand Old Party"; Koch, "Do Citizens Apply Gender Stereotypes to Infer Candidates' Ideological Orientations?"; Koch, "Gender Stereotypes and Citizens' Impressions of House Candidates' Ideological Orientations"; Lau and Redlawsk, "Advantages and Disadvantages of Cognitive Heuristics in Political Decision Making"; McDermott, "Voting Cues in Low-Information Elections"; McDermott, "Race and Gender Cues in Low-Information Elections"; Sanbonmatsu, "Gender Stereotypes and Vote Choice"; Sanbonmatsu and Dolan, "Do Gender Stereotypes Transcend Party?" But see Thompson and Steckenrider, "The Relative Irrelevance of Candidate Sex."

67. Koch, "Do Citizens Apply Gender Stereotypes to Infer Candidates' Ideological Orientations?" p. 414.

68. McDermott, "Voting Cues in Low-Information Elections," p. 271.

69. Koch, "Gender Stereotypes and Citizens' Impression of House Candidates' Ideological Orientations," p. 460. See also Atkeson, "Not All Cues Are Created Equal." But see Hayes, "When Gender and Party Collide."

70. Koch, "Gender Stereotypes and Citizens' Impression of House Candidates' Ideological Orientations," p. 455.

71. See, for example, Bystrom, "Confronting Stereotypes and Double Standards in Campaign Communication"; Mandel, *In the Running;* Lake "Name It, Change It"; "Turning Point, 2010."

72. Fenno, *Home Style,* p. 898.

73. Ibid. See, for example, Bystrom, "Advertising, Web Sites, and Media Coverage"; Dolan, Deckman, and Swers, *Women and Politics,* pp. 159–172.

74. Mandel, *In the Running,* p. 36.

75. Witt, Paget, and Matthews, *Running As a Woman,* p. 214.

76. Peoples and Brady, "Playing Partisan from Her Hill Perch."

77. "Turning Point, 2010."

78. Ibid.

79. Lake, "Name It, Change It," p. 27.

80. Witt, Paget, and Matthews, *Running As a Woman,* p. 214.

81. See Herrnson, Lay, and Stokes, "Women Running 'As Women'"; Iyengar et al., "Running As a Woman"; Sanbonmatsu, "Gender Stereotypes and Vote Choice"; Shames, "The 'Un-Candidates'"; Williams, "Gender, Political Advertising, and the 'Air Wars'"; Witt, Paget, and Matthews, *Running As a Woman.* But see Perkins and Fowlkes, "Opinion Representation Versus Social Representation."

82. See, for example, Stevens, "The Strength of These Women Shows in Their Numbers," p. 2625.

83. Koch, "Gender Stereotypes and Citizens' Impression of House Candidates' Ideological Orientations."

84. Atkeson, "Not All Cues Are Created Equal," p. 1042. But see Dolan, "Symbolic Mobilization?" Kathleen Dolan found that there is no systematic evidence that female candidates mobilize the public toward more political engagement, but she did find that there was a greater impact in House races than Senate races.

85. Hansen, "Talking About Politics"; High-Pippert, "Female Empowerment." See also Campbell and Wolbrecht, "See Jane Run"; Lawless, "Politics of Presence?" But see Stokes-Brown and Neal, "Does 'Running As a Woman' Mobilize Voters?"

86. See, for example, Cooperman and Oppenheimer, "The Gender Gap in the House of Representatives"; Palmer and Simon, "Breaking the Logjam"; Palmer

and Simon, "Political Ambition and Women in the US House of Representatives"; Rule, "Why Women Don't Run." But see Schwarz, "Election Behavior with High Female Representation."

87. The full statistical tests are available in Palmer and Simon, "When Women Run Against Women."

88. For each male-female comparison in Tables 5.4 to 5.8, we use a standard t-test for the difference in proportions.

89. Koszczuk and Stern, *CQ's Politics in America, 2006,* p. 485.

90. "Marsha Blackburn"; Sullivan, "Safe Territory," p. B1.

91. Barone and Cohen, *Almanac of American Politics, 2010,* p. 744.

92. Atkeson, "Not All Cues Are Created Equal"; Hansen, "Talking About Politics."

SIX

Red vs. Blue:
A History of the Party Gap

In 1966, the distribution of female House members between the two parties was virtually equal: six of the eleven women in the US House of Representatives were Democrats, while five were Republicans. In 2008, of the seventy-four women elected to the House, fifty-seven, or 77 percent, were Democrats, and only seventeen were Republicans. With the Republican takeover of the House in 2010, GOP women did catch up some: only 67 percent of the seventy-two women elected were Democrats, and 33 percent were Republicans. Even with the tremendous gains made by the Republican Party in 2010, this still meant that two-thirds of the women in the House were Democrats. Since the early 1970s, as explored in Chapter 2, the number of women running and winning primary and general elections has generally been increasing. But there is something else happening beneath these overall patterns of participation. What accounts for the development of this tremendous "party gap"?

Thus far, the forces that we have considered in understanding women's success as candidates have not been partisan. Neither the events of the 1970s that helped to trigger an increase in the activism of women as candidates, nor the factors that influenced women to pursue careers in elective office, are grounded in party differences. In this chapter, however, we show that the "arrested development" seen in the integration of women into Congress does have a partisan component. The observed change in women seeking and winning office highlighted in Chapter 2 has not been uniform across both parties. Since the early 1990s, the growth of women as candidates and officeholders has occurred disproportionately within the Democratic Party. Further, this Democratic advantage in electing women is not restricted to the US House; it is evident across multiple levels of the political hierarchy. Ultimately, the gap that has developed between the propor-

161

tions of Democratic and Republican women in Congress is not particularly well explained by looking at the overall electoral fortunes of the parties or by looking in the "pipeline." There are clues, however, that lie in the perceptions of female candidates held by party leaders.

■ The Growth of the Party Gap in Congress

Except for those localities that use nonpartisan elections, virtually all candidates for public office have a party label after their name. However, campaigns often downplay or barely mention party affiliation; in many cases, candidates try very hard to separate themselves from their party. As campaigns have become increasingly candidate-centered, particularly over the past three decades, many argue that political parties have lost much of their power and control over elections.[1] For example, in the 2010 Nevada race for the Senate, the state Republican Party endorsed Sue Lowden to challenge the extremely vulnerable Senate majority leader Harry Reid (D-NV). In January 2010, Reid had a 52 percent unfavorable rating among registered voters, and polls showed him losing to Lowden by 10 points.[2] Lowden was the Republican state party chair. During the primary, Lowden made national headlines when she criticized Barack Obama's healthcare reforms and argued that bartering chickens in exchange for a checkup would be a better way to pay for healthcare.[3] Despite the fact that Lowden was the state party leader, she lost the primary to Sharron Angle, a former member of the Nevada assembly. Angle's rift with Republican Party leaders was no secret during her campaign. She claimed that "no one was more shocked" than Republicans on Capitol Hill when she won: "When I went back to Washington, DC, they were still moaning and groaning and weeping and gnashing teeth over Sue Lowden. . . . Republicans have lost their standards, they've lost their principles."[4] Polls in June showed her with a 7-point lead over Reid.[5] After a "bitter destroy-the-opponent-at-all-costs" general election campaign that left voters "hating" both candidates, Reid won a fifth term with 53 percent of the vote.[6] Over 16,000 people voted for "None of These Candidates."

Parties do, however, still play a critical role in recruiting and providing assistance to candidates.[7] In fact, the 2008 Center for American Women and Politics (CAWP) Recruitment Study of state legislators found that party leaders and legislative officials were the most influential sources of encouragement for potential candidates—and also had the biggest impact when trying to discourage candidacies and talk people out of running.[8] The 2008 Citizen Political Ambition Study of potential candidates found that encouragement from party leaders and elected officials was the single most important predictor of whether or not someone considered running.[9]

Interestingly, the first women to run for Congress did so eschewing major party labels. Elizabeth Cady Stanton, the first woman to run for the US House in 1866, ran as an Independent. The first woman to run for the US Senate was Mary Elizabeth Lease, who ran in Kansas in 1893 as a Populist Party candidate. The Populist Party, also known as the People's Party, was one of the "most significant" third parties in US history.[10] As a paid traveling lecturer for the party, Lease gave hundreds of speeches in Kansas and across the country,[11] and the *Topeka State Journal* called her "the most famous woman orator of the century."[12] The character of Dorothy in *The Wizard of Oz* is rumored to be a representation of Lease.[13] When Lease ran for the Senate in 1893, senators were chosen by state legislatures. The *New York Times* noted that "her popularity with the rank and file of the [Populist] party will give her at least an equal chance with other aspirants."[14] The Kansas legislature, however, selected John Martin, a Democrat.[15]

Historically, the two major parties have been ambivalent toward women as voters and candidates.[16] Prior to the passage of the Nineteenth Amendment in 1920, which constitutionally guaranteed women the right to vote, to the extent that they paid attention at all, the national Democratic and Republican Party organizations feared that if women were enfranchised, they would form their own parties and separate groups, creating a "petticoat hierarchy which may at will upset all orderly slates and commit undreamed of executions at the polls."[17] For example, party leaders reacted to the proposed creation of the League of Women Voters "with horror."[18] When the Nineteenth Amendment finally passed, both parties attempted to give women leadership roles, particularly with regard to the mobilization of new female voters.[19] In the wake of the overwhelming defeat of the Democrats in 1920, the Democratic National Committee itself was "little more than a skeleton."[20] During the 1920s, the Democratic Party's very survival depended on the women who volunteered through the Women's Division and the National Woman's Democratic Club.[21] In 1918, the Republican Party created a Women's Division as a permanent part of the Republican National Committee (RNC). In addition, the RNC's Executive Committee was expanded to nineteen, in order to add eight women.[22] By 1930, "women had been absorbed and co-opted; the [two major] parties digested women with only a few burps."[23] In a 1928 interview that appeared in *Redbook,* Eleanor Roosevelt commented that "beneath the veneer of courtesy and outward show of consideration universally accorded women, there is a widespread male hostility . . . against sharing with them any actual control."[24]

One of the ways women quickly became involved in party politics was as delegates to the national conventions.[25] From 1932 to 1968, the proportion of women delegates to the Democratic Party's national convention fluctuated around 12 percent. At the Republican National Convention, women gradually increased from 6 percent of the delegates in 1928 to 18 percent of the delegates in 1968. However, women activists in each party had pushed the goal of having equal numbers of men and women as delegates beginning in the early 1920s.[26] For the Democrats, this would not happen until reforms advocated by the McGovern-Fraser Commission in the wake of the disastrous 1968 convention in Chicago. The commission recommended that women, racial minorities, and youth should be represented in state delegations "in reasonable relationship to their presence in the population of the state."[27] In 1972, 40 percent of the delegates at the national convention were women. In 1980, the Democratic Party changed its rules to mandate gender equity in state delegations, and women have composed approximately 50 percent of all delegates to the national convention since then.[28] While the Republican Party did not adopt a similar mandate, the party did yield to pressure for increasing the number of female delegates. In 1972 the proportion of female delegates increased to 30 percent, in 2004 women composed 40 percent of the delegates, and in 2008 a survey estimated the proportion of women at 32 percent.[29]

For the most part, national party commitments to recruiting and running women for public office have been mostly rhetoric.[30] In 1974, the Democrats created a "Campaign Conference" for women, with the goal of electing more female Democratic candidates. Twelve hundred women attended.[31] More recently, the parties began creating campaign training programs for women at the state level. In 1989, the Lugar Excellence in Public Service series was created, providing political leadership development programs for Republican women in Indiana.[32] By 2011, there were affiliated programs named after prominent Republican women in at least twelve other states. The Democrats began a similar training program, Emerge America, in 2002. A decade later, the programs run in nine states.[33]

In 2010, Republican Party leaders received a great deal of credit for going "out of their way to help female candidates."[34] As Sue Lynch, president of the National Federation of Republican Women, explained, "In the past, it has always been if a [female] candidate pops up, OK, great. Now we're asking women. I don't think anyone had ever asked."[35] For example, the National Republican Congressional Committee (NRCC) brought in Representative Cathy McMorris Rodgers (R-WA) to lead the party's efforts to recruit female candidates to run for the House. Representative Ileana Ros-Lehtinen (R-FL), a twenty-year congressional veteran, remarked that she "did see a stepped-up effort" by party leaders: "They put muscle and might behind it. I'm really happy that our conference woke up from our slumber."[36] Linda Divall, a pollster for the Republican National Committee, urged the party to recruit conservative women as a winning strategy, because they "could appeal to swing voters more successfully than conservative men," given their "outsider" appeal.[37] For example, Nikki Haley, in her successful South Carolina gubernatorial campaign, highlighted the fact that she was not part of the state capital's "frat party,"[38] creating a clear contrast to outgoing Republican governor Mark Sanford. Sanford was a rising star in the party and a 2012 presidential hopeful. In June 2009, he disappeared for almost a week; staff, family, and reporters could not reach him for four days. Eventually, he told his staff that the reason he was "off the grid" was because he was "hiking the Appalachian Trail." He was actually in Argentina visiting his mistress.[39] After an investigation into whether Sanford had used state money to fund his trips, the state legislature began impeachment proceedings, but instead voted to censure him. As one state representative put it, "We can't impeach for hypocrisy."[40] When Sanford's wife of twenty years told their two sons about what was happening, the thirteen-year-old said, "Oh my gosh. This is going to be worse than Eliot Spitzer."[41]

Given the rhetoric from both parties about recruiting female candidates, what do the patterns in the partisan distribution of female congressional candidates look like? Here we disaggregate the general trends of women running in primaries, winning primaries, and winning general elections by party. Figure 6.1 shows the proportion of female candidates that ran in each party's primaries. From 1956 to 1988, for over thirty years, women averaged about 5 percent of all Republican primary candidates and 6 percent of all Democratic primary candidates in a given election cycle. In fact, in seven of the seventeen election cycles, the difference between the proportions of female primary candidates in both parties was less than 1 percent. Beginning in 1990, however, the parties begin to drift apart. By 1996, the gap was significant, with women making up 17 percent of Democratic primary candidates and only 10 percent of Republican primary candidates. Since then, while the proportion of female Democratic primary candidates has continued to increase, reaching 23 percent in 2008, the proportion of female Republican primary candidates has stagnated at approximately 11 percent. The proportion of female Democratic primary candidates slightly declined in 2010 to 21 percent, but this was still greater than any other election cycle prior to 2008.

It is also important to note that for all the hoopla over 2010 being the "Year of the Republican Woman" and the efforts by the party to support fe-

**Figure 6.1   Women as a Proportion of Candidates Seeking
Their Party's Nomination to the US House, 1956–2010**

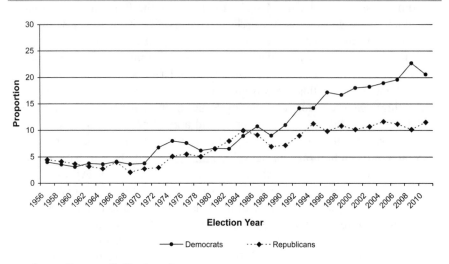

Source: Data compiled by the authors.

male candidates, there was no significant spike in women as a proportion
of Republican candidates; the proportion increased from 10 percent in
2008 to 11 percent in 2010. There was a dramatic increase in the raw number of Republican women who ran in primaries; in 2008 only sixty-four
Republican women ran, while in 2010 this more than doubled to 130, a
record number, nearly matching the 134 Democratic women who ran.
However, this dramatic increase in the number of female Republican candidates was matched with a dramatic increase in the number of male Republican candidates. In the 2008 election cycle, 637 Republicans ran in
primaries. In 2010, this nearly doubled, to 1,138. The number of Republican candidates seeking the nomination in 2010 was a historical high and
was likely a function of both the perceived vulnerability of Democrats as
well as the rise of the Tea Party. The political forces inducing Republican
candidates to run in 2010 were not confined to women. In fact, the proportion of female Republican primary candidates in 2010 was slightly
lower than in 2004, when 12 percent of all Republican primary candidates
were women. Thus the 2010 election did not depart from the twenty-year
trend. For the most part, the proportions of women running in Democratic
and Republican primaries move in near-identical fashion together until the
1990s, when they gradually begin to separate as the proportion of female

Republicans running in primaries levels off and the proportion of female Democrats continues to increase gradually.

The pattern among women winning primaries is similar, but with one noteworthy difference. As Figure 6.2 shows, the proportion of Republican and Democratic women who won House primaries was virtually the same from 1956 to 1990, not unlike the pattern for women running in primaries. During these eighteen election cycles, Republican women won a higher proportion of primaries than Democratic women in eight cycles, and Democratic women won a higher proportion of primaries than Republican women in ten cycles. In 1992, however, the parties suddenly diverged. The proportion of Democratic women winning primaries jumped from 10 percent to 16 percent, while the proportion of Republican women increased by only 1 percentage point, from 7 to 8. Since 1992, the gap between the parties has averaged more than 10 points. In the three most recent election cycles, the proportion of women nominated by the Democrats was more than twice the proportion nominated by the Republicans, 22 versus 11 percent in 2006, 23 versus 10 percent in 2008, the peak year for this party gap, and 22 versus 11 percent in 2010. Since 1992, women running in Republican primaries have not enjoyed the same level of success as Democratic

Figure 6.2   Women as a Proportion of Their Party's Nominees for the US House, 1956–2010

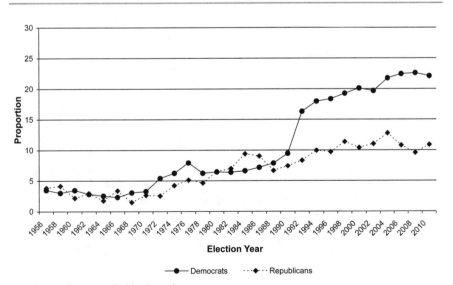

Source: Data compiled by the authors.

women. Republican women appear to be having a harder time winning their primaries.

The trends in the success of women in general election campaigns tell a remarkably similar story in Figure 6.3. Here we measure this success and the "female presence" among Democratic and Republican representatives by calculating the proportion of women in each party's delegation; in other words, we look at women as a percentage of their party's membership in the House. As in the case of primary contestants and nominees, there is no partisan gap from 1956 to 1990. Women as a proportion of all Democrats and Republicans in the House are relatively equal; in twelve of the eighteen election cycles during this period, the difference in the proportion of women that both parties sent to the House is less than 1 percent. Once again, we see a spike for Democratic women in 1992, with the proportion nearly doubling from 7 percent to 14 percent, while Republican women increase from 5 percent to only 7 percent of their party's delegation. Thereafter, the proportion of Democratic women continues to climb, and by 2010 women represent 25 percent of the Democrats in the House. Republican women made much more modest gains during this period, but even with the Republican sweep in 2010, they composed only 10 percent of their party's delegation in the House, less than half the proportion of the Democrats.

Figure 6.3   Women as a Proportion of Their Party's Delegation in the US House, 1956–2010

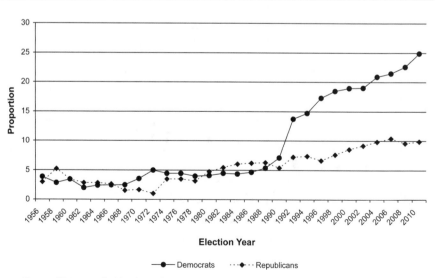

Source: Data compiled by the authors.

Among women running for the Senate, the now-familiar pattern emerges again. As Figures 6.4 and 6.5 show, the proportions of women running in primaries and winning primaries were relatively equal from 1958 until 1986.[42] A gap emerges in the 1988–1992 six-year cycle. This is largely attributable to the 1992 election cycle. In examining the individual elections in this six-year cycle, we find that in 1990 women composed only 6 percent of Democratic Senate primary candidates, while they composed 14 percent of Republican Senate primary candidates. In 1992, the parties switched places, with women as 20 percent of Democratic candidates and only 7 percent of Republican candidates. This switch was even more extreme among women who won primaries. In 1990, 6 percent of the Democrats who won their primaries were women, while an astonishing 18 percent of Republicans were women. Two years later, women composed 28 percent of Democratic Senate primary winners, and a mere 3 percent of Republican primary winners. As Figures 6.4 and 6.5 show, the gap among primary candidates and nominees reached its high point in the 2000–2004 elections. Women as a proportion of Democrats seeking the nomination surpassed the Republican proportion by a margin to 17 to 8 percent; the gap was even larger among nominees, 21 to 6 percent. In the most recent election cycles, 2006–2010, the gaps have narrowed, particularly among primary candidates. Of those Democrats seeking the nomination, 17 percent were women compared to 11

Figure 6.4 Women as a Proportion of Candidates Seeking Their Party's Nomination to the US Senate, 1958–2010

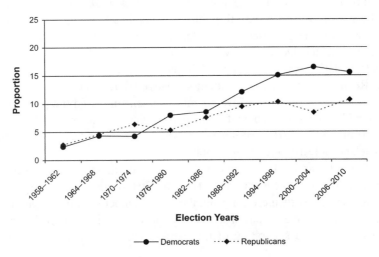

Source: Data compiled by the authors.

Figure 6.5   Women as a Proportion of Their Party's Nominees for the US Senate, 1958–2010

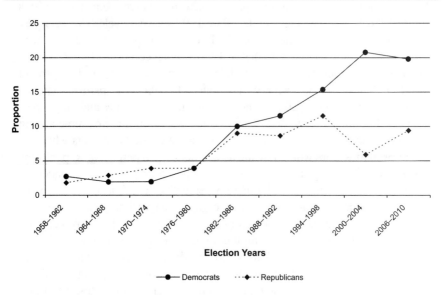

Source: Data compiled by the authors.

percent of the Republican candidates. Among those nominated, 20 percent of the Democrats were women compared to 9 percent of the Republicans.

Figure 6.6 shows the proportion of women in each party's delegation in the Senate. Prior to 1988, while the proportions of Democratic and Republican women were small, Republican women had an edge. In fact, Republican women composed a higher proportion of their party's delegation in the Senate than Democratic women in fourteen of the fifteen election cycles from 1958 to 1986. Only in 1976 did Democratic women fare better than Republican women. This situation changed during the 1988–1992 cycles, when the proportion of Democratic women surpassed the proportion of Republican women. Thereafter the gap widened. As a result of the elections from 2006 to 2010, women composed 22 percent of Democrats in the Senate and only 10 percent of Republicans.

The patterns we have examined suggest that there were two sets of forces operating in the election system. The first, originating in the 1970s, was associated with increasing numbers of Democratic and Republican women entering the electoral arena. The second, emerging in the early 1990s, triggered a separation of the parties. The fortunes of Republican

Figure 6.6   Women as a Proportion of Their Party's Delegation in the US Senate, 1958–2010

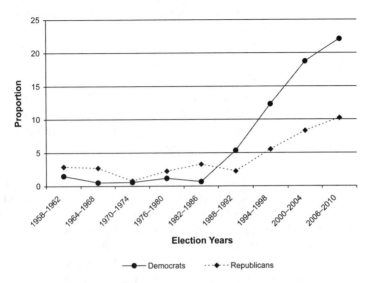

Source: Data compiled by the authors.

women leveled off or even declined, while Democratic women saw increasing success.

■ Explaining the Party Gap

As noted in Chapter 2, 1992 became known as the "Year of the Woman," and many analyses have correctly pointed out that the dramatic increase in the number of women winning a seat in Congress in this election cycle was largely a Democratic phenomenon.[43] On the other hand, the gap between the parties in the number of women running in congressional primaries predates 1992. And even if Democratic women had an unusually good year in 1992, why would the proportion of Republican women subsequently stall? Having illustrated the emergence and growth of a partisan gap in congressional primary and general elections, we next consider possible factors that may be useful in understanding these partisan trends: the overall success of the parties, the pipeline, and the perceptions of voters and party leaders.

The Success of the Parties

One possible explanation for the changes in the electoral success of women might be changes in the electoral success of the parties. In other words, when the Democratic Party has a good year and increases its delegation in the House, the number of women might increase as well. The same logic would apply to the Republicans. The expectation is that the overall success of a party is correlated with the success of its female delegation.

Figure 6.7 displays the proportion of each party's delegation in the House after each election from 1956 to 2010. Most noteworthy is that the size of the Democratic delegation actually dropped in 1992, with a loss of ten seats. The Democratic delegation then declined dramatically in the 1994 midterm election, with a loss of fifty-three seats. Yet in 1992 the proportion of women among Democrats increased from 7 percent to 14 percent. As Figure 6.3 shows, the proportion of women among Democrats continued to grow in the 1990s and 2000s, despite the party's minority status in the House. More generally, for the period from 1956 to 2010, the correlation between the proportion of Democrats in the House and women as a proportion of House Democrats is –0.73. This suggests that when Democrats fare poorly in the electoral arena, male Democrats tend to absorb the bulk of the electoral losses. The opposite appears to hold for Republicans. As Republicans gained and held majority-party status in the House, the proportion of women in the Republican delegation increased. In fact, for the 1956–2010 period, the correlation between the proportion of Republicans in the House and women as a proportion of Republicans is 0.58, suggesting that historically the presence of Republican women depends on the overall success of Republicans at the polls.

The implication is that when Democrats suffer at the polls, incumbent males are the "first to go." When Republicans suffer, the relationship is reversed, with incumbent women being the most likely electoral casualties.[44] Thus, shifts in the partisan makeup of Congress do not exert a uniform impact on the presence of female Democrats and Republicans in their party's delegation. In fact, the relationship is the opposite of what was expected for the Democrats.

The Pipeline

If trends in the overall success of the parties do not seem to match the trends in the success of the women within each party, another place to look is in the "pipeline." As noted in previous chapters, there is a hierarchy of elected offices, and many people aspiring to public office first run and serve at the state or local level before they run for the US Congress. In

Figure 6.7   Proportion of Democrats and Republicans in the US House, 1956–2010

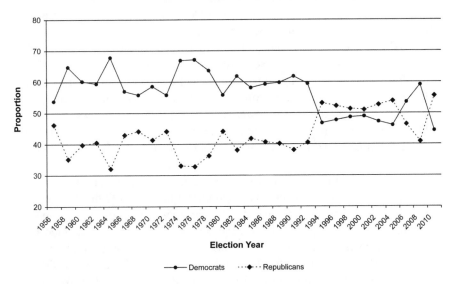

Election Year

●—— Democrats   ···◆··· Republicans

Source: Data compiled by the authors.

other words, there is a "career ladder" in politics; first, candidates run for the state house of representatives, then the state senate, then the US House of Representatives, then the US Senate.[45] This suggests, for example, that in state legislatures, there might be a spike in the number of Democratic women or a leveling-off of Republican women *before* 1992. This is because changes at lower levels of the office hierarchy should predate changes at the congressional level. In fact, if we look at the overall numbers of women serving in state legislatures, there was stagnation. It did not, however, occur before 1992. It happened from 1998 to 2006, when the proportion of female state legislators appeared to be stuck at 22 to 23 percent.[46] In 2010, women composed 25 percent of all state legislators.[47]

Figure 6.8 shows the proportion of women in state houses of representatives from 1958–2010.[48] Here again we see the same pattern, with a relatively narrow gap between the parties for the first thirty years of the series. However, one feature that stands out is the remarkable consistency in the higher proportion of Republican women in the lower chamber of state legislatures from 1958 to 1990. The average gap between the two parties is 2 percentage points. What is noticeably lacking is a surge in the number of Democratic women before 1992. In fact, Democratic women overtake Republican women in 1992, just as they did in the Congress; there is no surge that occurs prior to 1992. After that, the proportion of Republican women in state houses gradually declines, from 21 percent in 1992 to 18 percent in 2010, while the proportion of Democratic women substantially increases, from 22 percent to 32 percent.

While the trends for women elected to the upper chambers of state legislatures are similar, there are some differences worth noting. First, as Figure 6.9 shows, for the first thirty years of the series, the proportions of Democratic and Republican women in state senates are much closer together than the proportions in lower chambers. From 1964 to 1984, the difference is less than 1 point. But for the most part, except for 1974 and 1982, Republican women compose a higher percentage of their party's delegation than Democratic women. Second, the timing of the party switch is earlier. Democratic women slightly outnumber Republican women in 1988, by less than half a percentage point, but then in 1990 the gap grows to nearly 3 points. In other words, the party switch occurs in the upper chamber before it occurs in the lower chamber. This is not the expected sequence of changes. And the gap becomes even more pronounced than the gap in the lower chamber. By 2010, women compose 30 percent of Democratic state senators and only 15 percent of Republican state senators, a

Figure 6.8   Women as a Proportion of Their Party's Members in the Lower Chamber of State Legislatures, 1958–2010

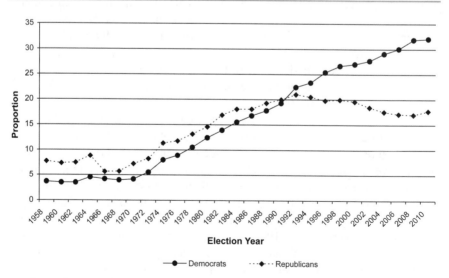

Source: Data compiled by the authors.

difference of 15 points. The proportion of Democratic women is double the proportion of Republican women in state senates.

The analysis suggests that, in the initial years of the twenty-first century, while the proportion of Democratic women in state legislatures was on the rise, it was not enough to counteract the decline in the proportion of Republican women. As a result, the overall proportion of women remained flat. There is no question that the pipeline theory helps us to understand the rates of electoral participation among women.[49] However, there is no sequential appearance in the rise of the gap moving from lower to higher levels in the office hierarchy. In fact, the gap appears in state senates just before it appears in state houses and assemblies. Across the four offices examined, from lower chambers of state legislatures to the US Senate, the actual sequence is best described as nearly simultaneous.

The Perceptions of Party Leaders

State party leaders are still overwhelmingly male. In 2009, only eleven state Democratic Party chairs and eight state Republican Party chairs were women.[50] And there is increasing evidence that "political elites continue to

Figure 6.9 Women as a Proportion of Their Party's Members in the Upper Chamber of State Legislatures, 1958–2010

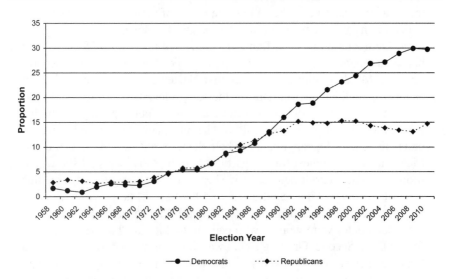

Source: Data compiled by the authors.

value men's political leadership more than women's."[51] Gender acts as a cue for party leaders in much the same way it does for voters: "candidate gender is one piece of information that party leaders may use to weigh the strengths and weaknesses of a potential candidate."[52] A recent study showed that in states where parties had substantial control over the recruitment of candidates, women were less likely to run for state legislature and more likely to drop out of campaigns.[53] The 2008 Citizen Political Ambition Study revealed that potential female candidates were less likely than potential male candidates to be encouraged to run by party leaders and elected officials. In fact, "politically active women who occupy the same professional spheres as politically active men are significantly less likely than men to report being sought out" by party leaders and elected officials to run for office.[54] A survey of female local elected officials in four states revealed that 64 percent of them agreed that party leaders discouraged potential female candidates from running because they were women. One woman in Ohio reported that she was told by party leaders that "women only serve on the decorating and coffee committee." Many others shared how they had endured insults such as "dumb housewife," "blonde bimbo," and "brainless bitch."[55] And there is evidence that women of color face even more challenges. Women of color in state legislatures reported substantially less party support for their candidacies and were more likely to encounter opposition from party leaders.[56]

In the rare instance when party leaders and elected officials make the recruitment of female candidates a priority, the results can be quite dramatic, as the example of the Minnesota house of representatives shows. In 2002, among the members in the Democratic Farmer Labor Party (DFL), or the Democratic Party in Minnesota, sixteen of the party's fifty-two state house members were women, or 31 percent. For the 2004 election, Representative Mindy Greiling, who was first elected in 1992, agreed to be in charge of candidate recruitment for the party's legislative caucus. She had been involved in candidate recruitment before, but typically what this meant was that party leaders would call her in a panic during the last weeks of an election cycle, begging her to help them recruit candidates in the districts that were toughest for her party to win. In 2004, she said she would head candidate recruitment only if she could "do it right." To her, this meant two things. First, candidates who had run in the previous election and lost would be asked if they would be willing to run again. Many of these candidates were women who had run in 2002 in "hopeless" districts for the DFL. Second, Greiling's goal was to recruit women who were good "fits" for her party's top twenty winnable districts. Greiling spent twenty to forty hours a week on the phone recruiting female candidates and, once they agreed to run, provided them with support, training, and mentors. After the 2004 election, the number of DFL women in the Minnesota house increased from sixteen to twenty-six, bringing the female composition of the party's delegation up to nearly 40 percent. And in 2006, women who had lost in the previous cycle were encouraged to run again, a strategy that continued to pay off, with the number of DFL women increasing to thirty-five. Despite her success in significantly increasing the size of her party's delegation, Greiling came under fire from male party leaders; she was accused of recruiting candidates who "did not fit the district," but mostly, she explained, "it was because I was recruiting women." By 2008, women composed nearly half of DFL members in the Minnesota house.[57] While Minnesota had a relatively high proportion of women in the state legislature to begin with, Greiling's efforts to make the recruitment of female candidates a priority had a substantial impact over a relatively short period of time; the number of women in her party's delegation doubled in just three election cycles.

However, taking into account the attitudes, perceptions, and priorities of party leaders does not explain the gap that has developed in the proportions of Democratic and Republican women in elective office. Much like the trend in Congress, the Republican Party has been increasingly successful in winning control of state legislatures, but the proportion of female Republican state legislators has declined from the peak seen in 1992, and the few increases that have happened from one election to another have not been all that dramatic. The 2010 midterm elections are a case in point. Across the nation, Republicans gained 571 seats in elections for the lower chamber of state legislatures and 134 seats in upper chambers. Despite these gains, the proportion of Republican women in lower chambers increased only from 17 percent in 2008 to 18 percent in 2010 and, in upper chambers, from 13 to 15 percent. And despite the Republican Party's stepped-up efforts to recruit women to run for Congress in 2010, the proportion of women in the party's delegation actually declined. Meanwhile, "the Democratic party, which has been losing seats, is seeing women become a larger share of its caucuses around the country."[58] All of this is particularly puzzling given that, in general, the Democratic Party has not been putting any more systematic effort into recruiting female candidates than the Republican Party. Neither party seems all that interested in making recruitment of women a priority. Yet the party gap has been increasing.

As it turns out, for state party leaders, "the main criterion driving the recruitment process is finding the candidate who can win.[59] Even among party leaders sympathetic to increasing women's representation, winning remains the primary goal."[60] However, party leaders are not gender-neutral in their assessments of male and female candidates and their ability to win. In fact, they "do not necessarily think that women are electable in all state legislative districts."[61] In some instances, women may have an advantage because they are perceived by voters as being more honest or "better" on an issue relevant to a particular constituency. In other instances, women may be at a disadvantage. The bottom line is that party leaders take into account what they believe to be the "hearts and minds" of voters in assessing a candidate's chances of winning.[62] Ultimately, "party leaders commonly believe women might have difficulty winning election to the House from some districts in their state; indeed, some party leaders believe that many such districts exist."[63] Thus an explanation for the differences in the success rates between Democratic and Republican women may lie in legislative districts.

▨ Conclusion

It has generally been considered a foregone conclusion that the number of women in elective office would continue to grow at a slow, steady pace. As we have shown in previous chapters, this assumption is not true. Beyond the unimpressive progress in the integration of women into Congress, the number of women serving in state legislatures stalled for nearly a decade at the turn of the twenty-first century. As Susan Carroll of the Center for American Women and Politics points out, "There is no invisible hand at work to insure that more women will seek and be elected to office with each subsequent election."[64]

Moreover, as we have shown in this chapter, the recent increases in the number of women in Congress are more of a Democratic than a Republican phenomenon. In fact, of all the women elected to the US House and Senate in history, two-thirds have been Democrats. This party gap favoring the Democrats is particularly noteworthy among women of color. Of the twenty-eight African American women who have served in the US House, all have been Democrats, as have six of the eight Latinas and five of the six Asian Pacific Islanders. Following the election of 2010, there were 340 women of color serving in state legislatures. The group is overwhelmingly Democratic: 98 percent of African Americans (235 of 240), 94 percent of Latinas (61 of 65), and 86 percent of Asian Pacific Islanders (30 of 35).[65] Given these numbers, as well as the other trends documented in this chapter, the Democratic Party has become much more of an "electoral home" for women than the Republican Party.

This is a substantial barrier if only one party provides increasing opportunities for female aspirants to win elective office. Our analysis here clearly illustrates that the slow, irregular, and undramatic pace of change is especially the case for Republican women. Even with the GOP's tremendous success in 2010, most of the female Republican recruits ran against Democratic incumbents, and very few of them were part of the party's "Young Guns" program, which provided additional funds and training to promising candidates.[66] Republican women sought the nomination in only twenty of forty-one districts with an open seat, and only two of these women won their primaries.

Republican women in Congress have become increasing vocal about their scarcity. As Representative Kay Granger (R-TX) explained, "We pass the word to make sure we're there at this ceremony or that photo-op, because there are fewer of us and we're spread more thinly."[67] Representative Marilyn Musgrave (R-CO) pointed out that there were no women on stage when President George W. Bush signed the partial-birth abortion ban in 2003. She was sitting in the audience: "I looked at the stage and said, 'You've got to be kidding me.'"[68]

Our analysis here serves as a prelude to the next chapter. Here we have shown that, in election cycles since the early 1990s, a party gap has developed and grown larger. The gap is not confined to a single office, but appears throughout the pipeline, in both chambers of state legislatures and both chambers of the US Congress. At the federal level, the gap includes those who seek their party's nomination, those who win their primary contests, and those who win seats in both the House and the Senate. Moreover, this gap cannot be attributed to a party's overall electoral fortunes, nor is it reflected in a sequential change in the hierarchy of offices in the pipeline. And there is very little evidence that gains in the proportion of female Democratic officeholders can be attributed to any systematic or deliberate efforts by Democratic Party leaders. In fact, neither party makes the recruitment of women a priority. If anything, there appears to be evidence to the contrary; the leaderships in both parties, to the extent that they pay attention to potential female candidates at all, can be quite discouraging. In this respect, little seems to have changed over the past century.

There is, however, some evidence that party leaders take account of voter perceptions in their predictions and assessments of the success of female candidates. In fact, party leaders believe that particular configurations of voters make it more or less likely that a woman (or a man) can win. In other words, they believe that in some districts women do better, and in some districts men do better. Accordingly, in the next chapter, we turn our attention to the constituency level and ask whether there are differences in the political geography of districts that elect women and men of either party.

▪ Notes

1. See, for example, Bibby and Schaffner, *Politics, Parties, and Elections in America;* Maisel and Brewer, *Parties and Elections in America;* Silbey, *The American Political Nation;* Wattenberg, *The Decline of American Political Parties.*

2. Myers, "Reid Hits New Low in Poll."

3. Montopoli, "Sue Lowden Stands by Chicken Health Care Barter Plan."

4. Siegel, "Sharron Angle Slams Republicans."

5. Condon, "Harry Reid on the Attack."

6. Damon and Demirjian, "Sen. Harry Ried Wins Fifth Term Against Anti-Incumbent Fervor."

7. See, for example, Maestas, Maisel, and Stone, "National Party Efforts to Recruit State Legislators to Run for the US House"; Moncrief, Squire, and Jewell, *Who Runs for the Legislature?;* Sanbonmatsu, *Where Women Run.*

8. Sanbonmatsu, Carroll, and Walsh, *Poised to Run,* pp. 11–12.

9. Fox and Lawless, "If Only They'd Ask."

10. Ness and Ciment, *The Encyclopedia of Third Parties in America,* p. 421.

11. Orr, "Mary Elizabeth Lease," p. 252.

12. Ibid., p. 248.

13. Attebery, *The Fantasy Tradition in American Literature,* pp. 86–87.

14. "Mrs. Mary E. Lease for Senator," *New York Times,* November 18, 1892, http://query.nytimes.com/mem/archive-free/pdf?res=F1091EF6355D15738DDD A10994D9415B8285F0D3 (accessed February 9, 2012).

15. "Topics in Kansas History."

16. For a discussion of parties, women, and theories of representation, see Sanbonmatsu, "Representation by Gender and Parties."

17. Chafe, *The American Woman,* p. 25.

18. Freeman, *A Room at a Time,* p. 124.

19. Anderson, *After Suffrage;* Fisher and Whitehead, "Women and National Party Organization"; Freeman, *A Room at a Time;* Gustafson, "Partisan Women in the Progressive Era"; Sanbonmatsu, *Democrats, Republicans, and the Politics of Women's Place.*

20. Freeman, *A Room at a Time,* p. 86. See also Harvey, *Votes Without Leverage.*

21. Freeman, *A Room at a Time,* p. 87.

22. Ibid., p. 97.

23. Ibid., p. 149.

24. Ibid. See also Edwards, *Angels in the Machinery;* Fisher and Whitehead, "Women and National Party Organization"; Gustafson, "Partisan Women in the Progressive Era." Women activists were also ambivalent toward the two major parties; Gustafson, "Partisan Women in the Progressive Era"; Gustafson, *Women and the Republican Party;* Voss-Hubbard, "The 'Third Party Tradition' Reconsidered."

25. Burrell, "Political Parties and Women's Organizations," p. 146.

26. Freeman, *A Room at a Time,* pp. 180–183.

27. Burrell, "Political Parties and Women's Organizations," p. 147.

28. Ibid.

29. The percentage for 2004 is from ibid. The percentage for 2008 is from Wayne, *The Road to the White House, 2012,* p. 179.

30. Burrell, "Political Parties and Women's Organizations," p. 152.

31. Ibid., p. 151.

32. "Our Objectives."

33. "A Fifty-State Strategy."

34. Bash, "Despite New Female Faces in Congress, Numbers in Decline."

35. Hennessey, "For GOP Women, 2010 May Not Be Their Year."

36. Bash, "Despite New Female Faces in Congress, Numbers in Decline."

37. McManus, "2010: The Year of the Conservative Woman?"

38. Ibid.

39. Barr, "South Carolina Gov. Mark Sanford Admits Affair."

40. O'Connor, "Panel Votes to Censure Sanford."

41. Maslin, "Facing Scandal, Keeping Faith."

42. As we did in Chapter 2, we group our Senate data here in six-year periods for the purposes of continuity and readability. When the data are disaggregated by year, the same patterns emerge.

43. See, for example, Cook, Thomas, and Wilcox, *The Year of the Woman.*

44. See also Simon and Palmer, "The Midterm Elections of 2010"; Simon and Palmer, "Women and Elections to the US House of Representatives."

45. See, for example, Burrell, *A Woman's Place Is In the House;* Carroll, *Women as Candidates in American Politics;* Sanbonmatsu, Carroll, and Walsh, *Poised to Run;* Welch, "Recruitment of Women to Public Office."

46. See Carroll, "2004 Elections and Women," pp. 23–25. See also Sanbonmatsu, "Gender Pools and Puzzles."

47. "Women in State Legislatures." Many states hold their elections in odd years. Using data from the Center for American Women and Politics, we coded the annual percentages of women slightly differently, in that we looked at when women were elected, not when they were sworn in.

48. The data from 1958 to 1970 were compiled from the Book of the States series. Unfortunately, data for 1956 are not available. The data from 1972 to 2010 were compiled from data provided by the Center for American Women and Politics and the National Council of State Legislators.

49. See Sanbonmatsu, "Gender Pools and Puzzles," for a critical analysis of the pipeline theory, also known as social eligibility theory.

50. Sanbonmatsu, Carroll, and Walsh, *Poised to Run,* p. 14. See also Clark, Hadley, and Darcy, "Political Ambition Among Men and Women State Party Leaders."

51. Niven, "Throwing Your Hat Out of the Ring," p. 4731. See also Niven, *The Missing Majority.*

52. Sanbonmatsu, *Where Women Run,* p. 183.

53. Sanbonmatsu, *Where Women Run.* See also Niven, "Throwing Your Hat Out of the Ring"; Bledsoe and Herring, "Victims of Circumstances."

54. Fox and Lawless, "If Only They'd Ask," p. 320.

55. Niven, "Party Elites and Women Candidates," p. 153.

56. Sanbonmatsu, Carroll, and Walsh, *Poised to Run,* p. 14. See also Darling, "African-American Women in State Elective Office in the South."

57. Author interview, July 19, 2010. Data on the Minnesota House of Representatives are from "State Fact Sheet–Minnesota," from the Center for American Women and Politics; and "Party Control of the Minnesota House of Representatives," from the Minnesota Legislative Reference Library.

58. Sanbonmatsu, *Where Women Run,* p. 197.

59. See, for example, Moncrief, Squire, and Jewell, *Who Runs for the Legislature?*

60. Sanbonmatsu, *Where Women Run,* p. 196.

61. Ibid., p. 184.

62. Ibid., p. 183.

63. Ibid. See also Sanbonmatsu, "Do Parties Know That 'Women Win'?"; Sanbonmatsu, *Democrats, Republicans, and the Politics of Women's Place.*

64. Carroll, "2004 Elections and Women," p. 25.

65. "Women of Color in Elective Office."

66. Franke-Ruta, "Record Number of Republican Women Are Running for House Seats."

67. Lovley, "GOP Women: A Minority in a Minority."

68. Ibid.

SEVEN

Demographics Is Destiny:
Where Women Are Elected

Two major conclusions emerge from Chapters 5 and 6. First, women face a more competitive environment than men when seeking reelection, and female incumbents are more likely than their male counterparts to face female challengers. Second, there is clearly a partisan dimension to the political glass ceiling. The implication is that female candidates tend to cluster in particular districts. What explains this? Can we identify the districts that are more likely to elect women? Do women run and win elections in districts that are different from those that elect men?

Congressional districts in the United States vary widely in their demographic characteristics. Candidates rely heavily on demographic data to create their campaign strategies, and they often hire consulting firms to provide them with detailed profiles and suggestions for targeting voters in their districts. However, we know very little about the demographic characteristics of the districts where women have been successful candidates. But even a cursory analysis of the geographic distribution of the current women in Congress suggests that there is a distinct political geography to the districts they represent: twenty-seven of the seventy-two female House members elected in 2010, or 38 percent, were from California and New York. Six more were from Florida. In other words, nearly half came from only three states. Female representatives are not randomly distributed across the country. As noted in Chapter 1, even the women elected in the mid-1950s tended to come from urban districts and large cities.

In this chapter we explore the relationship between the demographic character of districts and electoral success. We illustrate that, while the strategies pursued by both parties and the demographic coalitions that have supported them have changed, there are particular demographic characteristics that make a House district predictably Democratic or Republican; demographics play an important role in predicting the partisan outcome of House elections. We then use the same logic to show that there are particular demographic characteristics that make a House district more or less likely to elect a woman. And with a few exceptions, the differences in the districts that elect a man or a woman hold across time and the race of the House member. Female House members, whether they are Republican, Democratic, white/non-Hispanic, African American, or Hispanic, are successful in districts that are clearly distinct from those electing male House members. In effect, there are districts that are "women-friendly."[1]

■ The Importance of Demographics

Demographic characteristics play an integral part in predicting electoral success and understanding representation. Demographics are often used by both academics and practitioners to explain and forecast the outcome of presidential and congressional elections.[2] The first response of House incumbents to questions about their districts is usually a description of the demographics of their constituencies: the boundaries of the district, its socioeconomic and racial makeup, and its partisan and ideological leanings. As Richard Fenno noted in *Home Style,* "Every congressman, in his mind's eye, sees his geographic constituency in terms of some special configuration of such variables."[3] Some districts are more homogeneous than others, but no member of Congress sees "an undifferentiated glob" of constituents within their district's boundaries.[4]

The conventional wisdom among academics, political consultants, and candidates is that there are particular configurations of demographic characteristics associated with typical Democratic and Republican districts.[5] House districts that elect Democrats are more urban and blue-collar, and have a sizable minority population; House districts that elect Republicans are wealthier and more professional and, geographically, are substantially larger than those electing Democrats, indicating that they are more suburban and rural. As those in the business of politics say, "demographics is destiny."[6] More will be said about each of these particular demographics later, but the point we wish to make here is that the outcome of an election can be predicted based on a district's demographics.

Given that we can identify "party-friendly" districts, there are two possibilities with respect to the impact of these factors on the success of female candidates. First, those women elected to the House may find success in districts that conform to the conventional party profile of districts. In this instance, there would be nothing unique about districts that elect women to the House. Party would trump gender, in that female and male Democratic members would be elected from demographically similar districts, as would female and male Republican members. Alternatively, women may be elected from districts where one or more characteristics do not conform to the standard partisan profile; female and male Democratic members would be elected from demographically distinct districts, as would female and male Republican members. If this is the case, then "women-friendly" and "party-friendly" denote different kinds of districts.

Despite the centrality of demographics to understanding electoral politics, there are surprisingly few analyses of their impact on women's success, particularly at the federal level.[7] As a result, we know very little about the House districts *where* women win. In this chapter we examine the demographic characteristics that predict the partisanship of a district and then explore the extent to which these factors can predict whether a woman will win that district.

■ Shifting Party Strategies and Shifting Demographics

During the time period of our study, significant changes have occurred in both the strategies used by Democratic and Republican Party leaders and the constituency coalitions that form their bases. The shift in strategy is largely attributed to Karl Rove, chief adviser for George W. Bush's gubernatorial and presidential campaigns. Traditionally, to win presidential elections both parties moved toward the center, where most of the voters were.[8] Bill Clinton, for example, successfully used this strategy in 1992 and 1996.[9] However, in 2000 and 2004, instead of fighting for the center, the Republicans "raced for the base" and focused on mobilizing their most loyal supporters.[10] By 2008, the Democrats had also successfully employed this strategy.[11] Rather than moderating to appeal to the center, both parties are now running to the extremes. Similar trends can also be seen in Congress. Beginning in the 1980s, the Republicans, led by Representative Newt Gingrich (R-GA), adopted a much more confrontational approach with House Democrats. By the 1990s, both parties in Congress, rather than reaching across the aisle, concentrated on maintaining unity within their parties.[12] Civility in Congress became a thing of the past. Fifty years ago, for example, House speaker Sam Rayburn, a Texas Democrat, "served drinks at the end of the day to his Republican opponents."[13] Today, however, as University of Georgia political scientist Keith Poole explains, "They hate one another."[14] All of this both contributes to and reflects the polarization of US politics.[15]

Along with this came a shift in the kinds of voters that each party pursued. Since President Franklin Roosevelt's New Deal coalition, a vital part of the Democratic Party's support was ethnic, working-class voters residing in large cities such as Boston, New York, Philadelphia, Pittsburgh, Cleveland, Detroit, Milwaukee, and Chicago.[16] During the 1960s, support for the Democrats among African Americans, Hispanics, and women increased, partly in response to the party's advocacy of civil rights. But as President Lyndon Johnson predicted after he signed the Civil Rights Act of 1964, the Democratic Party would lose its hold over the "Solid South."[17] Similarly, the Republican Party base, which used to be made up of "WASPs," white Anglo-Saxon Protestants in the Northeast, has shifted toward Southern, rural Evangelicals.[18] Over the past fifty years, both parties have had to deal with tremendous demographic changes, including the decline in manufacturing and blue-collar jobs, the development of suburbs and exurbs, increasing education levels, increasing immigration, increasing numbers of women entering the work force, and even changing attitudes about marriage.[19]

Racial gerrymandering and the creation of majority-minority districts represent another significant change in the demography of House elections. In 1982, Congress amended the Voting Rights Act of 1965, mandating that minorities be able to "elect representatives of their choice."[20] The theory was that increasing the number of minorities in a district would increase the number of minorities elected to the House, because minority voters are much more likely than white voters to vote for minority candidates.[21] In fact, one study suggests that "only the percentage of blacks and Latinos in the district alters the probability of an African American winning election to the House."[22] African American and Latino candidates "almost never win election from white majority districts."[23] In 1992, the first round of elections under the Voting Rights Act mandate, districts were drawn—particularly in states across the South—to maximize the number of African American constituents. Eight of these districts were newly created, with an average black population of 58 percent. In addition, five existing districts were substantially redrawn, increasing their average black population from 34 percent to 57 percent. As a result, thirteen new African Americans were elected to the House, the largest increase in history; the number of black representatives increased from twenty-five to thirty-eight. This round of redistricting also created four new Hispanic-majority districts, along with two districts redrawn to substantially increase their Hispanic populations. All six of these districts were won by Hispanic candidates, increasing their overall number in the House to seventeen, a record high.[24] While there have been multiple constitutional challenges to racial gerrymandering, there is no question that this process has contributed to increasing the number of blacks and Hispanics in the House.[25]

To explore the association between demographics and the election of Democrats and Republicans to the House, we examine twelve commonly used demographic factors, organized into four categories: partisanship, geography, diversity, and socioeconomic factors. To explore changes over the past fifty years, we examine these relationships for three time periods: 1956 to 1990, 1992 to 2000, and 2002 to 2010. We use this temporal breakdown because there were relatively few women elected from 1956 to 1990, and isolating the last two redistricting periods permits us to examine the possible impact of demographic changes and shift in party strategies on the success of female House candidates.[26] Because race has a strong partisan dimension and plays a prominent role in the redistricting process, we first analyze the demographic characteristics of the districts that have elected white/non-Hispanic representatives, and then we analyze the characteristics of districts that have elected African American and Hispanic representatives.[27]

Partisanship

Party is the most important cue in the voting booth. Democratic voters overwhelmingly vote for Democratic candidates, and Republican voters overwhelmingly vote for Republican candidates.[28] For example, in the 2008 presidential election, 89 percent of those identifying themselves as Democrats voted for Barack Obama, and 90 percent of those identifying themselves as Republicans voted for John McCain.[29] Party labels provide voters with a shortcut that is used to infer candidate positions and their willingness to support a candidate.

As a measure of district partisanship, we use the proportion of the two-party vote won by the Republican candidate in presidential elections; higher percentages indicate that the district is more Republican, while lower percentages indicate that the district is more Democratic. Not surprisingly, as Table 7.1 shows, House districts electing Republicans have a higher average Republican share of the presidential vote. There has, however, been an important change: districts electing Democrats have become even more Democratic over time. During the 1956–1990 period, the average Republican share of the presidential vote was nearly 50 percent. In other words, districts electing Democratic House members were quite moderate, with many of them being swing districts. However, we see a substantial shift to the left during the 1992–2000 and 2002–2010 periods. Among the districts electing Democrats, the average Republican share of the presidential vote dropped to 42 percent. Districts electing Democrats

Table 7.1 The Shifting Demographics of House Districts Electing Democrats and Republicans, 1956–2010

	Districts Electing Democrats 1956–1990 (n = 4,372)	Districts Electing Republicans 1956–1990 (n = 3,080)	Districts Electing Democrats 1992–2000 (n = 836)	Districts Electing Republicans 1992–2000 (n = 1,056)	Districts Electing Democrats 2002–2010 (n = 803)	Districts Electing Republicans 2002–2010 (n = 1,056)
Partisanship						
Republican share of presidential vote	49.7%	59.6%[a]	42.3%	54.0%[a]	42.2%	58.5%[a]
Geography						
District size, square miles	2,290.0	3,055.0[a]	1,323.0	3,502.0[a]	1,266.0	4,033.0[a]
Urban residents	72.2%	65.2%[a]	81.3%	70.7%[a]	90.1%	73.5%[a]
Elected from the South	32.3%	15.4%[a]	23.2%	29.4%[a]	18.4%	36.1%[a]
Diversity						
Black residents	12.5%	5.3%[a]	9.2%	6.8%[a]	9.9%	7.6%[a]
Hispanic residents	4.9%	3.4%[a]	7.4%	5.7%[a]	11.2%	7.9%[a]
Foreign-born residents	5.8%	4.8%[a]	8.1%	5.3%[a]	12.5%	6.8%[a]
Socioeconomic						
Relative median income	96.7%	106.4%[a]	107.6%	110.3%[a]	109.3%	109.4%
Blue-collar workers	31.4%	30.1%[a]	14.0%	14.3%[a]	8.5%	9.3%[a]
College degrees	12.6%	14.8%[a]	20.6%	20.9%	26.2%	24.2%[a]
Married women	64.3%	67.1%[a]	55.6%	60.2%[a]	50.2%	55.9%[a]
School-age population	20.4%	20.7%[a]	14.7%	15.5%[a]	15.4%	16.1%[a]

Source: Data compiled by the authors.
Notes: Districts electing African Americans and Hispanics not included.
a. The difference between districts electing Democrats and Republicans is statistically significant with $p < 0.05$.

moved "farther away" from districts electing Republicans, reflecting the increased polarization of US politics over the past thirty years.

It is interesting to note that the development of the party gap among the women who serve in the House, discussed in Chapter 6, occurs at approximately the same time as the development of the party polarization among congressional districts. It would seem logical to expect that these two trends are somehow related and would affect the success of female candidates. Early studies with data from the 1970s and 1980s suggest that women of both parties do better in districts that are more liberal. Democratic women are more likely to be elected in the most liberal districts, while Republican women are more likely to be elected in more moderate districts.[30] Thus, our analysis here gives us an opportunity to further explore how gender and party interact.

Geography: District Size, Urbanization, and Region

Population density has been found to be an increasingly important factor in predicting elections, with Democratic candidates doing extremely well in core urban areas, and Republicans dominating outer-ring suburban, exurban, and rural areas.[31] In other words, as population density increases, Democratic candidates do better. In our analysis, we use two measures of population density: district size and urbanization, both of which show increasing polarization between districts that elect Democratic House members and those that elect Republican House members.

We measure geographic size by the total square miles of the district. As Table 7.1 shows, districts that elected Democrats have always been smaller than those that elected Republicans. However, the differences in size have substantially increased over time. During the 1956–1990 period, Democratic districts averaged about 2,300 square miles, and Republican districts averaged about 3,000 square miles. During the 2002–2010 period, Democratic districts shrank to approximately 1,300 square miles, while Republican districts grew to over 4,000 square miles; districts that elected Republican House members were more than three times bigger than districts that elected Democratic House members. In the 112th Congress (2011 session), the smallest House district in the country—New York's Eleventh District, in Brooklyn, only twelve square miles—was represented by Representative Yvette Clarke, an African American Democrat. Apart from those states that send only one representative to the House (such as South Dakota), the largest district in the nation was the Second District of Nevada, at 105,635 square miles. Since the creation of its boundaries in 2002, this district has never elected a woman.

There have been a few studies on the impact of district size on the success of women candidates, but the studies have been on state legislatures.[32] The logic is that the larger the district, measured in square miles, the harder it is to represent. Because constituents are dispersed in larger districts, more time is required to keep in contact with them. This is a particular problem for women. Because they are usually the primary caregivers of children even when they serve in public office, women are generally under more time constraints than men.[33] Women are more likely to juggle the roles of spouse, parent, and elected official than are their male counterparts. Thus women encounter more "geographic immobility" than men. For this reason, we expect that female House members will come from smaller, more geographically compact districts.

One of the biggest changes since World War II has been the move from rural areas and urban cores into the suburbs. In 1946, when Bill Levitt adapted Ford Motor Company's mass production methods to the housing industry, he "made it possible to provide inexpensive, attractive, single-unit housing for ordinary citizens, people who had never thought of themselves as middle-class before . . . he made the American Dream possible."[34] His Levittown housing development, the first of its kind in the nation, built on what had been potato farms in Long Island, had 1,400 contracts for new houses in one day.[35] Fifty years later, over half of all Americans lived in suburban areas.[36] The suburbs are no longer the stereotypical bastion of middle- and upper-class white families with two children and a dog; they are now incredibly complex, with many having the socioeconomic and cultural characteristics of urban areas.[37]

To tap these changes, we use a measure of urbanization, defined as the percentage of a district's population living in urban areas, as defined by the US Census. Given the more recent changes in suburban areas, many of these are now included in the Census definition of "urban."[38] Table 7.1 reveals two important trends. First, all districts have become more urban over time. Second, and perhaps more important, the rates of urbanization between districts electing Democrats and Republicans are quite different. Republican districts increased from 65 percent urban in the earliest period to 74 percent urban in the latest. Democratic districts increased from 72 percent urban to 90 percent urban. From 1956 to 1990, districts electing Democrats were on average only 7 percent more urban than districts electing Republicans. From 2002 to 2010, districts electing Democrats were 17 percentage points more urban than districts electing Republicans. According to the 2000 Census, there were forty-nine House districts that were 100 percent urban. In the 2010 House elections, Democrats won forty-five, or 92 percent, of these districts. There were forty-seven districts where less than 50 percent of the population lived in urban areas. The Republicans won thirty-five, or 74 percent, of these districts. The Fifth District of Kentucky, at 21 percent urban, was the least urban in the country and was represented by Republican Harold Rogers, who was first elected in 1980.

One of the few demographic factors that has received some attention in research on women in Congress is urbanization: female House members are more likely to represent urban districts.[39] Women are more likely to be recruited to run for office in urban areas because there is a "larger pool of activist women who are potential candidates" than in rural areas.[40] There are also more seats and thus more opportunities to run in areas with higher populations.[41] Democratic women in particular tend to rely on women's groups for campaign support, and these organizations tend to be located in larger urban centers.[42] EMILY's List, for example, has major offices in Washington, D.C., and Los Angeles. The Women's Campaign Fund has offices in Washington, D.C., and New York. In addition, women are more likely to be recruited and do well electorally in urban areas because these constituencies are most receptive to agendas emphasizing social welfare issues. These issues, which include funding for after-school programs, aid to dependent children, and other public assistance programs, are often major concerns in urban districts. Because women are perceived to be "better" on these issues, they are more likely to run and win.[43] The victory rates of female candidates in the 2010 elections provide some evidence for this. Women won nineteen of forty-nine elections, or 39 percent, in districts with 100 percent urban populations, and only five of forty-seven elections, or 11 percent, in districts with urban populations of less than 50 percent.

Perhaps the most significant change in US electoral politics involves the South.[44] In the 1956 House elections, Democrats won 99 of the 106 seats, or 93 percent, in the South. There were no African Americans or Hispanics among the winners. The 2010 midterm elections provide a dramatic contrast. Democrats won only 37 of the 131 seats, or 28 percent. Of these Democrats who won, 65 percent were minorities: twenty African Americans and four Hispanics. In our analysis, we define the South as the former states of the Confederacy: Alabama, Arkansas, Florida, Georgia, Louisiana, Mississippi, North Carolina, South Carolina, Tennessee, Texas, and Virginia. Table 7.1 shows, for each of the time periods, the proportions of the Democratic and Republican House delegations that were elected from the South. The trends in the table clearly show the shifting geography within each of the party's bases. From 1956 to 1990, nearly a third of all Democratic House members came from the South. By 2002, this had dropped to less than 20 percent. For the Republicans, from 1956 to 1990, only 15 percent of their House members came from the South. By the 2002–2010 period, 36 percent of their members came from the South.

Regional and cultural differences do play a role in determining the prevalence and success of female candidates.[45] While traditional attitudes toward women's roles have clearly changed over the past hundred years in the United States, cultural barriers that discourage women from running for office still remain, particularly in the South.[46] This is attributed to a unique political culture that confined "real political power to a small and self-perpetuating elite who often inherit their right to govern through family title or social position."[47] This traditionalism includes "a clear predisposition with regard to social conservatism and particularly women's rights."[48] As one historian explained, in the antebellum South, "even though the master's wife and daughters were white and members of the planter class, 'they were . . . in this rigidly hierarchical society, subjected to male rule.' . . . In fact, an educated and well-bred woman . . . was not even allowed to initiate a political conversation."[49] Despite the dramatic social and economic changes in the South, these regional distinctions "have shown remarkable resilience."[50] In the 1970s, Texas was the only state in the former Confederacy that voted to ratify the Equal Rights Amendment.[51] In 1984, Mississippi's legislature voted to "ratify" the Nineteenth Amendment, which constitutionally guaranteed women the right to vote, sixty-four years after the amendment had actually been added to the Constitution.[52] Texas did not remove "marital rape exemptions" from its sexual assault laws until 1994.[53] Until 2003, Florida had a "Scarlet Letter" law that required single women who were putting their babies up for adoption to "publish their sexual histories in a newspaper if they did not know the identity of the father."[54] We expect, then, that regional differences will help explain the success of women; female candidates will be more likely to seek and win House seats in districts outside the South.

Diversity: Race, Ethnicity, and Percentage Foreign-Born

One of the most profound changes in the demography of the United States in the twenty-first century will be the shift in its racial and ethnic composition.[55] According to the US Census, in 2010 non-Hispanic whites composed 64 percent of the population, down from 69 percent in 2000. The "number of Hispanics and Asians is soaring, the number of blacks is growing slowly and whites are almost at a standstill."[56] Four states—California, Hawaii, New Mexico, and Texas—are minority-majority states. Given that these groups are growing and their turnout rates are increasing, candidates, particularly Democrats, are paying them increasing attention. African

Americans have a solid history of supporting Democrats. In the presidential elections from 1976 to 2010, a majority of the Hispanic vote has gone to the Democratic candidate, ranging from a low of 53 percent in 2004 to a high of 72 percent in 1996.[57] While the differences here are not as pronounced as they are among the partisan and geographic measures, these factors also show how Democratic and Republican House districts are becoming more polarized.

As measures of district diversity, we use the percentages of residents who identified themselves in the US Census as African American, Hispanic or Latino, and foreign-born. Table 7.1 shows that, for the most part, diversity has been increasing over time across all House districts. The exception to this is the slight decline in black residents in Democratic districts. While this seems counterintuitive, it is attributable to the creation of majority-minority districts after the 1990 Census, which reduced the proportion of black and Hispanic voters in districts held by white/non-Hispanic Democrats.[58] However, it is still the case that districts electing Democrats are more racially and ethnically diverse than districts electing Republicans. According to the 2000 Census, the most diverse district was the Sixteenth District of New York, with a minority population of 93 percent, 60 percent Hispanic and 33 percent African American. In the 112th Congress (2011 session), this district was represented by Democrat José Serrano. The least diverse district was the Seventh District of Wisconsin, with a minority population just over 1 percent. In the 112th Congress, this district was represented by Republican Sean Duffy.

There are a few studies of the relationship between the diversity of a district and its likelihood of electing a woman, but those that have been undertaken analyze women elected in the 1970s and 1980s and provide conflicting results.[59] However, given the rising importance of racial and ethnic diversity in US politics, we include these measures in our analysis. We suspect that female House members will run and be elected in districts that are more racially diverse than those of their male counterparts.

Socioeconomic Factors: Income, Social Class, Education, Marriage, and School-Age Population

Just as the regional bases of the parties have changed, so has the role of wealth and social class. As a fundamental part of President Roosevelt's New Deal coalition, further secured in the 1960s by President Johnson's War on Poverty and Great Society, people with lower incomes supported Democratic candidates. Largely because of the higher taxes that programs like these would require, people with higher incomes supported Republicans. However, over the past thirty years, the relationship between income and party support has become more complex. Now Democrats do quite well among the wealthy, particularly outside of the South.[60] For example, in Mississippi, the poorest state in the nation, wealthy voters overwhelmingly supported Republican presidential candidate John McCain. However, voters in Connecticut, one of the richest states in the nation, uniformly supported Democrat Barack Obama across all income levels.[61] Obama won eight of the ten richest states and lost nine of the ten poorest states. Today, some wealthy districts vote Democratic and some wealthy districts vote Republican. In the aggregate, the differences in voting patterns based on wealth are disappearing. While Obama won among voters with annual incomes less than $50,000 by 22 points, he tied with McCain among voters with annual incomes above $50,000.[62]

As a measure of income, we use the relative median income of the congressional district, expressed as a percentage of the national median.[63] Values greater than 100 percent represent districts above the national median, and values less than 100 percent are those below the national median. The magnitude of the measure conveys the degree to which a district is rich or poor compared to all congressional districts in a given redistricting period. Table 7.1 shows the convergence over time of median income in districts electing Democrats and districts electing Republicans. As expected, during the 1956–1990 period, there were substantial differences in the median incomes of districts electing Democrats, 97 percent of the national average, and districts electing Republicans, 106 percent of the national average. By the 2002–2010 period, the differences had disappeared; both Democratic House members and Republican House members were elected in districts with incomes that were 109 percent of the national average. There are, of course, still massive disparities in wealth across districts. According to the 2000 Census, the poorest congressional district was the Sixteenth District of New York, with a median income of $19,311, represented in the 112th Congress, as mentioned earlier, by Democrat José Serrano. The wealthiest was the Eleventh District of Virginia, with a median income of $80,397. This district was also represented by a Democrat, Gerry Connolly, who took over the seat in 2008 after Republican Tom Davis retired. Across all congressional districts, median income was $41,060. Using our measure, the relative income in New York's Sixteenth District is 47 percent of the national average, and in Virginia's Eleventh it is 196 percent of the national average.

There is some evidence that women in Congress tend to be elected in wealthier districts.[64] One line of reasoning suggests that lower incomes make legislative service more attractive to men; because politics is an option for men, it "becomes more relevant when men's opportunities in other occupations [are] limited. . . . When income levels are greater for men, other occupations become more attractive even when state legislative salaries are high."[65] We expect that as the median income of a district increases, the likelihood that a female candidate will win should also increase.

Related to income is occupation and social class. Not surprisingly, the white "working class" historically voted Democratic and, given the prominence and importance of unions, was the heart of the original New Deal coalition. This demographic, however, has been shrinking. After World War II, blue-collar workers outnumbered white-collar workers. Today, there are three times as many white-collar workers as blue-collar workers.[66] Despite this decline, the white working class still plays an important role in electoral politics.[67] Over the past twenty years, Republicans have made major inroads among this demographic, at least in part because of their more traditional attitudes on social issues.[68] During the 2008 campaign, Obama was accused of being "elitist" by the leader of one of the largest unions in the nation. R. Thomas Buffenbarger, president of the International Association of Machinists and Aerospace Workers, called Obama supporters "latte-drinking, Prius-driving, Birkenstock-wearing, trust-fund babies."[69] As it turned out, there was a positive correlation between a state's support for Obama and its number of Starbucks stores.[70] But Buffenbarger's criticism fed into perceptions of Obama and other Democrats as out of touch with "working-class America." As one bumper sticker at a Kansas City gun show put it, "A working person that supports Democrats is like a chicken that supports Col. Sanders!"[71]

We use the percentage of blue-collar workers as our measure of social class. Not surprisingly, Table 7.1 shows that, overall, blue-collar jobs have been disappearing; the proportion of blue-collar workers in all districts has declined in the past fifty years, from 30 percent to 9 percent.[72] At the same time, while the differences have been small, party support among blue-collar workers has shifted. During the 1956–1990 period, Democrats had the edge among the working class, but by the 2002–2010 period, Republicans had the edge. The Seventeenth District of Ohio is among those that are the most working class, with blue-collar workers representing nearly 25 percent of the people in the district. Historically, the core of this district has been Youngstown and surrounding areas in Mahoning and Trumbull Counties.[73] Once the home of numerous steel mills, the district was heavily unionized, with the General Motors assembly plant in Lordstown a major employer. Since 1956, five men have represented the district, four Democrats and one Republican.[74] In contrast, with only 3 percent of its residents employed in blue-collar jobs, New York's Fourteenth District has one of the smallest working-class constituencies in the nation. The district, represented by Democrat Carolyn Maloney, includes the Upper East Side of Manhattan and is home to "people with more accumulated wealth than anywhere else in the world."[75]

There is evidence that women candidates are likely to be less successful in blue-collar, working-class districts.[76] In particular, the traditionalist and less-than-accepting attitudes toward female candidates among labor leaders and white ethnic groups who are influential in Democratic political machines have served as a substantial barrier.[77] For example, politics in New Jersey and Massachusetts is controlled by party bosses and county chairmen. In a 2010 column that appeared in the *Daily Beast,* James Carroll, a columnist for the *Boston Globe,* explained that Massachusetts, "the most liberal state in the nation . . . practices the politics of misogyny . . . no women need apply. . . . Democrats don't tap women for the top jobs, and neither do Republicans."[78] In the 112th Congress (2011 session), Massachusetts had one woman among its ten House members, Niki Tsongas (D-MA), who was first elected in a special election in 2007. In his recent memoir, former New Jersey governor James McGreevey explained that strip clubs are the "fraternal lodges" of politics in his state: "We used to order beer after beer at Cheeques, watching the dancers twirl on their poles while debating everything from local policy initiatives and tax ratables to the merits of silicone breast enhancements."[79] McGreevey resigned as governor in 2004 and made national headlines when he announced he was gay.[80] Given the attitudes associated with blue-collar culture, we expect that women candidates will do better in districts with fewer blue-collar workers.

Also related to income and social class is education. One of the reasons that the blue-collar sector has declined is because education levels have increased. In 1940, 75 percent of adults were high school dropouts, and only 5 percent of Americans had a college degree.[81] In 2008, only 14 percent of adults had not finished high school, and nearly 30 percent had a college degree.[82] Education has a somewhat unusual relationship with party identification among voters. Those with the least education, along with those with the most education, tend to support Democratic candidates. For example, in 2008, Democrat Barack Obama did well among those with a high school diploma or less, winning this group with 63 percent of the vote, but also did well among those with a postgraduate degree, winning this group with 58 percent of the vote. But among those with a college degree, support was nearly evenly split between Obama and Republican John McCain.[83]

To measure education, we use the proportion of residents age twenty-five or older who completed four or more years of college. As Table 7.1

shows, education levels have increased in all districts over the fifty years of our study. However, as expected, the differences between the parties are quite small, and during the 1992–2000 period the difference is not statistically significant. According to the 2000 Census, the proportion of people with college degrees is lowest in two districts, California's Twentieth and Texas's Twenty-ninth. In the 112th Congress (2011 session), both of these districts were represented by men, Democrats Jim Costa and Gene Green respectively. The district with the highest proportion of people with college degrees, at 57 percent, is the Fourteenth District of New York, represented by Democrat Carolyn Maloney since 1992.

While having a college degree may not predict whether someone will vote for a Democrat or Republican, we anticipate that as the proportion of residents with college degrees in a given district increases, women will be more likely to win the House seat for that district, and thus we include this measure in our analysis.[84] People with a college education are more likely to support a more egalitarian view of women and less likely to hold traditional attitudes about gender roles.[85] In addition, women with more education are more likely to run for office, and consequently districts with higher levels of education should be more fertile recruiting grounds.[86]

Just as social class and education levels tap into cultural attitudes, we also attempt to explore the impact of family arrangements on voters. While family structures have been transformed in the past fifty years, the centrality of the family with regard to its influence on politics has not.[87] Marriage rates have declined, because people are putting off marriage and divorce rates have increased.[88] Marital status has become an important predictor of vote choice, with Republicans doing well among those who are married, and Democrats doing well among those who are not.[89] For example, in 2008, among the married, McCain won 56 percent of the vote, and among those who were not married, Obama won 65 percent of the vote.[90] Birthrates have also declined, not only because people in general are having fewer children, but also because family size has substantially declined. At the height of the Baby Boom in 1957, the birthrate peaked at 3.65 children per woman. In the twenty-first century, the average American family has no minor children living in it.[91] This too has political ramifications. Those without children are more likely to vote for Democrats, while those with children, particularly those with more than two children, are more likely to vote for Republicans.[92]

In our analysis, we use two measures of family arrangements. The first is the proportion of women age sixteen or older who are married with their husband living in the household. This is a standard definition used by the US Census and excludes those women who are divorced and widowed.

The second measure is the proportion of residents in a House district enrolled in public elementary and high schools. As Table 7.1 shows, rates of marriage and birth have been declining over time. As expected, Republicans have consistently had a slight edge among the married and those with school-age children. In the most recent redistricting period, the Seventh District of Georgia had the highest marriage rate, 69 percent, and the Fifteenth District of New York had the lowest, at 24 percent; in the 112th Congress (2011 session), the districts were represented by Republican Rob Woodall and Democrat Charles Rangel respectively. During the 2002–2010 period, there were three districts whose school-age population exceeded 24 percent: the Fifteenth District of Texas, represented in the 112th Congress by Democrat Ruben Hinojosa; the First District of Utah, represented by Republican Rob Bishop; and the Third District of Utah, represented by Republican Jason Chaffetz. Among the districts with the smallest school-age population were New York's Fourteenth, represented by Democrat Carolyn Maloney, and Florida's Twenty-second, represented by Republican Allen West, an African American who defeated Democratic incumbent Ron Klein in 2010.

Because these factors tap into cultural attitudes, we include them in our analysis, but the impact of these demographics could play out in a variety of ways with regard to the success of women candidates. On the one hand, given that women candidates are perceived as more competent on issues involving education and children, the parents of school-age children might be more likely to vote for a woman candidate. On the other hand, families with stay-at-home moms might have more traditional attitudes about women; married couples with school-age children tend to live in suburban and exurban areas, where Republican political campaigns stressing traditional "family values" have been quite successful, making these couples less likely to support female candidates.[93] Another way this could play out is that the school-age population is small in districts with a high proportion of retired older voters, who tend to have more conservative attitudes about women's roles. But given the importance of these factors in determining whether a district is "friendly" toward a Democratic or Republican candidate, they may also be important in determining whether a district is "friendly" toward a male or female candidate.

We have shown that, while there have been changes in the strategies and coalitions pursued by both parties, there are particular demographic characteristics that help us understand the outcomes of House elections. As Table 7.1 demonstrates, there are sharp differences in the political geography of congressional districts that elect white/non-Hispanic Democrats compared to Republicans.

■ The Political Geography of Women's Success

Essentially, we know that there are configurations of demographic measures that make a district "party friendly." Are there configurations that make a district "women friendly"? In other words, are there particular demographic characteristics that influence whether a district will elect a man or a woman? In addition to examining changes over time, here we further explore the interaction of gender, race, and party. From 1956 to 2010, ninety-two of the ninety-six African Americans elected to the House, 96 percent, were Democrats. The four black Republicans were all men. Representative Gary Franks (R-CT) was first elected to an open seat in 1990, and Representative J. C. Watts (R-OK) won an open seat in 1994. The two remaining black Republicans, Representatives Allen West (R-FL) and Tim Scott (R-SC) won their first elections to the House in 2010.[94] West and Scott are the first African American Republicans elected from the South since the Reconstruction era. Although not as dramatic, there are also partisan differences in the election of Hispanic members. Among the forty-six Hispanics elected to the House since 1956, thirty-six, 78 percent, were Democrats and ten were Republicans, 22 percent. Only two of the ten Hispanic Republicans elected to the House were women, Representative Ileana Ros-Lehtinen (R-FL), first elected in 1989, and Representative Jaime Herrera Beutler (R-WA), who won her first election in 2010.

Given all of this, we first compare districts electing white/non-Hispanic men to those electing white/non-Hispanic women from 1956 to 2010. Second, we take a deeper look and compare the election of white/non-Hispanic men and women by party over our three time periods, to see if the changes in the demographic coalitions supporting the parties are related to the gender of the winning candidates. Third, because there were no black women and only two Hispanic women among the Republicans elected to the House, we compare those Democratic districts electing African American and Hispanic men and women; because of the prominence of racial gerrymandering in explaining the dramatic increase in the number of minority House members, we expect that the impact of demographics electing men and women in these districts may be different.

The Demographics of Districts
Electing White/Non-Hispanic Men and Women

Table 7.2 displays the demographics of districts that elected white/non-Hispanic men and women from 1956 to 2010. Districts electing white/non-Hispanic women are clearly distinct and have substantially different demographic profiles when compared to districts that elect white/non-Hispanic men. White/non-Hispanic women represent districts that vote more Democratic than the districts of their male counterparts. On average, the Republican share of the two-party vote in districts that elect men is 53 percent. However, in districts that elect women, the average Republican share of the vote is only 48 percent. This is quite striking, given that this includes districts that elect women of both parties, suggesting that Republican women do better in districts that lean Democratic. With regard to geography, women are elected from districts that are geographically smaller; the median size of districts electing men, 2,948 square miles, is nearly three times the size of districts that elect women. Women are also more likely to be elected from districts that are substantially more urban and are from outside the South.

There are differences in the level of diversity of districts electing white/non-Hispanic men and women as well. The districts that elect women have slightly smaller proportions of African American residents,

Table 7.2   House Districts Electing Men and Women, 1956–2010

	Districts Electing Men (n = 10,491)	Districts Electing Women (n = 712)
Partisanship		
Republican share of presidential vote	52.9%	47.5%[a]
Geography		
District size, square miles	2,948.0	1,026.5[a]
Urban residents	70.8%	89.0%[a]
Elected from the South	27.0%	12.2%[a]
Diversity		
Black residents	9.2%	7.7%[a]
Hispanic residents	4.0%	7.3%[a]
Foreign-born residents	6.0%	10.0%[a]
Socioeconomic		
Relative median income	102.7%	116.4%[a]
Blue-collar workers	25.0%	16.4%[a]
College degrees	17.5%	24.3%[a]
Married women	61.3%	55.7%[a]
School-age population	19.0%	16.4%[a]

Source: Data compiled by the authors.
Notes: Districts electing African Americans and Hispanics not included.
   a. The difference between districts electing men and women is statistically significant with $p < 0.05$.

but are more diverse with respect to both the Hispanic and foreign-born populations. The socioeconomic differences in districts that elect men and women are perhaps the most dramatic. Women are more likely to be elected from "upscale" districts. Compared to districts that elect men, districts that elect women are wealthier, with 116 percent of national median income versus 103 percent for men; have a smaller blue-collar work force, 16 percent versus 25 percent; and have more constituents with college degrees, 24 percent versus 18 percent. In addition, districts that elect women appear to be less "traditional" in the sense that they have fewer married women and smaller school-age populations.

Overall, Table 7.2 provides considerable evidence that districts electing nonminority women to the House are distinct from districts that elect nonminority men. This implies that there is a configuration of characteristics—a demographic profile—that make congressional districts "women-friendly." Such districts are more Democratic in presidential voting, smaller in size and more urban, outside the South, more racially and ethnically diverse, wealthier, and have a socioeconomic profile that can arguably be considered an indicator of more progressive attitudes about the roles of women. When compared to the "party-friendly" indicators in Table 7.1, it is clear that "party-friendly" and "women-friendly" are not the same concept. Women-friendly districts have their own unique political geographies.

To explore the idea of women-friendly districts in more depth, we compare districts electing Democratic men and women and districts electing Republican men and women. In addition, given the shifts that have occurred in the demographic coalitions that have supported the parties over the past several decades, it is important to explore changes over time. The first half of Table 7.3 presents the results for districts electing Democrats in each time period, and the second half presents the results for districts electing Republicans. Reading across the rows provides a portrait of intraparty differences on the demographic factors over time, while reading down the columns allows for interparty comparisons within a given time period.

Looking first at the districts that elected Democrats, the most prominent feature is the consistency in the differences between the House districts electing white/non-Hispanic men compared to women over time. Almost all of the twelve measures comparing districts electing men and women are statistically significant across all three time periods. There are only three exceptions: the proportion of black residents from 1956 to 1990, the proportion of Hispanic residents from 1956 to 1990, and the school-age population from 2002 to 2010.

Table 7.3 The Shifting Demographics of House Districts Electing Men and Women, by Party, 1956–2010

	Districts Electing Men 1956–1990 (n = 7,177)	Districts Electing Women 1956–1990 (n = 275)	Districts Electing Men 1992–2000 (n = 1,704)	Districts Electing Women 1992–2000 (n = 188)	Districts Electing Men 2002–2010 (n = 1,610)	Districts Electing Women 2002–2010 (n = 249)
Democrats						
Partisanship						
Republican share of presidential vote	49.8%	46.9%[a]	42.9%	38.7%[a]	43.4%	37.5%[a]
Geography						
District size, square miles	2,416.0	349.0[a]	1,550.0	472.0[a]	1,862.0	485.0[a]
Urban residents	71.3%	96.8%[a]	78.9%	95.9%[a]	79.1%	98.0%[a]
Elected from the South	33.0%	14.5%[a]	25.6%	8.0%[a]	21.4%	5.4%[a]
Diversity						
Black residents	12.5%	12.3%	9.3%	7.9%[a]	10.4%	8.0%[a]
Hispanic residents	4.9%	4.5%	7.2%	9.1%[a]	10.2%	15.5%[a]
Foreign-born residents	5.7%	8.3%[a]	7.5%	11.8%[a]	11.4%	17.3%[a]
Socioeconomic						
Relative median income	96.3%	107.4%[a]	104.8%	125.8%[a]	106.7%	120.9%[a]
Blue-collar workers	31.6%	27.5%[a]	14.5%	10.8%[a]	8.7%	7.5%[a]
College degrees	12.5%	15.5%[a]	19.6%	27.4%[a]	25.1%	31.2%[a]
Married women	64.6%	59.6%[a]	56.1%	52.3%[a]	50.8%	47.7%[a]
School-age population	20.4%	18.5%[a]	14.9%	13.1%[a]	15.6%	15.5%

continues

Table 7.3 continued

	Districts Electing Men 1956–1990 (n = 7,177)	Districts Electing Women 1956–1990 (n = 275)	Districts Electing Men 1992–2000 (n = 1,704)	Districts Electing Women 1992–2000 (n = 188)	Districts Electing Men 2002–2010 (n = 1,610)	Districts Electing Women 2002–2010 (n = 249)
Republicans						
Partisanship						
Republican share of presidential vote	59.6%	58.7%	54.2%	51.8%[a]	58.6%	57.5%
Geography						
District size, square miles	3,147.0	925.0[a]	3,660.0	1,403.0[a]	4,033.0	4,424.0
Urban residents	64.8%	75.6%[a]	67.4%	81.4%[a]	73.6%	72.4%
Elected from the South	16.0%	0.0%[a]	30.3%	17.1%[a]	36.3%	34.0%
Diversity						
Black residents	5.4%	4.1%[a]	6.9%	5.2%[a]	7.8%	6.3%[a]
Hispanic residents	3.6%	2.6%[a]	5.8%	5.6%	7.9%	8.1%
Foreign-born residents	4.7%	7.0%[a]	5.2%	6.6%[a]	6.9%	6.0%
Socioeconomic						
Relative median income	106.0%	116.4%[a]	109.3%	123.6%[a]	109.5%	108.4%
Blue-collar workers	30.2%	26.8%[a]	14.2%	12.0%[a]	9.3%	9.7%[a]
College degrees	14.7%	17.0%[a]	20.5%	25.0%[a]	24.2%	24.4%
Married women	67.1%	66.7%	60.2%	59.9%	55.9%	56.1%
School-age population	20.7%	19.7%[a]	15.6%	14.9%[a]	16.2%	15.7%[a]

Source: Data compiled by the authors.

Notes: Districts electing African Americans and Hispanics not included.

a. The difference between districts electing men and women is statistically significant with $p < 0.05$.

Democratic districts that elect women are consistently more Democratic than those that elect men. In fact, the differences between the Republican share of the presidential vote among the districts that elected men and
women increase in each time period. While all Democratic districts became
"less Republican" over time, by the 2002–2010 period Democratic women
come from districts that are substantially more Democratic than districts
that elected Democratic men. With respect to geography, Democratic districts electing women are smaller and, not surprisingly, more urban; districts
electing white/non-Hispanic women are almost 100 percent urban across all
three time periods. The districts where these women are successful are also
far more likely to be outside the South than the districts where men have
been successful. Democratic districts electing women have, since 1992, a
significantly lower proportion of black residents than those districts electing men. However, over the same time frame, Democratic districts electing
women have significantly larger Hispanic and foreign-born populations.
For Democratic men, the proportions of Hispanic and foreign-born constituents have doubled over time. For Democratic women, these proportions
have tripled. Thus, Democratic women have gradually represented districts
that have become more diverse.

Some of the most consistent and dramatic differences between the
Democratic districts electing men and women are seen among the socioeconomic factors. For example, Democratic women have always been
elected in wealthier districts than Democratic men. Median income in
Democratic districts actually peaked during the 1992–2000 period; median
income in districts electing nonminority men increased from 96 percent to
105 percent of the national average, but in districts electing women, it shot
up from 107 percent to 126 percent of the national average. In fact, during
the 1992–2000 period, Democratic women came from the wealthiest districts in the nation. During the 2002–2010 period, while median incomes
declined, the difference between districts electing men and women was
still 14 percent. Shifts in the proportion of blue-collar workers also reveal
dramatic changes. While the "working class" has been disappearing in all
Democratic districts, Democratic women have always been more successful in districts with lower proportions of blue-collar workers. White/non-
Hispanic Democratic women also come from districts with more
constituents who are less likely to have traditional attitudes about women.
Democratic women are elected in districts with a higher proportion of people with college degrees, fewer married couples, and smaller school-age
populations.

The differences since 1992 are particularly striking. Compared to male
Democrats and both male and female Republicans, female Democrats rep-

resent the most wealthy, most diverse, most educated, and least blue-collar districts, the vast majority of which are outside the South. In short, nonminority female Democrats are elected from the most upscale, "swanky," "bohemian" House districts in the nation, the kinds of districts most likely to have a Starbucks on every corner and a Prius in every garage.

Examination of the Republican districts presented in Table 7.3 reveals two stories. The first covers the two periods that extend from 1956 to 2000. Almost all of the twelve measures comparing districts electing Republican men and women are statistically significant across these two time periods. There are only four exceptions: the Republican share of the presidential vote and the proportion of married residents during the 1956–1990 period, and the percentage of Hispanic and married residents during the 1992–2000 period. While not as sharp as those found among the Democrats, it is clear that there are differences between Republican districts that elected white/non-Hispanic men and women from 1956 to 2000.

While the difference is not statistically significant during the 1956–1992 period, Republican women were successful in districts with a smaller Republican share of the presidential vote. In other words, nonminority Republican women were elected in districts that were more moderate. The geographic factors provide the most consistent differences. While Republican districts are larger than Democratic districts generally, Republican districts that elected a woman during these periods were decidedly smaller than the districts that elected males; the districts that elected men were almost triple the size of those that elected women. Unsurprisingly, Republican women also come from districts that have substantially larger urban populations. Women of the GOP are also substantially less likely to come from the South. In fact, during the 1956–1990 period, there were no Republican women in Southern districts. Districts that elected a Republican woman also had fewer black residents and larger foreign-born populations than those that elected Republican men.

During these earlier two periods, the socioeconomic factors highlight some interesting differences as well. Republican districts that elected a white/non-Hispanic woman before 2002 were significantly wealthier than districts that elected Republican men. Just as we saw in Democratic districts, median income peaked during the 1992–2000 period. In addition, the gains were the largest in those districts electing women. In districts electing Republican men, median income increased only from 106 percent of the national average to 109 percent. In districts electing Republican women, median income increased from 116 percent to 124 percent. From 1992 to 2000, the gap between districts electing men and women was 14 percent. Districts electing Republican women also had a smaller blue-collar work force compared to districts electing their male counterparts. In addition, these districts also had more constituents who were more likely to have nontraditional attitudes about women's roles, with higher proportions of college graduates and smaller school-age populations.

Through the election of 2000, then, the districts electing nonminority Republican women shared a number of characteristics with those electing Democratic women. These districts were smaller, more urban, more diverse, and less likely to be in the South. They were also wealthier, less blue-collar, and more educated, and had fewer school-age children. All of this suggests that white/non-Hispanic Republican women were elected in districts that were less stereotypically Republican than the districts of their male counterparts. Thus, until 2002, there is ample evidence to conclude that both Democratic and Republican women represented districts that had a distinct "women-friendly" profile.

The second story about Republican women focuses on the elections from 2002 to 2010. During this time, the distinctiveness of those districts electing Republican women disappears. As Table 7.3 illustrates, there are no statistically meaningful differences between the districts that elect Republican men and women in their Republican share of the presidential vote, square miles, the proportion of urban residents, median income, the proportion of Hispanic and foreign-born residents, proportion of residents with college degrees, or the proportion of married residents. One of the most dramatic shifts is in where women are successful: while there were no women elected in Southern districts during the 1952–1990 period, by the 2002–2010 period a third of all Republican women in the House were from the South, virtually equal to the proportion of men. The relationship between the political geography of a district and the election of Republican women dissolved during the period of 2002–2010.

This change is attributable, in part, to the turnover among Republican women that has occurred in just the last three election cycles. During the 2002–2010 period, sixteen Republican women left the House; nine retired and seven were incumbents defeated in their reelection bids. Twenty-one new Republican women won their first election to the House. There are dramatic differences in the district profiles of those Republican women who left and those who entered. Those women entering the House came from districts that were much larger (4,434 versus 2,355 square miles), less urban (65 percent versus 87 percent), and less wealthy (median incomes of 102 percent versus 119 percent of the national average), and had smaller proportions of college graduates (23 percent versus 29 percent). Among the women who left the House during this period, several represented constituencies that were classic examples of women-friendly districts, such as Connie Morella of Maryland (99 percent urban and a median income of

166 percent of the national average), Marge Roukema of New Jersey (81 percent urban and median income of 174 percent), Sue Kelly of New York (79 percent urban and median income of 157 percent), Deborah Pryce of Ohio (91 percent urban and median income of 107 percent), and Thelma Drake of Virginia (92 percent urban and median income of 108 percent).

It is also noteworthy that eleven of the sixteen departures by Republican women occurred during the Democratic "wave election" cycles of 2006 and 2008.[95] Eight of the eleven Republican women who left during these two elections were replaced by Democrats. In contrast, the eight Republican women who won their first election in the Republican "wave election" of 2010 came from districts that we would characterize as distinctly "unfriendly" toward female candidates. All of these Republican women won in districts previously held by Democrats with average urban populations of only 62 percent and median incomes of just 99 percent of the national average. Among these women were Martha Roby of Alabama (with a district that was only 50 percent urban and median income of 79 percent of the national average), Vicky Hartzler of Missouri (40 percent urban and median income of 84 percent), Renee Ellmers of North Carolina (49 percent urban and median income of 89 percent), and Diane Black of Tennessee (53 percent urban and median income of 97 percent).

The different profiles of the departing and arriving Republican women raise the question of whether this change is an aberration produced by the tremendous volatility created by three consecutive wave elections and, in particular, the uniqueness of the 2010 election, or whether changes in the character of electoral politics have dissolved the relationship between the political geography of a district and the election of Republican women. An answer to this question depends, at least in part, on the redistricting regimes that will be in place by 2012, as well as the character of national forces and party strategies operating in the 2012 election cycle and beyond.

The Demographics of Districts
Electing African American and Hispanic Men and Women

Having shown that white/non-Hispanic women represent districts that are distinct from those of their male counterparts, are there similar patterns among minority men and women? Among the ninety-six African American Democrats elected to the House from 1956 to 2010, twenty-seven, or 28 percent, were women. Among the thirty-six Hispanic Democratic House members, six, or 17 percent, were women. Table 7.4 presents the demographic measures for districts electing African American men and women and Hispanic men and women.[96]

Table 7.4   House Districts Electing African American and Hispanic Male and Female Democrats, 1956–2010

	Districts Electing Black Male Democrats (n = 472)	Districts Electing Black Female Democrats (n = 135)	Districts Electing Hispanic Male Democrats (n = 216)	Districts Electing Hispanic Female Democrats (n = 45)
Partisanship				
Republican share of presidential vote	22.4%	22.7%	36.5%	29.4%[a]
Geography				
District size, square miles	79.0	108.0	199.0	59.0[a]
Urban residents	100.0%	100.0%	98.3%	100.0%[a]
Elected from the South	29.9%	38.1%	40.7%	0.0%[a]
Diversity				
Black residents	57.2%	47.0%[a]	8.5%	5.2%[a]
Hispanic residents	8.1%	17.1%[a]	57.7%	64.5%[a]
Foreign-born residents	10.3%	15.3%[a]	21.0%	43.6%[a]
Socioeconomic				
Relative median income	86.7%	82.9%[a]	76.6%	88.5%[a]
Blue-collar workers	18.2%	15.7%[a]	18.4%	14.3%[a]
College degrees	16.1%	16.2%	11.7%	11.8%
Married women	41.7%	40.7%	54.1%	52.2%
School-age population	17.7%	18.7%[a]	20.6%	18.2%[a]

Source: Data compiled by the authors.

Note: a. The difference between districts electing men and women is statistically significant with $p < 0.05$.

As the table shows, among African American male and female House members, there are significant differences for six of the twelve demographic measures. Both African American men and women are elected from districts with very low levels of support for Republican presidential candidates, only 22 and 23 percent respectively. In fact, these districts are extremely safe; no black incumbent Democrat, male or female, has ever been defeated in a general election.[97] Geographically, these districts are quite small, and are 100 percent urban. Male and female African Americans are equally likely to be elected from districts in the South. There are, however, some noteworthy patterns with regard to the race and ethnicity of the constituents in these districts. Districts that have elected African American men have a substantially larger proportion of black residents than districts that have elected African American women, 57 percent compared to 47 percent, a 10-point gap. African American women, however, represent districts that have much larger Hispanic populations, 17 percent versus 9 percent for the districts represented by their male counterparts, and larger foreign-born populations, 15 percent versus 10 percent. African American women are elected from districts that are somewhat poorer, with a smaller blue-collar work force. Blacks and Hispanics elected as Democrats represent what could be considered historically "hyper-Democratic" districts. These districts rank as the most Democratic in their voting behavior, the most urban, and the most diverse, and, in the tradition of the New Deal alignment, represent constituents who are less wealthy and have less education.

Overall, then, there are distinctions between the Democratic districts electing black men compared to those electing women, but they are not as numerous as the distinctions between those electing white/non-Hispanic men compared to women. Importantly, however, it should also be noted that black and white/non-Hispanic women share several commonalities: they represent the portion of "urban America" that is highly partisan and diverse. And given the role that racial gerrymandering plays in these districts, it is quite surprising that there are as many differences as there are in the districts that have elected African American men compared to women. In other words, even among majority-minority districts, there are still differences between the districts that elect male compared to female House members.

Our concept of the "women-friendly" district also works quite well for understanding the election of Hispanic female House members. There are clear differences between the districts electing Hispanic Democratic men compared to women, which are, for the most part, similar to the differences found between districts electing white/non-Hispanic men compared to women. Table 7.4 shows that there are statistically significant differences for ten of the twelve demographic measures. Hispanic women are elected in districts that have even lower support for Republican presidential candidates than the districts that elect Hispanic men. Hispanic female Democrats come from the smallest districts in the nation, averaging only fifty-nine square miles; these districts are almost one-fourth the size of the districts electing Hispanic male Democrats. They are also 100 percent urban. None of these women come from districts in the South, while 41 percent of their male counterparts do. With respect to diversity, female Hispanics are elected in districts with significantly larger populations of Hispanic and foreign-born residents. Like white/non-Hispanic women, Latina House members come from districts that are wealthier and that have fewer blue-collar workers and school-age residents. Overall, then, the demographic factors that determine electoral success for Hispanic men compared to women mirror those for white/non-Hispanic men compared to women.

▓ Conclusion

Our analysis in Chapter 5 suggested that women candidates tended to cluster in particular districts; female incumbents were far more likely than male incumbents to face challenges from other women. Based on our findings in this chapter, we now have some insight into why this occurs. The districts that elect male candidates are quite different from those that elect female candidates. The demographics of a district not only predict whether a Democrat or Republican can win, but also can be used to predict whether a man or woman will win.

The demographic profiles of the districts that have elected white/non-Hispanic Democratic women are the most distinct. Compared to male Democrats, female Democrats represent districts that are smaller, more urban, more diverse, wealthier, more educated, less blue-collar, and significantly less likely to be in the South. In fact, the shifting demographic coalitions and polarization that have occurred over the past thirty years within the Democratic Party appear to be correlated with the success of white/non-Hispanic female Democratic candidates. For example, the Democratic Party has found increasing success in districts that are wealthy and have fewer working-class voters, especially in those kinds of districts outside the South. These are precisely the districts where Democratic female House members have found increasing success. Over the past fifty years, districts electing white/non-Hispanic Democrats have become increasingly supportive of Democratic presidential candidates, smaller and more urban, and more racially and ethnically diverse. The districts electing women are the most extreme examples of these trends.

The demographic profiles of the districts that have elected white/non-Hispanic Republican women are also distinct from those electing Republican men. The demographics of these districts are, in many respects, "less Republican," in that they are, for example, smaller, more urban, and more ethnically diverse. This may explain, at least in part, the development of the party gap that we explored in Chapter 6, and the lack of Republican women in the House relative to the number of Democratic women. It suggests that Republican women have, until recently, faced a "catch-22." The districts where they were most likely to win the primary were the districts where they were the least likely to win the general election; their gender was an advantage, but their party was a disadvantage.[98] It does appear, however, that the distinctiveness of the districts where Republican women have been successful may be in flux, given the volatility in the last three election cycles in our analysis. In the three consecutive wave elections of 2006, 2008, and 2010, there was a noticeable change in the kinds of districts where white/non-Hispanic Republican women were successful.

The demographic profiles of the districts that have elected Democratic African American and Hispanic women are also distinct from those electing their male counterparts. While the differences in the districts electing Hispanic female House members are clearer than for those electing black female House members, the fact that there are any differences at all is quite remarkable, given the role that racial gerrymandering plays in the election of minority House members.

Thus, while there are some caveats, the concept of women-friendly districts appears to hold across the race of House candidates and over time. As it turns out, incumbency may not be the only barrier to increasing the number of women in the House. Without doubt, as we explored in Chapter 2, female candidates—or any candidates for that matter—have a significantly better chance of winning an open seat than defeating an incumbent. The number of open seats in a given election cycle, however, is quite small. Moreover, as our analysis here shows, once the demographic characteristics of these seats are taken into account, the number of real opportunities for women, be they Democrat, Republican, white/non-Hispanic, African American, or Hispanic, could be even smaller.

■ Notes

1. We would like to acknowledge Barbara Burrell, who first used this terminology in her 1994 book, *A Woman's Place Is In the House.*

2. See, for example, Ardoin and Garand, "Measuring Constituency Ideology in US House Districts"; Bishop, *The Big Sort;* Black and Black, *The Rise of Southern Republicans;* Bond, "The Influence of Constituency Diversity on Electoral Competition in Voting for Congress"; Chinni and Gimpel, *Our Patchwork Nation;* Erikson, Wright, and McIver, *Statehouse Democracy;* Fiorina, *Representatives, Roll Calls, and Constituencies;* Judis and Teixeira, *The Emerging Democratic Majority;* Key, *Southern Politics in State and Nation;* Page et al., "Constituency, Party, and Representation in Congress"; Teixeira, *Red, Blue, and Purple America.*

3. Fenno, *Home Style,* p. 2.

4. Ibid., p. 3.

5. Flanigan and Zingale, *Political Behavior of the American Electorate,* 8th ed.; Koetzle, "The Impact of Constituency Diversity upon the Competitiveness of US House Elections."

6. We recognize that the grammatically correct phrase would be "demographics are destiny." However, the phrase used colloquially by many consultants and candidates is "demographics is destiny," which is why we use it here.

7. See Burrell, *A Woman's Place Is In the House.* There are some studies on women in state legislatures: Jones and Nelson, "Correlates of Women's Representation in Lower State Legislative Chambers"; Nechemias, "Geographic Mobility and Women's Access to State Legislatures"; Nechemias, "Changes in the Election of Women to US State Legislative Seats"; Norrander and Wilcox, "Change in Con-

tinuity in the Geography of Women State Legislators"; Rule, "Why Women Don't Run"; Rule, "Why More Women Are Legislators."

8. Downs, *An Economic Theory of Democracy.*

9. See, for example, Hale, "The Making of the New Democrats."

10. See, for example, Hackler and Pierson, *Off Center.*

11. Peters and Rosenthal, *Speaker Nancy Pelosi and the New American Politics,* p. 9.

12. Ibid., pp. 5–13.

13. Bishop, "A Steady Slide Toward a More Partisan Union."

14. Ibid.

15. See, for example, Eilperin, *Fight Club Politics;* Fiorina and Levendusky, "Disconnected"; Galston and Nivola, "Delineating the Problem"; Mann and Ornstein, *The Broken Branch;* Sinclair, *Party Wars.*

16. Flanigan and Zingale, *Political Behavior of the American Electorate,* 8th ed.

17. Peters and Rosenthal, *Speaker Nancy Pelosi and the New American Politics,* p. 5.

18. See, for example, Bishop, *The Big Sort;* Chinni and Gimpel, *Our Patchwork Nation;* Dionne, "Polarized by God?"; Frank, *What's the Matter with Kansas?;* Gelman, *Red State, Blue State, Rich State, Poor State;* Lublin, *The Republican South;* McTague and Layman, "Religion, Parties, and Voting Behavior"; Teixeira, *Red, Blue, and Purple America.*

19. See, for example, Teixeira, *Red, Blue, and Purple America.*

20. Canon, *Race, Redistricting, and Representation,* p. 1.

21. See, for example, Grofman and Handley, "Minority Population Proportion and the Black and Hispanic Congressional Success in the 1970s and 1980s"; Handley and Grofman, "The Impact of the Voting Rights Act on Minority Representation"; Lublin, *The Paradox of Representation;* Canon, *Race, Redistricting, and Representation.*

22. Lublin, *The Paradox of Representation,* p. 40.

23. Ibid., p. viii.

24. Ibid., pp. 22–23. See also Cameron, Epstein, and O'Halloran, "Do Majority-Minority Districts Maximize Substantive Black Representation in Congress?"; Fleisher and Bond, "Polarized Politics"; Swain, *Black Faces, Black Interests;* Whitby, *The Color of Representation.*

25. See, for example, *Shaw v. Reno; Miller v. Johnson;* and *LULAC v. Perry.*

26. We gathered the Republican share of the two-party presidential vote from relevant editions of the *Congressional Quarterly Almanac* and the *Almanac of American Politics.* We then cross-checked these results with data kindly supplied by Professor Gary Jacobson of the University of San Diego. For the 1956–2000 period, the measures of district size, urbanization, black and foreign-born residents, median income, blue-collar workers, and school-age population were obtained from the files compiled by Professor Scott Adler (http://sobek.colorado.edu/~esadler/Data.html). Our measures of the Hispanic population and college degrees were calculated from data made available by Professor David Lublin (www1.american.edu/dlublin/). For the 2002–2010 period, we used the congressional district data from the 2000 decennial Census (http://factfinder.census.gov) and followed, as closely as possible, the definitions used by Adler and Lublin. The data on married women were obtained from labor force statistics produced by the US Census Bureau's Current Population Survey (Series LNU00000315). The data on the Hispanic population, college de-

grees, and married women are available since 1972; all other measures cover the entire period from 1956 to 2010. Until full implementation of the "one person, one vote" rule mandated by *Baker v. Carr* and *Wesberry v. Sanders,* states often added a newly gained seat as an at-large or statewide district. Between 1956 and 1968, there were forty-five of these at-large elections. We exclude these from our analysis.

27. For nine of our twelve measures, we use the mean values: Republican share of the presidential vote, the proportion of black, Hispanic, and foreign-born residents, median income, blue-collar workers, residents with college degrees, married women, and school-age population. For these measures, we use a difference-in-means test to determine if the districts that elect Democrats and Republicans are statistically distinct. For two measures, district size and urbanization, because their distributions are unusual and skewed, we use their median values. When data are skewed, the median offers a more satisfactory measure of central tendency in a distribution. To test for group differences on these two measures, we use the Mann-Whitney test, which is the nonparametric counterpart of the difference-in-means test. For our measure of the South, we calculate the proportion of Democrats and Republicans elected from this region and use the resulting chi-square statistic from the cross-tabulation to determine statistical significance.

28. See, for example, Campbell et al., *The American Voter;* Flanigan and Zingale, *Political Behavior of the American Electorate,* 8th and 10th eds.; Lau and Redlawsk, "Advantages and Disadvantages of Cognitive Heuristics in Political Decision Making"; Lau and Sears, *Political Cognition;* Rahn, "The Role of Partisan Stereotypes in Information Processing About Political Candidates."

29. "President National Exit Poll."

30. Burrell, *A Woman's Place Is In the House,* pp. 48–51.

31. Lang, Sanchez, and Berube, "The New Suburban Politics."

32. Nechemias, "Geographic Mobility and Women's Access to State Legislatures." One study found that populous states with small legislatures had smaller proportions of women state legislators, which also suggests that district size acts as a constraint; Werner, "Women in the State Legislatures."

33. Fox, "Gender, Political Ambition, and the Decision Not to Run for Office"; Lawless and Fox, *It Still Takes a Candidate;* Sapiro, "Private Costs of Public Commitments or Public Costs of Private Commitments?"

34. Halberstam, *The Fifties,* p. 132.

35. Ibid., p. 135.

36. Lang, Sanchez, and Berube, "The New Suburban Politics."

37. Ibid. See also Bishop, *The Big Sort;* Chinni and Gimpel, *Our Patchwork Nation.*

38. Lang, Sanchez, and Berube, "The New Suburban Politics."

39. Burrell, "Women Candidates in Open-Seat Primaries for the US House"; Darcy and Schramm, "When Women Run Against Men"; Diamond, *Sex Roles in the State House;* Rule, "Why Women Don't Run"; Welch, "Are Women More Liberal Than Men in the US Congress?"; Welch et al., "The Effect of Candidate Gender on Election Outcomes in State Legislative Races." But see Kirkpatrick, *Political Woman;* Werner, "Women in the State Legislatures."

40. Darcy and Schramm, "When Women Run Against Men," p. 8.

41. Rule, "Why Women Don't Run," p. 71.

42. Darcy and Schramm, "When Women Run Against Men," p. 8.

43. Rule, "Why Women Don't Run," p. 65.

44. Black and Black, *The Rise of Southern Republicans;* Lublin, *The Republican South.*

45. Burrell, *A Woman's Place Is In the House,* p. 49.

46. Nuwer, "Southern Women Legislators and Patriarchy in the South"; Twenge, "Attitudes Towards Women."

47. Elazar, *American Federalism,* p. 93.

48. Wolbrecht, *The Politics of Women's Rights,* p. 187.

49. Nuwer, "Southern Women Legislators and Patriarchy in the House," p. 450.

50. Reed, *The Enduring South.*

51. Wolbrecht, *The Politics of Women's Rights,* p. 187.

52. Spruill and Wheeler, "The Equal Rights Amendment and Mississippi."

53. "Rape in Marriage."

54. Canedy, "Florida 'Scarlet Letter' Law Is Repealed by Gov. Bush."

55. See, for example, Barreto, "Si, Se Pueda!"; Frey, "Race, Immigration, and America's Changing Electorate"; Herron and Sekhon, "Black Candidates and Black Voters"; Leal et al., "The Latino Vote in the 2004 Election"; Wong, "Mobilizing Asian-American Voters."

56. Morello, "Census Count Finds Decreasing White Population in 15 States."

57. Results are from the national exit polls; for 1976 to 1988, they can be found in Stanley and Niemi, *Vital Statistics on American Politics,* 4th ed., and for 1992 to 2004 in Stanley and Niemi, *Vital Statistics on American Politics, 2009–2010.* The 2008 exits polls are available at www.cnn.com/ELECTION/2008/results/polls.main.

58. Bullock, *Redistricting,* pp. 49–86.

59. Welch, "Are Women More Liberal Than Men in the US Congress?"

60. Gelman, *Red State, Blue State, Rich State, Poor State.* See also Frank, *What's the Matter with Kansas?*

61. Gelman, *Red State, Blue State, Rich State, Poor State.* See also Brooks, *On Paradise Drive;* Chinni and Gimpel, *Our Patchwork Nation;* Frank, *What's the Matter with Kansas?*

62. "President National Exit Poll."

63. More specifically, simply using the median income in each district could be problematic given the upward trend in the measure over the decades of our analysis. For example, the median income across all congressional districts was $9,555 for the 1972–1980 districting period; this increased to $19,701 for 1982–1990, and increased again to $34,114 for 1992–2000. Median income across all congressional districts in the 2000 US Census was $41,060. To control for this drift, we use these national median values from each redistricting period and then divide each district's median by the national median. Thus the measure expresses median income in the district as a proportion of the median across all districts for each redistricting period. The interpretation of the measure is easy. Values greater than 100 percent represent districts over the national median, and values less than 100 percent represent those below the national median. The magnitude of the measure conveys the degree to which a district is rich or poor compared to all congressional districts in a given redistricting period. Over the time frame of our analysis, the values of the relative income measure range from 42.7 to 196.0 percent.

64. Burrell, *A Woman's Place Is In the House;* Nechemias, "Changes in the Election of Women to US State Legislative Seats"; Rule, "Why Women Don't Run"; Welch, "Are Women More Liberal Than Men in the US Congress?"

65. Rule, "Why Women Don't Run," p. 69.

66. Abramowitz and Teixeira, "The Decline of the White Working Class and the Rise of a Mass Upper-Middle Class," p. 110.

67. Abramowitz and Teixeira, "The Decline of the White Working Class and the Rise of a Mass Upper-Middle Class."

68. Frank, *What's the Matter with Kansas?*

69. MacGillis, "Obama Meets with Labor Leaders."

70. Gelman, "Where the Starbucks and Walmarts Are"; "Do Latte Drinkers Really Vote for Obama?"

71. Frank, *What's the Matter with Kansas?* p. 2.

72. While we do know that the proportion of blue-collar workers has declined over time, we want to point out that part of the decline in the blue-collar measure shown in Table 7.1 is also likely due to changing definitions of "blue-collar work" by the Census Bureau.

73. Barone and Cohen, *Almanac of American Politics, 2004,* pp. 1293–1296.

74. Michael Kirwan (D-OH, 1937–1970), Charles Carney (D-OH, 1970–1979), Lyle Williams (R-OH, 1979–1983), James Traficant (D-OH, 1983–2003), and Tim Ryan (D-OH, 2003–present).

75. Barone and Cohen, *Almanac of American Politics, 2002,* p. 1138.

76. Nechemias, "Changes in the Election of Women to US State Legislative Seats"; Welch and Studlar, "The Opportunity Structure for Women's Candidacies and Electability in Britain and the United States."

77. Rule, "Why Women Don't Run," p. 64; Welch and Studlar, "The Opportunity Structure for Women's Candidacies and Electability in Britain and the United States," p. 869. See also Sanbonmatsu, "Political Parties and the Recruitment of Women to State Legislatures"; Starr, "Bada Bing Club," pp. 10–12.

78. Carroll, "Misogynist Massachusetts."

79. Starr, "Bada Bing Club," p. 10.

80. McGreevey, *The Confession.*

81. Abramowitz and Teixeira, "The Decline of the White Working Class and the Rise of a Mass Upper-Middle Class."

82. National Center for Education Statistics, "Table 8: Percentage of Persons."

83. "President National Exit Poll."

84. Nechemias, "Changes in the Election of Women to US State Legislative Seats."

85. See, for example, Welch and Sigelman, "Changes in Public Attitudes Toward Women in Politics"; Arceneaux, "The 'Gender Gap' in State Legislative Representation."

86. Burrell, *A Woman's Place Is In the House.*

87. Smith, "Changes in Family Structure, Family Values, and Politics."

88. Ibid.

89. See, for example, Lake, Conway, and Whitney, *What Women Really Want;* Smith, "Changes in Family Structure, Family Values, and Politics"; "Unmarried Women Play Critical Role in Historic Election."

90. "Election Polls: Vote by Groups, 2008."

91. Smith, "Changes in Family Structure, Family Values, and Politics."

92. Ibid.

93. Lang, Sanchez, and Berube, "The New Suburban Politics," pp. 34–35; Smith, "Changes in Family Structure, Family Values, and Politics."

94. In the Republican primary, Scott defeated the sons of former governor Car-

roll Campbell and former senator Strom Thurmond; Barone and McCutcheon, *Almanac of American Politics, 2012,* p. 1450.

95. See, for example, Simon and Palmer, "Beyond Hillary"; Simon and Palmer, "Women and Elections to the US House of Representatives."

96. Given that 1992 was the first election after the creation of majority-minority districts, it would be very useful to conduct our analysis here over three time periods, as we did in Table 7.1. However, the small number of cases in the earliest period does not make this practical. In addition, it should be noted that Representative Cynthia McKinney (D-GA) is counted once in our total number of African American Democratic candidates here, although she was elected as a new member of the House on two occasions. She won her first election in the Eleventh District of Georgia in 1992. In the 2002 Democratic primary in the renumbered Fourth District of Georgia, she was defeated by Denise Majette, who went on to win the general election. When Majette vacated the seat in 2004 to run for the Senate, McKinney recaptured the seat. In 2006, McKinney lost her second primary election to Hank Johnson.

97. However, sixteen black Democratic incumbents have been defeated in the primaries. One black Republican, Gary Franks, was defeated in the general election in 1996, losing to Democrat Jim Maloney in the Fifth District of Connecticut.

98. See also Matland and King, "Women as Candidates in Congressional Elections."

EIGHT

Women of the Twenty-First Century

In many respects, Representative Debbie Wasserman Schultz (D-FL) personifies the changes that have occurred among the women running for Congress in the twenty-first century. Her career reveals not only how cultural attitudes about women's roles have changed, but also how the pipeline for political office has opened for women. In addition, she represents a district that is quintessentially women-friendly. In 1992, at the age of twenty-six, Wasserman Schultz successfully ran for the Florida state house of representatives, becoming the youngest woman elected in the state's history. She then became the mother of twins and successfully ran for the Florida state senate. In August 2003, she had a baby girl and hit the campaign trail again, this time for the US House.[1] "My generation," Wasserman Schultz explained, "is significantly unrepresented in terms of public policy and decision making. As a woman today, it's very different living through raising children and balancing work and family."[2]

Once in the House, Wasserman Schultz quickly rose through the ranks into leadership positions, and in the 112th Congress (2011 session) served as the vice chair of the House Democratic Steering and Policy Committee and as chief deputy whip. Representative Melissa Bean (D-IL), a former House colleague with whom Wasserman Schultz shared a town house, explained how Wasserman Schultz would fall asleep with "her head on her laptop or on top of her briefing book. Not only does she not quit. She won't even quit on herself."[3] Wasserman Schultz's fundraising abilities are legendary.[4] For her 2010 reelection campaign, while the average House incumbent raised $1.75 million, she brought in over $4.5 million.[5] In 2007, she was diagnosed with breast cancer. Even after multiple surgeries, she rarely took a day off and only told her immediate family and closest friends; "I didn't want it to define me. . . . I didn't want my name to be

Debbie Wasserman Schultz who is currently battling breast cancer."[6] To raise awareness—and money—she organized the first women's congressional softball team.[7] In April 2011, she became the second woman to chair the Democratic National Committee.[8] Some have speculated that she is on her way to becoming the second female speaker of the House.[9]

Wasserman Schultz's electoral history is also a prime example of how female candidates often find themselves running against other female candidates. The first time she ran for the House in the open seat race in 2004, Wasserman Schultz defeated Republican Margaret Hostetter, a Realtor who had never run for office before, with 70 percent of the vote. While Wasserman Schultz ran unopposed in 2006, Hostetter came back for a rematch in 2008 running as an Independent; Wasserman Schultz won with 77 percent of the vote. In 2010, Wasserman Schultz faced another female Republican, Karen Harrington, defeating her by 22 points.

The fact that Wasserman Schultz has faced multiple female opponents should come as no surprise given the nature of the district she represents. The Twentieth District of Florida is quite small, only 218 square miles, and 100 percent urban. In 2008, the district supported Barack Obama with 64 percent of the vote; the constituency is strongly Democratic. It is also quite diverse, with 8 percent of the residents being black, 21 percent being Hispanic, and 27 percent being foreign-born. The district is also upscale; median income is 107 percent of the national average, blue-collar workers compose only 7 percent of the work force, and 30 percent of its residents have earned college degrees. Wasserman Schultz comes from a district that is distinctly women-friendly.

■ The Rules of the Game

In 2010, with seventy-two women elected to the House and seventeen women serving in the Senate, there is no doubt that progress has been made. Women made up 17 percent of Congress. On the other hand, one could still say that women have "a very small share, though a very large stake, in political power."[10] Cultural norms and gender role expectations have changed, but there are still remnants, particularly when it comes to raising children and housework. On the other hand, the political pipeline is now open to women, and their career paths look much like those of their male colleagues. In addition, redistricting and demographic trends may actually provide more opportunities for women in the future. Table 8.1 provides a profile of the sixty women who were elected to the House for the first time between 2002 and 2010.

Table 8.1 Profile of the Sixty Women Elected to the US House Between 2002 and 2010

	Number of Women	Percentage
Race		
Women of color	15	25.0
Background		
Lawyer	21	35.0
Prior elective office experience		
Elected to local office	19	31.7
Elected to state house of representatives	25	41.7
Elected to state senate	19	31.7
Elected to statewide office	7	11.7
Other political experience		
Served in appointed administrative office	10	16.7
Served in party organization	2	3.3
Lateral entry		
Widow	1	1.7
No prior elective office experience	15	25.0
Party		
Democrat	37	61.7
Republican	23	38.3

Source: Data compiled by the authors.

Cultural Norms: No Longer a "Man's Game"

Cultural and social attitudes have transformed since the 1950s. A college degree is now regarded as important to the futures of both men and women. In 1950, only 24 percent of bachelor's degrees went to women; in 2008, 57 percent did.[11] In 1950, the average age of marriage for women was twenty; by 2008, it was twenty-six.[12] In 2008, only 2 percent of the respondents in the National Election Study believed that a woman's place was in the home.[13] Women composed 50 percent of the work force.[14] The proportion of married women in the work force was 59 percent, compared to 29 percent in 1956, and 64 percent of women with children under the age of six were in the work force.[15] The wage gap between men and women steadily declined, and by 2010 was the smallest in history: women earned 83 percent of what men earned. Single women between the ages of twenty-two and thirty actually earned 8 percent more than their male counterparts.[16]

Politics is no longer off-limits to women. Since the 1970s, the political participation of women has increased substantially. For the past two decades, voter turnout among women has consistently exceeded turnout among men by 2–3 percentage points. In the 2008 election, for example, 60 percent of women reported voting, compared to 56 percent of men; 7.6 million more women than men voted.[17] Women were as likely as men to engage in other kinds of political participation as well, including working on campaigns. In fact, women have more positive feelings than men about participating in campaigns, attending fundraisers, and going door-to-door to meet with constituents.[18] The 2008 Citizen Political Ambition Survey showed that among those in the "eligibility pool"—those who came from backgrounds and professions that made them the most likely to run for office—men and women had virtually equal political participation rates across a wide variety of activities, including giving money to a candidate, volunteering on a campaign, writing a letter to the editor, and serving on community boards.[19]

Black women, despite the formidable barriers blocking their political participation for most of the nineteenth and twentieth centuries, have more than caught up to black men and white women, particularly when it comes to running for office.[20] While none of the women elected between 1916 and 1956 were women of color, 25 percent of the women elected between 2002 and 2010 were, as Table 8.1 shows. For example, Representative Linda Sanchez (D-CA) ran for the House in 2002. She was the youngest of seven children. Her father was a mechanic and her mother was an elementary school teacher and, as Sanchez explained, they "wanted us to take advantage of all the opportunities they never had."[21] After graduating from law school at the University of California–Los Angeles, she became a civil rights attorney. Her sister, Loretta Sanchez (D-CA), successfully ran for the House in 1996, and Linda worked on her campaign. After Linda won her own House seat six years later, she said, "My passion is to get more women elected in politics. And if it's a Hispanic woman, it's even better."[22] The Sanchez sisters were the first and only pair of sisters to serve in Congress. In 2010, forty-one African Americans were elected to the House, including thirteen women; twenty-six Hispanics were elected to the House, including seven women.

Despite these changes, vestiges of old cultural norms remain. There is evidence that women of color are still dealing with the "double disadvantage." A survey of state legislators in 2000 showed that when African American women became party leaders or committee chairs, the influence of those positions actually declined; even when they reported good working relationships with legislative and party leaders, black women committee chairs were still excluded from the "real" power centers where decisions were made.[23] In addition, women are still substantially less likely to think about running for office in the first place. Speaking to a group of high school girls in 2010, Representative Gabrielle Giffords (D-AZ) explained that it is still "very challenging for women to see themselves right in the middle of it."[24] Even when they have the same résumés as men, women are less likely to think they are qualified to run for office; while women are no longer confined to "lickin' and stickin'" jobs on a campaign staff, they do not appear to be aware that their skills and backgrounds would make them good campaigners and legislators.[25] They are also less likely to be told by others, even members of their own families, that they should run for office.[26] On the positive side, although women are not encouraged to run for office as often as men, when they are encouraged, they are as likely to consider running.[27] Thus, internships, mentoring programs, and other informal recruitment methods—for example, something as simple as telling more women they should run—could have a substantial impact on the number of female candidates.[28]

Family connections still play an important role in the decisions female candidates make, but with one major change from the early part of the

Photo courtesy of Running Start and Ellie Van Houtte

Representative Linda Sanchez (D-CA) successfully ran for the House in 2002 with no prior elective office experience.

twentieth century: far fewer women follow their deceased husbands to a House seat. Between 1916 and 1956, well over a third of the women who served in the House were congressional widows. Table 8.1 shows that among the sixty women elected between 2002 and 2010, there was only one, Representative Doris Matsui (D-CA). In the 2005 special election held after the death of her husband from a rare bone marrow disease, Matsui defeated eleven opponents with 72 percent of the vote. Although she had never run for public office before, she served as deputy assistant to the president in the White House Office of Public Liaison from 1992 to 1998.[29] She successfully ran for her third full term in 2010.

In many respects, however, traditional attitudes about women's roles within the family have not changed that much. For women, housework and childcare still play major roles in the decision to pursue a political career, and women will often wait until their children are grown before they run.[30] As a result, women are still typically older than their male counterparts when they begin serving in Congress. Of the fifty-five women who were elected between 1916 and 1956, seven, or 13 percent, were under forty years old when they first ran for the House. Of the women who were first elected between 2002 and 2010, nine of the sixty, or 15 percent, were under forty years old when they first ran. The very first woman to successfully campaign for the House, Representative Jeannette Rankin (R-MT), was thirty-six when she ran in 1916. The youngest woman in the 112th Congress (2011 session) was Representative Jaime Herrera Beutler (R-WA). Prior to running for the House in 2010 at the age of thirty-two, she had worked as a legislative aide to Representative Cathy McMorris Rodgers (R-WA).[31] McMorris Rodgers had also started her congressional career young; she ran for the House when she was thirty-three.

While there are still relatively few young women in Congress, recently there has been a congressional "baby boom." Of the nine children born to female House members, five of them have been born since 2007. Voters still have a double standard when it comes to candidates with young children; they are more likely to question whether a mother with children can handle the demands of public office, while fathers are given a pass.[32] However, there are now many examples of women who have successfully combined politics and parenthood.

Entry Professions and the Pipeline

Over time, the backgrounds of the men and women who serve in Congress have converged; the career paths of women are becoming more like those of their male counterparts.[33] The entry professions of law and business are no longer blocked.[34] The proportion of law degrees awarded to women in

1956 was only 4 percent. In 2008, the proportion of law degrees awarded to women was 47 percent.[35] Prior to 1950, women were not accepted at Harvard Law School. In 2010, 48 percent of its students were women.[36] Women have also substantially increased their numbers in lower-level political offices. For the past three decades, there has been a relatively steady increase in the number of women serving in state legislatures. In 1971, 5 percent of state legislators were women. In 2010, 25 percent of state legislators were women,[37] and women of color composed 20 percent of all female state legislators.[38] In New Hampshire, women have come to dominate state politics. In 2008, the state became the first to have a legislative chamber with a majority of female members; the New Hampshire senate had thirteen women and eleven men. The president of the state senate was a woman. Nine of the state senate's fourteen committees were chaired by women. And the speaker of the New Hampshire house was a woman.[39] The political pipeline is now open.

As Table 8.1 illustrates, among the sixty women elected for the first time to the House between 2002 and 2010, twenty-one, or 35 percent, were lawyers. This is considerably greater than the 13 percent among the women

Photo courtesy of Running Start and Ellie Van Houtte

Representative Jaime Herrera Beutler (R-WA) was the youngest member of the 112th Congress (2011 session).

elected between 1916 and 1956. In the 112th Congress (2011 session), 40 percent of the men in Congress had law degrees, compared to 33 percent of the women.[40] Thirty-five of the sixty women, or 58 percent, served in their state legislatures before running for the US House (sixteen in the state house of representatives, ten in the state senate, and nine in both chambers). Overall then, 42 percent were elected to their state house of representatives and 32 percent were elected to their state senate. Among all the women elected between 1916 and 1956, only 16 percent had served in their state house of representatives, and 2 percent in their state senate. Iris Blitch (D-GA) was the only woman to serve in both state legislative chambers during the 1916 to 1956 era, whereas nine women of the twenty-first century have taken this route. For example, before she began her political career, Representative Giffords ran her family's tire business. In 2000, she successfully campaigned for the Arizona state house of representatives. Two years later, she ran for the state senate, becoming the youngest woman ever elected, at the age of thirty-two.[41] In 2006, she successfully ran for an open US House seat, defeating Republican Randy Graf, who had also served in the Arizona state senate. Shortly after winning her third term in an extremely close race, on January 8, 2011, Giffords was the victim of an assassination attempt while at a "Congress On Your Corner" event in a Tucson grocery store parking lot. She was talking to constituents about Medicare reimbursements when a young man walked up and opened fire, shooting Giffords in the head. Six people, including a federal judge, one of her staffers, and a nine-year-old girl, were killed. Thirteen more were injured.[42] Twenty-two-year-old Jared Lee Loughner was quickly identified as the shooter and was later determined to be paranoid schizophrenic, suffering from delusions and hallucinations.[43] Giffords survived, but was missing part of her brain. After spending several months in a rehabilitation center in Houston, on August 2 she surprised her colleagues by showing up on the House floor to vote on the controversial bill that would raise the debt ceiling.[44] While she has had trouble speaking, Giffords's recovery has been called "remarkable."[45] She resigned on January 25, 2012, after the House unanimously passed a bill she sponsored that gave federal law enforcement agencies more power to combat drug trafficking.[46]

As women gained access to the pipeline, the prominence of party experience in their backgrounds has declined. Between 1916 and 1956, 25 percent of the women elected to the House had worked for party organizations. However, among those elected in the past decade, only two have served in party organizations at the local, state, or national level. This suggests that women are now launching their political careers in lower-level elective office rather than serving apprenticeships in their parties.

Table 8.1 also shows that fifteen women, or 25 percent, were elected to the House without any prior elective office experience, which is a significant change; among the women who were elected in the first half of the twentieth century, only 11 percent had no prior elective office experience. While this suggests that female candidates have become "less qualified," this is actually another way that the political careers of men and women have been converging. In general, "lateral entry" into national office has increased over time; the traditional pipeline has become less relevant for all candidates. There are increasing numbers of "amateurs" who have never run for anything before becoming candidates for national office. For example, before she ran for the House, Loretta Sanchez worked in investment banking and as a strategist at a consulting firm. The closest thing she had to any political experience was working for the Orange County transportation authority for three years.[47] In 1996, she decided to run for the House and took on a nine-term incumbent, Representative Robert "B-1 Bob" Dornan (R-CA). She won by 984 votes. Dornan challenged the results and claimed that "the election was stolen through rampant illegal voting by noncitizens."[48] A fourteen-month investigation by the House Oversight Committee concluded that there were voting irregularities, but not enough to affect the outcome. Dornan challenged Sanchez in her 1998 reelection bid in what turned out to be the most expensive House race of the election cycle. The two candidates spent more than $6.4 million. Much of the election centered around the issue of abortion. Dornan, who was of Irish descent, called himself the "true Latino candidate" because of his pro-life position.[49] He lost badly, with only 39 percent of the vote. His concession speech turned into a tirade in which he spoke of a "fog of evil that has rolled across our country," and his daughter's boyfriend got into a fistfight with a police officer.[50]

Many of these first-time candidates capitalize on their celebrity status or spend a great deal of their own money to make up for their lack of political experience.[51] For example, as discussed in Chapter 4, some come from prominent political families, such as Representative Patrick Kennedy (D-RI) and Senator Ted Kennedy (D-MA). Before his Senate bid in 1994, Fred Thompson (R-TN) had a long career as an actor, with roles in *The Hunt for Red October, Cape Fear,* and *Die Hard II,* and guest appearances on *China Beach* and *Matlock.* Thompson resigned from the Senate in 2002 and landed the role of District Attorney Arthur Branch on *Law and Order.*[52] He ran for president in 2008. Fred Grandy (R-IA) played "Gopher" on *The Love Boat* for nine years before running for the House in 1986.[53] After playing "Cooter," the "good ole boy mechanic," on *The Dukes of Hazzard,* Ben Jones (D-GA) served for two terms in the House.[54] In 2008, Al Franken (D-MN), a comedy writer, author, and actor known for his "Stuart Smalley" character on *Saturday Night Live,* won an extremely close race for the Senate in Minnesota.[55] The 2010 election featured three Republican women who had never run for office before, but who, because of their success in the business world, were able to spend large sums of their own money to fund their campaigns. Carly Fiorina, the former CEO of Hewlett-Packard, spent $5.5 million of her own money to take on three-term incumbent senator Barbara Boxer (D-CA).[56] Linda McMahon, the former chief executive of World Wrestling Entertainment, spent over $50 million of her own money running for an open Senate seat in Connecticut.[57] Meg Whitman, former CEO of eBay and current CEO of Hewlett-Packard, spent over $140 million of her own money running for governor of California.[58] None of these women were successful. Whitman, however, did break the record for self-financing.[59]

Regardless of how they get there, once in Congress women are now as "careerist" as men and reap the advantages of incumbency. In the 112th Congress (2011 session), 22 percent of the male House members and 19 percent of the female House members had served for ten or more terms. The most senior woman, Representative Marcy Kaptur (D-OH), was first elected in 1982 and had served fifteen consecutive terms. Senator Barbara Mikulski (D-MD), first elected in 1986, was the most senior woman in the Senate; she ranked fourteenth in seniority among all her colleagues.[60] The average length of service in the House and Senate is longer for men than women, but the difference can be explained by the fact that most of the current women members have been elected since 1992. But the vast majority of women in Congress now seek long careers and are gradually accumulating the leadership roles and influence that come with long-term service.

Demographics and the Politics of Redistricting

Table 8.1 shows that 62 percent of the women elected in the twenty-first century have been Democrats, while 38 percent have been Republicans—virtually the same proportions that were elected in the first half of the twentieth century. This apparent similarity, however, masks significant changes in the party identification among the women who have served in the House, particularly since 1992. From 1916 to 1956, the difference between the number of Democratic and Republican women running in each election cycle was one or two, and Republican female candidates outnumbered Democratic female candidates in eight of the twenty-one election cycles. Since 1992, Republican women have never outnumbered Democratic women; as a proportion of their party's nominees, Democratic women have outnumbered Republican women two to one. As shown in Chapter 6, for the past two decades there has been a significant party gap in the number of women running and winning House elections.

Figure 8.1 shows another significant shift that has occurred: the Republican women elected since 2002 have been significantly more conservative than the Republican women of the early twentieth century.[61] Like Figure 1.1 in Chapter 1, Figure 8.1 provides a measure of ideology for House members based on their House floor roll call votes. The measure provides scores from 0 to 100; scores closer to 0 indicate representatives are more liberal, while numbers closer to 100 indicate representatives are more conservative.[62] Among all of the House members elected between 1916 and 1956, Figure 1.1 showed that women of both parties were to the left of their male counterparts: Democratic women were more liberal than Democratic men, and Republican women were more moderate than Republican men. However, Figure 8.1 reveals two major changes. First, while Democratic men and women have remained in virtually the same positions, all Republicans have moved to the right. Republican House members are much more conservative than those elected in the earlier period. Second, Republican women are now to the right of Republican men. While Republican men shifted 9 points to the right, female Republican House members shifted 16 points to the right.

This new pattern found in the voting records of female Republican House members is not terribly surprising, given our analysis in Chapter 7. Because of the change in the demographic profiles of the districts that have elected Republican women since 2002, it makes sense that these women have significantly more conservative voting records than women from earlier time periods.[63] The districts that have elected Republican women since 2002 are different from the districts that elected Republican women during the twentieth century. Given the centrality of demographics in determining the outcome of elections—and congressional voting behavior—redistricting and gerrymandering become all the more important in understanding

Figure 8.1   Ideology of Female and Male Members of the US House, 2002–2008

Most Liberal	Democrats		Republicans		Most Conservative
	Women	Men	Men	Women	
0.0	31.4	37.7	77.1	79.6	100.0

Source: Data compiled by Keith Poole and Howard Rosenthal, http://voteview.com/downloads.asp.

the integration of women into Congress. The process of redrawing district lines every ten years has the potential to shape the number of opportunities for female candidates.

With a few exceptions, redistricting is done by state legislatures. In most instances, special committees are created to draw the maps. The maps then make their way through the legislative process just like any other bill, requiring a majority vote in both chambers and the governor's signature. State legislators interested in running for Congress often serve on the committee in the legislature responsible for creating the maps. This gives them the opportunity to create a US House district that largely overlaps their current constituency, making the transition from state legislature to the House much easier. For example, Barbara Jordan was elected to the Texas state senate in 1966, making her the first African American to serve in that chamber since Reconstruction. In the round of redistricting following the 1970 Census, Jordan created a US House district in central Houston that contained most of her state senate district, and in 1972 became the first African American woman elected to the House from the former Confederacy.[64] In 1992, twenty years after Jordan, another African American woman in the Texas state senate, Eddie Bernice Johnson, chaired the state's redistricting committee and drew herself a US House district that overlapped her constituency in Dallas; she won with 72 percent of the vote.[65] Cynthia McKinney was elected to the Georgia house of representatives in 1988. She served on the state's redistricting committee, drew herself a House district that was 60 percent black, and won the seat in 1992.[66] In 1990, Karen Thurman served in the Florida state senate and chaired the state's redistricting committee. As a result of the 1990 Census, Florida gained four new seats. In the redistricting process, Thurman was instrumental in making sure that one of the new seats represented most of her state senate district.[67] When she ran in 1992 for the new House district she created, Thurman won with 53 percent of the vote, and did not have any serious competition in the next four election cycles. By 2000, however, the redistricting committee in the state legislature was controlled by Republicans. Ginny Brown-Waite was first elected to the Florida state senate in 1992, the year Thurman ran for Congress. Brown-Waite moved up the leadership ladder, becoming the Republican whip, and developed congressional aspirations of her own. The redistricting committee redrew Thurman's House district to include all of Brown-Waite's state senate district and exclude the more liberal part of the district around the University of Florida.[68] In 2002, with the new map in place, Brown-Waite narrowly defeated Thurman by less than 2 points. In 2011, Representative Dan Burton (R-IN) had his US House district redrawn by his brother, Indiana state representative Woody Burton, who happened to be serving on the state's redistricting committee.[69]

As discussed in Chapter 1, redistricting controversies in the 1960s focused on malapportionment and the resulting rural dominance in state legislatures. Debates in the 1990s focused upon racial gerrymandering and its impact on the representation of people of color in Congress.[70] While there is no doubt that racial gerrymandering has increased the number of minority members of Congress, there is also evidence that the creation of majority-minority districts has also had at least one unintended consequence: helping Republicans. In fact, some argue that racial gerrymandering actually gave Republicans the opportunity to take control of the House in 1994.[71] To create majority-minority districts, large numbers of African Americans are "packed" into a district. Because African Americans disproportionately vote Democratic, these seats elect Democratic House members by extremely large margins that, in essence, waste Democratic votes. Packing Democratic voters into one district creates opportunities for Republicans in other districts.[72] As a result, according to Michael McDonald, a professor at George Mason University and a redistricting consultant, racial gerrymandering has created an "unholy alliance" between minority and Republican members of state legislatures.[73] In 2011, for example, Republicans in the Ohio state legislature worked hard to get the support of African American Democrats to pass a new congressional map that would have given the GOP control of twelve of the state's sixteen House seats.[74]

The redistricting that occurred after the 2000 US Census refocused the debate on incumbent protection. In fact, "the nationwide theme of congressional line drawing was incumbent protection."[75] In 1992, eighty House members won their seats with less than 55 percent of the vote. In 2002, thirty-seven—fewer than half as many—House members won their seats with less than 55 percent of the vote. In 2000, the election cycle before the redistricting, there were fifty-seven House members who came from marginal seats. In 2002, after the redistricting, only three of these incumbent House members lost.[76] Incumbent protection plans are typically the product of bipartisan negotiations. For example, Republican representative and then speaker of the House Dennis Hastert and Democratic representative William Lipinski, both from Illinois, brokered a deal that "protected the reelection prospects of almost every Illinois incumbent."[77] In 2001, their proposal sailed through a state legislature that was under divided control of the parties.[78] Even in California, where Democrats controlled the state legislature, incumbent protection was the goal. In addition to protecting almost all of the safe Democratic House members, the seven marginal Democratic House members were given safe seats, and nineteen of the twenty Republicans in the California House delegation were also protected.[79]

Seats are made safer by adding more constituents who identify with the House member's party; Democratic members are given more Democratic voters, and Republican members are given more Republican voters, typically until they reach the 55–60 percent range. In addition to being used in racial gerrymandering, "packing" is a technique in which seats are made overly safe (that is, beyond the 55–60 percent range) by the opposition party in an effort to waste votes in one district while creating opportunities for themselves in other districts.[80] This method of "partisan gerrymandering" became a flashpoint in Texas. In 2000, the state legislature was under divided party control and passed an incumbent protection plan. The state's congressional delegation comprised seventeen Democrats and fifteen Republicans, despite the fact that, in the aggregate, voters in the state leaned Republican. In 2002, the Republicans gained control of both the state house and state senate and also held the governor's seat. In an unprecedented move, in May 2003, House majority leader Tom DeLay and Karl Rove, one of President George W. Bush's closest advisers, met with state legislators and proposed a new redistricting plan that would create twenty-two Republican House seats. Historically, no state had redrawn its district lines at this point in the ten-year cycle unless under orders from the federal courts. In response to this re-redistricting plan, Democrats in the state legislature walked out and took up temporary residence in Oklahoma, out of reach of the state troopers and Texas Rangers. After a bitter fight, which included another walkout to New Mexico by senate Democrats, the new map passed.[81] In 2004, the Texas congressional delegation included twenty Republicans and twelve Democrats.

The 2010 redistricting cycle appeared to be even more contentious than usual, but with a variety of approaches being taken among the states. This time around, the process in Texas included a controversial process called "bleaching," or packing districts with white/non-Hispanic voters.[82] In states that lost seats, such as Iowa, Louisiana, Michigan, and Ohio, several incumbents were forced to run against each other.[83] In Arizona, one of the few states that has an independent commission redraw district lines, Republican governor Jan Brewer initiated impeachment proceedings against the chair of the commission. In response, one Democratic Party leader called her "drunk with power" and said that the impeachment was "a brazen power grab that would rival any in Arizona history."[84] While there may not have been a "clear theme" in 2010, as one redistricting consultant explained, "all roads in redistricting lead to the courthouse." In Florida, voters approved a constitutional amendment that banned incumbent protection and partisan gerrymandering. Immediately after it passed,

Representatives Mario Diaz-Balart (R-FL) and Corrine Brown (D-FL) filed a lawsuit to have the amendment overturned.[85] The process in at least four other states, including Colorado, Minnesota, Nevada, and Texas, had also been pushed into state courts.[86]

The impact of redistricting on the political fortunes of female candidates has received very little, if any, systematic attention. However, in 2001, Virginia state senator Virginia Byrne accused the state legislature of "gender gerrymandering" and making it tougher for the women who had been elected in the northern part of the state to get reelected. Her colleague, Senator Linda Puller, agreed and said that in the latest round of redistricting, "they were harsher on us. It's still good ol' boys" drawing the lines.[87] Also in 2001, Minnesota's state legislature was unable to agree on a new map, so the process was turned over to a special redistricting panel made up of judges. In their order establishing the new district lines, the judicial panel took into account a complaint by women's groups that a few of the maps that had been proposed by the legislature disproportionately hurt female incumbents.[88]

But what would the impact of incumbent protection or partisan gerrymandering be on female candidates? Incumbent protection plans make it harder for any kind of turnover. If more incumbents are running for reelection in safe seats, it further limits opportunities for challengers, male or female. But when seats are made safer for incumbents or they are packed, the result is the same: districts become more extreme and less competitive. They have larger proportions of Democrats or Republicans. Our analysis in Chapter 7 showed that female Democratic candidates do better in districts that have more Democratic voters. Thus, female Democratic candidates can benefit from this kind of redistricting, provided that those additional elements that make a district women-friendly are included. On the other hand, the opposite may be true for at least some Republican women. Historically, the more Republican voters in a district, the less likely a female Republican candidate would run and win. Until recently, female Republican candidates did better in more moderate or swing districts. If these districts continue to disappear, opportunities for Republican women might disappear as well. On the other hand, as we saw in 2010, if women who are more conservative continue to run, we could see more opportunities for Republican women.

◾ Another Option: Women-Friendly Districts

In Chapter 7 we found that female candidates are more likely to win in districts that are different from those where male candidates win. Using the demographic factors from our previous analysis, we estimate here the probabilities that particular districts, with particular demographic profiles, will elect a woman.[89] The probabilities provide an easily interpretable measure of the women-friendliness of House districts: the higher the probability, the more a district can be considered women-friendly.

Table 8.2 provides a list of the twenty districts with the highest probability of electing a woman and their occupants in the 112th Congress (2011 session). Not unsurprisingly, all twenty districts elected Democrats in 2010. The table shows that the two districts with a probability greater than 0.50 are held by Representatives Carolyn Maloney (D-NY) and Nancy Pelosi (D-CA). In fact, nine of the districts are located in California and another six are in New York; 75 percent of these districts are in two states. The table also shows that not all women-friendly districts are held by women. In fact, twelve of these districts, 60 percent, are occupied by men. These are districts, however, where women would have a good chance of winning. Our earlier analysis emphasizes that while open seats are conventionally seen as the primary opportunities for women, open seats vary in their friendliness to women. If left basically unchanged by the redistricting process, the districts listed in Table 8.2, should the incumbents retire, would be the most receptive to female candidates. It is worth noting that seven of the male incumbents in these districts are sixty-four or older.

Table 8.3 lists the "lowest of the low," the twenty districts with the smallest probabilities of electing a woman in 2010. Here too are several obvious patterns among the districts that are most unfriendly to women. Nineteen of the twenty districts were won by Republicans. Representative Mike Ross of Arkansas, the only Democrat, was first elected to the House in 2000. He announced he would not seek reelection in 2012, in part because of the way his district was redrawn.[90] All of the districts in Table 8.3 are located in the South. None are held by a woman.

There are, of course, a few women who have won in "unfriendly" districts. There were three Republican women elected in 2010 who represented districts with probabilities of 0.04, just above the lowest of the low: Martha Roby from the Second District of Alabama, Diane Black from the Sixth District of Tennessee, and Virginia Foxx from the Fifth District of North Carolina. Foxx was first elected in 2004. Prior to running for the House, she served in the North Carolina senate and on her local school board.[91] Her campaign for the House was particularly nasty. She ran in a crowded Republican primary that featured eight candidates competing to fill the open seat vacated by Republican representative Richard Burr. She finished second to Winston-Salem city councilman Vernon Robinson, an African American Republican, and faced him in a runoff election. Robinson ran television ads featuring a Pakistani man, Kamran Akhtar, who was

Table 8.2 The Top Twenty Women-Friendly House Districts, 2010

State and District	Representative	Party	Probability of Electing a Woman
NY 14th	Carolyn Maloney	D	0.56
CA 8th	Nancy Pelosi	D	0.54
NY 15th	Charles Rangel	D	0.46
NY 8th	Jerrold Nadler	D	0.46
MA 8th	Michael Capuano	D	0.45
CA 30th	Henry Waxman	D	0.45
CA 14th	Anna Eshoo	D	0.44
MD 8th	Chris Van Hollen	D	0.41
CA 9th	Barbara Lee	D	0.40
CA 12th	Jackie Speier	D	0.40
CA 33rd	Karen Bass	D	0.40
WA 7th	Jim McDermott	D	0.40
NY 11th	Yvette Clarke	D	0.38
CA 15th	Mike Honda	D	0.38
CA 31st	Xavier Becerra	D	0.37
NY 12th	Nydia Velazquez	D	0.37
CA 28th	Howard Berman	D	0.36
NY 16th	José Serrano	D	0.36
IL 5th	Mike Quigley	D	0.35
IL 4th	Luis Gutierrez	D	0.35

Source: Data compiled by the authors.

Table 8.3 The Bottom Twenty Women-Friendly House Districts, 2010

State and District	Representative	Party	Probability of Electing a Woman
SC 3rd	Jeff Duncan	R	0.03
NC 10th	Patrick McHenry	R	0.03
VA 9th	Morgan Griffith	R	0.03
TX 4th	Ralph Hall	R	0.03
TX 11th	Michael Conaway	R	0.03
LA 7th	Charles Boustany	R	0.03
GA 10th	Paul Broun	R	0.03
AR 4th	Mike Ross	D	0.03
LA 5th	Rodney Alexander	R	0.03
MS 4th	Steven Palazzo	R	0.03
TX 1st	Louie Gohmert	R	0.03
TX 13th	Mac Thornberry	R	0.03
MS 1st	Alan Nunnelee	R	0.03
GA 8th	Austin Scott	R	0.03
AR 1st	Rick Crawford	R	0.03
LA 3rd	Jeffery Landry	R	0.03
TN 1st	Phil Roe	R	0.03
TN 4th	Scott DesJarlais	R	0.03
GA 9th	Tom Graves	R	0.02
AL 4th	Robert Aderholt	R	0.02

Source: Data compiled by the authors.

caught by police in downtown Charlotte filming office buildings and charged with immigration violations. In the ad, Robinson states, "I'm Vernon Robinson and I approve this message because Akhtar didn't come here to live the American dream. He came here to kill you."[92] In another ad, he compared Foxx to Hillary Clinton: "Hillary Clinton voted for racial quotas, higher taxes, gay rights and the abortion bills. So did Virginia Foxx."[93] His aggressive tactics backfired, and Foxx won the runoff by 10 percentage points. She then easily defeated her Democratic opponent, Jim Harrell, in the general election.

Using our model, we can also explore how the probability of electing a woman and the distribution of women-friendly and women-unfriendly districts has changed over time. For each congressional district in each of the four redistricting cycles since 1972, we calculated the probability of electing a woman. In order to get a sense of how many women-friendly and women-unfriendly districts there were in each time period, we grouped the district probabilities into categories that range from less than 0.05 to greater than 0.40. Figure 8.2 presents the distributions for the redistricting periods from 1972 forward.[94] The change depicted in the figure is quite dramatic. In the period from 1972 to 1980, the average probability of electing a woman was 0.04 with a maximum probability of 0.25. The likelihood that a female candidate would win was less than 0.05 in 324 of the 435 House districts. In other words, nearly three-quarters of all House districts had demographic profiles that made them extremely unlikely to support a female candidate.

However, in the most recent redistricting cycle, from 2002 to 2010, the mean probability increased to 0.14, which is still rather low, but it is a substantial increase and, as we noted earlier, there were two districts above 0.50, both of which were held by women. The number of districts with a probability less than 0.05 dropped to sixty-one, only 14 percent of all House districts. There were thirty-three districts with a probability of 0.30 or greater.

Figure 8.2 shows that the prospects of electing a woman to the US House have increased over time. We can see this not only in the higher averages and maximum probabilities, but also in the less skewed shape of the distributions over time. Moreover, it is expected that the trends shown in Figure 8.2 will continue. The engine that drives our analysis is demography, and recent demographic trends bode well for women seeking a House seat. Changes in racial and ethnic diversity, education, and the work force suggest a continued growth in the number of women-friendly congressional districts. The 2012 round of redistricting will once again have to account for these shifting demographics, shaping future opportunities for female candidates for the next decade.

■ Conclusion: A Century of Change

The US electoral arena is unique: it is the only place in the United States where women and men engage in direct, public competition.[95] Sports are segregated by sex. Even the Academy Awards are segregated by sex. But in a campaign, men and women go head to head, winner-take-all. Campaigns featuring a female candidate for the US House and Senate have grown to be less of a "rare event," but they have yet to become a common event. Our purpose has been to explore a century of change in an effort to answer a key question: Why has the pace of electing women to Congress been so slow?

We take for granted today that members of Congress serve for long periods of time, and there is no doubt that incumbents are virtually unbeatable. But it is important to remember that this is a twentieth-century phenomenon. Careerism in Congress did not develop until the early 1900s. In fact, members of the House began seeking long careers just as women were entering the political arena. The first woman to win a seat in the House, Representative Jeannette Rankin (R-MT), ran in 1916. Ten years prior, only about 10 percent of all members served six or more terms. By

Figure 8.2 Probability of Electing a Woman to the US House, by Decade, 1972–2010

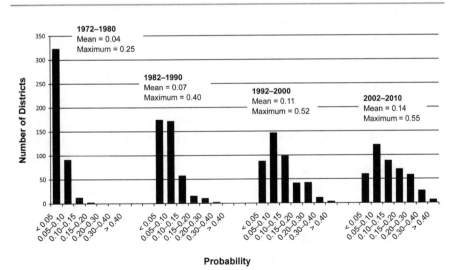

Source: Data compiled by the authors.

1926, more than 20 percent served six or more terms. Just as the first women were running for Congress, the development of careerism made it more difficult for them to succeed. And by the 1970s, when the United States finally began to see real increases in the number of women running, the power of incumbency was firmly in place: more than 40 percent of members were serving six or more terms. Long careers were the norm. This is a tremendous barrier for anyone—male or female—who wants to run, and consequently incumbency plays a major role in determining the remarkably slow pace of the integration of women into Congress.

There is, however, more to the story. There is no doubt that once women are in Congress, they reap the benefits of incumbency as much as men do. In fact, female incumbents historically have done a bit better than male incumbents: they are slightly more likely to win reelection and they win by bigger margins. However, this obscures what is happening beneath the surface. Female incumbents are challenged in their own primaries more often than male incumbents. In addition, there is typically a "free-for-all" in the opposition-party primary. Women in the House rarely get a "free pass," easily sailing through their reelection campaigns with no competition in their primaries or general elections. In short, female incumbents attract more competition than male incumbents do; they have to work harder to maintain their seats. The advantages of incumbency are not gender-neutral.

One other prominent explanation for the lack of women in Congress is the pipeline theory, the idea being that we have to wait for women to run for and get experience in lower-level public offices before they run for national office. While the pipeline is important, it is an incomplete explanation, especially when we disaggregate historical trends by party. Once party is taken into account, there is no obvious sequential pattern in the number of women winning in state houses of representatives, then state senates, then the US House, and then the US Senate. What we can see, however, is that since the 1990s the increasing number of women elected to Congress has largely been a Democratic phenomenon; there is a major "party gap." If the road to Congress goes through only one party, this further slows the integration of women.

In our analysis of female incumbents, the increased competition they face is partially explained by the fact that they are more likely to face female opponents. In other words, women are far more likely to run against each other. One of the ramifications is that if women are just running against other women, there are no net gains in the number of female House members. But why would we find women running against other women? Why do so many of the women in the House come from so few states? Why has such a huge party gap developed? The answer to all of these questions is related to the kinds of districts where female candidates run and are successful. There are very clear differences between the House districts that elect men and the House districts that elect women. Just as demographics can be used to predict whether a Republican or Democrat will win, demographics can be used to predict whether a man or woman will win. There are districts that are women-friendly. Female candidates, whether they are Democrat, Republican, white/non-Hispanic, African American, or Hispanic, are more likely to be successful in districts that are smaller, more urban, more racially and ethnically diverse, more educated, and less blue-collar. Thus, incumbency is not the only factor that determines who will win a House seat; the demographic profile of the district will also play a major role in determining whether a man or woman can win that seat. The American public, however, is becoming more urban, more diverse, more educated, and less blue-collar, suggesting that opportunities for female candidates will continue to increase. The future is likely to grow more women-friendly. If so, this will continue and perhaps accelerate the century of change we have documented.

▨ Notes

1. "Biography," Congresswoman Debbie Wasserman Schultz; "Wasserman Schultz, Debbie"; author interview, November 14, 2004.
2. Alvarez, "In a Life Filled with Firsts."
3. Ibid.
4. McElwaine, "Meet the DNC's Feisty New Chair."
5. "Representative Debbie Wasserman Schultz."
6. Alvarez, "In a Life Filled with Firsts."
7. McElwaine, "Meet the DNC's Feisty New Chair."
8. Alvarez, "In a Life Filled with Firsts."
9. McElwaine, "Meet the DNC's Feisty New Chair."
10. Kirkpatrick, *Political Woman*, p. 3.
11. National Center for Education Statistics, "Table 279: Degrees Conferred."
12. "Families and Living Arrangements."
13. "Equal Role for Women."
14. Cauchon, "Gender Pay Gap Is Smallest on Record."
15. US Department of Labor, Bureau of Labor Statistics, "Table 4: Employment Status"; "Labor Force Participation Rates Among Mothers."
16. Wiseman, "Young, Single, Childless Women Out-Earn Male Counterparts."
17. US Department of Commerce, Bureau of the Census, "Table 4.b: Reported Voting and Registration."
18. Conway, Steuernagel, and Ahern, *Women and Political Participation;* Fox, "Gender, Political Ambition, and the Decision Not to Run for Office"; Fox, Lawless, and Feeley, "Gender and the Decision to Run for Office."
19. Fox and Lawless, *It Still Takes a Candidate,* pp. 46–47.
20. Clayton and Stallings, "Black Women in Congress"; Cohen, "A Portrait of

Continuing Marginality"; Darcy and Hadley, "Black Women in Politics"; Darling, "African-American Women in State Elective Office in the South"; Handley and Grofman, "The Impact of the Voting Rights Act on Minority Representation"; Moncrief, Thompson, and Schuhmann, "Gender, Race, and the State Legislature"; Smooth, "African American Women and Electoral Politics"; Swain, *Black Faces, Black Interests;* Williams, "The Civil Rights–Black Power Legacy."

21. *Women in Congress,* p. 904.

22. Ibid., p. 905.

23. Smooth, "Gender, Race, and the Exercise of Power and Influence."

24. Speech at Running Start event, Washington, D.C., July 21, 2010.

25. Conway, Steuernagel, and Ahern, *Women and Political Participation;* Lawless and Fox, *It Still Takes a Candidate.*

26. Lawless and Fox, *It Still Takes a Candidate.*

27. Fox, "Gender, Political Ambition, and the Decision Not to Run for Office"; Lawless and Fox, *It Still Takes a Candidate.*

28. For example, Running Start (www.runningstartonline.org) is a nonprofit organization that trains high school girls how to run for political office. "She Should Run" (www.sheshouldrun.org) is a program created by the Women's Campaign Forum that uses new media to ask more women to run. See also Rozell, "Helping Women Run and Win"; Sanbonmatsu, Carroll, and Walsh, *Poised to Run.*

29. "The Honorable Doris O. Matsui."

30. Bledsoe and Herring, "Victims of Circumstances"; Fox, "Gender, Political Ambition, and the Decision Not to Run for Office"; Fox, Lawless, and Feeley, "Gender and the Decision to Run for Office"; Lawless and Fox, *It Still Takes a Candidate.*

31. "Biography," Congresswoman Jaime Herrera Beutler.

32. Stalsburg, "Voting for Mom."

33. Dolan and Ford, "Change and Continuity Among Women State Legislators"; Dolan and Ford, "Are All Women State Legislators Alike?"; Gertzog, *Congressional Women;* Thompson, "Career Convergence." But see Sanbonmatsu, "Gender Pools and Puzzles."

34. Epstein, *Women in Law;* Williams, "Women, Law, and Politics."

35. National Center for Education Statistics, "Table 291: First-Professional Degrees Conferred."

36. Weiss, "Men Outnumber Women at Most Top Law Schools."

37. "Women in State Legislatures."

38. Sanbonmatsu, Carroll, and Walsh, *Poised to Run,* p. 6.

39. Date, "N.H. First State with Female Majority in Senate."

40. Numbers calculated from data we collected, combined with data from Manning, *Membership of the 112th Congress.*

41. "Biography," Congresswoman Gabrielle Giffords.

42. Lacy and Herszenhorn, "In Attack's Wake, Political Repercussions."

43. Cloherty, Thomas, and Balderick, "Jared Lee Loughner Mentally Incompetent to Stand Trial."

44. Dick, "Giffords, History, and True Arizona Grit."

45. "Asheville Rehab Workers."

46. Sonmez, "Gabrielle Giffords Resigns from the House in Emotional Farewell."

47. *Women in Congress,* p. 906.

48. Koszczuk, "Proof of Illegal Voters Falls Short," p. 330.

49. "Sanchez Claims Victory in Nation's Most Expensive Race."

50. Gerber, "Dornan Loses Solidly."

51. Canon, *Actors, Athletes, and Astronauts.*

52. "Fred Dalton Thompson."

53. "Fred Grandy."

54. Jones, *Redneck Boy in the Promised Land.*

55. "Franken, Al."

56. "Total Raised and Spent: 2010 Race, California Senate."

57. "Total Raised and Spent: 2010 Race, Connecticut Senate."

58. James, "California Governor's Race Shows Limits of Money."

59. Ibid.

60. "Senate Seniority List–112th Congress."

61. A study of Republican women in state legislatures found similar trends; Carroll, "Have Women State Legislators in the United States Become More Conservative?"

62. As in Chapter 1, these scores are calculated from Professors Keith Poole and Howard Rosenthal's data, available at http://voteview.com/downloads.asp. The original scores range from –1 (most liberal) to 1 (most conservative), but for ease of interpretation and comparison we transformed the scores to a scale ranging from 0 to 100.

63. See, for example, Gerrity, Osborn, and Mendez, "Women and Representation"; Simon and Palmer, "The Roll Call Behavior of the Men and Women in the US House of Representatives."

64. Barone, Ujifusa, and Matthews, *Almanac of American Politics, 1974,* p. 1003.

65. Foerstel, *Biographical Dictionary of Congressional Women,* p. 135.

66. Ibid., p. 181. This district was then the subject of a lawsuit filed by white voters challenging the constitutionality of "racial gerrymandering" and, according to the Supreme Court in *Miller v. Johnson,* had to be redrawn. In 1996, McKinney was reelected in her new district, which was now 65 percent white; Moore, "Majority-Minority District."

67. Foerstel, *Biographical Dictionary of Congressional Women,* p. 270.

68. "Brown-Waite, Ginny."

69. Toeplitz, "When Redistricting's All In the Family."

70. See, for example, Canon, *Race, Redistricting, and Representation;* Epstein and O'Halloran, "A Social Science Approach to Race, Redistricting, and Representation"; Galderisi, *Redistricting in the New Millennium;* Lublin, *The Paradox of Representation;* Lublin, "Racial Redistricting and African-American Representation."

71. See, for example, Bullock, "Affirmative Action Districts"; Guinier, "Don't Scapegoat the Gerrymander," p. 36; Hill, "Do Black Majority Districts Aid Republicans?"

72. Hill, "Do Black Majority Districts Aid Republicans?"

73. Author interview, March 17, 2004.

74. Joseph, "Ohio Redistricting Battle Heats Up."

75. Benenson, Giroux, and Allen, "Safe House," p. 1274; Giroux, "Remaps' Clear Trend," p. 2627; Scammon, McGillivray, and Cook, "Analysis of the Elections of 2002"; Cox and Katz, *Elbridge Gerry's Salamander.* But see Friedman and Holden, "The Rising Incumbent Reelection Rate."

76. Connie Morella (R-MD), Bill Luther (D-MN), and Jim Maloney (D-CT); Scammon, McGillivray, and Cook, "Analysis of the Elections of 2002," p. 2.

77. Giroux, "Remaps' Clear Trend," p. 2627.

78. Ibid.

79. Giroux, "California Democrats' Remap Puts Two of Their Own in Tough Spots," p. 2224.

80. Jost, "Redistricting Disputes," pp. 221–247.

81. Gaddie, "The Texas Redistricting"; Jost, "Redistricting Disputes."

82. "Between the Lines."

83. Ibid.; Miller, "Michigan Democrats Weary over Redistricting."

84. Livingston, "Arizona Governor Starts Impeachment Process Against Redistricting Panel."

85. Miller, "Redistricting Reform Is Tough Task Every Time."

86. Toeplitz and Trygstad, "Redistricting Woes Plague State Legislatures."

87. Melton, "Byrne Strikes a Nerve in Richmond," p. C5.

88. "Final Order."

89. In our statistical model here, the dependent variable in the analysis is dichotomous and denotes whether a district elected a man (coded 0) or a woman (coded 1). The independent variables include eleven of the twelve measures used in the analysis presented in Chapter 7; we exclude here the measure of district size because it is highly correlated with the proportion of urban residents. We add one additional binary variable that denotes whether a district represented a new seat awarded to a state during the reapportionment process. Excluding the small number of at-large elections and districts where there are missing data produces a database of 11,692 House elections from 1956 to 2010. We estimated the model using probit, a standard technique when the dependent variable is dichotomous. All of the estimated coefficients are statistically significant and properly signed. The overall fit of the model, as measured by the Wald chi-square statistic (718.6 with eleven degrees of freedom) is very satisfactory. We also performed an additional check on this model. The dependent variable here, whether a district elects a man or a woman, is quite skewed; across the time frame of our analysis, a woman was elected in less than 8 percent of all contests for a House seat. Accordingly, we cross-checked our results by reestimating the model using a logit technique that adjusts for rare events; see Tomz, King, and Zeng, *RELOGIT: Rare Events Logistical Regression;* King and Zeng, "Logistic Regression in Rare Events Data." The results of this exercise reveal that these techniques produce no appreciable differences in the significance of the coefficients.

90. Joseph, "Rep. Mike Ross to Retire."

91. "Foxx, Virginia Ann."

92. "Robinson Accuses Arrested Pakistani of Terrorism in New Ad."

93. Christensen, "Candidate's Zeal Divides," p. A1.

94. We begin with the 1972–1980 redistricting period, because it was the first in which the requirements of "one person, one vote" mandated by *Baker v. Carr* and *Wesberry v. Sanders* were fully implemented. In addition, we did examine the distributions for the 1956–1960 and 1962–1970 periods, and they differ very little from the distribution of 1972–1980 shown in Figure 8.1.

95. Bledsoe and Herring, "Victims of Circumstances," p. 213.

Bibliography

"About Tulsi." VoteTulsi.com. http://votetulsi.com/tulsi-gabbard (accessed August 10, 2011).

Abramowitz, Alan, and Ruy Teixeira. "The Decline of the White Working Class and the Rise of a Mass Upper-Middle Class." In *Red, Blue, and Purple America: The Future of Election Demographics,* edited by Ruy Teixeira. Washington, DC: Brookings Institution, 2008.

Adair, Bill, Adam C. Smith, and Anita Kumar. "Lawmaker Quits Amid Scandal." *St. Petersburg Times,* September 30, 2006.

"Alaska Certifies Sen. Murkowski's Re-elections." CNN.com, December 30, 2010. http://articles.cnn.com/2010-12-30/politics/alaska.senate.race_1_vote-count-names-on-write-in-ballots-write-in-votes?_s=PM:POLITICS (accessed July 20, 2011).

Alberts, Sheldon. "Limbaugh Remains Defiant After Saying Fox Faked Illness." *Montreal Gazette,* October 26, 2006.

Alexander, Deborah, and Kristi Anderson. "Gender as a Factor in the Attribution of Leadership Traits." *Political Research Quarterly* 46 (1993): 527–545.

Allison, Wes. "House Leader Hit with Indictment." *St. Petersburg Times,* September 29, 2005.

Alpern, Sara. "Center Stage: Helen Gahagan Douglas, a Life." *American Historical Review* 98 (1993): 967–968.

Alpert, Bruce. "Critics of Sen. Mary Landrieu Presented As Examples by Sexism Watchdogs." *Times Picayune,* Nola.com, September 6, 2010. www.nola.com/politics/index.ssf/2010/09/critics_of_sen_mary_landrieu_p.html (accessed September 14, 2011).

Alvarez, Lizette. "In a Life Filled with Firsts, One More." NewYorkTimes.com, April 24, 2011. www.nytimes.com/2011/04/25/us/politics/25wasserman.html?pagewanted=all (accessed October 28, 2011).

Ambrose, Stephen. *Nixon: The Education of a Politician, 1913–1962.* New York: Simon and Schuster, 1987.

Amundson, Kirsten. *The Silenced Majority: Women and American Democracy.* Englewood Cliffs, NJ: Prentice Hall, 1971.

Andersen, Kristi, and Stuart Thorson. "Congressional Turnover and the Election of Women." *Western Political Quarterly* 37 (1984): 143–156.

Anderson, Kristi. *After Suffrage: Women in Partisan and Electoral Politics Before the New Deal.* Chicago: University of Chicago Press, 1996.

Andolina, Molly, Krista Jenkins, Cliff Zukin, and Scott Keeter. "Habits from Home, Lessons from School: Influences on Youth Civic Engagement." *PS: Political Science and Politics* 36 (2003): 275–280.

"Andre Carson Wins Special Election." wthr.com, March 11, 2008. www.wthr .com/story/8001860/andre-carson-wins-special-election?redirected=true (accessed July 20, 2011).

Arceneaux, Kevin. "The 'Gender Gap' in State Legislative Representation: New Data to Tackle an Old Question." *Political Research Quarterly* 54 (2001): 143–160.

Ardoin, Phillip, and James Garand. "Measuring Constituency Ideology in US House Districts: A Top-Down Simulation." *Journal of Politics* 65 (2003): 1165–1189.

"Asheville Rehab Workers: US Rep. Gabrielle Giffords' Case 'Remarkable.'" Citizen-Times.com, October 25, 2011. www.citizen-times.com/article/2011 1025/NEWS/310250029/Asheville-s-rehab-expertise-good-fit-Rep-Giffords ?odyssey=tab%7Ctopnews%7Ctext%7CFrontpage (accessed October 20, 2011).

Atkeson, Lonna Rae. "Not All Cues Are Created Equal: The Conditional Impact of Female Candidates on Political Engagement." *Journal of Politics* 65 (2003): 1040–1061.

Attebery, Brian. *The Fantasy Tradition in American Literature: From Irving to Le Guin.* Bloomington: Indiana University Press, 1980.

Babington, Charles, and Jonathan Weisman. "Rep. Foley Quits in Page Scandal." WashingtonPost.com, September 30, 2006. www.washingtonpost.com /wp-dyn/content/article/2006/09/29/AR2006092901574.html (accessed August 10, 2011).

Baker, Ross. *House and Senate.* 2nd ed. New York: Norton, 1995.

Balz, Dan. "Hillary Clinton Opens Presidential Bid." *Washington Post,* January 12, 2007.

Banner, Lois. *Elizabeth Cady Stanton: A Radical for Women's Rights.* Boston: Little, Brown, 1980.

Barone, Michael, and Richard Cohen. *Almanac of American Politics, 2002, 2004, 2006.* Washington, DC: National Journal, 2001, 2003, 2005.

———. *Almanac of American Politics, 2010.* Washington, DC: National Journal, 2009.

Barone, Michael, and Chuck McCutcheon. *Almanac of American Politics, 2012.* Washington, DC: National Journal, 2011.

Barone, Michael, and Grant Ujifusa. *Almanac of American Politics, 1986, 1994, 1996, 1998, 2000.* Washington, DC: National Journal, 1985, 1993, 1995, 1997, 1999.

Barone, Michael, Grant Ujifusa, and Douglas Matthews. *Almanac of American Politics, 1974.* Boston: Gambit, 1973.

Barr, Andy. "South Carolina Gov. Mark Sanford Admits Affair." Politico.com, June 24, 2009. www.politico.com/news/stories/0609/24146.html (accessed August 20, 2011).

Barreto, Matt. "Si, Se Pueda! Latino Candidates and the Mobilization of Latino Voters." *American Political Science Review* 101 (2007): 425–441.

Barrett, Edith. "The Policy Priorities of African American Women in State Legislatures." *Legislative Studies Quarterly* 20 (1995): 223–247.

Bash, Dana. "Despite New Female Faces in Congress, Numbers in Decline." CNN.com, November 10, 2010. http://articles.cnn.com/2010-11-10/politics /congress.women_1_republican-women-female-candidates-republican -woman?_s=PM:POLITICS (accessed August 20, 2011).

———. "What's New on Capitol Hill? Motherhood." CNN.com, May 8, 2009. http://articles.cnn.com/2009-05-08/living/congress.babies_1_capitol-hill -day-care-female-lawmakers?_s=PM:LIVING (accessed August 10, 2011).

"The Battle for America's Front Yard." *National Geographic,* June 2004.

Becker, Jo, and Spencer Hsu. "Credit Firm Gave Moran Favorable Loan Deal." *Washington Post,* July 7, 2002.

Benenson, Bob, Gregory Giroux, and Jonathan Allen. "Safe House: Incumbents Face Worry-Free Election." *CQ Weekly,* May 17, 2002.

Berch, Neil. "Women Incumbents, Elite Bias, and Voter Response in the 1996 and 1998 US House Elections." *Women & Politics* 26 (2004): 21–33.

———. "The 'Year of the Woman' in Context: A Test of Six Explanations." *American Politics Quarterly* 24 (1996): 169–193.

Bernstein, Robert. "Might Women Have the Edge in Open-Seat House Primaries?" *Women & Politics* 17 (1997): 1–26.

———. "Why Are There So Few Women in the House?" *Western Political Quarterly* 39 (1986): 155–164.

"Between the Lines: First Maps Make Incumbents Uncomfortable." RollCall.com, April 5, 2011. www.rollcall.com/issues/56_105/-204596-1.html (accessed November 4, 2011).

Bibby, John, and Brian Schaffner. *Politics, Parties, and Elections in America.* 6th ed. Boston: Wadsworth, 2008.

Bingham, Clara. *Women on the Hill.* New York: Times, 1997.

Biographical Directory of the American Congress. Washington, DC: US Government Printing Office, 1971.

Biographical Directory of the United States Congress. http://bioguide.congress.gov.

"Biography." Chief Deputy Whip Diana DeGette. http://degette.house.gov /index.php?option=com_content&view=article&id=125&Itemid=91 (accessed August 15, 2011).

———. Congresswoman Debbie Wasserman Schultz. http://wassermanschultz .house.gov/about/biography.shtml (accessed August 15, 2011).

———. Congresswoman Gabrielle Giffords. http://giffords.house.gov/about (accessed October 20, 2011).

———. Congresswoman Jaime Herrera Beutler. http://herrerabeutler.house.gov /Biography (accessed October 20, 2011).

———. Congresswoman Mazie K. Hirono. http://hirono.house.gov /AboutMazie/Biography.htm (accessed August 10, 2007).

———. Congresswoman Tammy Baldwin. http://tammybaldwin.house.gov/about /biography.shtml (accessed October 1, 2011).

Bishop, Bill. *The Big Sort: Why the Clustering of Like-minded America Is Tearing Us Apart.* New York: Houghton Mifflin, 2008.

———. "A Steady Slide Toward a More Partisan Union." AustinAmerican Statesman.com, May 30, 2004. www.statesman.com/specialreports/content /specialreports/greatdivide/0530divide.html (accessed October 29, 2011).

Black, Earl, and Merle Black. *The Rise of Southern Republicans.* Cambridge: Harvard University Press, 2002.

Black Americans in Congress. Washington, DC: Office of the Clerk of the US House of Representatives. http://baic.house.gov (accessed October 20, 2011).

Bledsoe, Timothy, and Mary Herring. "Victims of Circumstances: Women in Pursuit of Political Office." *American Political Science Review* 84 (1990): 213–223.

"Boehner's Tears." YouTube.com. www.youtube.com/watch?v=iUQPqDCDaCE (accessed September 15, 2011).

Boles, Janet. *The Politics of the Equal Rights Amendment.* New York: Longman, 1979.

Bond, Jon. "The Influence of Constituency Diversity on Electoral Competition in Voting for Congress, 1974–1978." *Legislative Studies Quarterly* 8 (1983): 201–217.

Bousquet, Steve, and Anita Kumar. "Castor, Martinez Keep Senate Race Attacks Coming." *St. Petersburg Times,* October 29, 2004.

Boxer, Barbara. *Strangers in the Senate: Politics and the New Revolution of Women in America.* Washington, DC: National Press, 1993.

Braden, Maria. *Women Politicians and the Media.* Lexington: University of Kentucky Press, 1996.

Brady, David, Kara Buckley, and Douglas Rivers. "The Roots of Careerism in the US House of Representatives." *Legislative Studies Quarterly* 24 (1999): 489–510.

Breslau, Karen. "Hillary Tears Up." *Newsweek,* January 6, 2008. www.thedaily beast.com/newsweek/2008/01/06/hillary-tears-up.html (accessed September 15, 2011).

Bresnahan, John, and Glenn Thrush. "Rep. Eric Massa to Resign." Politico.com, March 5, 2010. www.politico.com/news/stories/0310/34001.html (accessed August 10, 2011).

Brooks, David. *On Paradise Drive.* New York: Simon and Schuster, 2004.

Brooks, Deborah Jordan. "Testing the Double Standard for Candidate Emotionality: Voter Reactions to the Tears and Anger of Male and Female Politicians." *Journal of Politics* 73 (2011): 597–615.

Brown, Clyde, Neil Heighberger, and Peter Shocket. "Gender-Based Differences in Perceptions of Male and Female City Council Candidates." *Women & Politics* 13 (1993): 1–17.

"Brown-Waite, Ginny." In *CQ's Politics in America, 2006: The 109th Congress,* edited by Jacki Koszczuk and H. Amy Stern. Washington, DC: CQ Press, 2005. http://library.cqpress.com/congress/document.php?id=pia109-Brown-Waite.

Brudnick, Ida. "Congressional Salaries and Allowances." Washington, DC: Congressional Research Service, June 28, 2011. www.senate.gov /CRSReports/crs-publish.cfm?pid=%270E%2C*PL[%3D%23P%20 %20%0A (accessed July 7, 2011).

Bullock, Charles. "Affirmative Action Districts: In Whose Face Will They Blow Up?" *Campaigns and Elections* 16 (1995): 22–23.

——. "House Careerists: Changing Patterns of Longevity and Attrition." *American Political Science Review* 66 (1972): 1295–3000.

——. *Redistricting: The Most Political Activity in America.* New York: Rowman and Littlefield, 2010.

Bullock, Charles, and Patricia Lee Findley Heys. "Recruitment of Women for Congress: A Research Note." *Western Political Quarterly* 25 (1972): 416–423.

Burns, Nancy, Kay Schlozman, and Sidney Verba. *The Private Roots of Public Action: Gender, Equality, and Political Participation.* Cambridge: Harvard University Press, 2001.

Burrell, Barbara. "The Political Opportunity of Women Candidates for the US House of Representatives in 1984." *Women & Politics* 8 (1988): 51–68.

———. "Political Parties and Women's Organizations: Bringing Women into the Electoral Arena." In *Gender and Elections: Shaping the Future of American Politics,* edited by Susan Carroll and Richard Fox. New York: Cambridge University Press, 2006.

———. *A Woman's Place Is In the House: Campaigning for Congress in the Feminist Era.* Ann Arbor: University of Michigan Press, 1994.

———. "Women Candidates in Open-Seat Primaries for the US House, 1968–1990." *Legislative Studies Quarterly* 17 (1992): 493–508.

"Byrd, Robert Carlyle." *Biographical Directory of the United States Congress.* http://bioguide.congress.gov/scripts/biodisplay.pl?index=B001210 (accessed August 15, 2011).

Bystrom, Dianne. "Advertising, Web Sites, and Media Coverage: Gender and Communication Along the Campaign Trail." In *Gender and Elections: Shaping the Future of American Politics,* edited by Susan Carroll and Richard Fox. New York: Cambridge University Press, 2006.

———. "Confronting Stereotypes and Double Standards in Campaign Communication." In *Legislative Women: Getting Elected, Getting Ahead,* edited by Beth Reingold. Boulder: Lynne Rienner, 2008.

Bystrom, Dianne, et al. *Gender and Candidate Communication.* New York: Routledge, 2004.

"Cady, Daniel." *Biographical Directory of the United States Congress.* http://bioguide.congress.gov/scripts/biodisplay.pl?index=C000014 (accessed June 6, 2009).

Cain, Bruce, John Ferejohn, and Morris Fiorina. *The Personal Vote: Constituency Service and Electoral Independence.* Cambridge: Harvard University Press, 1987.

Cameron, Charles, David Epstein, and Sharyn O'Halloran. "Do Majority-Minority Districts Maximize Substantive Black Representation in Congress?" *American Political Science Review* 90 (1996): 794–812.

Campbell, Angus, et al. *The American Voter.* Chicago: University of Chicago Press, 1960.

Campbell, David E., and Christina Wolbrecht. "See Jane Run: Women Politicians as Role Models for Adolescents." *Journal of Politics* 68 (2006): 233–247.

Canedy, Dana. "Florida 'Scarlet Letter' Law Is Repealed by Gov. Bush." NewYorkTimes.com, May 31, 2003. www.nytimes.com/2003/05/31/us/florida-scarlet-letter-law-is-repealed-by-gov-bush.html?ref=danacanedy (accessed September 20, 2011).

Canon, David. *Actors, Athletes, and Astronauts.* Chicago: University of Chicago Press, 1990.

———. *Race, Redistricting, and Representation: The Unintended Consequences of Black Majority Districts.* Chicago: University of Chicago Press, 1999.

Carmines, Edward, and James Stimson. *Issue Evolution: Race and the Transformation of American Politics.* Princeton: Princeton University Press, 1989.

"Carnahan, Jean." *CQ's Politics in America, 2002: The 107th Congress.* Washington, DC: CQ Press, 2001. http://library.cqpress.com/elections /pia107-0453058594 (accessed July 30, 2007).

Carroll, James. "Misogynist Massachusetts." *Daily Beast,* January 19, 2010. www.thedailybeast.com/articles/2010/01/19/misogynist-massachusetts.html (accessed September 25, 2011).

Carroll, Susan. "Have Women State Legislators in the United States Become More Conservative?" *Atlantis* 27 (2003): 128–139.

———. "Political Elites and Sex Differences in Political Ambition: A Reconsideration." *Journal of Politics* 47 (1985): 1231–1243.

———. "Reflections on Gender and Hillary Clinton's Presidential Campaign: The Good, the Bad, and the Misogenic." *Politics & Gender* 5 (2009): 1–20.

———. "2004 Elections and Women: An Analysis of Statewide and State Legislative Election Results." *Spectrum: The Journal of State Government* 78 (2005): 23–25.

———. *Women as Candidates in American Politics.* Bloomington: Indiana University Press, 1994.

Carroll, Susan, and Ronnee Schreiber. "Media Coverage of Women in the 103rd Congress." In *Women, Media, and Politics,* edited by Pippa Norris. New York: Oxford University Press, 1997.

Carson, Jamie, Erik Engstrom, and Jason Roberts. "Candidate Quality, the Personal Vote, and the Incumbency Advantage in Congress." *American Political Science Review* 101 (2007): 289–301.

Cauchon, Dennis. "Gender Pay Gap Is Smallest on Record." USAToday.com, September 13, 2010. www.usatoday.com/money/workplace/2010-09-13 -wage-gaps_N.htm (accessed October 15, 2011).

Chafe, William. *The American Woman: Her Changing Social, Economic and Political Roles, 1920–1970.* New York: Oxford University Press, 1972.

Chamberlin, Hope. *A Minority of Members: Women in the United States Congress.* New York: Praeger, 1973.

"Chandra Levy's Killer Gets 60 Years." MSNBC.com, February 11, 2011. www.msnbc.msn.com/id/41529499/ns/us_news-crime_and_courts/t/chandra -levys-killer-gets-years (accessed July 8, 2011).

Chaney, Carole, and Barbara Sinclair. "Women and the 1992 House Elections." In *The Year of the Woman: Myths and Reality,* edited by Elizabeth Adell Cook, Sue Thomas, and Clyde Wilcox. Boulder: Westview, 1994.

Chinni, Dante, and James Gimpel. *Our Patchwork Nation.* New York: Gotham, 2010.

Chisholm, Shirley. *Unbought and Unbossed: An Autobiography.* New York: Houghton Mifflin, 1970.

Christensen, Rob. "Candidate's Zeal Divides." *Raleigh News and Observer,* August 13, 2004.

Cillizza, Chris. "For GOP's Female Candidates, a Big-Name Den Mother." *Washington Post,* May 17, 2010.

Clark, Janet, Charles Hadley, and Robert Darcy. "Political Ambition Among Men and Women State Party Leaders." *American Politics Quarterly* 17 (1989): 194–207.

Clayton, Dewey. "African American Women and Their Quest for Congress." *Journal of Black Studies* 33 (2003): 354–388.

Clayton, Dewey, and Angela Stallings. "Black Women in Congress: Striking the Balance." *Journal of Black Studies* 30 (2000): 574–603.

Clift, Eleanor, and Tom Brazaitis. *Madam President.* 1st ed., 2nd ed. New York: Scribner, 2000, 2003.

Cloherty, Jack, Pierre Thomas, and Thomas Balderick. "Jared Lee Loughner Mentally Incompetent to Stand Trial in Giffords Shootings." ABCNews.com, May 25, 2011. http://abcnews.go.com/US/loughner-mentally-incompetent -stand-trial-giffords-shootings/story?id=13687399 (accessed October 20, 2011).

Clubok, Alfred, Norman Wilensky, and Forrest Berghorn. "Family Relationships, Congressional Recruitment, and Political Modernization." *Journal of Politics* 31 (1969): 1035–1062.

Cockerham, Sean. "Murkowski Concedes GOP Senate Race to Miller." *Anchorage Daily News,* adn.com, September 1, 2010. www.adn.com/2010/08/31 /1433454/murkowski-concedes-senate-race.html (accessed July 20, 2011).

Cohen, Cathy. "A Portrait of Continuing Marginality: The Study of Women of Color in American Politics." In *Women and American Politics: New Questions, New Directions,* edited by Susan Carroll. New York: Oxford University Press, 2003.

Cohen, Richard. "Member Moms." *National Journal,* April 7, 2007.

Condon, Stephanie. "Haley Endorsed by Blogger Who Claimed Affair with Her." CBCNews.com, June 18, 2010. www.cbsnews.com/8300-503544_162 -503544.html?keyword=nikki+haley (accessed August 12, 2011).

———. "Harry Reid on the Attack, but Still Lags Sharron Angle in Polls." CBSNews.com, June 25, 2010. www.cbsnews.com/8301-503544_162 -20008886-503544.html (accessed August 20, 2011).

"Congresswoman Balances Bills with Birth." CBSNews.com, April 21, 2007. www.bookrags.com/news/congresswoman-balances-bills-with-moc/ (accessed April 23, 2007).

Constantini, Edmond. "Political Women and Political Ambition." *American Journal of Politics* 34 (1990): 741–770.

Conway, M. Margaret. *Political Participation in the United States.* 3rd ed. Washington, DC: CQ Press, 2000.

Conway, M. Margaret, Gertrude Steuernagel, and David Ahern. *Women and Political Participation.* Washington, DC: CQ Press, 1997.

Cook, Elizabeth Adell. "Voter Reactions to Women Candidates." In *Women and Elective Office: Past, Present, and Future,* edited by Sue Thomas and Clyde Wilcox. New York: Oxford University Press, 1998.

Cook, Elizabeth Adell, Sue Thomas, and Clyde Wilcox. *The Year of the Woman: Myths and Reality.* Boulder: Westview, 1994.

Cook, Elizabeth Adell, and Clyde Wilcox. "Women Voters in the Year of the Woman." In *Democracy's Feast: Elections in America,* edited by Herbert Weisberg. Chatham, NJ: Chatham House, 1995.

Cooper, Michael, and Elisabeth Bumiller. "Alaskan Is McCain's Choice; First Woman on GOP Ticket." NewYorkTimes.com, August 29, 2008. www.nytimes.com/2008/08/30/us/politics/29palin.html?pagewanted=all (accessed October 13, 2011).

Cooperman, Rosalyn, and Bruce Oppenheimer. "The Gender Gap in the House of

Representatives." In *Congress Reconsidered,* 7th ed., edited by Lawrence Dodd and Bruce Oppenheimer. Washington, DC: CQ Press, 2001.

Costain, Anne. *Inviting Women's Rebellion: A Political Process Interpretation of the Women's Movement.* Baltimore: Johns Hopkins University Press, 1992.

Cox, Gary, and Jonathan Katz. *Elbridge Gerry's Salamander: The Electoral Consequences of the Reapportionment Revolution.* New York: Cambridge University Press, 2002.

CQ's Guide to 1990 Congressional Redistricting. Washington, DC: CQ Press, 1993.

Damon, Anjeanette, and Karoun Demirjian. "Sen. Harry Ried Wins Fifth Term Against Anti-Incumbent Fervor." LasVegasSun.com, November 2, 2010. www.lasvegassun.com/news/2010/nov/02/harry-reid-takes-lead-over -sharron-angle (accessed August 20, 2011).

Darcy, R., and James Choike. "A Formal Analysis of Legislative Turnover: Women Candidates and Legislative Representation." *American Journal of Political Science* 30 (1986): 237–255.

Darcy, R., and Charles Hadley. "Black Women in Politics: The Puzzle of Success." *Social Science Quarterly* 69 (1988): 629–645.

Darcy, R., and Sarah Slavin Schramm. "When Women Run Against Men." *Public Opinion Quarterly* 41 (1977): 1–12.

Darcy, R., Susan Welch, and Janet Clark. *Women, Elections, and Representation.* 2nd ed. Lincoln: University of Nebraska Press, 1994.

Darling, Marsha. "African-American Women in State Elective Office in the South." In *Women and Elective Office: Past, Present, and Future,* edited by Sue Thomas and Clyde Wilcox. New York: Oxford University Press, 1998.

Date, Terry. "N.H. First State with Female Majority in Senate." EagleTribune.com, November 6, 2008. www.eagletribune.com/newhampshire/x1876453397/N -H-first-state-with-female-majority-in-Senate (accessed October 15, 2011).

Davidson, Roger, and Walter Oleszek. *Congress and Its Members.* 5th ed., 9th ed. Washington, DC: CQ Press, 1996, 2004.

Davidson, Roger, Walter Oleszek, and Frances Lee. *Congress and Its Members.* 11th ed. Washington, DC: CQ Press, 2008.

Davis, Flora. *Moving the Mountain: The Women's Movement in America Since 1960.* New York: Simon and Schuster, 1991.

Deber, Raisa. "The Fault Dear Brutus: Women as Congressional Candidates in Pennsylvania." *Journal of Politics* 44 (1982): 463–479.

Deckman, Melissa, and Louis Goldstein. "Style or Substance? An Examination of Media Coverage of Hillary Clinton and Sarah Palin in the 2008 Presidential Elections." Presentation at the Japanese American Women's Symposium, Tokyo, 2009.

Deering, Christopher, and Stephen Smith. *Committees in Congress.* 3rd ed. Washington, DC: CQ Press, 1997.

deFiebre, Conrad. "Janklow Case: He Did Politics His Way; Roughshod Style Made Him SD Icon." *Minneapolis Star Tribune,* December 14, 2003.

Delli Carpini, Michael, and Ester Fuchs. "The Year of the Woman? Candidates, Voters, and the 1992 Elections." *Political Science Quarterly* 108 (1993): 29–36.

Demirjian, Karoun. "Sen. John Ensign to Resign, Dean Heller Likely Replacement." LasVegasSun.com, April 21, 2011. www.lasvegassun.com/news/2011/apr/21 /report-sen-john-ensign-step-down-friday (accessed September 20, 2011).

Dewar, Helen. "NY Senate Primary Gets Muddy Near the Wire." *Washington Post,* August 30, 1992.

Diamond, Irene. *Sex Roles in the State House.* New Haven: Yale University Press, 1977.

Dick, Jason. "Giffords, History, and True Arizona Grit." RollCall.com, August 3, 2011. www.rollcall.com/issues/57_19/giffords-history-and-true-arizona-grit -207978-1.html (accessed October 20, 2011).

Dickenson, James, and Paul Taylor. "Widow of Burton Will Seek Election to His House Seat." *Washington Post,* April 19, 1983.

"Dingell, John D." *CQ's Politics in America, 2006: The 109th Congress.* Washington, DC: CQ Press, 2005. http://library.cqpress.com/congress /pia109-Dingell-John-D (accessed July 15, 2005).

"Dingell, John David." *Biographical Directory of the United States Congress.* www.bioguide.congress.gov/scripts/biodisplay.pl?index=D000354 (accessed October 1, 2011).

"Dingell, John David, Jr.." *Biographical Directory of the United States Congress.* www.bioguide.congress.gov/scripts/biodisplay.pl?index=D000355 (accessed October 1, 2011).

Dionne, E. J. "Polarized by God? American Politics and the Religious Divide." In *Red and Blue Nation? Characteristics and Causes of America's Polarized Politics,* edited by Pietro Nivola and David Brady. Washington, DC: Brookings Institution, 2006.

"Do Latte Drinkers Really Vote for Obama?" UrbanSpoon.com, April 15, 2008. www.urbanspoon.com/blog/23/Do-latte-drinkers-really-vote-for-Obama.html (accessed October 1, 2011).

"Dodge, Augustus." *Biographical Directory of the United States Congress.* http://bioguide.congress.gov/scripts/biodisplay.pl?index=D000394 (accessed October 18, 2011).

"Dodge, Henry." *Biographical Directory of the United States Congress.* http://bioguide.congress.gov/scripts/biodisplay.pl?index=D000396 (accessed October 18, 2011).

Dolan, Julie, Melissa Deckman, and Michele Swers. *Women and Politics: Paths to Power and Political Influence.* Upper Saddle River, NJ: Pearson Prentice Hall, 2007.

Dolan, Kathleen. "Electoral Context, Issues, and Voting for Women in the 1990s." In *Women and Congress: Running, Winning, and Ruling,* edited by Karen O'Connor. Binghamton, NY: Haworth, 2001.

———. "Symbolic Mobilization? The Impact of Candidate Sex." In *Legislative Women: Getting Elected, Getting Ahead,* edited by Beth Reingold. Boulder: Lynne Rienner, 2008.

———. *Voting for Women: How the Public Evaluates Women Candidates.* Boulder: Westview, 2004.

———. "Voting for Women in the 'Year of the Woman.'" *American Journal of Political Science* 42 (1998): 272–293.

Dolan, Kathleen, and Lynne Ford. "Are All Women State Legislators Alike?" In *Women and Elective Office: Past, Present, and Future,* edited by Sue Thomas and Clyde Wilcox. New York: Oxford University Press, 1998.

———. "Change and Continuity Among Women State Legislators: Evidence from Three Decades." *Political Research Quarterly* 50 (1997): 137–151.

Dowd, Maureen. "Can Hillary Clinton Cry Her Way Back to the White House?" NewYorkTimes.com, January 9, 2008. www.nytimes.com/2008/01/09 /opinion/08dowd.html (accessed September 15, 2011).

Downs, Anthony. *An Economic Theory of Democracy.* New York: Addison Wesley, 1997.

Druckman, James, Martin Kifer, and Michael Parkin. "Campaign Communications in US Congressional Elections." *American Political Science Review* 103 (2009): 343–366.

Duerst-Lahti, Georgia. "The Bottleneck: Women Becoming Candidates." In *Women and Elective Office: Past, Present, and Future,* edited by Sue Thomas and Clyde Wilcox. New York: Oxford University Press, 1998.

Edwards, Rebecca. *Angels in the Machinery.* New York: Oxford University Press, 1997.

Ehrenhart, Alan, ed. *Politics in America, 1982.* Washington, DC: CQ Press, 1981.

Eilperin, Juliet. *Fight Club Politics.* Lanham: Rowman and Littlefield, 2006.

Elazar, Daniel. *American Federalism: A View from the States.* New York: Crowell, 1966.

"Election Polls: Vote by Groups, 2008." Gallup.com. www.gallup.com/poll /112132/election-polls-vote-groups-2008.aspx (accessed October 28, 2011).

"EMILY's List 2008 PAC Summary Data." OpenSecrets.org. www.opensecrets .org/pacs/lookup2.php?strID=C00193433&cycle=2008 (accessed August 10, 2011).

Epstein, Cynthia Fuchs. *Women in Law.* 2nd ed. Chicago: University of Illinois Press, 1993.

Epstein, David, and Sharyn O'Halloran. "A Social Science Approach to Race, Redistricting, and Representation." *American Political Science Review* 93 (1999): 187–191.

"Equal Role for Women, 1972–2008." *The ANES Guide to Public Opinion and Electoral Behavior.* www.electionstudies.org/nesguide/toptable/tab4c_1.htm (accessed October 14, 2011).

Erikson, Robert, Gerald Wright, and John McIver. *Statehouse Democracy: Public Opinion and Policy in the American States.* New York: Cambridge University Press, 1993.

Eulau, Heinz. "The Political Socialization of American State Legislators." In *Legislative Behavior: A Reader in Theory and Research,* edited by John Wahlke and Heinz Eulau, Glencoe, IL: Free Press, 1959.

Fahrenthold, David, and Paul Kane. "Rep. Anthony Weiner Resigns." Washington Post.com, June 16, 2011. www.washingtonpost.com/politics/anthony-weiner-to -resign-thursday/2011/06/16/AGrPONXH_story.html (accessed August 10, 2011).

Falk, Erika. *Women for President: Media Bias in Eight Campaigns.* Urbana: University of Illinois Press, 2008.

"Familial Connections of Women Representatives and Senators in Congress." Washington, DC: Office of the Clerk of the US House of Representatives. http://womenincongress.house.gov/historical-data/familial-connections-in -congress.html#table8 (accessed October 1, 2011).

"Families and Living Arrangements: Historical Time Series, Estimated Median Age by First Marriage, by Sex." US Bureau of the Census. Washington, DC: US Department of Commerce, Bureau of the Census. www.census.gov /population/www/socdemo/hh-fam.html#ht (accessed October 15, 2011).

Fears, Darryl. "On a Mission in a Political Second Act; Bush's Record Forced Her to Run, Braun Says." *Washington Post,* July 13, 2003.

Fenn, Jennifer. "Swift Sent Women a Bad Message." *Lowell Sun,* March 22, 2002.

Fenno, Richard. *Congress at the Grassroots: Representational Change in the South, 1970–1998.* Chapel Hill: University of North Carolina Press, 2000.

———. *Congressmen in Committees.* Boston: Little, Brown, 1973.

———. *Home Style: House Members in Their Districts.* Boston: Little, Brown, 1978.

———. *Senators on the Campaign Trail.* Norman: University of Oklahoma Press, 1996.

"A Fifty-State Strategy." Emerge America. www.emergeamerica.org/affiliates (accessed May 30, 2011).

"Final Order: Adopting a Legislative Redistricting Plan." State of Minnesota Special Redistricting Panel, C0-01-160, March 19, 2002.

Fiorina, Morris. *Congress: Keystone of the Washington Establishment.* 2nd ed. New Haven: Yale University Press, 1989.

———. *Representatives, Roll Calls, and Constituencies.* Lexington, MA: Heath, 1974.

Fiorina, Morris, and Matthew Levendusky. "Disconnected: The Political Class Versus the People." In *Red and Blue Nation? Characteristics and Causes of America's Polarized Politics,* edited by Pietro Novila and David Brady. Washington, DC: Brookings Institution, 2006.

Fisher, Marguerite, and Betty Whitehead. "Women and National Party Organization." *American Political Science Review* 38 (1944): 895–903.

Flanigan, William, and Nancy Zingale. *Political Behavior of the American Electorate.* 8th ed., 10th ed. Washington, DC: CQ Press, 1994, 2002.

Fleisher, Richard, and Jon Bond. "Polarized Politics: Does It Matter?" In *Polarized Politics: Congress and the President in a Partisan Era,* edited by Jon Bond and Richard Fleisher. Washington, DC: CQ Press, 2000.

Foerstel, Karen. *Biographical Dictionary of Congressional Women.* Westport: Greenwood, 1999.

Foerstel, Karen, and Herbert Foerstel. *Climbing the Hill: Gender Conflict in Congress.* Westport: Praeger, 1996.

Foner, Eric. *Freedom's Lawmakers: A Directory of Black Officeholders During Reconstruction.* Baton Rouge: Louisiana State University Press, 1996.

Fowler, Linda, and Jennifer Lawless. "Looking for Sex in All the Wrong Places: Press Coverage and the Electoral Fortunes of Gubernatorial Candidates." *Perspectives on Politics* 7 (2009): 519–536.

Fowler, Linda, and Robert McClure. *Political Ambition: Who Decides to Run for Congress.* New Haven: Yale University Press, 1989.

Fowlkes, Diane, Jerry Perkins, and Sue Tolleson Rinehart. "Gender Roles and Party Roles." *American Political Science Review* 3 (1979): 772–780.

Fox, Richard. "Gender, Political Ambition, and the Decision Not to Run for Office." New Brunswick, NJ: Rutgers University, Center for American Women and Politics, Eagleton Institute of Politics, 2003. www.rci.rutgers.edu /~cawp/Research/Reports/Fox2003.pdf.

———. *Gender Dynamics in Congressional Elections.* Thousand Oaks, CA: Sage, 1997.

Fox, Richard, and Jennifer Lawless. "If Only They'd Ask: Gender, Recruitment, and Political Ambition." *Journal of Politics* 72 (2010): 310–326.

Fox, Richard, Jennifer Lawless, and Courtney Feeley. "Gender and the Decision to Run for Office." *Legislative Studies Quarterly* 26 (2001): 411–435.

Fox, Richard, and Zoe Oxley. "Gender Stereotyping in State Executive Elections: Candidates Selection and Success." *Journal of Politics* 65 (2003): 833–850.

Fox and Friends. "For Crying Out Loud." FoxNews.com, January 8, 2008. http://greenroom.blogs.foxnews.com/2008/01/08/for-crying-out-loud (accessed September 15, 2011).

"Foxx, Virginia Ann." *Biographical Directory of the United States Congress.* http://bioguide.congress.gov/scripts/biodisplay.pl?index=F000450 (accessed November 8, 2011).

Francis, Wayne, and Lawrence Kenny. *Up the Political Ladder: Career Paths in US Politics.* Thousand Oaks, CA: Sage, 2000.

Frank, Thomas. *What's the Matter with Kansas?* New York: Metropolitan, 2004.

Franke-Ruta, Garance. "Record Number of Republican Women Are Running for House Seats." WashingtonPost.com, May 1, 2010. www.washingtonpost.com/wp-dyn/content/article/2010/04/29/AR2010042903222.html (accessed August 20, 2011).

Frankel, Bruce. "Anything Goes in NY Primary." *USA Today,* September 11, 1992.

"Franken, Al." *Biographical Directory of the United States Congress.* http://bioguide.congress.gov/scripts/biodisplay.pl?index=F000457 (accessed November 4, 2011).

"Fred Dalton Thompson." imdb.com. www.imdb.com/name/nm0000669/bio (accessed October 20, 2011).

"Fred Grandy." imdb.com. www.imdb.com/name/nm0334948 (accessed October 20, 2011).

Freeman, Jo (Joanne). *Affairs of Honor: National Politics in the New Republic.* New Haven: Yale University Press, 2001.

———. *The Politics of Women's Liberation.* New York: David McKay, 1975.

———. *A Room at a Time: How Women Entered Party Politics.* New York: Rowman and Littlefield, 2000.

———. *The Women Who Ran for President.* JoFreeman.com. www.jofreeman.com/politics/womprez03.htm (accessed July 6, 2011).

"Frelinghuysen, Frederick." *Biographical Directory of the United States Congress.* www.bioguide.congress.gov/scripts/biodisplay.pl?index=F000368 (accessed October 1, 2011).

"Frelinghuysen, Frederick Theodore." *Biographical Directory of the United States Congress.* www.bioguide.congress.gov/scripts/biodisplay.pl?index=F000373 (accessed October 1, 2011).

"Frelinghuysen, Joseph Sherman." *Biographical Directory of the United States Congress.* www.bioguide.congress.gov/scripts/biodisplay.pl?index=F000373 (accessed October 1, 2011).

"Frelinghuysen, Peter Hood Ballantine." *Biographical Directory of the United States Congress.* www.bioguide.congress.gov/scripts/biodisplay.pl?index=F000373 (accessed October 1, 2011).

"Frelinghuysen, Rodney." *Biographical Directory of the United States Congress.* www.bioguide.congress.gov/scripts/biodisplay.pl?index=F000373 (accessed October 1, 2011).

"Frelinghuysen, Theodore." *Biographical Directory of the United States Congress.*

www.bioguide.congress.gov/scripts/biodisplay.pl?index=F000373 (accessed October 1, 2011).

Frey, William. "Race, Immigration, and America's Changing Electorate." In *Red, Blue, and Purple America: The Future of Election Demographics,* edited by Ruy Teixeira. Washington, DC: Brookings Institution, 2008.

Fridkin, Kim, and Patrick Kenney. "The Role of Gender Stereotypes in US Senate Elections." *Politics & Gender* 5 (2009): 301–324.

Friedman, John, and Richard Holden. "The Rising Incumbent Reelection Rate: What's Gerrymandering Got to Do with It?" *Journal of Politics* 71 (2009): 593–611.

Friedman, Sally. "House Committee Assignments of Women and Minority Newcomers, 1965–1994." *Legislative Studies Quarterly* 21 (1996): 73–81.

Froman, Lewis. *The Congressional Process.* Boston: Little, Brown, 1967.

Fulton, Sarah, Cherie Maestas, L. Sandy Maisel, and Walter Stone. "The Sense of a Woman: Gender, Ambition, and the Decision to Run for Congress." *Political Research Quarterly* 59 (2006): 235–248.

Gaddie, Ronald Keith. "The Texas Redistricting, Measure for Measure." In *Extensions: Congressional Redistricting,* edited by Ronald Peters. Norman: University of Oklahoma Press, 2004.

Gaddie, Ronald Keith, and Charles Bullock. "Congressional Elections and the Year of the Woman: Structural and Elite Influences on Female Candidates." *Social Science Quarterly* 76 (1995): 749–762.

Galderisi, Peter, ed. *Redistricting in the New Millennium.* New York: Lexington Books, 2005.

"Gallup Poll, 1935–1971." Wilmington, DE: Scholarly Resources, 1973.

Galston, William, and Pietro Nivola. "Delineating the Problem." In *Red and Blue Nation? Characteristics and Causes of America's Polarized Politics,* edited by Pietro Novila and David Brady. Washington, DC: Brookings Institution, 2006.

Gamarekian, Barbara. "'The Popular Burton' and Her Mission." *New York Times,* July 29, 1983.

Gardner, Amy. "Jim Moran Calls GOP the 'Taliban Ticket.'" WashingtonPost.com, November 2, 2009. http://voices.washingtonpost.com/virginiapolitics/2009/11/jim_moran_calls_gop_the_taliba.html (accessed August 10, 2011).

Garrett, Sam. *Campaign Crises: Detours on the Road to Congress.* Boulder: Lynne Rienner, 2010.

Gelman, Andrew. *Red State, Blue State, Rich State, Poor State.* Princeton: Princeton University Press, 2009.

———. "Where the Starbucks and Walmarts Are." AndrewGelman.com, March 3, 2008. http://andrewgelman.com/2008/03/where_the_starb (accessed October 1, 2011).

"George Henry White." *Black Americans in Congress.* Washington, DC: Office of the Clerk of the US House of Representatives. http://baic.house.gov/member-profiles/profile.html?intID=22 (accessed October 20, 2011).

Geraghty, Jim. "Moranic Record." *National Review Online,* March 12, 2003. www.nationalreview.com/comment/comment-geraghty031203.asp.

Gerber, Larry. "Dornan Loses Solidly, Not Quietly." *Associated Press,* November 4, 1998.

Gerrity, Jessica, Tracy Osborn, and Jeanette Morehouse Mendez. "Women and Representation: A Different View of the District?" *Politics & Gender* 3 (2007):179–200.

Gertzog, Irwin. *Congressional Women: Their Recruitment, Integration, and Behavior.* 2nd ed. Westport: Praeger, 1995.

———. "The Matrimonial Connection: The Nomination of Congressmen's Widows for the House of Representatives." *Journal of Politics* 42 (1980): 820–833.

Gertzog, Irwin, and Michele Simard. "Women and 'Hopeless' Congressional Candidacies: Nomination Frequency, 1916–1978." *American Politics Quarterly* 9 (1991): 449–466.

Gilbert, Sophie. "Go Ahead—It's Okay to Cry." Washingtonian.com, March 1, 2010. www.washingtonian.com/blogarticles/18556.html (accessed September 15, 2011).

Giles, Kevin. *Flight of the Dove: The Story of Jeannette Rankin.* Beaverton, OR: Touchstone, 1980.

Gill, LaVerne McCain. *African American Women in Congress: Forming and Transforming History.* New Brunswick, NJ: Rutgers University Press, 1997.

Gillon, Steven. *That's Not What We Meant to Do: Reform and Its Unintended Consequences in Twentieth-Century America.* New York: Norton, 2000.

Giroux, Gregory. "California Democrats' Remap Puts Two of Their Own in Tough Spots." *CQ Weekly,* September 22, 2001.

———. "Remaps' Clear Trend: Incumbent Protection." *CQ Weekly,* November 3, 2001.

Givhan, Robin. "Hillary Clinton's Tentative Dip Into New Neckline Territory." WashingtonPost.com, July 20, 2007. www.washingtonpost.com/wp-dyn/content/article/2007/07/19/AR2007071902668.html (accessed October 13, 2011).

Groer, Annie. "Congress as a Family Business: Brothers (and Sisters and Sons) in Arms." PoliticsDaily.com, November, 2010. www.politicsdaily.com/2010/11/09/congress-as-a-family-business-brothers-and-sisters-and-sons-i (accessed October 18, 2011).

Grofman, Bernard, and Lisa Handley. "Minority Population Proportion and the Black and Hispanic Congressional Success in the 1970s and 1980s." *American Politics Quarterly* 17 (1989): 436–445.

Gruberg, Martin. *Women in Politics: A Source Book.* New York: Academic Press, 1968.

"Guide to House and Senate Members." Washington, DC: US Government Printing Office. www.memberguide.gpoaccess.gov/GetMembersSearch.aspx (accessed October 18, 2011).

Guinier, Lani. "Don't Scapegoat the Gerrymander." *New York Times Magazine,* January 8, 1995.

Gulati, Jeff, and Christine Williams. "Communicating with Constituents in 140 Characters or Less: Twitter and the Diffusion of Technology Innovation in the United States Congress." Social Science Research Network, April 23, 2010. http://ssrn.com/abstract=1628247.

Gustafson, Melanie. "Partisan Women in the Progressive Era: The Struggle for Inclusion in American Political Parties." *Journal of Women's History* 9 (1997): 8–30.

————. *Women and the Republican Party, 1854–1924.* Urbana: University of Illinois Press, 2001.

Haas, Karen. "List of Standing Committees and Select Committees and Their Subcommittees." Washington, DC: Office of the Clerk of the US House of Representatives, August 3, 2011.

————. "Seniority List of the United States House of Representatives One Hundred Twelfth Congress." Washington, DC: Office of the Clerk of the US House of Representatives, August 3, 2011.

Hackler, Jacob, and Paul Pierson. *Off Center: The Republican Revolution and the Erosion of American Democracy.* New Haven: Yale University Press, 2005.

Haga, Chuck. "'Come Home,' Coya Dies." *Minneapolis Star Tribune,* October 11, 1996.

Halberstam, David. *The Fifties.* New York: Fawcett Columbine, 1993.

Hale, Jon. "The Making of the New Democrats." *Political Science Quarterly* 110 (1995): 207–232.

Handley, Lisa, and Bernard Grofman. "The Impact of the Voting Rights Act on Minority Representation: Black Office Holding in Southern State Legislatures and Congressional Delegations." In *Quiet Revolution in the South: The Impact of the Voting Rights Act, 1965–1990,* edited by Chandler Davidson and Bernard Grofman. Princeton: Princeton University Press, 1994.

Hansen, Susan. "Talking About Politics: Gender and Contextual Effects on Political Proselytizing." *Journal of Politics* 59 (1997): 73–103.

Hardy, Michael, and Karen McCurdy. "Representational Threshold: Women in Congressional Committees." Paper presented at the annual meeting of the Southern Political Science Association, New Orleans, January 2005.

Hardy-Fanta, Carol, ed. *Latina Politics, Latino Politics: Gender, Culture, and Political Participation in Boston.* Philadelphia: Temple University Press, 1993.

Harrison, Cynthia. *On Account of Sex: The Politics of Women's Issues, 1945–1968.* Berkeley: University of California Press, 1988.

Harvey, Anna. *Votes Without Leverage: Women in American Electoral Politics, 1920–1970.* New York: Cambridge University Press, 1998.

Hayes, Danny. "When Gender and Party Collide: Stereotyping in Candidate Trait Attribution." *Politics & Gender* 7 (2011): 133–165.

Haynes, Audrey, and Brian Pitt. "Making an Impression: New Media in the 2008 Presidential Nomination Campaigns." *PS: Political Science and Politics* 42 (2009): 53–58.

Healy, Patrick. "On Eve of Primary, Clinton's Campaign Shows Stress." NewYorkTimes.com, January 8, 2008. www.nytimes.com/2008/01/08/us /politics/08clinton.html (accessed September 15, 2011).

Heaney, Michael. "Blogging Congress: Technological Change and the Politics of the Congressional Press Galleries." *PS: Political Science and Politics* 41 (2008): 422–426.

Heldman, Caroline, Susan Carroll, and Stephanie Olson. "'She Brought Only a Skirt': Print Media Coverage of Elizabeth Dole's Bid for the Republican Presidential Nomination." *Political Communication* 22 (2005): 315–335.

Hennessey, Kathleen. "For GOP Women, 2010 May Not Be Their Year." LosAngelesTimes.com, July 24, 2010. http://articles.latimes.com/2010/jul/24 /nation/la-na-gop-women-20100725 (accessed August 20, 2011).

————. "GOP Women Still Have Work to Do." *Los Angeles Times,* July 25, 2010.

Henry, Mark. "Bono's Mother Doesn't Want His Widow Elected." *Riverside Press Enterprise* (California), March 28, 1998.

————. "Phone Call Discouraged Election Run." *Riverside Press Enterprise* (Riverside, California), March 31, 1998.

Hernandez, Raymond. "Ex-Congressman Describes Tickle Fights with Aides." NewYorkTimes.com, March 9, 2010. www.nytimes.com/2010/03/10 /nyregion/10massa.html (accessed August 10, 2011).

Herrnson, Paul. *Congressional Elections: Campaigning at Home and in Washington.* 4th ed. Washington, DC: CQ Press, 2004.

Herrnson, Paul, J. Celeste Lay, and Atiya Kai Stokes. "Women Running 'As Women': Candidate Gender, Campaign Issues, and Voter-Targeting Strategies." *Journal of Politics* 65 (2003): 244–255.

Herron, Michael, and Jasjeet Sekhon. "Black Candidates and Black Voters: Assessing the Impact of Candidate Race on Uncounted Vote Rates." *Journal of Politics* 67 (2005): 154–177.

Hess, Stephen. *America's Political Dynasties: From Adams to Kennedy.* Garden City, NY: Doubleday, 1966.

————. "America's Top Dynasty?" WashingtonPost.com, September 13, 2009. www.washingtonpost.com/wp-dyn/content/article/2009/09/11/AR2009 091101831.html (accessed August 10, 2011).

High-Pippert, Angela. "Female Empowerment: The Influence of Women Representing Women." *Women & Politics* 19 (1998): 53–67.

Hill, David. "Political Culture and Female Political Representation." *Journal of Politics* 43 (1981): 159–168.

Hill, Kevin. "Do Black Majority Districts Aid Republicans?" *Journal of Politics* 57 (1995): 384–401.

Historical Statistics of the United States. Washington, DC: US Department of Commerce, Bureau of the Census, various years.

Hoffman, Kim, Carrie Palmer, and Ronald Keith Gaddie. "Candidate Sex and Congressional Elections: Open Seats Before, During, and After the Year of the Woman." In *Women and Congress: Running, Winning, and Ruling,* edited by Karen O'Connor. Binghamton, NY: Haworth, 2001.

Hole, Judith, and Ellen Levine. *Rebirth of Feminism.* New York: Quadrangle, 1971.

Holtzman, Elizabeth, with Cynthia Cooper. *Who Said It Would Be Easy? One Woman's Life in the Political Arena.* New York: Arcade, 1996.

"The Honorable Doris O. Matsui." Congresswoman Doris Matsui. http://matsui .house.gov/index.php?option=com_content&view=article&id=332&Itemid =57 (accessed October 20, 2011).

Hook, Janet. "Will the Flood of Retirements Arrive in 1992? Maybe Not." *CQ Weekly,* January 12, 1991.

Huddy, Leonie, and Nayda Terkildsen. "The Consequences of Gender Stereotypes for Women Candidates at Different Levels and Types of Office." *Political Research Quarterly* 46 (1993): 503–525.

————. "Gender Stereotypes and the Perception of Male and Female Candidates." *American Journal of Political Science* 37 (1993): 119–147.

Hulse, Carl, and David Herszenhorn. "Rangel Steps Aside from Post During Ethics Inquiry." NewYorkTimes.com, March 3, 2010. www.nytimes.com/2010/03 /04/nyregion/04rangel.html (accessed August 10, 2011).

"I Had a One-Night Stand with Christine O'Donnell." Gawker.com, October 28,

2010. http://gawker.com/5674353/i-had-a-one+night-stand-with-christine -odonnell (accessed September 10, 2011).

Inskip, Leonard. "A Revival of Sorts for Minnesota's Knutson." *Minneapolis Star Tribune,* February 4, 1997.

Iyengar, Shanto, et al. "Running As a Woman: Gender Stereotyping in Political Campaigns." In *Women, Media, and Politics,* edited by Pippa Norris. New York: Oxford University Press, 1997.

Jacobson, Gary. *The Politics of Congressional Elections.* 4th ed., 7th ed. New York: HarperCollins, 1997, 2009.

James, Frank. "California Governor's Race Shows Limits of Money." NationalPublicRadio.org. www.npr.org/blogs/itsallpolitics/2010/11/03/131030498 /california-governor-s-race-shows-limits-of-money (accessed October 20, 2011).

Jamieson, Kathleen Hall. *Beyond the Double Bind: Women and Leadership.* New York: Oxford University Press, 1995.

"Janklow Trial Begins, Could Shake Up State's Political Scene." *Bulletin's Frontrunner* (McLean, VA), December 2, 2003.

Jaschik, Scott. "For First Time, More Women Than Men Earn PhD." USAToday.com, September 14, 2010. www.usatoday.com/news/education/2010-09-15-women phd14_st_N.htm (accessed October 1, 2011).

Jenkins, Chris, and R. H. Melton. "Contrite, Combatative Moran on the Ropes: Congressman Fights to Survive." *Washington Post,* March 16, 2003.

Jennings, M. Kent, and Richard Niemi. *Generations and Politics: A Panel Study of Young Adults and Their Parents.* Princeton: Princeton University Press, 1981.

Jennings, M. Kent, Laura Stoker, and Jake Bowers. "Politics Across Generations: Family Transmission Reexamined." *Journal of Politics* 71 (2009): 782–799.

Jennings, M. Kent, and Norman Thomas. "Men and Women in Party Elites: Social Roles and Political Resources." *Midwest Journal of Political Science* 12 (1968): 462–492.

"Jo Ann Davis Dies at 57; Represented Virginia in Congress." NewYorkTimes.com, October 8, 2007; www.nytimes.com/2007/10/08/us/08davis.html (accessed July 15, 2011).

"Jo Ann Davis' Husband May Seek Her Congressional Seat." FreeRepublic.com, October 8, 2007. www.freerepublic.com/focus/f-news/1908474/posts (accessed July 15, 2011).

"John Boehner: Real Men Do Cry." CBSNews.com, *60 Minutes Overtime,* December 10, 2010. www.cbsnews.com/8301-504803_162-20025417-1039 1709.html (accessed September 15, 2011).

Jones, Allison North, and Ellen Gedalius. "Martinez 'Humbled to Be' US Senator." *Tampa Tribune,* November 4, 2004.

Jones, Ben. *Redneck Boy in the Promised Land: The Confessions of "Crazy Cooter."* New York: Crown, 2008.

Jones, Woodrow, and Albert Nelson. "Correlates of Women's Representation in Lower State Legislative Chambers." *Social Behavior and Personality* 1 (1981): 9–15.

Joseph, Cameron. "Ohio Redistricting Battle Heats Up." TheHill.com, October 20, 2011. http://thehill.com/blogs/ballot-box/house-races/188721-ohio-redistricting -battle-heats-up (accessed November 4, 2011).

———. "Rep. Mike Ross to Retire." TheHill.com, July 25, 2011. http://thehill.com/blogs/ballot-box/house-races/173233-rep-mike-ross-to -announce-political-future (accessed November 4, 2011).

Jost, Kenneth. "Redistricting Disputes." *CQ Researcher,* March 12, 2004.

Judis, John, and Ruy Teixeira. *The Emerging Democratic Majority.* New York: Scribner, 2002.

Kahn, Kim Fridkin. "Characteristics of Press Coverage in Senate and Gubernatorial Elections: Information Available to Voters." *Legislative Studies Quarterly* 20 (1995): 23–35.

———. *The Political Consequences of Being a Woman.* New York: Columbia University Press, 1996.

Kahn, Kim Fridkin, and Edie Goldenberg. "Women Candidates in the News: An Examination of Gender Differences in US Senate Campaign Coverage." *Public Opinion Quarterly* 55 (1991): 180–199.

Kane, Paul. "Charlie Rangel Censure Recommended by House Ethics Committee." WashingtonPost.com, November 19, 2010. www.washington post.com/wp-dyn/content/article/2010/11/18/AR2010111800478.html?sid =ST2010111805447 (accessed August 10, 2011).

———. "Mike Castle Won't Endorse Christine O'Donnell for Senate, Citing 'Smears.'" WashingtonPost.com, September 17, 2010. www.washingtonpost .com/wp-dyn/content/article/2010/09/16/AR2010091604717.html (accessed July 7, 2010).

Kane, Paul, and Ben Pershing. "Rep. Maxine Waters of California Probably Broke Ethics Rules, House Panel Finds." WashingtonPost.com, August 3, 2010. www.washingtonpost.com/wp-dyn/content/article/2010/08/02/AR2010 080204084.html (accessed August 10, 2011).

Kaptur, Marcy. *Women of Congress: A Twentieth-Century Odyssey.* Washington, DC: CQ Press, 1996.

Karl, Jonathan. "In South Dakota: Another Sarah Palin?" ABCNews.com, October 12, 2010. http://abcnews.go.com/Politics/2010_Elections/elections-2010 -south-dakota-sarah-palin/story?id=11860378 (accessed July 31, 2011).

———. "John Boehner Cries Amid Government Shutdown Standoff." ABCNews.com, April 6, 2011. http://abcnews.go.com/blogs/politics/2011/04 /boehner-cries-over-looming-government-shutdown (accessed September 15, 2011).

Katz, Jonathan, and Brian Sala. "Careerism, Committee Assignments, and the Electoral Connection." *American Political Science Review* 90 (1996): 21–33.

Kaufman, Karen, and John Petrocik. "The Changing Politics of American Men: Understanding the Sources of the Gender Gap." *American Journal of Political Science* 43 (1999): 864–887.

Kazee, Thomas, ed. *Who Runs for Congress? Ambition, Context, and Candidate Emergence.* Washington, DC: CQ Press, 1994.

"Kennedy, Edward Moore (Ted)." *Biographical Directory of the United States Congress.* http://bioguide.congress.gov/scripts/biodisplay.pl?index=K000105 (accessed October 18, 2011).

"Kennedy, Patrick Joseph." *Biographical Directory of the United States Congress.* http://bioguide.congress.gov/scripts/biodisplay.pl?index=K000113 (accessed October 18, 2011).

"Kennedy, Robert Francis." *Biographical Directory of the United States Congress.* http://bioguide.congress.gov/scripts/biodisplay.pl?index=K000114 (accessed October 18, 2011).

Kernell, Samuel. "Toward Understanding 19th Century Congressional Careers:

Ambition, Competition, and Rotation." *American Journal of Political Science* 21 (1977): 669–693.

Key, V. O. *Southern Politics in State and Nation.* New York: Knopf, 1949.

Kincaid, Diane. "Over His Dead Body: A Positive Perspective on Widows in the US Congress." *Western Political Quarterly* 31 (1978): 96–104.

King, David, and Richard Matland. "Sex and the Grand Old Party: An Experimental Investigation of the Effect of Candidate Sex on Support for a Republican Candidate." *American Politics Research* 31 (2003): 595–612.

King, Gary, and Langche Zeng. "Logistic Regression in Rare Events Data." *Political Analysis* 9 (2001): 1–27.

Kirkpatrick, Jeane. *Political Woman.* New York: Basic, 1974.

Kleefeld, Eric. "O'Donnell Blasts Castle's 'Un-Manly' Tactics." TalkingPoints Memo.com, September 10, 2010. www.webcitation.org/5u8syuHZT (accessed July 7, 2011).

Koch, Jeffrey. "Do Citizens Apply Gender Stereotypes to Infer Candidates' Ideological Orientations?" *Journal of Politics* 62 (2000): 414–429.

———. "Gender Stereotypes and Citizens' Impressions of House Candidates' Ideological Orientations." *American Journal of Political Science* 46 (2002): 453–462.

Kocieniewski, David. "Congressman Pays Back Tax on Dominican Republic Villa." NewYorkTimes.com, September 19, 2008. www.nytimes.com/2008 /09/20/nyregion/20rangel.html?bl=&ei=5087&en=e988142cbc6e5775&ex=1 222056000&adxnnl=1&adxnnlx=1313191619-YUScPzE1KnaS7gbk W2q20Q (accessed August 10, 2011).

———. "House Ethics Committee Votes to Begin an Inquiry on Rangel." NewYorkTimes.com, September 24, 2008. www.nytimes.com/2008/09/25 /washington/25rangel.html (accessed August 10, 2011).

Koetzle, William. "The Impact of Constituency Diversity upon the Competitiveness of US House Elections, 1962–1996." *Legislative Studies Quarterly* 23 (1998): 561–573.

Komarovsky, Mirra. "Cultural Contradictions and Sex Roles." *American Journal of Sociology* 52 (1946): 184–189.

Kornblut, Anne. "Clinton Shatters Record for Fundraising." *Washington Post,* April 2, 2007.

———. *Notes from the Cracked Ceiling: Hillary Clinton, Sarah Palin, and What It Will Take for a Woman to Win.* New York: Crown, 2009.

Koszczuk, Jacki. "Proof of Illegal Voters Falls Short, Keeping Sanchez in House." *CQ Weekly,* February 7, 1998.

Koszczuk, Jacki, and H. Amy Stern, eds. *CQ's Politics in America, 2006: The 109th Congress.* Washington, DC: CQ Press, 2005.

Kropf, Martha, and John Boiney. "The Electoral Glass Ceiling? Gender, Viability, and the News in US Senate Campaigns." In *Women and Congress: Running, Winning, and Ruling,* edited by Karen O'Connor. Binghamton, NY: Haworth, 2001.

Kumar, Anita, and Joni James. "Harris Announces Run for US Senate." *St. Petersburg Times,* June 8, 2005.

Kuntz, Phil. "Overdrafts Were a Potent Charge." *CQ Weekly,* November 7, 1992.

———. "Uproar over Bank Scandal Goads House to Cut Perks." *CQ Weekly,* October 5, 1991.

"Labor Force Participation Rates Among Mothers." Washington, DC: US Department of Labor, Bureau of Labor Statistics, May 7, 2010. www.bls.gov /opub/ted/2010/ted_20100507.htm (accessed October 15, 2011).

Lacy, Marc, and David Herszenhorn. "In Attack's Wake, Political Repercussions." NewYorkTimes.com. www.nytimes.com/2011/01/09/us/politics/09giffords .html?pagewanted=all (accessed October 20, 2011).

Lai, James, Wendy Tam Cho, Thomas Kim, and Okiyoshi Takeda. "Asian-Pacific American Campaigns, Elections, and Elected Officials." *PS: Political Science and Politics* 34 (2001): 611–617.

Lake, Celinda. "Name It, Change It: Findings from an Online Dial Survey of 800 Likely Voters Nationwide." Washington, DC: Lake Research Partners, 2010.

Lake, Celinda, Kellyanne Conway, and Catherine Whitney. *What Women Really Want: How American Women Are Quietly Erasing Political, Racial, Class, and Religious Lines to Change the Way We Live.* New York: Free Press, 2005.

Lamson, Peggy. *Few Are Chosen.* Boston: Houghton Mifflin, 1968.

Lane, Robert. *Political Life.* Glencoe, IL: Free Press, 1959.

Lang, Robert, Thomas Sanchez, and Alan Berube. "The New Suburban Politics: A County-Based Analysis of Metropolitan Voting Trends Since 2000." In *Red, Blue, and Purple America: The Future of Election Demographics,* edited by Ruy Teixeira. Washington, DC: Brookings Institution, 2008.

Lassen, David, and Adam Brown. "Twitter: The Electoral Connection." *Social Science Computer Review,* September 2010. http://ssc.sagepub.com/content /early/2010/09/16/0894439310382749.abstract (accessed September 10, 2011).

Lau, Richard, and David Redlawsk. "Advantages and Disadvantages of Cognitive Heuristics in Political Decision Making." *American Journal of Political Science* 45 (2001): 951–971.

Lau, Richard, and David Sears, eds. *Political Cognition.* Hillsdale, NJ: Erlbaum, 1986.

Lawless, Jennifer. "Politics of Presence? Congresswomen and Symbolic Representation." *Political Research Quarterly* 57 (2004): 81–99.

Lawless, Jennifer, and Richard Fox. *It Still Takes a Candidate: Why Women Don't Run for Office.* New York: Cambridge University Press, 2010.

Lawrence, Regina, and Melody Rose. *Hillary Clinton's Race for the White House: Gender Politics and Media on the Campaign Trail.* Boulder: Lynne Rienner, 2010.

Leal, David, Matt Barreto, Jongho Lee, and Rodolfo O. de la Garza. "The Latino Vote in the 2004 Election." *PS: Political Science and Politics* 38 (2005): 41–49.

Lee, Christopher. "Rangel's Pet Cause Bears His Own Name." WashingtonPost.com, July 15, 2008. www.washingtonpost.com/wp-dyn/content/article/2008/07/14 /AR2008071402546.html (accessed August 10, 2011).

Leeper, Mark. "The Impact of Prejudice on Female Candidates: An Experimental Look at Voter Inference." *American Politics Quarterly* 19 (1991): 248–261.

Lengel, Allan. "Discovery May Alter Questions for Condit." *Washington Post,* May 24, 2002.

Lengel, Allan, and Petula Dvorak. "Condit Offers Long-Awaited Comment Tonight." *Washington Post,* August 23, 2001.

Lewis, Ann. "Hillary for President." July 27, 2007. www.washingtonpost.com/wp -srv/artsandliving/daily/graphics/hillary_for_president_072807.pdf (accessed October 13, 2011).

Lipman, Larry. "Ex-Harris Aides Reveal Why They Became 'Exes.'" *Palm Beach Post,* August 6, 2006.

Livingston, Abby. "Arizona Governor Starts Impeachment Process Against Redistricting Panel." RollCall.com, October 26, 2011. www.rollcall.com/news /arizona_governor_jan_brewer_starts_impeachment_against_redistricting _panel-209840-1.html (accessed November 4, 2011).

Locke, Mamie. "From Three-fifths to Zero." In *Women Transforming Politics,* edited by Cathy Cohen, Kathleen Jones, and Joan Tronto. New York: New York University Press, 1997.

Lopach, James, and Jean Luckowski. *Jeannette Rankin: A Political Woman.* Boulder: University Press of Colorado, 2005.

Lovley, Erika. "GOP Women: A Minority in a Minority." Politico.com, May 10, 2009. www.politico.com/news/stories/0509/22342.html (accessed August 20, 2011).

Lublin, David. *The Paradox of Representation: Racial Gerrymandering and Minority Interests in Congress.* Princeton: Princeton University Press, 1997.

———. "Racial Redistricting and African-American Representation: A Critique of 'Do Majority-Minority Districts Maximize Substantive Black Representation in Congress?'" *American Political Science Review* 93 (1999): 183–186.

———. *The Republican South: Democratization and Partisan Change.* Princeton: Princeton University Press, 2004.

Luce, Clare Boothe. *Stuffed Shirts.* New York: Liveright, 1933.

MacGillis, Alec. "Obama Meets with Labor Leaders." WashingtonPost.com, June 19, 2008. www.washingtonpost.com/wp-dyn/content/article/2008/06/18/AR 2008061802935.html (accessed October 1, 2011).

Maddaus, Gene. "Congress a Family Affair?" *Long Beach Press Telegram,* May 12, 2007.

Maestas, Cherie, Sandy Maisel, and Walter Stone. "National Party Efforts to Recruit State Legislators to Run for the US House." *Legislative Studies Quarterly* 30 (2005): 277–300.

Maisel, Sandy, and Mark Brewer. *Parties and Elections in America.* 5th ed. New York: Rowman and Littlefield, 2008.

Mandel, Ruth. *In the Running: The New Woman Candidate.* New Haven: Ticknor and Fields, 1981.

Mandel, Ruth, and Katherine Kleeman. *Political Generation Next: America's Young Elected Leaders.* New Brunswick, NJ: Rutgers University, Center for American Women and Politics, Eagleton Institute of Politics, 2004.

Mann, Thomas, and Norman Ornstein. *The Broken Branch.* New York: Oxford University Press, 2006.

Manning, Jennifer. *Membership of the 112th Congress: A Profile.* Washington, DC: Congressional Research Service, 2011.

Mansbridge, Jane. *Why We Lost the ERA.* Chicago: University of Chicago Press, 1986.

March, William, and Keith Epstein. "Bile Flows As Tight Senate Race Heads to End." *Tampa Tribune,* October 29, 2004.

Margolies-Mezvinsky, Marjorie. *A Woman's Place: The Freshmen Women Who Changed the Face of Congress.* New York: Crown, 1994.

Markon, Jerry. "Ex-Rep. Jefferson (D-La) Gets 13 Years in Freezer Cash Case." WashingtonPost.com, November 14, 2009. www.washingtonpost.com/wp -dyn/content/article/2009/11/13/AR2009111301266.html (accessed August 10, 2011).

"Marsha Blackburn: Campaign Finance/Money-Contributions-Congressman, 2004." OpenSecrets.org. www.opensecrets.org/politicians/summary.asp?CID =N00003105&cycle=2004 (accessed July 3, 2005).

Martinez-Ebers, Valerie, Linda Lopez, and Ricardo Ramirez. "Representing Gender and Ethnicity: Strategic Intersectionality." In *Legislative Women: Getting Elected, Getting Ahead,* edited by Beth Reingold. Boulder: Lynne Rienner, 2008.

"Maryland Senate: Delores Goodwin Kelley." *Maryland State Archives,* 2011. http://mdarchives.state.md.us/msa/mdmanual/05sen/html/msa12170.html (accessed October 20, 2011).

Maslin, Janet. "Facing Scandal, Keeping Faith." NewYorkTimes.com, February 3, 2010. www.nytimes.com/2010/02/04/books/04book.html (accessed August 20, 2011).

Matland, Richard, and David King. "Women as Candidates in Congressional Elections." In *Women Transforming Congress,* edited by Cindy Simon Rosenthal. Norman: University of Oklahoma Press, 2002.

Matthews, Donald. *US Senators and Their World.* Chapel Hill: University of North Carolina Press, 1960.

Mauer, Richard, Nicole Tsong, and Paula Dobbyn. "Murkowski Up; Votes to Come." *Anchorage Daily News,* November 3, 2004.

Mayer, William. *The Changing American Mind.* Ann Arbor: University of Michigan Press, 1992.

Mayhew, David. *Congress: The Electoral Connection.* New Haven: Yale University Press, 1974.

McCurdy, Karen. "The Institutional Role of Women Serving in Congress, 1960–2000." In *Representation of Minority Groups in the US,* edited by Charles Menifield. Lanham: Austin and Winfield, 2001.

McDermott, Monika. "Race and Gender Cues in Low-Information Elections." *Political Research Quarterly* 51 (1998): 895–918.

———. "Voting Cues in Low-Information Elections: Candidate Gender as a Social Information Variable in Contemporary US Elections." *American Journal of Political Science* 41 (1997): 270–283.

McElwaine, Sandra. "Meet the DNC's Feisty New Chair, Debbie Wasserman Schultz." TheDailyBeast.com, May 3, 2011. www.thedailybeast.com/articles /2011/05/04/debbie-wasserman-schultz-democratic-national-committees -feisty-new-chair.html (accessed October 28, 2011).

McGlen, Nancy, et al. *Women, Politics, and American Society.* 4th ed. Upper Saddle River, NJ: Prentice Hall, 2005.

McGreevey, James. *The Confession.* New York: HarperCollins, 2006.

McIntosh, Hugh, Daniel Hart, and James Youniss. "The Influence of Family Political Discussion on Youth Civic Engagement: Which Parent Qualities Matter?" *PS: Political Science and Politics* 40 (2007): 495–499.

McKinley, James. "DeLay Sentenced to 3 Years in Conspiracy and Money-Laundering Case." NewYorkTimes.com, January 10, 2011. www.nytimes .com/2011/01/11/us/politics/11delay.html (accessed August 10, 2011).

McManus, Doyle. "2010: The Year of the Conservative Woman?" LosAngelesTimes.com, June 10, 2010. http://articles.latimes.com/2010/jun/10/opinion/la-oe-mcmanus-20100610 (accessed August 20, 2011).

McTague, John, and Geoffrey Layman. "Religion, Parties, and Voting Behavior: A Political Explanation of Religious Influence." In *The Oxford Handbook of Religion and American Politics,* edited by Corwin Smidt, Lyman Kellstedt, and James Guth. New York: Oxford University Press, 2009.

Melton, R. H. "Byrne Strikes a Nerve in Richmond: Fairfax Senator Says Colleagues Are Trying to Force Out Democratic Women." *Washington Post,* April 15, 2001.

Mervin, David. "United States Senate Norms and the Majority Whip Election of 1969." *Journal of American Studies* 9 (1975): 321–333.

Mezey, Susan Gluck. *Elusive Equality: Women's Rights, Public Policy, and the Law.* 2nd ed. Boulder: Lynne Rienner, 2011.

Mikulski, Barbara, et al. *Nine and Counting: The Women of the Senate.* New York: Morrow, 2000.

Milbank, Dana. "So $90,000 Was in the Freezer; What's Wrong with That?" WashingtonPost.com, May 23, 2006. www.washingtonpost.com/wp-dyn/content/article/2006/05/22/AR2006052201536.html (accessed August 10, 2011).

Miller, Clem. *Member of the House: Letters of a Congressman.* New York: Scribner, 1962.

Miller, Melissa, Jeffrey Peake, and Brittany Anne Boulton. "Testing the *Saturday Night Live* Hypothesis: Fairness and Bias in Newspaper Coverage of Hillary Clinton's Presidential Campaign." *Politics & Gender* 6 (2010): 169–198.

Miller, Tricia. "Michigan Democrats Weary over Redistricting." RollCall.com, March 3, 2011. www.rollcall.com/issues/56_90/-203803-1.html (accessed November 4, 2011).

———. "Redistricting Reform Is Tough Task Every Time." RollCall.com, December 14, 2010. www.rollcall.com/issues/56_59/-201450-1.html (accessed November 4, 2011).

Mills, Paul. "Mr. Vacationland and Why We Can't Forget the Lady from Rumford." *Lewiston Sun Journal,* September 3, 2000.

"Miss Rankin—Sobbing—Votes No." *New York Times,* April 6, 1917.

Mitchell, Greg. *Tricky Dick and the Pink Lady: Richard Nixon vs. Helen Gahagan Douglas—Sexual Politics and the Red Scare, 1950.* New York: Random, 1998.

Molinari, Susan. *Representative Mom: Balancing Budgets, Bill, and Baby in the US Congress.* New York: Doubleday, 1998.

Moncrief, Gary, Peverill Squire, and Malcolm Jewell. *Who Runs for the Legislature?* Upper Saddle River, NJ: Prentice Hall, 2001.

Moncrief, Gary, Joel Thompson, and Robert Schuhmann. "Gender, Race, and the State Legislature: A Research Note on the Double Disadvantage Hypothesis." *Social Science Journal* 28 (1991): 481–487.

Montopoli, Brian. "Sue Lowden Stands by Chicken Health Care Barter Plan." CBSNews.com, April 22, 2010. www.cbsnews.com/8301-503544_162-20003163-503544.html (accessed August 20, 2011).

Moore, J. L. "Majority-Minority District." *Elections A to Z.* Washington, DC: CQ Press, 2003. http://library.cqpress.com/elections/elaz2d-156-7490-402760 (accessed July 26, 2005).

Morello, Carol. "Census Count Finds Decreasing White Population in 15 States."

WashingtonPost.com, September 29, 2011. www.washingtonpost.com/local /census-count-finds-decreasing-white-population-in-15-states/2011/09/29 /gIQA2aDJ8K_story.html (accessed October 2, 2011).

Mueller, Melinda, and Barbara Poole. "A New Year of the Woman? Women Candidates for US House Seats in 2004." Paper presented at the annual meeting of the Southern Political Science Association, New Orleans, January 2005.

Myers, Laura. "Reid Hits New Low in Poll." LasVegasReviewJournal.com, January 9, 2010. www.lvrj.com/news/reid-hits-new-low-in-poll-81060702.html (accessed August 20, 2011).

"Name It, Change It: Awards for the Most Sexist Media Coverage in the 2010 Elections." NameItChangeIt.org. www.nameitchangeit.org/blog/entry/the -name-it.-change-it.-awards-for-most-sexist-media-coverage-in-the-2 (accessed September 15, 2011).

National Center for Education Statistics. "Table 8: Percentage of Persons Age 25 and Over and 25 to 29, by Race/Ethnicity, Years of School Completed, and Sex: Selected Years, 1910 Through 2010." http://nces.ed.gov/programs/digest /d10/tables/dt10_008.asp (accessed October 28, 2011).

———. "Table 279: Degrees Conferred by Degree-Granting Institutions." http://nces.ed.gov/programs/digest/d10/tables/dt10_279.asp (accessed October 1, 2011).

———. "Table 291: First-Professional Degrees Conferred by Degree-Granting Institutions, by Sex of Student, Control of Institution, and Field of Study: Selected Years, 1985–86 Through 2008–09." http://nces.ed.gov/programs /digest/d10/tables/dt10_291.asp (accessed October 15, 2011).

Nechemias, Carol. "Changes in the Election of Women to US State Legislative Seats." *Legislative Studies Quarterly* 12 (1987): 125–142.

———. "Geographic Mobility and Women's Access to State Legislatures." *Western Political Quarterly* 38 (1985): 119–131.

Ness, Immanuel, and James Ciment, eds. *The Encyclopedia of Third Parties in America.* Armonk, NY: Sharpe, 2000.

"New Member Pictorial Directory." Washington, DC: 112th Congress New Member Orientation, Committee on House Administration, November 9, 2011. www.gpoaccess.gov/pictorial/112th/pdf/fulldoc.pdf (accessed October 18, 2011).

"New Member Profile: Elijah E. Cummings, D-Md. (7)." *CQ Weekly,* April 20, 1996.

Newport, Frank. "Update: Hillary Rodham Clinton and the 2008 Election." *Gallup Poll News Service,* June 7, 2005.

"Niki Tsongas, Long Bio." Congresswoman Niki Tsongas. http://tsongas.house .gov/index.cfm?sectionid=54&sectiontree=8,54 (accessed July 24, 2011).

Niven, David. *The Missing Majority: The Recruitment of Women as State Legislative Candidates.* Westport: Praeger.

———. "Party Elites and Women Candidates: The Shape of Bias." In *Women, Gender, and Politics: A Reader,* edited by Mona Lena Krook and Sarah Childs. New York: Oxford University Press, 2010.

———. "Throwing Your Hat Out of the Ring: Negative Recruitment and the Gender Imbalance in State Legislative Candidacy." *Politics & Gender* 2 (2006): 473–489.

Niven, David, and Jeremy Zilber. "'How Does She Have Time for Kids and

Congress?' Views on Gender and Media Coverage from House Offices." In *Women and Congress: Running, Winning, and Ruling,* edited by Karen O'Connor. Binghamton, NY: Haworth, 2001.

Norman, Michael. "Mrs. Fenwick and Lautenberg Meet in Final Debate." *New York Times,* November 1, 1982.

———. "Rep. Fenwick Tries to Figure Out Why She Lost." *New York Times,* November 4, 1982.

Norrander, Barbara, and Clyde Wilcox. "Change in Continuity in the Geography of Women State Legislators." In *Women and Elective Office: Past, Present, and Future,* 2nd ed., edited by Sue Thomas and Clyde Wilcox. New York: Oxford University Press, 2005.

Norris, Pippa. "Women Leaders Worldwide: A Splash of Color in the Photo Op." In *Women, Media, and Politics,* edited by Pippa Norris. New York: Oxford University Press, 1997.

Nuwer, Deanne Stephens. "Southern Women Legislators and Patriarchy in the South." *Southeastern Political Review* 28 (2000): 449–468.

Oakley, Mary Ann. *Elizabeth Cady Stanton.* Long Island, NY: Feminist Press, 1972.

"Obama Blames Economy for Democratic 'Shellacking.'" CNN.com, November 3, 2010. http://articles.cnn.com/2010-11-03/politics/election.obama_1_president -barack-obama-majorities-in-both-chambers-republicans?_s=PM:POLITICS (accessed July 7, 2011).

O'Connor, John. "Panel Votes to Censure Sanford, but Against Impeachment." TheState.com (South Carolina), December 10, 2009. www.thestate.com /2009/12/10/1063834/panel-votes-to-censure-sanford.html (accessed August 20, 2011).

O'Hanlon, Ann, and Patricia Davis. "Parents File Complaint Against Va.'s Moran." WashingtonPost.com, April 13, 2000. www.washingtonpost.com /ac2/wp-dyn/A3237-2000Apr12?language=printer (accessed August 10, 2011).

Oleszek, Walter. *Congressional Procedures and the Policy Process.* 6th ed. Washington, DC: CQ Press, 2004.

Ornstein, Norman, ed. *Congress in Change: Evolution and Reform.* New York: Praeger, 1975.

Orr, Brooke Speer. "Mary Elizabeth Lease: Gendered Discourse and Populist Party Politics in Gilded Age America." *Kansas History: A Journal of the Central Plains* 29 (2006–2007): 246–265.

"Our Objectives." Lugar Excellence in Public Service Series. www.lugarseries .com/objectives.php (accessed May 30, 2011).

Page, Benjamin, et al. "Constituency, Party, and Representation in Congress." *Public Opinion Quarterly* 48 (1984): 741–756.

Paglia, Camille. "Hillary Without Tears." Salon.com, January 10, 2008. www.salon.com/news/opinion/camille_paglia/2008/01/10/hillary/index.html (accessed September 15, 2011).

Palmer, Barbara, and Dennis Simon. "Breaking the Logjam: The Emergence of Women as Congressional Candidates." In *Women and Congress: Running, Winning, and Ruling,* edited by Karen O'Connor. Binghamton, NY: Haworth, 2001.

———. "Political Ambition and Women in the US House of Representatives, 1916–2000." *Political Research Quarterly* 56 (2003): 127–138.

———. "When Women Run Against Women: The Hidden Influence of Female

Incumbents in Elections to the US House of Representatives, 1956–2002." *Politics and Gender* 1 (2005): 39–63.

Parsons, Stanley, William Beach, and Michael Dubin. *United States Congressional Districts, 1843–1883.* Santa Barbara, CA: Greenwood, 1986.

"Party Control of the Minnesota House of Representatives." Minnesota Legislative Reference Library. www.leg.state.mn.us/lrl/histleg/caucus.aspx (accessed October 20, 2011).

Patrick, Steven. "Traficant Refuses to Go Quietly Despite Calls for His Resignation." *CQ Weekly,* April 13, 2002.

Paul, David, and Jessi Smith. "Subtle Sexism? Examining Vote Preferences When Women Run Against Men for the Presidency." *Journal of Women, Politics, and Policy* 29 (2008): 451–476.

"Paul, Rand." *Biographical Directory of the United States Congress.* http://bioguide.congress.gov/scripts/biodisplay.pl?index=P000603 (accessed October 18, 2011).

"Paul, Ronald Ernest." *Biographical Directory of the United States Congress.* http://bioguide.congress.gov/scripts/biodisplay.pl?index=P000583 (accessed October 18, 2011).

Peoples, Steve, and Jessica Brady. "Playing Partisan from Her Hill Perch." RollCall.com, May 9, 2011. www.rollcall.com/issues/56_118/wasserman _schultz_dnc_chairwoman-205431-1.html (accessed September 15, 2011).

Perkins, Jerry, and Diane Fowlkes. "Opinion Representation Versus Social Representation: Or Why Women Can't Run As Women and Win." *American Political Science Review* 74 (1980): 92–103.

Peters, Ronald, and Cindy Simon Rosenthal. *Speaker Nancy Pelosi and the New American Politics.* New York: Oxford University Press, 2010.

Petrocik, John. "Issue Ownership in Presidential Elections, with a 1980 Case Study." *American Journal of Political Science* 40 (1996): 825–850.

Phillips, Frank. "Shake-Up in the Governor's Race: Swift Yields to Romney Saying 'Something Had to Give,' Exits Race for Governor." *Boston Globe,* March 20, 2002.

Pitt, Leonard. "Mrs. Deeds Goes to Washington." *Reviews in American History* 21 (1993): 477–481.

Polsby, Nelson. "Goodbye to the Senate's Inner Club." In *Congress in Change: Evolution and Reform,* edited by Norman Ornstein: New York: Praeger, 1975.

———. "The Institutionalization of the US House of Representatives." *American Political Science Review* 52 (1968): 124–143.

"President National Exit Poll." CNN.com, Election Center 2008. www.cnn.com /ELECTION/2008/results/polls/#USP00p1 (accessed October 28, 2011).

Prestage, Jewel. "Black Women State Legislators: A Profile." In *A Portrait of Marginality: The Political Behavior of American Women,* edited by Marianne Githens and Jewel Prestage. New York: David McKay, 1977.

———. "The Case of African American Women and Politics." *PS: Political Science and Politics* 27 (1994): 720–721.

Price, H. Douglas. "Congress and the Evolution of Legislative Professionalism." In *Change in Congress,* edited by Norman Ornstein. New York: Praeger, 1975.

Quinn, Sally. "Maryon Allen: The Southern Girl in the Senate." *Washington Post,* July 30, 1978.

Rahn, Wendy. "The Role of Partisan Stereotypes in Information Processing About

Political Candidates." *American Journal of Political Science* 37 (1993): 472–496.

"Rand, Ron Paul Make History." MSNBC.com, November 2, 2010. http://firstread .msnbc.msn.com/_news/2010/11/02/5397817-rand-ron-paul-make-history (accessed October 18, 2011).

"Rape in Marriage." Texas Association Against Sexual Assault. www.taasa.org /images/materials/RapeInMarriage.pdf?PHPSESSID=19ee0821cbbe5500cd2 114c3fd2f6810 (accessed September 20, 2011).

Reed, John Shelton. *The Enduring South: Subcultural Persistence in Mass Society.* Chapel Hill: University of North Carolina Press, 1986.

"Report: Pensacola Republicans Say Scarborough Courted for Senate." *Associated Press State and Local Wire,* August 16, 2005.

"Representative Debbie Wasserman Schultz, 2010 Election Cycle." OpenSecrets.org. www.openSecrets.org/politicians/summary.php?cycle=2010&type=I&cid=N00 026106&newMem=N (accessed October 28, 2010).

"Reps. Connie Mack, Mary Bono Wed." USAToday.com, December 16, 2007. www.usatoday.com/news/washington/2007-12-16-bonomack_N.htm (accessed July 15, 2011).

"Republican Leadership." www.gop.gov/republicans/leadership (accessed August 10, 2011).

Reyes, B. J. "Case Wins Hawaii's 2nd Congressional District." *Associated Press State and Local Wire,* January 5, 2003.

"Robinson Accuses Arrested Pakistani of Terrorism in New Ad." *Associated Press State and Local Wire,* August 15, 2004.

Roddy, Dennis. "Admission of Guilt: Waldholtz Admits Financial Violations, Apologizes to All but Ex-Wife." *Pittsburgh Post Gazette,* June 6, 1996.

Rohde, David. "Risk-Bearing and Progressive Ambition: The Case of Members of the United States House of Representatives." *American Journal of Political Science* 23 (1979): 1–26.

"Ros-Lehtinen Hangs Up on Obama, Twice." Politico.com, December 3, 2008. www.politico.com/blogs/thecrypt/1208/RosLehtinen_hangs_up_on_Obama _Twice.html (accessed July 11, 2011).

Rosenthal, Cindy Simon. "Climbing Higher: Opportunities and Obstacles Within the Party System." In *Legislative Women: Getting Elected, Getting Ahead,* edited by Beth Reingold. Boulder: Lynne Rienner, 2008.

Ross, Shelly. *Fall from Grace: Sex, Scandal, and Corruption in American Politics from 1702 to the Present.* New York: Ballantine, 1988.

Rozell, Mark. "Helping Women Run and Win: Feminist Groups, Candidate Recruitment, and Training." *Women & Politics* 21 (2000): 101–116.

Rucker, Philip. "In South Dakota, Democrats' Own 'Mama Grizzly' vs. 'The Next Sarah Palin.'" WashingtonPost.com, August 23, 2010. www.washingtonpost .com/wp-dyn/content/article/2010/08/22/AR2010082203217.html (accessed September 10, 2011).

Rule, Wilma. "Why More Women Are Legislators: A Research Note." *Western Political Quarterly* 43 (1990): 437–448.

———. "Why Women Don't Run: The Critical and Contextual Factors in Women's Legislative Recruitment." *Western Political Quarterly* 34 (1981): 60–77.

Rusk, Jerrold. "The Effect of the Australian Ballot on Split Ticket Voting, 1876–1908." *American Political Science Review* 64 (1970): 1220–1238.

Rutenberg, Jim. "An Idea, with 4 Words, That Was Supposed to Soothe the Tone of Ads but Did Not." *New York Times,* October 30, 2004.

Ruth, Daniel. "Memo to Harris Staff Members: Keep Digging." *Tampa Tribune,* August 31, 2006.

Sanbonmatsu, Kira. *Democrats, Republicans, and the Politics of Women's Place.* Ann Arbor: University of Michigan Press, 2004.

———. "Do Parties Know That 'Women Win'? Party Leader Beliefs About Women's Electoral Chances." *Politics & Gender* 2 (2006): 431–450.

———. "Gender Pools and Puzzles: Charting a 'Women's Path' to the Legislature." *Politics & Gender* 2 (2006): 387–400.

———. "Gender Stereotypes and Vote Choice." *American Journal of Political Science* 46 (2002): 20–34.

———. "Political Parties and the Recruitment of Women to State Legislatures." *Journal of Politics* 64 (2002): 791–809.

———. "Representation by Gender and Parties." In *Political Women and American Democracy,* edited by Christina Wolbrecht, Karen Beckwith, and Lisa Baldez. New York: Cambridge University Press, 2008.

———. *Where Women Run: Gender and Party in the American States.* Ann Arbor: University of Michigan Press, 2006.

Sanbonmatsu, Kira, Susan Carroll, and Debbie Walsh. *Poised to Run: Women's Pathways to the State Legislatures.* New Brunswick, NJ: Rutgers University, Center for American Women and Politics, Eagleton Institute of Politics, 2009.

Sanbonmatsu, Kira, and Kathy Dolan. "Do Gender Stereotypes Transcend Party?" *Political Research Quarterly* 62 (2009): 486–494.

"Sanchez Claims Victory in Nation's Most Expensive Race." *Associated Press,* November 4, 1998.

Sapiro, Virginia. *The Political Integration of Women.* Urbana: University of Illinois Press, 1983.

———. "Private Costs of Public Commitments or Public Costs of Private Commitments? Family Roles Versus Political Ambition." *American Journal of Political Science* 26 (1982): 265–279.

Scammon, Richard, A. V. McGillivray, and R. Cook. "Analysis of the Elections of 2002." In *American Votes,* vol. 25. Washington, DC: CQ Press, 2003.

Schlesinger, Joseph. *Ambition and Politics: Political Careers in the United States.* Chicago: Rand McNally, 1966.

Schmidt, Susan, and James Grimaldi. "Ney Sentenced to 30 Months in Prison for Abramoff Deals." WashingtonPost.com, January 20, 2007. www.washington post.com/wp-dyn/content/article/2007/01/19/AR2007011900162.html (accessed August 10, 2011).

Schroeder, Pat. *Twenty-four Years of House Work and the Place Is Still a Mess.* Kansas City, MO: Andrews McMeel, 1999.

Schwarz, Jay. "Election Behavior with High Female Representation: A Regression Discontinuity Analysis." Social Science Research Network, 2010. http://ssrn.com/abstract=1569929 (accessed September 15, 2011).

Scobie, Ingrid Winther. *Center Stage: Helen Gahagan Douglas, a Life.* New York: Oxford University Press, 1992.

Seligman, Lester. "Political Recruitment and Party Structure: A Case Study." *American Political Science Review* 5 (1961): 77–86.

Seltzer, Richard, Jody Newman, and Melissa Voorhees Leighton. *Sex as a Political Variable.* Boulder: Lynne Rienner, 1997.

"Senate Seniority List—112th Congress." RollCall.com. www.rollcall.com /politics/senateseniority.html (accessed October 20, 2011).

Shames, Shauna. "The 'Un-Candidates': Gender and Outsider Signals in Women's Political Advertisements." *Women & Politics* 25 (2003): 115–147.

Shenon, Philip. "Lawmaker Admits He Took Illegal Gifts." NewYorkTimes.com, September 16, 2006. www.nytimes.com/2006/09/16/us/16ney.html (accessed August 10, 2011).

———. "Ohio Republican Tied to Abramoff Abandons Reelection Bid." *New York Times,* August 8, 2006.

Sherman, Jake, and John Bresnahan. "Rep. Chris Lee Resigns over Suggestive Photo." Politico.com, February 9, 2011. www.politico.com/news/stories/0211 /49202.html (accessed August 10, 2011).

Sidlow, Edward. *Challenging the Incumbent: An Underdog's Undertaking.* Washington, DC: CQ Press, 2004.

Siegel, Elyse. "Sharron Angle Slams Republicans for 'Losing Their Principles,' Says She's 'Not Sure' If She Can Win." HuffingtonPost.com, October 4, 2010. www.huffingtonpost.com/2010/10/04/sharron-angle-slams-repub_n _748682.html (accessed August 20, 2011).

Silbey, Joel. *The American Political Nation.* Stanford: Stanford University Press, 1991.

Simon, Dennis. "Electoral and Ideological Change in the South: The Case of the US House of Representatives, 1952–2000." Paper presented at the annual meeting of the Southern Political Science Association, New Orleans, January 2004.

Simon, Dennis, and Barbara Palmer. "Beyond Hillary: Female Congressional Candidates in 2008 and the Political Geography of Women's Success." Paper presented at the annual meeting of the Southern Political Science Association, New Orleans, January 2009.

———. "Gender, Party, and Political Change: The Evolution of a Democratic Advantage." Presentation at the APSAnet eSymposium "An Open Boundaries Workshop: Women in Politics in a Comparative Perspective." *PS Online* 37 (2004). www.apsanet.org/imgtest/EvolutionDemocraticAdvan-Palmer.pdf.

———. "The Midterm Elections of 2010: Another 'Year of the Woman?'" Paper presented at the annual meeting of the Southern Political Science Association, New Orleans, January 2011.

———. "The Roll Call Behavior of the Men and Women in the US House of Representatives." *Politics & Gender* 6 (2010): 225–246.

———. "Women and Elections to the US House of Representatives: The Midterm Elections of 1994 and 2006." Paper presented at the annual meeting of the Southern Political Science Association, New Orleans, January 2008.

———. "Women as Third Party Candidates in Elections to the US House of Representatives." Paper presented at the annual meeting of the Southern Political Science Association, New Orleans, January 2010.

Sinclair, Barbara. *Party Wars.* Norman: University of Oklahoma Press, 2006.

Smith, Jeffrey. "DeLay Indicted in Texas Finance Probe." WashingtonPost.com, September 29, 2005. www.washingtonpost.com/wp-dyn/content/article/2005 /09/28/AR2005092800270.html (accessed August 10, 2011).

———. "The DeLay-Abramoff Money Trail." WashingtonPost.com, December 31, 2005. www.washingtonpost.com/wp-dyn/content/article/2005/12/30/AR2005 123001480.html (accessed August 10, 2001).

Smith, Tom. "Changes in Family Structure, Family Values, and Politics, 1972–2006." In *Red, Blue, and Purple America: The Future of Election*

Demographics, edited by Ruy Teixeira. Washington, DC: Brookings Institution, 2008.

Smooth, Wendy. "African American Women and Electoral Politics: Journeying from the Shadows to the Spotlight." In *Gender and Elections: Shaping the Future of American Politics,* edited by Sue Carroll and Richard Fox. New York: Cambridge University Press, 2006.

———. "Gender, Race, and the Exercise of Power and Influence." In *Legislative Women: Getting Elected, Getting Ahead,* edited by Beth Reingold. Boulder: Lynne Rienner, 2008.

Solowiej, Lisa, and Thomas Brunell. "The Entrance of Women to the US Congress: The Widow Effect." *Political Research Quarterly* 56 (2003): 283–292.

Somashekhar, Sandhya. "In Alaska's Senate Race, Murkowsi's Write-In Bid Bears Fruit." WashingtonPost.com, November 4, 2010. www.washingtonpost.com /wp-dyn/content/article/2010/11/03/AR2010110308817.html (accessed July 20, 2011).

Sonmez, Felicia. "Gabrielle Giffords Resigns from the House in Emotional Farewell," WashingtonPost.com, January 26, 2012. www.washingtonpost.com (accessed February 17, 2012).

"Special Election Results, United States Representative in Congress, 37th District, Final Canvass." Office of the California Secretary of State, June 26, 2007. www.sos.ca.gov/elections/elections_cd37.htm (accessed August 4, 2007).

"Special Report: CQ's Guide to the Committees." *CQ Weekly,* April 16, 2007.

Spruill, Marjorie, and Jesse Wheeler. "The Equal Rights Amendment and Mississippi." *Mississippi History Now.* Mississippi Historical Society, 2000– 2012. http://mshistory.k12.ms.us/articles/226/the-equal-rights-amendment -and-mississippi (accessed September 20, 2011).

Stalsburg, Brittany. "Voting for Mom: The Political Consequences of Being a Parent for Male and Female Candidates." *Politics & Gender* 6 (2010): 373– 404.

Stanley, Alessandra. "In Primary Race for Senate, Ads Are Costly and Caustic." *New York Times,* September 13, 1992.

Stanley, Harold, and Richard Niemi. *Vital Statistics on American Politics.* 4th ed. Washington, DC: CQ Press, 1993.

———. *Vital Statistics on American Politics, 2009–2010.* Washington, DC: CQ Press, 2010.

Stanton, Elizabeth Cady, Susan B. Anthony, and Matilda Gage. *History of Woman Suffrage.* Vol. 2. New York: E. O. Jenkins, 1881.

Stanton, Theodore, and Harriot Stanton Blatch, eds. *Elizabeth Cady Stanton As Revealed in Her Letters, Diary and Reminiscences.* Vol. 2. New York: Arno, 1969.

Starr, Alexandra. "Bada Bing Club." *New Republic,* April 23, 2007.

"State Fact Sheet—Minnesota." New Brunswick, NJ: Rutgers University, Center for American Women and Politics, Eagleton Institute of Politics, 2010.

Statistical Abstract of the United States. Washington, DC: US Department of Commerce, Bureau of the Census, various years.

Steinhorn, Leonard. *The Greater Generation: In Defense of the Baby Boom Legacy.* New York: St. Martin's, 2006.

Stevens, Allison. "The Strength of These Women Shows in Their Numbers." *CQ Weekly,* October 25, 2003.

Stokes-Brown, Atiya Kai, and Melissa Olivia Neal. "Does 'Running As a Woman' Mobilize Voters?" In *Legislative Women: Getting Elected, Getting Ahead*, edited by Beth Reingold. Boulder: Lynne Rienner, 2008.

Stolberg, Sheryl Gay. "When It Comes to Scandal, Girls Won't Be Boys." NewYorkTimes.com, June 11, 2011. www.nytimes.com/2011/06/12/weekin review/12women.html?pagewanted=all (accessed August 10, 2011).

Struble, Robert. "House Turnover and the Principle of Rotation." *Political Science Quarterly* 94 (1979): 649–667.

"Stunner in New Hampshire: Clinton Defeats Obama." MSNBC.com, January 9, 2008. www.msnbc.msn.com/id/22551718/ns/politics-decision_08/t/stunner-nh -clinton-defeats-obama/#.TnOODNR2C0k (accessed September 15, 2011).

Sullivan, Bartholomew. "Safe Territory: Redrawing of Congressional District Lines Puts Incumbents in Driver's Seat." *Memphis Commercial Appeal*, October 27, 2004.

Sullivan, Joseph. "US Senate Race Tops Jersey Elections." *New York Times*, October 31, 1982.

Swain, Carol. *Black Faces, Black Interests: The Representation of African-Americans in Congress*. Cambridge: Harvard University Press, 1993.

Swers, Michelle. "Research on Women in Legislatures: What Have We Learned, Where Are We Going?" In *Women in Congress: Running, Winning, Ruling*, edited by Karen O'Connor. Binghamton, NY: Haworth, 2001.

———. "Understanding the Policy Impact of Electing Women: Evidence from Research on Congress and State Legislatures." *PS: Political Science and Politics* 26 (2001): 217–219.

Swift, Elaine, Robert Brookshire, David Canon, Evelyn Fink, and John Hibbing, comps. *Database of Congressional Historical Statistics*. Study no. 3371. Ann Arbor, MI: Interuniversity Consortium for Political Research, 2004.

"Tar Heel, NC Has Election, but No One Bothers to Run." Citizen-Times.com, July 15, 2011. www.citizen-times.com/article/20110715/POLITICS/307150058 /Tar-Heel-NC-has-election-no-one-bothers-run (accessed August 1, 2011).

Taylor, Paul. "Women and Political Leadership." Washington, DC: Pew Research Center, September 28, 2009. http://pewsocialtrends.org/files/2010/10/gender -leadership.pdf (accessed September 15, 2011).

Teixeira, Ruy, ed. *Red, Blue, and Purple America: The Future of Election Demographics*. Washington, DC: Brookings Institution, 2008.

"Texas Politics: The Legislative Branch." University of Texas. www.laits .utexas.edu/txp_media/html/leg/0205.html (accessed July 7, 2011).

Thompson, Joan Hulce. "Career Convergence: Election of Women and Men to the House of Representatives, 1916–1975." *Women & Politics* 5 (1985): 69–90.

Thompson, Seth, and Janie Steckenrider. "The Relative Irrelevance of Candidate Sex." *Women & Politics* 17 (1997): 71–92.

"Thurmond, James Strom." *Biographical Directory of the United States Congress*. http://bioguide.congress.gov/scripts/biodisplay.pl?index=T000254 (accessed October 20, 2011).

Toeplitz, Shira. "When Redistricting's All In the Family." RollCall.com, June 9, 2011. www.rollcall.com/issues/56_136/State-redistricting-is-all-in-the-family -206308-1.html (accessed November 1, 2011).

Toeplitz, Shira, and Kyle Trygstad. "Redistricting Woes Plague State Legislatures." RollCall.com, September 9, 2011. www.rollcall.com/features

/Guide-to-Congress_2011/guide/Redistricting-Woes-Plague-State
-Legislatures-208579-1.html (accessed November 4, 2011).

Tolchin, Susan, and Martin Tolchin. *Clout: Womanpower and Politics.* New York: Coward, McCann, and Geoghegan, 1974.

Tomz, Michael, Gary King, and Langche Zeng. *RELOGIT: Rare Events Logistical Regression.* Ver. 1.1. Cambridge: Harvard University Press, 1999.

"Topics in Kansas History: Politics and Government." Kansas State Historical Society. www.kshs.org/research/topics/politics/essay_senators.htm (accessed June 5, 2009).

Torry, Jack. "From His Cell, Traficant Still a Force in Election." *Columbus Dispatch,* November 2, 2002.

"Total Raised and Spent: 2006 Race, Florida District 18." OpenSecrets.org. www.opensecrets.org/races/summary.asp?id=FL18&cycle=2006 (accessed October 20, 2011).

"Total Raised and Spent: 2010 Race, California Senate." OpenSecrets.org. www.opensecrets.org/races/summary.php?cycle=2010&id=CAS1 (accessed October 20, 2011).

"Total Raised and Spent: 2010 Race, Connecticut Senate." OpenSecrets.org. www.opensecrets.org/races/summary.php?id=CTS2&cycle=2010 (accessed July 31, 2011).

"Traficant, James A., Jr." *CQ's Politics in America, 2002: The 107th Congress.* Washington, DC: CQ Press, 2001. http://library.cqpress.com/congress/pia107-0453055393 (accessed July 15, 2005).

Traister, Rebecca. *Big Girls Don't Cry: The Election That Changed Everything for American Women.* New York: Free Press, 2010.

Traub, James. "Party Like It's 1994." *New York Times Magazine,* March 12, 2006.

Tsong, Nicole, and Sean Cockerham. "ANWR, Tax Issue Separate Debaters." *Anchorage Daily News,* October 29, 2004.

Turner, Wallace. "Burton's Widow Among 4 Considering Race for Congress Seat." *New York Times,* April 18, 1983.

"Turning Point, 2010." Barbara Lee Family Foundation. www.barbaraleefoundation.org/our-research/topics/turning-point-2010 (accessed September 15, 2011).

Twenge, Jean. "Attitudes Towards Women, 1970–1995." *Psychology of Women Quarterly* 21 (1997): 35–51.

"2010 Overview: Incumbent Advantage." OpenSecrets.org. www.opensecrets.org/overview/incumbs.php (accessed July 7, 2010).

"2010 Overview: Stats at a Glance." OpenSecrets.org. www.opensecrets.org/overview/index.php?cycle=2010&Type=A&Display=A (accessed July 31, 2011).

"Unmarried Women Play Critical Role in Historic Election." Greenberg Quinlan Rosner Research, WomensVoicesWomenVote.org. http://wvwv.org/research/2008-election-research/unmarried-women-change-america (accessed October 28, 2011).

US Department of Commerce, Bureau of the Census. "Table 4.b: Reported Voting and Registration of the Voting-Age Population, by Sex, Race and Hispanic Origin, for States: November 2008." www.census.gov/hhes/www/socdemo/voting/publications/p20/2008/tables.html (accessed October 15, 2011).

US Department of Labor, Bureau of Labor Statistics. "Table 4: Employment Status by Marital Status and Sex." www.bls.gov/cps/wlf-table4-2009.pdf (accessed October 15, 2011).

Voss-Hubbard, Mark. "The 'Third Party Tradition' Reconsidered: Third Parties and American Public Life, 1830–1900." *Journal of American History* 20 (1999): 121–150.

Wagman, Jake, Matthew Franck, and Virginia Young. "McCaskill Prevailed Despite Cash Gap." *St. Louis Post-Dispatch,* December 9, 2006.

Wallace, Jeremy. "At Final Hour, 3 Republicans Join Senate Race." *Sarasota Herald-Tribune,* May 13, 2006.

———. "Harris Unfazed by Apparent Party Pressure." *Sarasota Herald-Tribune,* June 25, 2005.

"Washburn, Cadwallader Colden." *Biographical Directory of the United States Congress.* http://bioguide.congress.gov/scripts/biodisplay.pl?index=W000170 (accessed October 18, 2011).

"Washburn, Israel, Jr." *Biographical Directory of the United States Congress.* http://bioguide.congress.gov/scripts/biodisplay.pl?index=W000173 (accessed October 18, 2011).

"Washburn, William Drew." *Biographical Directory of the United States Congress.* http://bioguide.congress.gov/scripts/biodisplay.pl?index=W000175 (accessed October 18, 2011).

"Washburne, Elihu Benjamin." *Biographical Directory of the United States Congress.* http://bioguide.congress.gov/scripts/biodisplay.pl?index=W000176 (accessed October 18, 2011).

"Wasserman Schultz, Debbie." *Biographical Directory of the United States Congress.* http://bioguide.congress.gov/scripts/biodisplay.pl?index=W000797 (accessed October 28, 2011).

Watson, Robert, and Ann Gordon. *Anticipating Madam President.* Boulder: Lynne Rienner, 2003.

Wattenberg, Martin. *The Decline of American Political Parties, 1952–1988.* Cambridge: Harvard University Press, 1990.

Wayne, Stephen. *The Road to the White House, 2000.* New York: Wadsworth, 1999.

———. *The Road to the White House, 2012.* New York: Wadsworth, 2011.

Weiner, Rachel. "Sarah Palin Not Running for President." WashingtonPost.com, October 5, 2011. www.washingtonpost.com/blogs/the-fix/post/sarah-palin -not-running-for-president/2011/10/05/gIQAzr9MOL_blog.html (accessed November 4, 2011).

Weisman, Jonathan. "House Ethics Panel Begins Bribery Probe; Congressmen from Ohio and Louisiana Targeted; DeLay Escapes with Resignation." *Washington Post,* May 18, 2006.

Weisman, Jonathan, and Chris Cillizza. "DeLay to Resign From Congress." WashingtonPost.com, April 4, 2006. www.washingtonpost.com/wp-dyn /content/article/2006/04/03/AR2006040301787.html (accessed August 10, 2011).

Weisman, Jonathan, and Shailagh Murray. "Democrats Take Control on Hill." WashingtonPost.com, January 5, 2007. www.washingtonpost.com/wp-dyn/content/article/2007/01/04/AR2007010400802.html (accessed October 13, 2011).

Weiss, Debra Cassens. "Men Outnumber Women at Most Top Law Schools." ABAJournal.com, May 9, 2011. www.abajournal.com/news/article/men _outnumber_women_at_most_top_law_schoolsbut_the_imbalance_is_greater _at (accessed October 15, 2011).

Welch, Susan. "Are Women More Liberal Than Men in the US Congress?" *Legislative Studies Quarterly* 10 (1985): 125–134.

———. "Recruitment of Women to Public Office." *Western Political Quarterly* 31 (1978): 372–380.

Welch, Susan, and Lee Sigelman. "Changes in Public Attitudes Toward Women in Politics." *Social Science Quarterly* 63 (1982): 312–321.

Welch, Susan, and Donley Studlar. "The Opportunity Structure for Women's Candidacies and Electability in Britain and the United States." *Political Research Quarterly* 49 (1996): 861–874.

Welch, Susan, et al. "The Effect of Candidate Gender on Election Outcomes in State Legislative Races." *Western Political Quarterly* 38 (1985): 464–475.

Werner, Emmy. "Women in Congress, 1917–1964." *Western Political Quarterly* 19 (1966): 16–30.

———. "Women in the State Legislatures." *Western Political Quarterly* 19 (1968): 40–50.

"What to Believe: US Senate Ads." *St. Louis Post-Dispatch,* November 1, 2006.

Whitby, Kenny. *The Color of Representation: Congressional Behavior and Black Interests.* Ann Arbor: University of Michigan Press, 1997.

White, Theodore H. *The Making of the President, 1972.* New York: Atheneum, 1973.

White, William S. *The Citadel: The Story of the US Senate.* New York: Harper and Brothers, 1956.

"Widow of Rep. Burton Is Elected in California Congressional Race." *New York Times,* June 23, 1983.

Wilcox, Clyde. "Why Was 1992 the 'Year of the Woman'? Explaining Women's Gains in 1992." In *The Year of the Woman: Myths and Reality,* edited by Elizabeth Adell Cook, Sue Thomas, and Clyde Wilcox. Boulder: Westview, 1994.

Williams, Christine. "Women, Law, and Politics: Recruitment Patterns in the Fifty States." *Women & Politics* 10 (1990): 103–123.

Williams, Leonard. "Gender, Political Advertising, and the 'Air Wars.'" In *Women and Elective Office: Past, Present, and Future,* edited by Sue Thomas and Clyde Wilcox. New York: Oxford University Press, 1998.

Williams, Linda. "The Civil Rights–Black Power Legacy: Black Women Elected Officials at the Local, State, and National Levels." In *Sisters in the Struggle: African American Women in the Civil Rights–Black Power Movement,* edited by Bettye Collier-Thomas and V. P. Franklin. New York: New York University Press, 2001.

Williams, Shirley, and Edward Lascher, eds. *Ambition and Beyond: Career Paths of American Politicians.* Berkeley: University of California Press, 1993.

Wilson, Marie. *Closing the Leadership Gap: Why Women Can and Must Help Run the World.* New York: Viking, 2004.

Wing, Nick. "John Boehner Tries Not to Cry." HuffingtonPost.com, November 3, 2010. www.huffingtonpost.com/2010/11/02/john-boehner-cries-speech_n _778042.html (accessed September 15, 2011).

Wiseman, Paul. "Young, Single, Childless Women Out-Earn Male Counterparts." USAToday.com, September 2, 2010. www.usatoday.com/money/workplace /2010-09-01-single-women_N.htm (accessed October 15, 2011).

Witt, Linda, Karen Paget, and Glenna Matthews. *Running As a Woman: Gender and Power in American Politics.* New York: Free Press, 1995.

Wolbrecht, Christina. *The Politics of Women's Rights: Parties, Positions, and Change.* Princeton: Princeton University Press, 2000.

"Women of Color in Elective Office, 2011." New Brunswick, NJ: Rutgers University, Center for American Women and Politics, Eagleton Institute of Politics, 2011.

Women in Congress, 1917–2006. Office of the Clerk of the US House of Representatives. Washington, DC: US Government Printing Office, 2006.

"Women in State Legislatures, 2010." New Brunswick, NJ: Rutgers University, Center for American Women and Politics, Eagleton Institute of Politics, 2010.

"Women in the US Senate, 1922–2011." New Brunswick, NJ: Rutgers University, Center for American Women and Politics, Eagleton Institute of Politics, 2011.

"Women Who Have Chaired Congressional Committees, 1923–Present." Washington, DC: Office of the Clerk of the US House of Representatives, 2011. http://womenincongress.house.gov/historical-data/congressional-committee-chairs.html (accessed July 31, 2011).

"Women's History Month: A New Reason to Celebrate Louisiana Women's History Every Day." www.senate.gov/~landrieu/whm/boggs.html (accessed March 30, 2005).

Wong, Janelle. "Mobilizing Asian-American Voters: A Field Experiment." *Annals of the American Academy of Political and Social Science* 601 (2005): 102–114.

Woodward, Bob. *The Agenda: Inside the Clinton White House.* New York: Simon and Schuster, 1994.

Yanez, Luisa. "Actress Plans Fundraising Concert for Patlak." *Miami Herald,* September 16, 2006.

———. "A Venerable Politician—And a Celebrity, Too." *Miami Herald,* August 20, 2006.

Young, James Sterling. *The Washington Community, 1800–1828.* New York: Columbia University Press, 1966.

Index

Abel, Hazel, 39tab, 59n68
Abramoff, Jack, 35, 71
Abzug, Bella, 32, 47tab
Akaka, Daniel, 47tab, 50, 56
Allen, Maryon, 101–102
Angle, Sharron, 44, 162

Baker, Irene Bailey, 95tab, 105,
    110tab
Baker, Jr., Howard, 104tab, 105–106,
    110tab
Baker v. Carr, 17, 18, 213n26, 240n94
Baldwin, Tammy, 47tab, 50, 117tab
Bass, Karen, 54tab, 233tab
Bean, Melissa, 147, 217
Beck, Glenn, 71–72, 136
Berkley, Shelley, 47tab, 50, 114
Berman, Howard, 55, 233tab
Black, Diane, 207, 232
Blitch, Iris, 6–7, 12, 224
Boggs, Corrine "Lindy," 95tab, 100,
    120
Boggs, Hale, 100, 120
Bolton, Frances, 17, 18–19; as con-
    gressional widow, 97; House
    service of, 82tab, 95tab, 109,
    110tab
Bolton, Oliver, 109, 110tab
Bono, Mary, 103, 114. *See also* Mack,
    Mary Bono

Bowring, Eva, 101tab, 59n68
Boxer, Barbara, 39tab, 47tab, 114,
    129tab, 141, 226
Brown, Corinne, 54tab, 82tab, 231
Bryan, William Jennings, 106, 108tab
Burke, Yvonne Brathwaite, 54tab, 113
Burton, Sala, 95tab, 99
Bush, George H. W., 33, 49, 129, 139
Bush, George W., 35, 53, 71, 102,
    179, 185, 230
Byron, Katharine, 95tab, 110tab, 117tab

Cantwell, Maria, 35, 39tab, 60n97,
    117tab
Capps, Lois, 95tab, 97
Caraway, Hattie, 5, 6photo, 101
careerism: development of, 21, 65, 77,
    235–236; House eras of, 78–81;
    and incumbents, 78, 80; and
    women in Congress, 81–83, 84,
    226
Carnahan, Jean, 101tab, 102, 110tab
Carson, Julia, 54tab, 111
Celler, Emanuel, 19, 32–33
Center for American Women and
    Politics (CAWP) Recruitment
    Study, 112, 162
Chavez, Linda, 127, 129tab
Chisholm, Shirley, 3tab, 11, 32, 51,
    52photo, 53, 54tab

Church, Marguerite, 17, 95tab
Citizen Political Ambition Study
    (CPAS), 112, 162, 176, 220
Civil Rights Act: of 1957, 6, 17; of
    1964, 7, 31, 186
Clarke, Yvette, 54tab, 189, 233tab
Clinton, Bill, 1, 34, 35, 56, 113, 185
Clinton, Hillary Rodham: in the
    media, 135, 139, 234; as secretary
    of state, 72, 115; in the Senate,
    39tab; as presidential candidate,
    1, 2
Collins, Cardiss, 54tab, 81, 82tab,
    95tab, 100
Collins, Susan, 39tab, 129tab
congressional widows: advantages of,
    92; in the House of
    Representatives, 13, 99–100, 222;
    statistics on, 96–97, 98, 100,
    101tab; in the Senate, 100–103;
    stereotype of, 22, 92, 97–98. *See
    also* family connections, in
    Congress
Cormier, Lucia, 128–129
CPAS. *See* Citizen Political Ambition
    Study
cultural norms, 7–11, 218, 219–222

D'Amato, Alfonse, 47tab, 130
Davis, Jo Ann, 103, 152
DeGette, Diana, 117tab, 118, 125n135
DeLay, Tom, 35, 70–71, 230
Democratic incumbents: female chal-
    lengers to, 148–150; opposition-
    party nomination competition,
    147, 148, 149tab; and uncontest-
    ed elections, 145–146
demographics: of districts electing
    African American and Hispanic
    representatives, 207–209, 208tab,
    211; of districts electing
    white/non-Hispanic representa-
    tives, 199–201, 210; diversity of
    congressional districts, 187,
    188tab, 192–193; and election
    forecasting, 184–185, 210; geog-
    raphy of congressional districts,
    187, 188tab, 189–192; partisan-
    ship of congressional districts,

187–189; socioeconomic factors
    of congressional districts, 187,
    188tab, 193–198; of women-
    friendly districts, 23, 24, 237. *See
    also* women-friendly districts
Dingell, Jr., John, 67, 81, 93
diversity, 187, 188tab, 192–193
Dole, Bob, 104tab, 129
Dole, Elizabeth, 39tab, 104tab, 129
Douglas, Helen Gahagan, 13–15,
    46–47

Education Amendments, 7, 32. *See
    also* Title IX
education rates, 64–65, 219. *See also*
    law degrees
Edwards, Elaine, 59n68, 101tab, 103
Eisenhower, Dwight, 5–6, 9, 41
Emerson, Jo Ann, 95tab, 97, 120
EMILY's List, 41–42, 43, 191
Emmanuel, Rahm, 35, 54
entry professions, 11–13, 222–226
Equal Rights Amendment (ERA), 7,
    32–33, 48, 192
ERA. *See* Equal Rights Amendment
Eshoo, Anna, 82tab, 233tab

family connections, in Congress:
    brothers, 110, 111, 123n95; chil-
    dren of members, 105, 113tab,
    114, 115, 120; fathers and daugh-
    ters, 106–109; fathers and sons,
    110–111, 123n77; grandson and
    grandmother, 111; mothers and
    sons, 109, 110tab; political fami-
    lies, 93–94, 119–120, 225; sisters,
    111, 220; spouses, 103–105, 113;
    wives succeeding husbands,
    94–96. *See also* congressional
    widows
Felton, Rebecca Latimer, 3tab, 4,
    101tab, 104tab
female incumbents: electoral security
    of, 150–154; female challengers
    to, 128, 130–132, 148–150, 152,
    154; the free pass, 145, 146,
    151–154, 236; and marginal dis-
    tricts, 150, 151tab, 153–154;
    opposition-party nomination com-

petition, 22, 147, 148, 151, 154, 236; reelection compared to male incumbents, 22, 128, 132–133, 133tab, 236; and safe districts, 150–153; and uncontested elections, 145–146, 148, 151–154. *See also* incumbents
Fenwick, Millicent, 47tab, 48, 60n108
Ferraro, Geraldine, 2, 130
Fiorina, Carly, 44, 129tab, 226
Foley, Mark, 35, 71
Foxx, Virginia, 232, 234
frank, the, 65–66
Franks, Gary, 199, 216n96
free pass: defined, 68tab, 69; and female incumbents, 145, 146, 151–154, 236; House incumbents with, 68tab; and male incumbents, 22, 128, 145, 146, 151; Senate incumbents with, 68tab
Friedan, Betty, 31, 32

Gabbard, Tulsi, 50, 124n129
gender gerrymandering, 231. *See also* partisan gerrymandering; racial gerrymandering
gender stereotypes, 7, 21, 84, 142, 144. *See also* sex-role stereotypes
geography, 187, 188tab, 189–192
gerrymandering, 227. *See also* gender gerrymandering; partisan gerrymandering; racial gerrymandering
Gibbs, Florence, 95tab, 97
Giffords, Gabrielle, 117tab, 125n135, 221, 224
Gillibrand, Kirsten, 101tab, 113tab, 115, 117tab
Granahan, Kathryn, 17, 18, 95tab
Granger, Kay, 83, 179
Graves, Dixie, 101tab, 103
Green, Edith, 7, 17, 18, 82tab
Greene, Enid, 113. *See also* Waldholtz, Enid Greene
Greiling, Mindy, 176–177
Griffiths, Martha, 7, 32, 33, 82tab
Gudger, Jr., James, 96, 108tab

Hagan, Kay, 39tab, 129
Haley, Nikki, 74, 165

Hall, Ralph, 67, 233tab
Hanna, Mark, 103, 108tab
Harris, Katherine, 36, 47tab, 49
Hastert, Dennis, 73, 229
Herrera Beutler, Jaime, 53, 54tab, 117tab, 199, 222, 223photo
Herseth Sandlin, Stephanie, 119photo; family, 104tab, 113tab, 115; House races, 116, 118, 136, 154; House service, 117tab
Hill, Anita, 33, 43, 55. *See also* Thomas-Hill hearings
Hirono, Mazie, 47tab, 50, 54tab
Holtzman, Elizabeth, 32, 47tab, 116, 117tab, 124n129, 130
Huck, Winnifred, 106, 108tab
Humphrey, Hubert H., 13, 41
Humphrey, Muriel, 41, 101
Hutchison, Kay Bailey, 39tab, 129tab

ideology, 16–17, 141–142, 227
incumbents: advantages for, 65–66; and careerism, 78, 80; and congressional committee system, 83; with the free pass, 68tab, 70; House reelection rates, 66–69; marginal, 150, 151tab, 153–154; and political action committees, 66, 91; and redistricting, 67, 71, 229–231; safe, 150–153; and safe seats, 67, 69, 133, 151; scandals of, 70–75; Senate reelection rates, 68tab, 69–70; and women as political candidates, 21, 84, 236. *See also* Democratic incumbents; female incumbents; male incumbents; Republican incumbents

Jacobs, Andrew, 103, 104tab
Johnson, Eddie Bernice, 54, 82tab, 228
Johnson, Lyndon, 36, 67, 100, 118, 186, 193
Johnson, Nancy, 82tab, 131
Jordan, Barbara, 51, 54tab, 117tab, 228

Kaptur, Marcy, 81, 82tab, 117tab, 226
Kassebaum, Nancy Landon, 39tab, 104tab, 105–106, 108tab

Kee, James, 109, 110tab
Kee, Maude, 95, 109, 110tab
Kelly, Edna, 17, 19
Kennedy, John F., 18, 31, 47, 100, 110, 129, 132
Kennedy, Joseph P., 47, 110
Kennedy, Patrick, 110, 225
Kennedy, Ted, 110, 225
Keys, Martha, 103, 104tab
Knowles, Tony, 106, 109
Knutson, Coya, 9–10

Landon, Alf, 106, 108tab
Landrieu, Mary, 13, 39tab, 115, 129tab, 135
Langley, John, 96, 121n32
Langley, Katherine, 95tab, 96, 108tab, 117tab, 121n32
Lautenberg, Frank, 47tab, 48
law degrees, 63–64, 222–223, 224. *See also* education rates
Lease, Mary Elizabeth, 3tab, 163
Lee, Barbara, 54tab, 233tab
Limbaugh, Rush, 44, 135
Lincoln, Abraham, 79–80
Lincoln, Blanche Lambert, 39tab, 60n97, 113tab, 114, 116, 117tab
Lloyd, Marilyn, 82, 94, 96tab
Long, Rose McConnell, 101, 110tab
Luce, Clare Boothe, 13, 14photo, 15, 108tab, 117tab

Mack, Mary Bono, 95tab, 97, 104tab, 117tab, 118. *See also* Bono, Mary
Mack IV, Connie, 103, 104tab
Majette, Denise, 47tab, 54tab, 216n96
majority-minority districts, 153, 186, 193, 209, 216n96, 229–230
malapportionment, 17–18, 229
male incumbents: the free pass, 22, 128, 145, 146, 151; and marginal districts, 150, 151tab, 153–154; opposition-party nomination competition, 147, 151; reelection compared to female incumbents, 22, 133, 133tab, 236; and safe districts, 150–152, 153; and uncontested elections, 145–146, 151, 153. *See also* Democratic

incumbents; female incumbents; incumbents; Republican incumbents
Maloney, Carolyn, 82tab, 196, 197, 198, 232, 233tab
marginal district, 150, 154
marginal incumbents, 150, 151tab, 153–154
Margolies-Mezvinsky, Marjorie, 34–35, 104tab
Martin, Lynn, 47tab, 91
Massa, Eric, 71–72
Matsui, Doris, 54tab, 95tab, 97, 222
McCain, John, 1–2, 187, 194, 196, 197
McCaskill, Claire, 39tab, 44
McCormick, Medill, 104tab, 105
McCormick, Ruth Hanna, 107photo; family members in Congress, 103–105, 108tab; House service, 94, 95tab, 105; Senate run, 47tab, 105
McGovern-Fraser Commission, 32, 164
McKinney, Cynthia, 54tab, 58n49, 117tab, 131, 216n96, 228, 239n66
McMahon, Linda, 46, 226
McMorris Rodgers, Cathy, 113tab, 114, 117tab, 118, 164, 222
Meek, Carrie, 54tab, 109, 110tab
Meek, Kendrick, 109, 110tab
Mikulski, Barbara: campaign image, 142; Senate elections, 39tab, 42, 47tab, 127–128, 129tab; Senate seniority, 226
Millender-McDonald, Juanita, 54tab, 111
Mink, Patsy: and the Democratic National Committee, 13; House campaigns and elections, 3tab, 7, 114, 131; House service of, 55tab, 56, 117tab; posthumous election in 2002, 56, 103; Senate run by, 47tab, 56
Molinari, Susan: age elected to House, 124n129; family, 103, 104tab, 106, 108tab, 113; House service of, 117tab; media coverage of, 134

Moran, Jim, 72–73
Morella, Connie, 152, 153tab, 206,
    240n76
Moseley Braun, Carol, 3tab, 7, 39tab,
    53, 55–56
Murkowski, Frank, 106, 108tab, 109
Murkowski, Lisa, 101tab, 106, 108tab,
    109, 112
Murray, Patty, 39tab, 43, 47tab,
    129tab, 143
Muskie, Edmund, 139–140

Nelson, Bill, 36, 47tab, 49
Neuberger, Maurine, 39tab, 41, 59n68,
    102–103
Ney, Bob, 35, 71
Nineteenth Amendment, 11, 163, 192
Nixon, Richard, 32, 46–47, 129
Noem, Kristi, 117tab, 118, 136–137
Nolan, Mae Ella, 83, 95tab, 97, 117tab
Norton, Mary Teresa, 6photo, 82tab

Obama, Barack, 115, 118, 162; 2008
    presidential election, 187, 194,
    195, 197, 218; 2008 presidential
    primaries, 1, 2, 139; 2010
    midterm elections, 36; 2011 State
    of the Union address, 140; tele-
    phone call to Rep. Ros-Lehtinen,
    53–55
O'Day, Caroline, 6photo, 18, 128, 130
O'Donnell, Christine, 44–45, 137
Oldfield, Pearl, 95tab, 97, 98photo
Owen, Ruth Bryan, 106, 107photo,
    108tab

packing, 229, 230
PACs. *See* political action committees
Palin, Sarah, 1–2, 37, 44, 109, 116
partisan gerrymandering, 230–231.
    See also racial gerrymandering
partisanship, 187–189
party-friendly districts, 184–185, 187,
    188tab, 201. *See also* demograph-
    ics; women-friendly districts
party gap: demographic explanations
    for, 210; in female House candi-
    dates, 165–168; in female House
    delegations, 22–23, 161, 168,

178; in female Senate candidates,
    169–170; in female Senate dele-
    gations, 170, 171fig, 178; and
    party polarization, 189; in state
    legislatures, 23, 173–175, 178,
    179
party polarization. *See* polarization
Paul, Rand, 110–111
Paul, Ron, 110–111
Paxon, Bill, 103, 104tab, 113
Pearce, Steve, 47tab, 49
Pelosi, Nancy: family, 106, 108tab,
    112; House campaigns and elec-
    tions, 99, 131; House district
    characteristics, 232, 233tab;
    House service of, 82tab; as speak-
    er of the House, 1, 2, 36, 83
Pfost, Gracie, 7, 47tab
Pingree, Chellie, 83, 93, 129tab
polarization, 185, 189, 193, 210
political action committees (PACs),
    32, 34, 66, 91, 129. *See also*
    EMILY's List; Women's
    Campaign Fund
Pyle, Gladys, 3tab, 38, 39tab

racial gerrymandering: and majority-
    minority districts, 186–187, 209,
    229, 230, 239n66; and minority
    House members, 153, 186–187,
    199, 211, 229
Rangel, Charles, 73–74, 198, 233tab
Rankin, Jeannette, 4photo; and
    Caroline O'Day, 128; and the
    House of Representatives, 2–3,
    18, 82, 116, 117tab, 222, 235;
    media coverage of, 134–135, 137,
    138; Senate run by, 3, 47tab;
    votes against World Wars I and II,
    3, 137, 138
Rayburn, Sam, 18, 185
Reagan, Ronald, 47, 129, 132, 139
reapportionment, 18, 53, 75, 240n89
redistricting: and incumbents, 67, 71,
    229–231; and minority con-
    stituents, 186; by state legisla-
    tures, 67, 71, 228–231; and
    women in Congress, 18–19, 23,
    227–231

Reece, Louise, 95tab, 108tab
Republican incumbents: female challengers to, 148–150; and opposition-party nomination competition, 147, 148, 149tab; and uncontested elections, 145–146
Richardson, Laura, 54tab, 111
Rivers, Lynn, 67, 117tab
Robertson, Alice, 134–135, 136photo
Robinson, Vernon, 232, 234
Roby, Martha, 117tab, 207, 232
Rogers, Edith Nourse, 6photo, 81, 82tab, 95tab, 99–100
Roosevelt, Eleanor, 14, 31, 128, 163
Roosevelt, Franklin Delano, 36, 38, 186, 193
Roosevelt, Theodore, 80, 118
Ros-Lehtinen, Ileana: House leadership, 55, 84, 118, 164; House service, 3tab, 54tab, 82tab, 117tab, 199; President Obama's telephone call to, 53–55
Ross, Mike, 232, 233tab
Roukema, Margaret, 82tab, 207
Rove, Karl, 49, 185, 230
Roybal-Allard, Lucille, 54tab, 82tab, 106, 108tab

safe district, 151, 154. *See also* safe incumbents
safe incumbents, 150–153. *See also* safe district
safe margin, 68tab, 69, 133tab
safe seats: defined, 67, 156n15; incumbents, 67, 69, 133, 151; and redistricting, 229–230, 231
Saiki, Patricia Fukuda, 47tab, 53, 54tab
Sanchez, Linda, 54tab, 111, 113tab, 117tab, 118, 220, 221photo
Sanchez, Loretta, 54tab, 111, 117tab, 125n135, 220, 225
Sandlin, Max, 67, 104tab
Schneider, Claudine, 47tab, 117tab
Schroeder, Patricia, 10, 82tab, 114, 117tab, 131, 137, 139
Scott, Tim, 199, 216n94
Serrano, José, 193, 194, 233tab
sex-role stereotypes, 134, 140, 142, 143. *See also* gender stereotypes

Shepherd, Karen, 35, 113
Simms, Albert Gallatin, 104tab, 105
Smith, Clyde, 39–40
Smith, Linda, 47tab, 117tab, 129tab
Smith, Margaret Chase, 40photo; 1948 Senate election, 3tab, 5, 38, 39tab, 40, 47tab; 1960 Senate election, 128–129; House service, 38–40, 95tab; presidential run, 41; Senate service, 40–41, 57, 59n68
Snowe, Olympia, 39tab, 47tab, 104tab, 117tab, 124n129, 129tab
socioeconomic factors, 187, 188tab, 193–198
Specter, Arlen, 43–44
Stabenow, Debbie, 39tab, 47tab
Stanley, Winnifred, 18, 117tab
Stanton, Elizabeth Cady, 2, 3tab, 163
state legislatures, 78; and malapportionment, 17; party gap in, 23, 173–175, 178, 179; and the pipeline, 12, 45; redistricting by, 67, 71, 228–231; women in, 177, 178, 219tab, 220, 223, 224
Sullivan, Leonor, 7, 17, 82tab, 94, 95tab, 100
Swift, Jane, 137–138

Talent, Jim, 44, 102
Tea Party, 44, 45, 109, 111, 166
Thomas, Clarence, 33, 55. *See also* Thomas-Hill hearings
Thomas-Hill hearings, 33–34, 43, 55, 76
Thurmond, Strom, 81, 216n94
Title IX, 7, 32, 56, 64
Truman, Harry, 36, 47
Tsongas, Niki, 94, 95tab, 97, 153, 196

Van Hollen, Chris, 152, 233tab
Velazquez, Nydia, 54tab, 82tab, 117tab, 233tab
voter perception, 140–142, 145, 178, 179
Voting Rights Act of 1965, 11, 186

Waldholtz, Enid Greene, 113, 117tab
Wasserman Schultz, Debbie, 115, 116, 117tab, 118, 142, 217–218
Waters, Maxine, 54tab, 74, 82tab

wave election: of 1964, 66–67; of
     2006, 35, 36, 77, 133, 207, 210;
     of 2008, 36, 77, 133, 207, 210; of
     2010, 66–67, 77, 133, 210;
     defined, 66–67; effect on incum-
     bents, 76
Wesberry v. Sanders, 17, 18, 213n26,
     240n94
West, Allen, 198, 199
Wilson, Heather, 47tab, 49, 60n97,
     117tab
women-friendly districts: for
     Democrats, 201, 202tab,
     204–205, 206; demographics of,
     23, 24, 237; and election of
     Hispanic female House members,
209; example of, 217–218; identi-
     fying, 184, 185; least friendly,
     233tab; measure of woman-
     friendliness, 232–234; most
     friendly, 233tab; and redistricting,
     231; for Republicans, 201,
     203tab, 205–207. *See also* demo-
     graphics; party-friendly districts
Women's Campaign Fund, 32, 191

Yeakel, Lynn, 43–44
Year of the Angry White Male, 34, 35
Year of the Republican Woman, 21,
     35, 37, 165
Year of the Woman, 21, 29, 33, 42, 76,
     171

About the Book

Since 1916, when the first woman was elected to the US Congress, fewer than 10 percent of all members have been women. Why is this number so extraordinarily small? And how has the presence of women in the electoral arena changed over the past hundred years? Barbara Palmer and Dennis Simon combine a rich analytical narrative, data on nearly 40,000 candidates, and colorful stories from the campaign trail in the most thorough accounting of women's performance in House and Senate elections ever presented.

The authors go beyond the conventional wisdom as they explore the continuing underrepresentation of women in Congress. In the process, they show how the "rules of the game"—together with an important cluster of demographic characteristics that can make a district more or less "women friendly"—have shaped opportunities for female candidates across a century of US history.

Barbara Palmer is associate professor of political science at Baldwin-Wallace College. **Dennis Simon** is Altshuler Distinguished Teaching Professor in the Department of Political Science at Southern Methodist University.